THE SON KING

MADAWI AL-RASHEED

The Son King

Reform and Repression in Saudi Arabia

OXFORD

UNIVERSITY PRESS

Oxford University Press is a department of the
University of Oxford. It furthers the University's objective
of excellence in research, scholarship, and education
by publishing worldwide.

Oxford   New York

Auckland   Cape Town   Dar es Salaam   Hong Kong   Karachi
Kuala Lumpur   Madrid   Melbourne   Mexico City   Nairobi
New Delhi   Shanghai   Taipei   Toronto

With offices in

Argentina   Austria   Brazil   Chile   Czech Republic   France   Greece
Guatemala   Hungary   Italy   Japan   Poland   Portugal   Singapore
South Korea   Switzerland   Thailand   Turkey   Ukraine   Vietnam

Oxford is a registered trade mark of Oxford University Press
in the UK and certain other countries.

Published in the United States of America by
Oxford University Press
198 Madison Avenue, New York, NY 10016

Library of Congress Cataloging-in-Publication Data is available
Madawi Al-Rasheed.
The Son King: Reform and Repression in Saudi Arabia.
ISBN: 9780197558140

Printed in the United Kingdom on acid-free paper
by Bell and Bain Ltd, Glasgow

CONTENTS

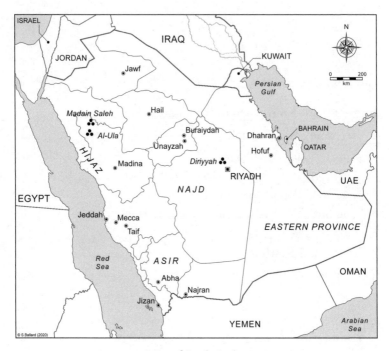

Map of Saudi Arabia

LIST OF ILLUSTRATIONS

1. Hatice Cengiz and Jamal Khashoggi in 2018, courtesy of Hatice Cengiz.
2. Author's correspondence with Jamal Khashoggi on Twitter Direct Messages.
3. Exiled Omar al-Zahrani, Canada, 2019, courtesy of Omar al-Zahrani.
4. *I Am My Own Guardian*, by Saudi artist Ms Saffaa, courtesy of Ms Saffaa.
5. Exiled Muhammad al-Massari, Muhammad al-Omari and Sahar al-Fifi in discussion, 2019, courtesy of Diwan London.
6. Exiled Abdullah al-Juraywi and journalist Safa al-Ahmad attending the Diaspora Conference, December 2019, courtesy of Diwan London.
7. Saudi exiles hold a demonstration outside the Saudi embassy in support of detained activists, December 2019, courtesy of Diwan London.
8. Outside the Saudi embassy in London, December 2019, courtesy of Diwan London.
9. Yahya Assiri, director of Diwan London, at the centre of a demonstration outside the Saudi embassy in London, December 2019, courtesy of Diwan London.

INTRODUCTION

KNOWLEDGE IN THE TIME OF OIL

On 2 October 2018, Saudi journalist Jamal Khashoggi entered the Saudi consulate in Istanbul and was never seen again. Investigations by Turkish authorities and UN sources concluded that the journalist was murdered inside the consulate by Saudi operatives acting on behalf of the regime, who then dismembered and disposed of his body. Saudi authorities initially denied murdering the journalist, but later accepted that he was murdered as a result of a crime committed by Saudi security agents who had been sent to Istanbul. Successive Saudi statements did not make it clear whether the operatives had been instructed to kidnap or murder Khashoggi.[1] Two years on from the murder, the Saudi regime is yet to accept full responsibility and name the high official who gave orders either to kidnap Khashoggi or to murder him. The kidnapping narrative is dubious, simply because the operatives seem to have come to Istanbul prepared for a more sinister mission.

Could such a thing have occurred under the auspices of Crown Prince Muhammad ibn Salman, the rising star who has amassed much power since 2015, when King Salman promoted him to the highest positions in government? How could a monarchy long described by its Western allies and partners as a benevolent authoritarian regime dare to go as far as committing a crime of this magnitude and brutality in the sanctuary of its own consulate? Have we all misunderstood the real Saudi Arabia under the rule of the new crown prince? Have there been serious gaps in our academic knowledge and media reporting on the country since 2015, beyond the visions of its current ruler, oil wealth, investment opportunities and arms sales? Why did observers fail to anticipate the brutality of the new realm, when many Saudi critics, including royalty, have been jailed since 2017?

In the past, academic knowledge about Saudi Arabia exclusively privileged the study of oil, the monarchy and religion. These factors are framed as explaining aspects of the country's past and current development (or lack thereof), its centrality to Western interests and its potential threat to international order. It is assumed that only the progressive Al Saud leadership can manage the vast oil resources and curb the excesses of the country's religious zealots. But both abundant oil and radical religion, in the form of the literalist Wahhabi tradition, fall short of telling us the full story about how people navigate their past and present, and also look to the future, in the framework of a repressive centralized monarchy.[2]

The Son King delves into new social and political outcomes beyond the scope of radical religion, oil and the current progressive leadership. It specifically explores the combination of reform and repression under the rule of the new crown prince, Muhammad ibn Salman, and the way these developments have brought on unexpected outcomes. It narrates how Saudi society in the twenty-first century is subjected to unprecedented repression, targeting its youth, women, tribes, regions, religious scholars, professionals, journalists and many others who simply hold different views on the country's present and future.

Although they do not provide a complete picture of the country's political landscape, oil and religion are what have made

INTRODUCTION

Saudi Arabia so important to others beyond its borders. For the West, the kingdom's oil, cash and market have offered opportunities making up for the loss of empires and colonies since the Second World War. When looking beyond the obvious importance of oil to the West and Asia, Adam Hanieh's work fills a vacuum in our understanding of how the Gulf's new capital shapes the political economy of the Middle East.[3] The kingdom was also constructed as an important country for all Muslims, who perform their annual pilgrimage to its holy cities, Mecca and Madina, and who pray in the direction of the former five times a day. Research and reporting about the country produced a mix of optimism, wishful thinking and, since 9/11, a damning assessment of its role in spreading radical Wahhabi interpretations around the globe. But even that episode failed to result in a real assessment of the role of Saudi Arabia's leaders in producing waves of religious radicalism, as part of a foreign policy initially introduced after the oil boom of the 1970s, with the consent of many of the regime's Western partners.[4]

In academic scholarship, literature about Saudi Arabia beyond a focus on oil and religion has started appearing only recently. Since 2000 new research has focused on the younger generation, capturing both the youth's opportunities and the restrictions on their aspirations. Mai Yamani's work traces social transformation among young people, which has taken place at unprecedented speed.[5] Pascal Menoret draws our attention to how regime modernization and development of urban space has created a marginalized and impoverished youth cohort that took to the streets to reclaim them. 'Joy riding', a common practice in certain neighbourhoods of Riyadh, was labelled deviance by regime educators and sociologists, but Menoret's analysis highlights important outcomes of urban development plans and social engineering that have pushed the poor into the dangerous sphere of assertive masculinity.[6] Amélie Le Renard has shown how young Saudi women navigate the same urban space and penetrate the new modernized city, with its multiple shopping centres, where women subvert and resist patriarchal traditions.[7] The work of Sean Foley goes beyond Islam and oil as two prisms that allegedly explain Saudi Arabia to outsiders. Foley's documentation of the flourishing creative arts, now co-opted by the state, moves away from the usual focus on Saudi radicalization.[8] A recent study of young Saudi men informs us about the aspirations, optimism, contested nationalism and reservations of the youth regarding the current regime initiatives to empower them.[9] A study of controversial Saudi heresies on Twitter turns the alleged radicalism of Saudi society on its head as it documents new expressions of doubt, agnosticism and atheism, and the emergence of humanism among the youth.[10]

Of course, there is also a growing trend that unapologetically accepts the narrative that the leadership has been empowering young Saudis, especially women, since 2015. This academic literature uncritically reproduces media optimism about the potential of Saudi Arabia's new reformist leadership. For example, regime policy to empower women is often blown out of proportion at the expense of realistic, careful and nuanced arguments about the country's so-called progressive crown prince, massive oil reserves and the alleged entrenched radicalism of its society that the prince is now curbing.[11]

This book goes beyond the overtly emphasized international significance of Saudi Arabia, its progressive leadership, oil and religion to explore new trends at a time when its youth enjoy greater visibility and at the same time endure pervasive repression under the young crown prince. It fills a vacuum in our knowledge about the politics of Saudi youth who have opted for exile as a result of successive waves of repression and restrictions on freedom. It is unique in being the first study of an 'incipient diaspora', struggling with the dislocation of exile and uprooting, at a time when Saudi Arabia is being constructed as a new kingdom empowering youth, developing its heritage beyond Islam, and opening up economic and social spheres that had been shut for decades. It answers the question of why not just old regime supporters, but also young Saudi men and women, are leaving the country when its leadership pledges to empower them.

Crown Prince 'MBS' and the New Branding

The Son King explores the politics of a regime that until the murder of Khashoggi was not considered brutal, deploying repressive methods akin to those that flourished in the rest of the Arab world under authoritarian republics. Unlike assessments of the repressive republican Arab regimes, many observers considered Saudi rulers to have a strong legitimacy of a traditional nature, cemented by a functioning social contract between princes and commoners, and benefiting from lavish oil subsidies and welfare services. This narrative was typical of 'knowledge in the time of oil', when Saudi Arabia became so important for its Western partners. The latter regarded it as a bastion of stability, not only domestically but across the Arab region. Its abundant oil wealth and the much-appreciated potential market for foreign investment, arms exports, global capital and, more recently, a flourishing entertainment industry for Western performers were enough to maintain partnership with the regime. Under Muhammad ibn Salman, in the eyes of many foreign observers, Saudi Arabia entered a new era of openness, prosperity, economic diversification and ample opportunities for investment and tourism. Representations of the young future king mixed serious assessment with public-relations propaganda, wishful thinking and manipulation of knowledge about the country, all done by its crown prince and accepted by outside media at face value.

The hype about the promise of moving the succession to the second-generation princes and appointing the young Muhammad ibn Salman as crown prince developed into the 'cult of the Son King'. In Western media, his long name was abbreviated to MBS to facilitate quick recognition and branding. He became an iconic visionary, not only inside the country but globally, from Washington to Tokyo. The cult had many disciples, both paid and unpaid, who spread images and myths about his great reforms and invited sceptical audiences to join in celebrating the transformation brought about by the young and charismatic Arab prince. The regime's pervasive media efforts to consolidate the cult of 'MBS' resemble what Paul Veyne describes as euergetism. The concept, which flourished in ancient Greece and Rome, concerned cities that honoured eminent persons who, through their money or public activity, 'did good to the city'.[12] For this cult to be visible and effective, it has to be founded on 'bread and circuses', combining money, power, entertainment and prestige. When the state machine felt or believed that it was threatened by certain interests of its subjects, especially the youth, the crown prince swiftly introduced his subjects to mass entertainment and promised more bread.

The prince wanted Saudis to move beyond dependence on oil by becoming entrepreneurs. He also provided ample opportunities for the circus as part of new mass culture. He embodies Juvenal's prediction that 'now that no one buys our votes, the public has long since cast off its cares; the people that once bestowed commands, consulship, legions and all else, now meddles no more and longs eagerly for just two things—Bread and Circuses'.[13] When the circus is entirely made abroad and imported at a high cost, neither old Marxist approaches that condemn mass culture nor liberal perspectives celebrating its potential for progress are sufficient to explain the new and swift decision to import foreign entertainment into Saudi Arabia wholesale. The introduction of entertainment was undoubtedly the work of foreign consultants who operated within the neoliberal framework, and a response to decades of accusations that Saudi Arabia was imposing a strict religious regime on its modern citizens. Previous restrictions were believed to have contributed to the breeding of terrorism. Hence the crown prince wanted to abandon that past and plunge Saudis swiftly into entertainment as a diversion from the previous social and religious control. While entertainment is part of the diversification of the economy, it is nevertheless also a great distraction from more urgent thoughts and aspirations. Saudis are sold the illusion of freedom in the circus, while the prince amasses new income and ensures that his subjects replace religious observance with legitimate 'decadence'. However, he is not outside the circus, a mere importer of its many attractions. In fact, he is at the heart of mass culture and entertainment. While international boxing champions and singers are imported for colossal sums, it is the prince himself who becomes the main celebrity, starring at each event. Items of his clothing, posture and body language are analysed and commented on in great detail, and images of his shoes and unusual coat immediately begin to circulate on social media by his fans. In the heart of the circus, we see him encircled by aides, world media and local journalists eager to capture a glimpse of the celebrity prince.

Many autocrats resist large-scale mass culture because they believe that 'if we allow the people to have festivals, innocent enough affairs in themselves, they will suppose that they are free to do whatever they like, and they will no longer be willing to obey or to fight'.[14] But the crown prince's solution was to provide public enjoyment confined to certain limited moments, for example the Riyadh and Diriyyah Festivals, which are turned into patriotic events. Such spectacles of power, featuring popular Western concerts, car races, boxing matches, football events, cinema and theatre, assert the crown prince's right to be obeyed, and this needs to be actualized and expressed in conspicuous consumption in controlled conditions. For this purpose, the prince established the Entertainment Authority, which controls fun and festivals and delivers them at specific seasons and places. Needless to say, the new entertainment, from concerts to boxing matches, proved a good distraction for an eager millennial generation so far deprived of fun. While the cult of 'MBS' flourished abroad, the abbreviation of his full name was not used domestically, and only those opposed to his policies referred to him as MBS, thus appropriating the branded name and turning it against his propaganda.

While most Saudi kings developed their own personality cults—for example, King Abdullah was known as the king of humanity and King Salman as the king of decisiveness—these cults had all been local. By contrast, MBS's efforts to gain international recognition made his abbreviated and branded acronyms recognizable across the world and in many cities.[15] The image of President Donald Trump waving a chart detailing how much 'MBS' paid and was willing to pay into the US economy on the latter's visit to the White House became iconic, as it celebrates the promise of 'bread' being spread beyond Saudi borders. Successive British prime ministers have often reminded the critics of arms sales to Saudi Arabia that 'we need the trade', and for this reason, the red carpet was rolled out when the prince visited London. The globalization of the crown prince helps to project his leadership in ways that facilitate the realization of his many promises, above all to end Saudi Arabia's dependence on oil and draw international investment and capital to the country. His images have been circulated internationally since 2017 and have appeared on buses and taxis in places such as London. This helped gain him eminence and recognition abroad, as eventually his cult went global.

Locally, the branded prince consolidated his cult of personality and associated himself with new, modern imagery, designed

INTRODUCTION

to generate loyalty to himself rather than to a nation that is still struggling to define its national identity. His cult manifested in the proliferation of images, social media posts and sponsored media articles that promoted him as the new face of a country, now constructed as stagnating under a succession of ageing monarchs and in need of serious transformation from above. While previous kings had appeared at camel races and poetry pageants, the new crown prince presided over newly introduced car races, youth conferences and boxing matches. His cult became sacrosanct, as any critical voices were either silenced by house arrest or put in jail. Critics who fled the country became targets of intimidation campaigns abroad. A long-time servant of the regime and a loyal journalist, Khashoggi chose exile in Washington, DC, to seek the freedom he had been denied at home. His unfortunate and brutal murder began to draw attention to the reality of life under the 'Son King'. Moreover, his murder begs the question as to why a loyal and privileged servant of the throne, and an ardent defender of monarchs, chose to flee the country in anticipation of his own detention. His murder could not be explained simply in terms of falling out with the new crown prince, who wanted to marginalize the old guard of the Saudi media empire and bring in his own coterie; it reflected a new brutality of a magnitude to which the world remained oblivious as long as it remained inside the country. But the murder in the consulate was like the globalization of the cult of the crown prince: the violence of the new regime became global too.

The sudden rise of Muhammad ibn Salman can only be understood in the context of the power vacuum created after the death of several senior princes, brothers of the king, amongst them Nayif and Sultan, who both passed away during King Abdullah's reign. For several decades before 2015, Saudi Arabia was ruled as a kingdom of multiple fiefdoms headed by such senior princes. Power and authority rested within more or less autonomous circles, each of which was headed by a powerful senior prince. This long-standing arrangement gave the impression that power-sharing was honoured within the senior branches of the house of Saud, which prided itself on 'ruling by consent' of the most senior princes. However, with the death of many senior princes, Salman became king in 2015, with important brothers eager to take senior positions in government. It was not, however, difficult for him to sack crown princes such as Muqrin—his brother—and Muhammad ibn Nayif, as the remaining brothers were not strong enough to contest his decision. His most eligible brother, Ahmad, was never a candidate as he had withdrawn from public office years earlier. So Salman was able to go ahead and promote his son to the position of crown prince with apparent ease. This bold move came to haunt Muhammad from 2017, pushing him not only to humiliate potential rival princes with tactics such as arrest, but also to continue to monitor the internal affairs of the ruling house for fear of a 'coup', or simply the withholding of the oath of allegiance. Despite the vacuum he filled, Muhammad ibn Salman will continue to be dogged by potential rivals challenging his authority, especially when the ageing King Salman passes away.

The Duality of Reform and Repression

I offer an understanding of Saudi Arabia beyond common wisdom about successive monarchs and their visions for transforming the country from tradition to modernity. My prime focus is the contradiction between repression and reform that has become a central prism through which to understand Saudi Arabia under the current ruler. My aim is to capture the consequences of that duality, which has pushed many respectable academics, media pundits and policy makers to argue that it is inevitable, implying that reforming the Saudi economy and society is necessarily a violent act that has to be carried out by an authoritarian—some would argue brutal—new crown prince. His regime is better understood as a liberal autocracy in which only superficial limited social liberalism is allowed to flourish. Such assertions about the inevitability of repression as a precondition for a new tolerant Islam, gender equality, a vibrant liberal economy, a fun culture and an empowered entrepreneurial youth build on old, defunct and unfashionable academic positions about inevitable oriental despotism.[16] Embedded in this old knowledge paradigm is the belief that a socially conservative, religiously radical and economically lazy society can never shed the shackles of the past without repression and coercion.

In discussions about the potential of Saudi society, we are told that the employment of its youth in the private sector is hindered by their laziness. The myth of the 'lazy native' is well entrenched in the minds of many observers of Saudi Arabia, much as it was the language of domination and repression used to describe Malays under foreign rule.[17] The prosperous young Saudi man is often constructed as an idle citizen who has become dependent on state handouts and, with guaranteed employment in the public sector, is an unmotivated underperformer. While Malays had to be drugged by opium to survive the harsh working conditions in the jungle, the Saudi was initially drugged by oil wealth. Now he is under the spell of Western popular culture to reach a new level of consciousness suitable for a modern liberal nation under an eclectic, albeit brutal, crown prince. The innate social conservatism and essentialized radical religious nature of the Saudis need to be violently uprooted by a top-down revolutionary and visionary leader, if Saudi Arabia is to become a truly modern country. Only then it can be born again as an open and tolerant society. Such assumptions miss important social trends that had emerged among Saudis even before the rise of the crown prince.

In addition to the alleged laziness of the Saudi, we are told he is incapable of reaching a level of citizenship beyond his archaic but persistent tribal affiliation, sectarian identity, regionalism and sexism. His national identity rests on shaky ground, a fact to be added to his shortcomings. But only a few observers tackled the absence of national identity beyond essentialized tribalism, and in ways that focus attention on how successive regimes oscillated between promoting a pan-Islamic identity at the expense of strengthening national belonging, and erasing local identities in the pursuit of a religious project to purify and eventually salvage the Arabian population from its alleged lapsed beliefs and observance.[18] Now, Saudis are forced to reinvent themselves as belonging to a new Saudi nation, defined from above and popularized in ways that generate new xenophobia and even lead to accusing critics of committing treason against God, king and nation. While the reforms of the crown prince are conducted as a mission in the name of the Saudi nation, the repression is equally the result of an ill-defined populist nationalism, propagated on social media by the prince and his many aides. The murder of Khashoggi was simply one outcome of an aggressive hyper-nationalist agenda, the purpose of which is to consolidate the power of a newly appointed prince who does not seem to enjoy consensus among his own family, let alone the Saudi people.[19]

As the crown prince was branded MBS, the Saudi nation has been reinvented and rebranded as *al-saoudiyya al-othma*, 'the Great Saudi Arabia'.[20] The branding of Saudi Arabia as great reminds us of Edward Said's words:

> Nationalism then justifies, retrospectively as well as prospectively, a history selectively strung together in a narrative form: thus all nationalisms have their founding fathers, their basic, quasi-religious texts, their rhetoric of belonging, their historical and geographical landmarks, their official enemies and heroes. This collective ethos forms what Pierre Bourdieu, the French sociologist, calls the *habitus*,

the coherent amalgam of practices linking habit with inhabitance. In time, successful nationalisms consign truth exclusively to themselves and relegate falsehood and inferiority to outsiders.[21]

Launching the new nation found a niche under a young founding father, a youthful crown prince instead of an ageing patriarch such as King Salman. The prince's disciples forge their own quasi-religious–nationalist Twitter hashtags about the greatness of the nation and its young reformer.

As the young Saudi male was constructed as an icon of laziness, conservatism and terrorism, young Saudi women were hailed by the regime, its intellectuals and outside observers as either victims of an oppressive male-dominated society or as heroes who had challenged the supremacy of men in the privacy of their homes or in public, thanks to the efforts of a progressive leadership. Feminist activists became known to outside audiences as symbols of bravery and freedom, while inside the country they were vilified as traitors who challenge society's dominant religion, patriarchy and values. Women activists and feminists entered the public sphere initially through social media, and later as a result of activism on the ground. Many amongst them held discussion forums, as well as training sessions for public participation and mobilization. They organized themselves to challenge the ban on driving and campaigned for an end to the guardianship system. They highlighted the plight of young girls sold in marriage to old men and girls abused by their own relatives and criticized the failure of state institutions, shelters and the judiciary to bring them justice. The regime-appointed judiciary failed to deliver justice in the cases of divorce and custody of children. Women went to court to force judges to allow them to marry when their male guardians refused to grant them permission. They were occasionally successful, but in many cases, state-appointed judges upheld the authority of fathers and brothers over their daughters and sisters. Judges even went as far as forcing couples to divorce or annul their marriages when such marriages did not conform to the rules of tribal endogamy and compatibility of lineages. Activists were imprisoned for engaging in national mobilization. Gender inequality unified all Saudis and went beyond old regional, sectarian, class and tribal divides. Feminists became a national security threat because they promoted an agenda that appealed to most Saudi women and many men.

A Twitter Nation

Free public debate, political representation and independent media had always been limited, but they totally vanished under the rule of the new prince. Deprived of the right to civil resistance, demonstrations, sit-ins and peaceful protest, Saudi society found refuge in social media. Its diverse fragments became active participants on social media from Twitter to YouTube. Saudis registered their presence as engaged vocal citizenry with their own creative ideas, criticism and contribution to debates about domestic, regional and global issues. Since 2011 both men and women activists have used social media to launch campaigns against gender inequality in general and to demand the lifting of the ban on driving and the abolition of the guardianship laws. Men highlighted the unemployment and housing shortages and campaigned for salary increases. They publicized the plight of abused women and those in underage marriages, highlighting the failure of state institutions—despite the crown prince's claims about women's empowerment—to provide safe shelters for girls who leave their homes after being subjected to physical and sexual violence. By 2015 a new phenomenon known as the 'runaway girls' had become hotly debated as young girls fled the country and sought safe refuge abroad. To draw attention to this new trend, the girls and their supporters took to social media, which enabled the globalization of Saudi women's causes. Saudi activists themselves reached out to global media to publicize their causes, and in return global media adopted their many grievances and amplified their plight. This was a clear case of what Lisa Wynn and Ms Saffaa call the appropriation and transnationalization of their struggles,[22] leading to greater regime scrutiny and repression at home. Global media is yet to exert enough pressure to result in the freeing of women activists held in prisons since 2018, or to put enough pressure on the regime to release other critics from prison.

New communications technology, embraced by the crown prince when he threw away his old Nokia phone and replaced it with a smartphone, in a gesture designed to emphasize his own modernity and empower grassroots contribution to public debate, became a tool of repression. The crown prince invested heavily in social media as propaganda for populist nationalism. But Saudis paid a high price for using them to voice alternative narratives and opinions. As Saudi Arabia has the highest level of Twitter users in the world,[23] spies of the regime are charged with infiltrating it to gather data on Saudi critics, activists and dissidents. In November 2019 the San Francisco Federal court charged two ex-Twitter employees with gathering data on 6,000 accounts for the Saudi regime. One of the key figures in the spy ring is allegedly a young Saudi who worked with the prince's close aides.[24] The regime commissioned prestigious management consultancy firms to monitor and report on influential online critics of the prince's many visions and transformation programmes, all advertised on social media and Twitter hashtags.[25] Social media became a trap to catch dissidents, but also an enabling tool to unite a new diaspora of Saudi exiles and asylum seekers scattered in several continents from North America to Australia, as we shall see in this book.

Contemporary forms of Saudi communication platforms include old print media and satellite audio-visuals, but in recent years new social media such as Twitter, Facebook, Instagram, Snapchat, Telegram and YouTube allowed a space beyond official channels for a short period of time, after which the regime realized the explosion in their usage in what were deemed to be subversive ways. Social media allowed rapid, flexible and individualistic ways of maintaining contact, initiating new networks and sustaining relations across ideological divides, regions and communities within the country. Writing at the advent of these emerging platforms, Eickelman and Anderson argued that communications technology contributed to creating new public spheres that are independent, autonomous and outside the control of traditional authority such as the state and other powerful figures in the community. This new public sphere became discursive, performative and participative. The new spaces created new authority figures, multiple voices and interpretations, contributing to diversity. These voices challenged traditional sources of authority, knowledge and information in the Muslim world and became an important outcome of the new communication technology revolution.[26] They also contributed to fostering transnational networks of solidarity, knowledge sharing and loyalty. Such aspects of the communications revolution were tested during the 2011 Arab uprisings and created a new public sphere.[27] Commentators forecast the efficient organizing potential of social media, but regimes were quick to respond. As they controlled access to the internet, they were able to cut it off and leave participants without connection as soon as protest erupted. It was only a matter of time until authoritarian regimes grasped the enabling potential of social media and endeavoured to control and monitor participants. Eventually, in Saudi Arabia many users ended up in prison simply for posting articles on Facebook or tweeting commentary, poetry and images that undermine and expose the official propaganda.

The regime proved more resourceful, more capable and wealthier than the users in controlling social media among participants, who depended for access on state-controlled communications monopolies in general. The Saudi regime under the crown prince created special Twitter farms to monitor dissent and build a data bank on dissidents.[28] His many aides invited citizens to help draw up a list of subversive voices online and promised to silence them forever as they are dubbed traitors who need to be punished for the sake of the nation. Young and old Saudis were imprisoned simply because they bypassed the 'Red Lines', a common charge against those who criticized the king or high-ranking princes, or simply offered new opinions on the newly introduced policies of the crown prince, for example Vision 2030, the Social Transformation Programmes, the Entertainment Authority, and other initiatives.

While new social media bridged the language gap, it allowed the participation of all literate people, especially those without specialist literacy, such as the language of religious scholars and interpreters of religious texts. Furthermore, posted images became a medium to convey messages even without words. Images of beggars in the main Saudi cities, collapsing infrastructure such as roads and schools, abusive men in the privacy of their own homes, and the excesses of religious surveillance of the population spread across the cyber sphere, exposing cracks in the official propaganda about modernization, security and prosperity. Young Saudis also became active in producing video clips, comedy and art performances to challenge the sterile official media. Saudi satire and comic songs in support of women driving spread across the world. Art that challenged male dominance was posted on special web pages to undermine the restrictions on women.

The regime feared most messages including calls for mobilization and activism, which were easily transmitted across localities at high speed. Individual grievances and personal stories, complete with images and sounds, travelled quickly across the globe, thus enabling the sender to reach a huge audience at a very low financial cost. These local events and experiences became global concerns, thanks to a population very active on Twitter.

There was also the emergence of new solidarities and loyalties. In some respects, Saudi society became increasingly an imagined virtual circle, within which one communicates regularly. But from 2015 this became increasingly dangerous for those conveying messages critical of the regime. In addition to being a source of support, social media also became a platform for the regime to insult critics and threaten them with prison sentences.

The rise of social media helped to break the isolation of many Saudis, who are deprived of legal civil society, political parties and independent associations. It allowed regular sharing of news, ideas, political opinions and experiences, becoming an alternative source of knowledge and a 'parliament' in the time of oil for many Saudis and outsiders. This proved to be important in situations where citizens are marginalized in public platforms and denied political representation. As the regime encouraged antagonism between groups domestically along divides such as liberal and Islamist, *muwatin* (national) and foreign, men and women, Sunni and Shia, and along regional lines, Saudis found a platform to express their diversity and encourage unity against the regime's divisive policies and strategies. Those who called for national politics and formed civil society organizations with strong online presence were immediately suppressed through detention and trials, followed by long prison sentences and bans on travel, and were subjected to campaigns tarnishing their reputations as they were labelled traitors and agents of foreign enemy governments.

A New Diaspora of Saudi Exiles

For the first time in its modern history an 'incipient Saudi diaspora' is in the making. In this book, I adopt a definition of diaspora as 'a social-political formation, created as a result of either voluntary or forced migration, whose members regard themselves as of the same ethno-national origin and who permanently reside as minorities in one or several host countries'.[29] Unlike voluntary diasporas, the Saudi version consists mainly of exiles who are directly or indirectly forced to leave the country. With so many prisoners of conscience incarcerated, unexplained disappearances, suspicious deaths in detention, and an unusually excessive number of executions, beheadings, and even crucifixions, Saudis began to flee the country in great numbers. While it is difficult to estimate the extent of this new diaspora with precision, an unpublished regime report estimated that in the near future there will be around 50,000 exiles abroad.[30] They will seek refuge in North America, Australia, Europe, Arab countries such as Lebanon and Qatar, and Turkey. The latter recently emerged as a temporary destination for exiles seeking permanent residence in a third country. Many exiles had been 'dormant' in their host countries, fearing retaliation by the regime against their families at home, or the confiscation of their assets and financial investments in Saudi Arabia. The recent repression compelled them to come out and openly declare their opposition to the regime. Since 2015 older activists have joined earlier exiles who had sought asylum in the 1990s in Western capitals. They were followed by a new cohort of students who had been sent on government scholarships to study abroad but feared to return if they had been vocal on social media against the regime. Young men and women in their twenties left the country immediately after the murder of Khashoggi.

Saudi women, allegedly empowered by the crown prince under his new policy to end gender inequality, have also fled the country in recent years. In exile they too may be isolated for various reasons, but they are able to participate in the diaspora's public sphere and debate without too much effort. Social media allow diaspora women to engage in conversations that were difficult at home except in authorized spaces and under the control of the higher authority. Social media and the internet have proved to be enabling tools in the diaspora but also a curse at home. In the diaspora they have allowed Saudi women to regroup, organize lobbying activities and disseminate criticism back to the homeland. The unexpected and unprecedented phenomenon of the 'runaway girls' drew attention to the plight of women and the emerging Saudi female diaspora, thanks to social media.

While Saudis at home face repression when they engage in national politics and forge cross-ideological, gender, sectarian and tribal solidarities, by its own nature and circumstances the emerging diaspora is united by common repression. Members seek out newly formed solidarities based on their own needs as exiles. According to Sheffer, in such situations 'a degree of cohesion emerges within those groups ... and group cohesion is founded on the primordial, cultural and instrumental elements in their collective identities'. Saudi exiles immediately realized that 'survival, continuity and prosperity of diasporas, their common sentiments and sense of unity must overcome generational, educational, social and ideological differences and gaps that always exist within diaspora groups'.[31] Khashoggi was one of the first critics to suffer the loneliness of exile in Washington and the pain of dislocation and estrangement from his own family in the homeland. After he arrived in Washington, his wife divorced him and he became estranged from his two sons. At the age of fifty-nine he reached out to young exile Omar al-Zahrani in Canada, thus forging intergenerational solidarity and unity that allowed collective action across the two countries and direct activism towards the homeland, as we shall see in this book. While social media allowed easy transnational organization and lobbying, in addition to being a tool in the hands of the regime for its own propaganda and spying on dissidents, the diaspora is yet to use it successfully to win the battle for greater freedoms, dignity and justice, as we shall see. Furthermore, I caution in this book against an overemphasis on the new solidarities, as schisms within the diaspora resurface, either because of divisive strategies by the regime or because members of the diaspora themselves maintain their own ideological orientations and refuse to compromise and forge overarching solidarities.

The murder of Khashoggi exposed the regime's effort to undermine and divide the diaspora. Early attempts started in the 1990s when Saudis masquerading as opposition figures infiltrated the Islamist Committee for Legitimate Rights in Saudi Arabia and precipitated a schism between its two exiled activists, Saad al-Faqih and Muhammad al-Massari, a rift that has not yet healed. In the 1990s it was easy to break up the unity of exiles simply because of their different ideological orientations, which were masked by an overall identity as Islamists.

In addition to these well-known and expected strategies to undermine the exiles and their diasporic politics, the regime uses specific methods to cut the diaspora from the homeland at the level of family and the country as a whole. Group punishment of the families of exiles in Saudi Arabia is very common. Travel bans, imprisonment and interrogations of those family members and friends left behind are frequent, and exiles narrate their own guilt and agony over what befalls their kin in Saudi Arabia as a result of their flight. Family members who send money to support their young sons and daughters in exile are severely punished, and the flow of support from exiles to needy family members at home is severely curtailed. A London exile who sent his mother a small sum of money to support her narrates how she was immediately arrested. Children as young as four are banned from travel to join their fathers abroad and are often returned from the airport by immigration officers in the kingdom. The regime exerts pressure on family members to disown their sons and daughters who have sought asylum abroad, thus breaking family units and precipitating long-lasting schisms. All these measures prompt the Saudi diaspora to seek solidarity and establish an organizational framework abroad to alleviate the heavy price its members pay for speaking out against a regime that brands itself as a force for reform.

The regime unsurprisingly uses the internet to tarnish the reputation of the diaspora. Its trolls on social media, especially Twitter, describe the diaspora as an insignificant coterie of jihadis or immoral feminists. Labelling the diaspora as a closet jihadi cohort is meant to frighten Western host countries and deprive the diaspora members of safe havens. Such accusations are meant to warn host governments about the 'danger' of Saudi exiles. As this diaspora is produced by a regime still considered an important ally and partner of Western countries, a contradictory situation arises simply because members of the diaspora chose to settle in the same countries that support and empower the regime that has pushed them to take the difficult decision to leave. But 'whether by their nature diaspora are aggressive and dangerous or whether essentially they are defensive, in which case it would be unjust to regard them as inherently harmful to their host countries',[32] the regime continues to vilify them. The diverse Saudi diaspora is aware of the accusations and tries hard to prove its innocence, especially in its activism and social media engagements.

The second label—immoral feminists—is directed towards the homeland, where the exodus of women in particular exposes the myth of the reformist prince who is determined to empower and protect women. Casting exiled women as seeking immoral pursuits in the West creates an everlasting rift between them and society, even setting them apart from their own families. The label tarnishes the reputation of fathers and brothers whose girls flee. They face the loss of social capital, honour and prestige. This is intended to act as a deterrent against future exodus. As young girls escape, they leave behind male relatives who 'lose face'. The latter are expected to disown their daughters to re-establish their honour and be able to face society again.

The diaspora naturally emerges in the regime discourse as a collection of traitors who had 'sold' their souls to enemy governments, thus casting doubt on their loyalty to their homeland. Enemy governments allegedly sponsoring the diaspora are as diverse as the conflicts of the regime with neighbouring states. Such conflicts have become prolific and persistent under the crown prince. In the 1990s Iraq, Iran, Libya and Qatar were all accused of sponsoring and empowering the Saudi opposition. Since 2015 Turkey, Iran and Qatar have been accused of supporting the diaspora and its emerging visible organizational activities. In all these accusations, the diaspora exiles are depicted as outside the body of the nation, which has been newly branded under the populist nationalism of the crown prince. They, however, respond to negative branding by calling themselves *soudiyun fi al-mahjar*, Saudis in the diaspora, thus emphasizing their belonging to the ethno-Saudi nation. This book captures the moment of exile and repression under the pretext of reform.

During the 2011 Arab uprisings there were positive assessments of social media's ability to mobilize and organize people. I accepted its connectivity and networking, but I remained sceptical about its mobilization potential in Saudi Arabia. I wrote, 'The euphoria surrounding the new communication technology, social networking and virtual connectivity proved its limitations in the Saudi context. On a practical level, it seems that the state was able to manipulate such electronic networks and control the outcome.'[33] As the emerging diaspora has no choice but to rely heavily on social media, my early scepticism remains valid in 2020. The diaspora can undermine regime propaganda, but it is not yet capable of instigating real mobilization on the ground in the homeland. In fact, many exiles now hesitate to call from abroad for real mobilization, such as the limited calls for protest in 2011. As that episode led to many Saudi protesters being shot by security forces in the Eastern Province and the arrest of others elsewhere when they responded to calls from outside, many in the diaspora now consider it unethical to call for protest from the relative safety of their host countries.

My Position and Methodology

I am not new to exile, having inherited the status as a teenager and endured it as an adult. In 1975 my father left Saudi Arabia following the assassination of King Faisal by his nephew Faisal ibn Musaid. The assassin's mother was my paternal aunt. My uncle, Miteb, was not only a maternal uncle of the assassin but also a dear friend as they were both close in age. My uncle was arrested immediately, as the Saudi regime suspected that the Al-Rashid maternal kin of Faisal ibn Musaid might have plotted the assassination with the Al Saud prince. My father decided to leave the country after interrogation. As we shall see in the book, the regime concluded that the assassin acted alone. My uncle was released after eighteen months and left the country to seek asylum in Iraq. The relationship between my family and the Al Saud was poisoned forever and the rift was never mended. My father occasionally returned to Saudi Arabia after several years in exile in Lebanon and France, but eventually he decided to stay abroad until he passed away in 2014.

The regime exerted pressure on the whole family by refusing to renew our passports, always claiming that we had to return to Riyadh to seek authorization from the Ministry of Interior. Regular delays in renewing our passports resulted in me being stranded in Lebanon at the age of twenty during the Israeli invasion in 1982. While bombs were falling on West Beirut, where I was living, close to the International College and the American University of Beirut, I sent my passport with a close friend to the consulate, asking them to extend it for six months so that I could join my parents, who had settled in France. My father had moved to France in 1979 when Saudi agents kidnapped dissident Nasir al-Said in Beirut, taking advantage of the chaos of its civil war and lawlessness. Al-Said disappeared, and his family still does not know what happened to him. Beirut became unsafe, and eventually my family moved to a safer place. I refused to leave and, against my father's will, stayed in Beirut. I had already been uprooted once and resisted a second exile in a foreign country. But by 1982 it had become difficult to remain in Lebanon under invasion. I acquired a new passport from an Arab country at their consulate in Beirut and left for France via Damascus in June 1982.

Exile in Beirut was an enriching experience even during the worst bombings, militia shootings, snipers and total chaos. But like in all civil wars, there were always moments of calm and reflection. I was active at school and university as an editor of student magazines, during which period I began to develop an anti-Saudi consciousness. My short articles, poetry and stories became my homeland. Articulating the experience of exile in words was one of the most satisfying solutions, which alleviated the sense of dislocation and alienation. But that solution abruptly ended as the Israeli invasion disrupted the new *habitus* I had become accustomed to. The invasion resulted in my second dislocation and settlement in France. Arriving in Paris, I felt out of place, and it was only a matter of months before I left for Britain to continue my higher education.

Britain in the early 1980s was dominated by the new Thatcherite era and its discontents. I felt totally disconnected from my new location. I focused on my studies and proceeded to continue my education. In 1989 I obtained a doctorate from Cambridge University in political anthropology. I became interested in how states are formed in tribal societies, why the Saudi state succeeded when others failed in the Arabian Peninsula, and what role religion played in the unification of the kingdom.[34] 'The homeland' turned into an academic project that has continued until the present day. But tribal politics seemed a distant past that did not satisfy my own personal quest to understand exile. It was simply a historical prelude to a current crisis—that of multiple dislocations. I searched for a project to study exiles.

I moved to London in 1990, and at the time I felt that I was the only Saudi exile in town. I decided to conduct a research project on Iraqi diaspora exiles, who had been arriving in Britain since the 1950s. I interviewed Iraqi Arabs, Kurds, Shia, Sunnis and Christians who had fled their country for political reasons. I intermingled with asylum seekers, refugees and the wealthy elite, all of whom had fled under duress. Many asylum seekers showed me the scars of torture on their bodies and told me stories about dangerous journeys across mountains in search of safe havens. They talked about broken families, downward mobility and regrouping in the diaspora. They also explained how Iraq's ethnic, political and class divisions in the homeland are reproduced in the diaspora. Writing about Iraqi exiles satisfied my personal quest to dig deeper into the lives of the dislocated and the alienated and to document their resilience as they reconstruct their lives in exile (*al-manfa*).[35] More importantly, my research dismissed the romance associated with intellectual exiles whose literary, poetic and philosophical writings portray a world alien to others. My research opened my eyes to a world of suffering and endurance under repression at home and uncertainty abroad. What partially alleviated the plight of Iraqis was the fact that they joined a growing diaspora community that had already established its own institutions and help-centres, in addition to the headquarters of its diverse political parties.

In 1994 two Saudi Islamists, Saad al-Faqih and Muhammad al-Massari, unexpectedly turned up in London and began to give interviews to the media. They joined several Shia activists such as Hamza al-Hassan, Fuad Ibrahim and Tawfiq al-Saif, who had fled the country after 1979 following an uprising in their region. They all became an opposition in exile. I asked my father to facilitate my access to the small number of Saudi exiles who had settled in London. They were all Islamists, and I hesitated to contact them directly with a view to interviewing them for a research project. Together with my sister, Loulouwa, who was writing a political science dissertation in Paris, and later moved to writing about Iraq in the 1990s,[36] I began the process of visiting exiles in north London and writing about their political projects and the events that led to their flight.[37] However, there was no Saudi community then, and all we did was document the activists' demands and explain their political agenda. The act of researching the exiled Sunnis and Shia was an opportunity to reconnect with a homeland and document the new political trends that evolved under the cover of authoritarian rule.

Writing about the London exiles, I maintained a reasonable academic distance that allowed me to write about both the Sunni and the Shia Islamists. I discovered that they did not forge new solidarities in exile, much as they had not done in the homeland. Their experience of exile in the 1990s failed to create new connections that cut across sectarian divides. In fact, new schisms started appearing even among exiles who belonged to the same ideological group. Several Shia exiles reconciled with the regime and returned to Saudi Arabia. However, after disappointment as the regime failed to honour its pledges to the community, some of them returned to London. Among the Sunni Islamists, a clash of personalities and incompatible political agendas, together with persistent regime attempts to split their unity, succeeded in precipitating a long-lasting rift. Among this cohort of exiles, no women were visible. The wives and daughters of the exiles were not part of our research project.

Since 2015, and with increased repressive measures deployed against critics of all political persuasions and of none, a Saudi diaspora has been in the process of emerging, not only in London, but also in Europe, North America and Australia. While a small minority of those exiles belong to various shades of Islamism, the majority are simply critics of the regime who feared retaliation and consequently decided to leave the country. Others are women who left in pursuit of feminist liberation and secular projects. Unlike the early cohort of exiles, the newcomers are very young, dispersed and diverse. Their immediate atomization and dispersal across continents are gradually giving way to regrouping. While the early exiles effectively used the fax machine to flood Saudi Arabia's[38] government departments with critical statements, the newcomers use social media to forge networks of support and cooperation and to connect with the homeland. They have become active in undermining the so-called reforms of the new crown prince through the production of alternative knowledge about the country and his policies.

Even before the current exodus, many disgruntled Saudis maintained contact with me either in person or by email. They sent documents providing evidence of corruption in state institutions, personal grievances and injustices, and, in the case of women, serious abuse of their rights as citizens. The wives of senior princes and one of the wives of King Abdullah initiated meetings with me. They told me about their own grievances as estranged and humiliated divorcees. I listened but could not write about such personal stories from one single source.

Writing about exiles is above all a personal quest to explore its meaning and experience, and to situate it in the academic discourse on the topic. Since 2015 I have conducted interviews with Saudis in the diaspora, attended their meetings and conferences, corresponded with them across many countries and met many amongst them in person. I have met them in Britain, Europe, the USA, Australia and Lebanon. Each interview lasted several hours. I translated the Arabic transcript of the interview into

English and sent it back to the interviewees to check its accuracy. They sent me documents that they had submitted to immigration officers in their host countries in support of their asylum applications. Others asked me to write supporting academic letters to their lawyers to strengthen their application for asylum and convince sceptical immigration officers. I even appeared in court to support a solicitor defending a Saudi exile whose host country decided to repatriate him, although he faced imprisonment there. I used my knowledge of Saudi Arabia to support exiles in their long journey. I present here the voices of many but not all exiles.

I cannot claim to be a quasi-objective academic, totally detached from the plight of my own compatriots. The stories of their exile document the hard choices young men and women make under repression. In the text, many well-known exiles are named as they gave me permission to do so. Many others shaped this book, and their voices are documented but their names are not mentioned. They fear retaliation by the regime against their families inside Saudi Arabia. They should remain anonymous.

I was not simply the outsider-interviewer. As young Saudi exiles launched their own media programmes online, they asked me to be interviewed. I agreed to discuss Saudi history and current affairs and received questions from online audiences based on my academic publications. I did not want this book to be a one-way process in which exiles become an empirical sample or a case study for the purpose of academic research. My voice and their many voices intermingle in this book to produce an account of a shared experience. My interviewers were interested not only in my published academic work but also my own personal journey into exile. As young exiles interviewed me, I shared my own personal experiences so that others became familiar with my early example of dislocation. This interactive method enriched the book and satisfied exiles' curiosity about my own life. As it became very difficult to speak to Saudis inside the country, I decided not to reach out to them in this book. I was worried about their safety, given that on a previous occasion the regime charged a few activists in the kingdom with the crime of reading my work and storing my articles on their computers.[39]

The book also relies on a plethora of written sources and regime documents that became increasingly available in hard copy and online. New regime foundations, policy statements and media appearances of both the crown prince and other officials are consulted as a source of information about the new realm. The regime increased its visibility online, and its postings became accessible to outsiders. Both the regime and its critics relied heavily on social media platforms such as Twitter to disseminate divergent narratives about the new kingdom. The book also draws on my own previous work on the country's history and society published over thirty years, in addition to secondary sources by historians, anthropologists and political scientists.

Organization of the Book

As the new crown prince pledges to correct the mistakes of the past, the book starts with a swift introduction to this past, starting with how a vast territory in the Arabian Peninsula became Saudi Arabia in the early twentieth century. Drawing on my own and other historical monographs, Chapter 1 highlights the centrality of violence in the creation of the state; like all state projects, a fair amount of violence accompanied Saudi state formation. But the project in the country was achieved by a different kind of 'sword', that of the Al Saud and the revival of the Wahhabi tradition. This specific history impinged on state consolidation, social development and national identity—or lack thereof—until the present day. The chapter later focuses on important moments in the twentieth century when many actors challenged the nascent state. It also explores how oil wealth and Western support consolidated the project of state building. It is hoped that the chapter explains how and why the new crown prince has pledged to free Saudi Arabia from the burden of this history while reinventing it at the same time. He promises a complete break from the past while retaining the central role of his family in the process of 'becoming Saudi Arabia'. Today, the Wahhabi tradition exists in a contentious relationship with power. It is neither abandoned completely nor wholeheartedly endorsed. It is still invoked in specific contexts, for example the 2015 war on Yemen, in which Saudi–Wahhabi sectarian rhetoric resurfaced as a tool to demonize Zaydi Yemenis, or to mobilize Saudis against Shia activism and their alleged Iranian backers.

The pledge to transform the kingdom has been well received by analysts and commentators since 2015, when Prince Muhammad ibn Salman was promoted to various high-ranking government jobs. Chapter 2 surveys the media's optimistic and overtly congratulatory assessment of the emerging realm. The new regime deployed a pervasive and aggressive campaign to convince outside journalists, academics and experts that a reformist era was being ushered in with the introduction of new royal visions. Chapter 3 introduces Muhammad ibn Salman, the mastermind of the new reforms, exploring the consolidation of his cult, which eventually led to the murder of Jamal Khashoggi, the 'Man of the Palace', a loyal journalist who had spent his career defending the realm but fell out with the new leadership in 2017. Reform and repression became connected in the new era of the crown prince. Having failed to secure the unanimous support of his own royal family, the new prince launched his project to create a Saudi nation. His populist nationalism is discussed in Chapter 4, where I trace the multiple stages of nation building, leading to the current phase of populist Saudi nationalism. This populist nationalism led to a succession of purges against members of the royal family, the Islamists, the youth and feminists.

While the current nationalism is meant to unify and forge solidarities, Chapter 5 shows how the prince's populist nationalism
continued the historical marginalization of the sub-nationals, who
constitute the diverse population with its multiple tribes, regions,
sects and immigrants. Immigrants are never included as a unit for
analysis in monographs on Saudi Arabia and feature only in
demographic reports, labour-force surveys and in the rhetoric that
dominates regime Saudization policies. But their inclusion in this
chapter as human agents who intermingle with Saudi society
rather than simply performing jobs that Saudis allegedly cannot
or do not want to do enriches our understanding of a population
of almost 10 million immigrants and permanent residents.

As empowering women becomes central in regime propaganda
and policies, Chapter 6 examines the contradiction of reform and
repression as it affects women's lives, especially feminists and
activists. It focuses specifically on how the struggle and mobilization of women is appropriated by the regime in an attempt to
claim success and credit for the recent policies that allow women
to drive, increase their employment opportunities and free them
from the historical burden of male guardians. But such reformist
initiatives take place amid a pervasive campaign to silence and
imprison feminists, and even criminalize feminism.

Chapter 7 explores the aspirations of young male exiles who
together with exiled women are now part of an incipient diaspora
scattered over many continents. From young students to middle-
aged activists, new forms of diaspora political engagement are
emerging and challenging old opposition ideologies online. A
redefinition of Islamism, Arab nationalism and feminism is taking place among connected activists in ways that the regime
wants to penetrate and silence—even to the extent of murdering
an activist abroad. The chapter captures a new moment in Saudi
state–society relations and explores the success and shortcomings
of activism in the diaspora.

INTRODUCTION

The book concludes by challenging the assumption that repression is inevitably needed to pursue reform. The vibrancy of the Saudis discussed in this book attests to their readiness to imagine alternative political systems in which democracy, free speech, civil society, gender equality and above all the civil state can develop in their own homeland.

1

BECOMING SAUDI ARABIA

We took it by the sword.

Al Saud saying

Every year Saudis celebrate their National Day on 23 September. Shrouded in heated debate and controversy, this special date in the calendar marks the establishment of the Kingdom of Saudi Arabia in 1932. In the early years, the day usually passed without any celebration. Religious scholars considered the National Day an alien tradition in a country where only the two Islamic festivals, Id al-Fitr, after the fasting month of Ramadan, and Id al-Adha, after the pilgrimage season, are legitimate occasions for celebration. Similarly, the birth of the Prophet Muhammad and the Islamic Hijra new year, celebrated across the Muslim world, used to pass without festivities.[1] But, since the late 1980s, every year on 23 September green flags are raised in the streets, operas are performed and poetry is recited. Conferences are held to mark the contribution of the ruling Al Saud family to the creation of the kingdom. In recent decades, and particularly in 2019, the National Day celebrations have become more vigorous, with processions in the streets of Riyadh, the capital, in Jeddah, in Dammam, and elsewhere. Young people make the most of the spirit of festivity, dancing in the streets and having fun, mixing freely with the opposite sex in public places.[2] The new wave of festivities is amplified by social media under the patronage of Crown Prince Muhammad ibn Salman, whose private office promotes YouTube recordings of glorious past monarchs and their consistent efforts to build the individual and the nation. Either being in English or having subtitles, such recordings are also meant for the consumption of foreign observers and interested audiences.[3]

The day was chosen to mark the establishment of the kingdom by Abdul Aziz ibn Saud (d. 1953; hereafter Ibn Saud). He completed the unification of several regions under his banner and merged them into one political entity. The name *al-mamlaka al-arabiyya al-saudiyya* (Kingdom of Saudi Arabia) replaced the previous long name, the Kingdom of Hijaz and of Najd and its Dependencies. George Rendel, head of the British Foreign Office Eastern Department, claimed that the name was his personal choice, feeling that Ibn Saud first wanted to name his state after himself (*saudiyya*) but dismissed it for its awkwardness among the international community. Rendel came up with 'Saudi Arabia'.[4]

By adopting Rendel's suggestion, Ibn Saud must have wanted to emphasize two aspects of the new realm: monarchical rule (kingship) and its 'Saudi' identity. The new name marked a departure from past naming practices by which the diverse regions of the Arabian Peninsula had been known, so the regions Hijaz and Najd were dropped from the denomination. Moreover, these regions had not previously been ruled by kings. Local leaders had been known as sharifs (in Mecca), emirs (princes in local oases), imams (prayer leaders in Ibn Saud's ancestral home in Diriyyah in the eighteenth century), and sultans (Ibn Saud before 1932). The title sultan was adopted by Ibn Saud briefly before the unification of the kingdom, when he was known as the

Sultan of Najd and its Dependencies. After 1932 the Hijaz, Najd, Hasa and the Northern Provinces became one realm under the rule of one family and one king. The people of those territories began to be referred to as Saudis, thus transferring the name of the new rulers to the rest of the population. Notwithstanding the British role in its choice, the name itself became controversial, as we shall see later in this book. From 1932 the new realm extended over 2 million square kilometres.

In 2019 official Saudi sources estimated that the population reached 33,413,660.[5] Accurate statistics on foreign labour, estimated in 2018 at 37 per cent of the population, are often difficult to come by because 'Saudi authorities conceal data pertaining to the nationality of foreign residents in official publications, for fear that the numeric domination of some nationalities would encourage socio-political claims'.[6]

The Al Saud family fled central Arabia in the late nineteenth century when their capital, Riyadh, was conquered by a rival chieftain, Muhammad ibn Rashid, who defeated them in 1891.[7] Ibn Saud was a young man at the time. His father, Abdul Rahman, took his family and settled with the Al Sabah rulers of Kuwait. The latter signed a treaty of protection with Britain in 1899. The Al Saud family hoped perhaps that being in Kuwait would allow them the opportunity to draw on the Al Sabah's experience of dealing with foreign powers with a view to getting help to return to Riyadh. The family began to cultivate relations with tribal groups, and by 1902 Ibn Saud had launched a successful attack on Riyadh and regained his family's power base.

From Riyadh the Al Saud revived their ambition to expand further in Arabia. Their first major attack was on Qasim, still controlled by their Rashidi rivals. By 1906 Ibn Saud had incorporated this region in the new realm after a famous battle, Rawdat Muhanna. The victory in Qasim was supported by the Al Sabah emirs of Kuwait and approved by the British, who were watching battles in central Arabia with a view to getting closer to those who potentially opposed the weak Ottoman presence there.

In 1913 Ibn Saud turned his attention to Hasa, the eastern province, a region where the Ottomans maintained a weak presence, sent mainly from Basra in Iraq in the late nineteenth century. The attack targeted the 1,200 Ottoman soldiers in Hafuf, who had been stationed there after the annexation of the region by the Ottomans in 1870.[8] Despite having antagonized the Ottomans, Ibn Saud signed a treaty with them, which bestowed on him the title of Pasha of Najd according to an Ottoman imperial *firman*. The active maritime trade of that region of the Persian Gulf was considered important as Riyadh had no access to the sea. It depended entirely on limited local agriculture and caravan trade beyond its borders.

The conquest of Hasa brought Al Saud authority to the shores of the Gulf, and after that they were able to count on new custom revenues from ports in that region. Furthermore, it brought under their control a substantial Shia minority that had been living there for centuries.[9] This conquest remained controversial until it was recognized by the British authorities who had established connections in Kuwait and other Gulf countries in order to secure maritime trade with India. Britain confirmed Ibn Saud's conquest, thus securing the eastern borders of his nascent Riyadh emirate. But Britain considered Ibn Saud an Ottoman vassal and declined to conclude a treaty with him similar to those signed with local Gulf chiefs. Only when the First World War started in 1914 did Britain feel free to initiate serious negotiations with Ibn Saud with a view to signing a treaty of protection.

The rise of the contemporary Saudi state was thus a process that had its roots in the First World War and culminated in the establishment of the kingdom in 1932. The Saudi leadership prides itself on having 'unified' the people of Arabia. Arabia had not had the experience of straightforward nineteenth-century imperialism or early twentieth-century colonialism. Unlike most of the Arab lands that became independent states in the twentieth century, such as Algeria, Syria, Iraq and Egypt, Saudi Arabia and its leaders did not launch a national liberation campaign to free their territory from foreign domination.

The territory that is now known as Saudi Arabia did not have enough resources to lure foreign occupiers or conquerors. Its most important region before the discovery of oil in 1933 was the Hijaz, the seat of the two holy cities of Mecca and Madina.[10] This region had been nominally ruled by the Ottoman sultans in Istanbul since the sixteenth century, with the Sharifian Hashemite family, which traces its descent from the Prophet Muhammad, acting on their behalf in Mecca. While many national leaders in Arab countries were heads of liberation movements, the leaders of Saudi Arabia were from the very beginning close allies of foreign powers, mainly the British, who displaced the Ottoman Empire in 1918, and after the Second World War the USA. The region that Ibn Saud conquered in Hasa on the shores of the Persian Gulf had already been important for Britain and its presence in India. While Britain had signed protection treaties with Gulf sheikhs, it was hesitant to enter into negotiations with the chiefs of the interior of Arabia who had nominally been under Ottoman rule. It was only with the outbreak of the First World War that Britain was freed from being seen as undermining the integrity of the Ottoman Empire and started looking for local allies whom it could use against the Ottomans.

This important fact prompts many observers to think that the kingdom was simply a British creation. It was British support for and arming of the Al Saud that led to the stabilization of their realm and the fixing of its borders on the map. After the outbreak of the First World War, and as early as 1915, Britain was hoping to recruit local chiefs in Arabia and to encourage them to stage a rebellion against the Ottoman Empire that would end the nominal Ottoman suzerainty over what is now Saudi Arabia. The Ottoman presence was felt only in the Hijaz, where Mecca and Madina were, and in Hasa, where Ottoman troops were stationed, but in the interior of Arabia it was truly insignificant, especially in the central Najd province where the Al Saud originated. The Ottomans appointed themselves protectors of the sacred precinct in Mecca and the pilgrimage routes. They appointed Hashemite sharifs to rule over the region on their behalf. They also maintained a military presence in the Hijaz to protect pilgrims and symbolically assert their guardianship over the holy places. In reality, unlike the more economically vital northern territories of Lebanon, Syria, Palestine and Iraq, neither the Hijaz nor the rest of Arabia was fully integrated in the Ottoman Empire.

As early as 1913 Britain conducted secret meetings with the Hashemites in the Hijaz, and in 1915 with Ibn Saud in order to precipitate a rebellion against the Ottomans in the holy places. Aware of how controversial it would have been, both in the Middle East and in British India, to send its troops to free the holy places from Ottoman rule, Britain sent emissaries to Arabian chiefs to encourage local rebellions.

Prominent British personalities in the secret communication with local Arabian chiefs are often remembered, and some of them have become legendary: Captain William Shakespear, killed in battle while fighting with Ibn Saud; T. E. Lawrence (Lawrence of Arabia), whose name is synonymous with the 1916 Arab Revolt; Gertrude Bell, known as the maker of Arab kings; and St John Philby, close adviser of Ibn Saud for several decades, were but a few names associated with that era when Britain was searching for local allies to defeat the Ottomans. Sending British troops to evict the Ottoman garrisons stationed in the Hijaz would have provoked the anger of the most critical Muslim mass under British rule at the time: Indian Muslims. Many Muslims held the view that non-Muslims should not be allowed to enter the holy places. Consequently, Britain conducted these secret meetings with local chiefs such as Sharif Hussein of Mecca and Ibn Saud. The former was promised the title 'King of the Arabs' should he cooperate with the British and stage a tribal rebellion against the Ottomans that could free both the Hijaz and territories as far as present-day Jordan from their rule. Ibn Saud was also promised recognition as the ruler of swathes of land in the interior of Arabia.

On 26 May 1915 Ibn Saud finally signed the Anglo–Saudi Treaty. Britain acknowledged Najd, Hasa, Qatif and Jubayl and their dependencies as the territory of Ibn Saud. Aggression towards them would result in British aid to Ibn Saud. On signing the treaty, Ibn Saud was given 1,000 rifles and £20,000. The treaty granted him a monthly stipend of £5,000 and regular shipments of rifles and machine guns. In return, Ibn Saud was to pledge not to attack any Gulf chiefdom under the protection of Britain or to enter into negotiations with other superpowers.[11] This was the beginning of British interference in the local affairs of central Arabia. Although the borders of Ibn Saud's new territories were ambiguous and fluid, the treaty empowered him enough to continue his conquest of Arabia.

More importantly, British negotiations with local chiefs were in fact taking place in the western part of Ibn Saud's realm, in the Hijaz, where the Ottomans had built the famous Hijaz railway from Damascus to Madina. It was meant to improve the integration of the holy places within the Ottoman Empire and facilitate the movement of pilgrims, troops and goods between the holy cities and the Ottoman administration in the north. Hoping to secure the promised title 'King of the Arabs', Sharif Hussein of Mecca was prompted to announce the 1916 Arab Revolt, after tribal groups were amassed by the famous Lawrence of Arabia. One of their objectives was to disrupt and destroy the

lines of communication between the Hijaz and the northern territories of the Ottoman Empire. Attacking the Hijaz railway was
important. Under Hashemite leadership, several Hijazi tribes—
Shararat, Huwaitat, Harb and others—declared war on the
Ottomans, now seen through the lens of a newly formed Arab
consciousness, in direct opposition to the increasing Turkishness
of the Ottomans. Islamic solidarity was not enough to thwart
rebellion against the Ottoman sultan, who had declared a jihad
against the infidels with the outbreak of the war. Arab Hijazi
tribes began attacking the sultan's garrisons in the region, and by
1918 Madina was freed from the Ottomans.

Ibn Saud, however, hesitated to announce a similar revolt
against the Ottomans, but his neutrality in the conflict between
Britain and the Ottomans was extremely important for the
British. By 1915 he was in communication with Sir Percy Cox,
British Gulf Resident in Kuwait. Ibn Saud was not prepared to
challenge the Ottomans directly—his homeland in Najd had not
seen an Ottoman soldier since Muhammad Ali of Egypt's invasion of Arabia on behalf of the Ottoman sultan in Istanbul in
1818. His father Abdul Rahman received a stipend from the
Ottoman governor in Iraq at the end of the nineteenth century.
As mentioned above, Ibn Saud himself was given the title of
Pasha of Najd, an Ottoman title that symbolically tied him to the
sultans in Istanbul. But he remained neutral in the war between
Britain and its Arab allies on the one hand and the Ottomans on
the other. While this war was raging to the west of Riyadh,
which he had reconquered and retrieved from the control of his
Rashidi arch-enemies in 1902, Ibn Saud hesitated to join the
Sharif of Mecca in declaring war on the Ottomans. His role
during the war was limited to attacking tribal chiefs who had
sided with the Ottomans during the war, such as his rivals the
Rashids of Hail. His contribution to the British war effort was
limited to keeping local allies of the Ottomans engaged with

warfare in the Peninsula, thus preventing them from lending support to the Ottoman Empire in the north.

Between 1915 and 1921, after securing the Eastern Province, Ibn Saud focused his energies on defeating his rivals beyond Qasim in northern Arabia. He waged wars against the Rashidi emirate (1836–1921), which remained an Ottoman ally, and defeated its ruler, Muhammad ibn Rashid in Hail in the north, thus ending several decades of Rashidi rule over the northern central province of Arabia. But the greatest prize was to conquer the Hijaz and defeat his rivals, the Hashemites, who had already been allies of the British. He started encroaching on the Hijaz as early as 1918, but the final victory was achieved seven years later, in 1925.

British support of local Arabian rulers during the First World War was inconsistent, and treacherous from the point of view of those who lost power immediately when the war ended in 1918. Sharif Hussein of Mecca was the first casualty of this war in the region. He was forced to abdicate in favour of his son Ali and was eventually evicted from the Hijaz by Ibn Saud in 1924, with the British offering the sharif no support to defend his realm. The British also failed to honour their pledge to declare the sharif 'King of the Arabs' as a reward for staging the 1916 Arab Revolt. After the war, his sons Faisal and Abdullah were placed as kings in the newly created countries, Faisal in Iraq and Abdullah in Transjordan. But Hussein, the ageing father, spent his last years in exile in Cyprus, his dream of becoming king extinguished forever. Together with members of his household, he was transported by boat from Jeddah to the Mediterranean island by the British. His departure from Arabia marked the end of several centuries of Hashemite rule over the holy city of Mecca and the Hijaz. Ibn Saud declared his conquest of the Hijaz a victory in 1925 after he evicted Sharif Ali, the son of Hussein, from the holy city.

While British support for Ibn Saud was crucial in upsetting the military balance between him and his rivals in Arabia at the time—the Hashemites of the Hijaz and the Rashids in Hail—it is important to emphasize the role of local actors in the story of state formation that led to the emergence of Ibn Saud as sole leader and the demise of the others. It is too simplistic to claim that Saudi Arabia was merely a British creation, thus denying agency to all those who contributed to its formation.

Local Actors

The Al Saud, a family that named several Arabian regions after itself, promote a certain interpretation of history that justifies their new hegemony. Of course, military victories were crucial in spreading Saudi domination over vast territories and people who had no obligation to accept the new conquerors. But the Al Saud make the claim that the project of unifying Arabia was nothing but reclaiming by the sword what had been theirs in the past. Their view of this past dates back to the eighteenth century when their ancestors were local chiefs, not in Riyadh but in a neighbouring town by the name of Diriyyah.[12] Their legendary historiography points to their first expansion from this small and insignificant town to territories as far as Mecca in the west, Iraq and Syria in the north, the shores of the Persian Gulf in the east, and the mountains of Yemen in the south. This first episode of expansion is called the first Saudi state (1744–1818). With fluctuating borders, the state was fragile and on the verge of collapse at different historical moments. Nevertheless, this first experiment in state formation anchors the Al Saud's claim to rule Arabia in that first moment. While the expansion lasted for almost half a century, it ended in the total annihilation of their capital and the end of their rule over Arabia by 1818.

While in the past it was common for Arabian chiefs to expand their realms, there was something different about the Al Saud experiment in the eighteenth century. Unlike other ambitious local chiefs, the Al Saud expansion was based on an Islamic revival. The raids they carried out were justified as a jihad against those unorthodox Muslims who inhabited Arabia. Now known as Wahhabism, this ideology was a religious revivalist movement founded in the eighteenth century by Muhammad ibn Abd al-Wahhab (1703–91). An Islamic preacher, Ibn Abd al-Wahhab had limited success in enlisting strong local rulers in central Arabia until he arrived in Diriyyah, where in 1744 Muhammad ibn Saud was the local ruler. Other Arabian chiefs had rejected the vigorous preaching of Ibn Abd al-Wahhab, who wanted to purify Islam from what he believed to be innovations such as saint worship, tomb visiting and the veneration of holy men. Such practices did exist in Arabia, but not on the scale that Saudi–Wahhabi propaganda claims.[13] Their narrative paints a dark picture of Arabian society and its religious practices before Ibn Abd al-Wahhab started preaching his new interpretations of Islam. Even today schoolchildren are taught that their ancestors were *mushrikun*, polytheists, who had lost the purity of Islamic faith and rituals as practised during the time of the Prophet. Thanks to the preacher and the military support of the Al Saud, Saudi history books claim, Arabians were saved and their Islam was restored to the true path.

Muhammad ibn Abd al-Wahhab needed to strike an alliance with a leader who would adopt this interpretation of the society's religion and pledge to spread the new faith. He struck an alliance with the Al Saud in 1744, when he found refuge with a local ruler from the family. The former wanted support to continue his religious mission to deliver Arabian society from blasphemy and polytheism, while the latter saw embracing the faith as an opportunity for territorial expansion and booty. The camaraderie between the religious preacher and the ruler of Diriyyah provided both opportunity and disaster.

The narrative about the lax pre-Saudi Arabian society is so persistent that it justifies offering allegiance to the saviours, the Al Saud, who adopted Wahhabism and swore allegiance to Ibn Abd al-Wahhab and the religious scholars. From 1744 letters were sent to other Arabian chiefs, calling upon them to embrace the new reformed Islam; if they ignored or rejected the call, the Saudi–Wahhabi forces marched on their villages and oases and conquered their territories. They killed rulers and villagers, poisoned wells and burnt fields. Their soldiers, people who embraced the Wahhabi religious call to save others from blasphemy and unorthodoxy, spread fear in Arabia as they expanded in all directions. Only those who accepted subjugation and paid Islamic tax (*zakat*) to the Al Saud were spared. Conquered villages were sent preachers who acted as judges applying Islamic law. They stoned and lashed transgressors. Missing the communal Friday prayer was justification for severe punishment. Punishment for adultery was death by stoning. Theft was punished by the chopping off of hands. This was done to establish 'law and order' and to apply sharia, Islamic law, according to a very strict interpretation, unseen in Arabia before the rise of the Wahhabi movement.

The founders of this first Islamic state perceived themselves as reviving the state that the Prophet Muhammad had established in Madina in the seventh century. There were great differences, however, as Muhammad's state was inclusive and incorporated non-Muslims, for example Christians and Jews. The Wahhabi state's mission was to annihilate difference and impose one interpretation of Islam on those who came under its control. The new Wahhabi state's borders were in a permanent state of flux as local communities waited for opportunities to free themselves from Saudi–Wahhabi rule.

The expansion continued for several decades until the Saudi–Wahhabi forces reached the gates of Mecca where Muslim pilgrims gathered every year. Pilgrims came from all over the Muslim world, bringing with them their own Islamic interpretations and practices, which Wahhabis considered an aberration amounting to blasphemy. They wanted to purify Meccan society and the Holy Mosque from what they regarded as 'deviance'. By 1803–4 Saudi forces had established control over Mecca, and its sharif, Ghalib, accepted defeat. He became a representative of the Al Saud. In 1804 they reached Madina and started a campaign of destruction. Domed tombs of companions of the Prophet were razed to the ground, as Wahhabis considered buildings on graves signs of blasphemy, especially if Muslims worshipped near them. The Saudi–Wahhabi forces repeated in the Hijaz what they had done in Karbala in Iraq in 1801. While the Hijaz was mostly populated by Muslims who were Sunnis like the Wahhabis, in Mesopotamia, and especially in Karbala, they encountered Shia communities and different religious practices, both of which represented in their theology a serious aberration of Islam. There they raided and plundered, in the process gathering booty, eventually retreating to their central Arabian stronghold in Diriyyah.

Such daring raids in the Hijaz and Mesopotamia alarmed the Ottoman Empire, whose sultan in Istanbul saw himself as the protector of the Muslim realm, especially the holy places of Mecca and Madina. Saudi–Wahhabi expansion was regarded as a rebellion against the sultan's authority and prestige. Without hesitation but with some delay, the Ottoman sultan entrusted the governor of Egypt, Muhammad Ali, with the task of eliminating the menace, which had been ignored until it threatened the very legitimacy of the Ottoman sultan and undermined his ability to protect the annual pilgrimage to Mecca. Muhammad Ali sent his son Ibrahim with a strong military force to eliminate the Wahhabis and their overlords in Diriyyah, their capital. By 1818 the mission was accomplished with the capture of the last Saudi ruler, Abdullah, who was sent to Istanbul, where he was beheaded. Diriyyah was plundered by the Egyptian troops, and many Wahhabi *ulama* (religious scholars) were massacred. The Saudis never forgave the Ottomans for the atrocities in their homeland. To begin with, they never accepted that the Ottoman sultans were true Muslims. Their *ulama* had already written treatises against the Ottomans' Sufism, which was also considered an aberration of Islam. Central Arabia was, nevertheless, an inhospitable terrain for Ottoman soldiers, and many had died of disease and the harsh climate by the time they destroyed the Wahhabis and their Saudi patrons.

In the mid-nineteenth century a weak Saudi–Wahhabi revival began to be re-established in central Arabia (1824–91). But the ambitions of its leaders were limited, as they avoided provoking another Ottoman invasion. Saudi historiography emphasizes that a second state was created this time in a new capital, Riyadh. This second episode failed to achieve expansion on a large scale and was riddled by internal disputes among the Al Saud rulers until they were defeated, this time by local chiefs. The Rashids in the north benefited from the power vacuum in Najd after the fall of Diriyyah in 1818 and began to expand in Arabia at the expense of the weak second Saudi–Wahhabi revival. The Rashids in Hail, led by Muhammad, reached Riyadh and ousted its Al Saud rulers in 1891. The Al Saud, having lost their capital, fled the region in search of refuge, waiting for the appropriate moment to strike back and return to their ancestral homeland. They initially took refuge with al-Murrah tribe in eastern Arabia, and later in Kuwait, where Ibn Saud settled for over a decade until his return to Riyadh in 1902.

The eighteenth- and nineteenth-century experiments in state building provide the rationale behind the Kingdom of Saudi Arabia. As the two previous polities were strongly dependent on the legitimacy of religious revival, the current state and its founder, Ibn Saud, wanted to repeat the experiment with the help of the same powerful ideology: the Wahhabi movement and its pledge to purify Islam. It was only at the third attempt that a kingdom that began to look like a state was consolidated.

Old Strategies

When he returned to Riyadh in 1902, Ibn Saud deployed the old strategies that his ancestors had used in their eighteenth- and nineteenth-century revivals. The claim that 'we took it by the sword' continued to inspire the Saudi dream to return to their homeland. Ibn Saud surrounded himself with Wahhabi clerics who believed in the narrative that the sword was to be deployed in the service of re-Islamizing Arabia, and he pledged to abide by their rulings. Consequently, he was able to appear as the pious Imam of his Muslim followers. His family had already married into the al-Wahhab family, and their genealogies merged over several decades. Ibn Saud pledged to expand the borders of the 'pious' Muslim community beyond Riyadh and its environs, a project that was enthusiastically taken up by his Wahhabi allies. In return for their support, he vowed to honour the clerics as the protectors of piety, morality, law and good Islamic conduct, exactly as his ancestors had done in the eighteenth and nineteenth centuries. Ibn Saud must have believed that the magical power of Wahhabism would help him to regain his ancestors' power: from then on, Wahhabis were the judges, the leaders of prayers and the enforcers of obedience. With British subsidies and what he could amass in taxes, Ibn Saud employed them to preach, theorize and justify his new jihad against all those Arabian Muslims whose practices were deemed corrupt. After securing the allegiance of settled communities, he sent Wahhabi clerics to the tribal hinterland. He wanted the Wahhabis to educate the people and ensure their obedience to his rule, while he was left to deal with politics and tribal alliances. They also left him to negotiate with foreign powers, such as the British, whom the Wahhabis regarded as infidels. As long as Ibn Saud's relations with the so-called infidels were discreet, the Wahhabis turned a blind eye, but it was only a matter of time before they realized that their Imam, as they called him, had strong ties with Britain.

To relaunch expansion in Arabia, a new tribal force, the Ikhwan (brothers in faith), indoctrinated by the Wahhabi clerics with their uncompromising interpretation of Islam, was created. The Ikhwan conjure up images of ferocity and inflexible attitudes. But, most importantly, they were one of the tools used by Ibn Saud to spread his hegemony over Arabia. They were his tribal jihadi warriors who were programmed to establish the Islamic state.

Ibn Saud's Ikhwan was the first Islamist jihadi militia created in the twentieth century. Most of its members belonged to famous Arabian tribes. The first recruits appeared in 1912. They consisted of successfully indoctrinated tribes, who were requested to abandon their nomadism and set up home in special settlements where they could receive the clerics and gain an Islamic education. They were also paid a stipend to compensate them for loss of income from nomadism and raids. While agriculture failed to appeal to these tribes in the settlements, they became ferocious warriors, to be dispatched to subdue those regions and people who had been labelled impure Muslims. Ibn Saud feared the shifting loyalties of such tribes, who could easily have abandoned his project or switched allegiance to his rivals. But the clerics ensured that they remained under control. The project proved to be difficult, and it was only a matter of time before these dispersed tribes staged a rebellion against the leader who had brought them together under an Islamic banner. They turned the indoctrination of Ibn Saud's clerics against him, using Wahhabi teachings to undermine his fragile realm.

By 1927 the Ikhwan were showing signs of unrest under Ibn Saud's leadership. This resulted from two contradictory perceptions of the conquest. Ibn Saud himself was restoring his ancestors' rule over Arabia after the collapse of their realm in the nineteenth century. In contrast, the Ikhwan had been indoctrinated with the idea that their raids were a jihad against those Muslims whose faith was corrupt. It was their duty to spread Islam again in Arabia, as the Prophet Muhammad did in the seventh century. And their tribal leaders expected to be compensated for their role as military commanders with sinecures as chiefs in the newly conquered territories, as the Prophet had done. But Ibn Saud envisaged a kingdom in which the Al Saud were the only legitimate rulers. He was not going to succumb to pressure and appoint tribal leaders of Otaiba, Ajman and Mutair, among others, as governors in the provinces—roles that were reserved for his brothers, sons and other powerful relatives. The three Ikhwan tribal leaders—Faisal al-Duwaish, the best-known rebel, Sultan Ibn Bijad and Ibn Hithlaiyn—felt betrayed by Ibn Saud. They had no doubt expected to be appointed emirs in the three major regions that had been conquered: Najd, Hijaz and Hasa. On one occasion in 1927, al-Duwaish marched to meet Ibn Saud with 150 armed men. He was described as fierce and arrogant and regarded himself as Ibn Saud's equal rather than his mere military commander. Negotiations with the Ikhwan leaders went badly, and eventually they started expanding in areas that were bound to get Ibn Saud into trouble with his protectors, the British authorities stationed in Kuwait and Iraq. In 1928 Ibn Saud summoned loyal preachers to issue a fatwa, or religious ruling, condemning the rebels, who were described as having misunderstood Islam and acted against the consensus of the Muslim *umma* and its legitimate ruler. Such rulings continued to inspire Saudi clerics and justified repressing any opposition to Al Saud rule by declaring protest an abhorred rebellion against the legitimate Muslim ruler. The clerics drew the conclusion that the rebels should be fought until they accepted Ibn Saud's authority. This opinion justified the military campaign that Ibn Saud began to launch against the rebels, following them to the borders of Kuwait, where the British Royal Air Force assisted in bombing their camps and capturing their leaders. The British captured Faisal al-Duwaish and handed him over to Ibn Saud, who put him in prison, where he later died.

The Ikhwan were finally defeated as Ibn Saud eliminated potential rivals from within the force that had helped him to expand his realm. Thus, in 1932, it seemed that the kingdom's name needed to be overtly Saudi, lest others entertain the idea that the realm was theirs too. Leadership of the kingdom, the regions and the most important positions were to belong to the Al Saud and nobody else. The character of the new state was now defined as a Saudi dynasty rather than a tribal or regional confederation. The leadership would continue to pledge support for the Wahhabi clerics as long as they did not deviate from the original pact between the Al Saud ancestors and the founder of the Wahhabi movement in the eighteenth century. A strong centralized state run from Riyadh endeavoured to eliminate regional autonomy and diversity. After 1932 there was only one king, the arbiter of all matters of state and provinces, and one interpretation of Islam, the Wahhabi tradition.

The pacification of the Ikhwan in the eastern region of Arabia was followed by another minor tribal rebellion in the west. Hamid ibn Rifadah of the Hijazi Billi tribe started an uprising in the Hijaz, allegedly supported by Abdullah, the son of the deposed Sharif Hussein of Mecca, who was now king in Transjordan, and the Free Party of the Hijaz, founded by Hijazis who refused to accept Ibn Saud in their territory and fled to Transjordan with the Hashemites. They did not accept the loss of the Hijaz to Ibn Saud in 1925 and entertained hopes of a return to their ancestral region. Such aspirations failed, as the Hashemites in both Transjordan and Iraq were under British rule, and so was Ibn Saud. Britain maintained its control in all three countries. The Hijazi tribal rebellion was crushed, and Ibn Saud declared his kingdom a polity for him and his descendants. To make this a permanent feature of the new realm, he appointed his son Saud as crown prince in 1933 and placed princes as governors of the conquered provinces. Kingship was then to pass from Saud to his most eligible brother, thus confirming an unusual horizontal line of succession that remained a constant feature in Saudi Arabia until 2017, when King Salman appointed his own son Muhammad, rather than a brother, as crown prince. King Salman did what his father had done in 1933—he marginalized his remaining brothers and appointed his own son to succeed him.

By 1932, only Kuwait, Oman and the other small emirates of the Gulf shores remained outside Saudi control in Arabia. There was also Yemen, where an old imamate remained independent of British control. The first Saudi–Yemen war broke out in 1934, as Ibn Saud and Imam Yahya of Sanaa competed over the southernmost regions of Saudi Arabia in Asir. The conflict was resolved, and each party respected the borders that were drawn up between the two countries. However, claims and counterclaims remained a thorny issue between the kingdom and Yemen. The most recent bombardment of Yemen by a Saudi-led coalition in 2015 rekindled this old history with the Yemeni Houthis, reminding their people of how the Saudis annexed territories they regard as theirs.

The process of becoming Saudi Arabia was contested and took almost thirty years to complete. In its early years it faced serious challenges, such as the tribal rebellions mentioned above. The fact that most of the severe trials emanated from the very forces that were crucial for its creation is telling. Throughout the twentieth century this challenge became a recurrent feature of Saudi Arabia's modern history, as later modern-day jihadis, armed with early

Wahhabi theology about the righteous Muslim leader, his proper
relations with infidels, his obligation to remain faithful to Islam,
and his responsibility to honour his pledge to lead a pure Islamic
state, resorted to violence to undermine Al Saud rule exactly as
their predecessors had in 1927. Notwithstanding the different
historical context between that era and present-day Saudi Arabia,
certain continuities remained apparent. The more the Saudi rulers
were seen as dependent on external powers, the more their legitimacy was questioned by their own loyal Wahhabis. The cycles
repeated themselves and reached a climax with the rise of contemporary terrorism, including that of al-Qaida and the Islamic
State group. Both recent movements were inspired by the early
Saudi state of the eighteenth century and its theology.

Another important feature in emerging Saudi Arabia was its
reliance from the very beginning on the support of external powers. The Saudi rulers never considered Britain as a colonial power
or an occupier. In fact, they were so dependent on Britain that
their most loyal Ikhwan forces began to question the relationship
in 1927. The Ikhwan faced their demise at the hands of Britain,
which handed them over to Ibn Saud. The British played a
prominent role not only in naming the realm Saudi Arabia but
more importantly in supporting it during times of duress. This
historical relationship is cherished by both sides and remains so
in the present day, as Britain is the second-most important
exporter of arms to the kingdom after the USA.

Another challenge to the process of becoming Saudi Arabia
presented itself immediately after the establishment of the kingdom. With the world recession of 1933, few pilgrims were able
to make the journey to Mecca. As their numbers dwindled, so
did Ibn Saud's income from taxing them. After the expansion of
the territories, Ibn Saud lacked the resources to keep the various
forces that had helped him establish the realm rewarded and
satisfied. He could not offer the conquered territories anything

other than meagre and erratic subsidies, while taxing them at the same time. Yet he and his clerics expected the people of Arabia to be grateful for their efforts to educate them in true Islam as preached by the clerics. Their narrow interpretation of Islam and inspiration from the jurisprudence of early Muslim scholars, such as Ahmad ibn Hanbal, resulted in the stifling of diversity of religious interpretations, especially in the Hijaz, where Shafi'i, Maliki and Hanafi jurisprudence had been taught in its local mosque schools (*madrasas*). The Wahhabi tradition and the teachings of its clerics later became the only curriculum taught in religious schools. The revenues that Ibn Saud amassed from the Hasa and the Hijaz were not sufficient, and it was only with the discovery of oil in 1933 that he was able to count on a source of income, extracted by an American oil company and independent of the will of the conquered people. Ibn Saud was now free from any pressure to succumb to the will of the people, including the clerics. With oil, he was no longer dependent on taxing merchants, the Bedouin and other constituencies.

The discovery of oil in Ibn Saud's territories happened in 1933. He granted the oil-exploration contract to American oil company Exxon, thanks to the efforts of St John Philby, whom the British had dispatched to Ibn Saud in 1918 and who remained as his adviser until the death of Ibn Saud in 1953. Ibn Saud demanded a stipend from the oil company in gold on signing the exploration contract. The stipend was used to maintain the realm and enrich his own royal household. But it was only after the Second World War that oil was pumped in commercial quantities and Saudi Arabia became important for the rest of the world. It is at this juncture that British influence in the kingdom began to be replaced by that of the USA, whose oil companies facilitated diplomatic relations with Ibn Saud, most importantly to protect the oilfields in the Eastern Province, where most of Saudi oil industry is located.[14] The USA was drawn into Saudi Arabia after the discovery of oil, thanks to petroleum executives and their interest in securing a territory that later became known as the location of 25 per cent of world energy reserves.

Challenges to the New State, 1953–2011

With oil revenues starting to make an impact and succession to the throne guaranteed to remain in the hands of Ibn Saud's sons, the ageing king died in 1953, leaving behind forty-four sons. Crown Prince Saud became king as planned. He ruled until 1964. During his reign, cracks at the top leadership level began to surface. King Saud and his brother Crown Prince Faisal entered into a fierce battle over how to manage oil revenues and who among the princes should be promoted to important high positions. Ibn Saud wanted all his sons to accede to kingship in due course, but this went against each successive king's desire to promote his own sons, rather than his brothers, to the highest positions. Faisal was a strong crown prince who was determined to exclude Saud's sons from the succession. Saud continued to promote his own sons, but Faisal protested. Saud was accused of mismanaging oil revenues, spending most of them on his own palaces, children, and many wives and concubines. Faisal now became the pious, austere, careful and shrewd contester who planned to oust the irresponsible King Saud. The brothers could not agree on how to manage finances and policies, so eventually Faisal summoned the Riyadh religious scholars and extracted a fatwa from them justifying forcing his brother to abdicate. Saud was not easily removed but, in 1964, as the Saudi National Guard was ordered by Faisal to surround his palace, he succumbed to the pressure and was driven to the airport. He left for Vienna with a small number of his wives and young children and would die in Athens in 1969. This was the first succession dispute between the Saudi brothers that threatened the king-

dom at a difficult time when other regional forces and movements were equally determined to undermine and even overthrow the Saudi regime.

How to manage the new state revenues, create institutions,
educate the population, establish an army, manage relations with
the Arab and Muslim world, and maintain the trust of foreign
allies became urgent issues for successive Saudi kings. The oil
industry in the Eastern Province built its own settlement, which
came to be known as Aramco camp. Aramco shipped American
executives, skilled labour, managers, geologists and secretaries to
the camp, while local Bedouin were hastily brought in trucks
from other regions to work on the oil sites while living in tin-
roofed shelters. As there was not enough local labour, and many
Saudis initially hesitated to migrate to the Eastern Province, the
oil company brought in workers from other Arab countries who
were attracted by the new job opportunities or fleeing turmoil in
a region still under Western domination. With the discovery of
oil, Saudi Arabia had become important beyond its borders. It
was fully integrated into the global capitalist economy as an
energy source that many in the industrial world depended on.
While in the past Arabian tribes had migrated to the fertile
northern territories in Syria and Iraq for their livelihood, oil
made Saudi Arabia a country receiving immigrants.

The heartland of Najd lacked an educated elite to manage state
affairs, but it had many preachers, traders and craftsmen, all of
whom lived in oases and towns. The state initially relied on experienced Hijazis who had much more exposure to states and
empires while under Ottoman and Sharifian rule. Saudi kings
supplemented Hijazis with foreign Arab bureaucrats who had
fled their countries during the turbulent years of anti-colonial
struggle. Egyptians, Syrians, Lebanese, Libyans and, after 1948,
Palestinians were recruited to work in the oil industry and the
expanding new state bureaucracies. Many became ambassadors,

such as the Egyptian Hafez Wahba in London; historians documenting the victory of Ibn Saud, such as the American Lebanese Amin al-Rihani and Kheyr al-Din Zirkili; teachers in schools; and bureaucrats in newly established ministries. It took several decades for Saudis to move into newly created government jobs. Most Saudis of the early generation were educated by foreign Arabs. It was only in the 1980s that Saudi schools, especially those created for women in the early 1960s, began to replace their foreign teachers with local women.

In the late 1950s and 1960s, Muslim Brotherhood cadres suffering persecution in countries such as Egypt and Iraq sought refuge in Saudi Arabia, where they staffed religious and educational institutions.[15] They came to play an important role in creating contacts between Saudi Arabia and the rest of the Muslim world, especially during the Cold War, when Saudi Arabia faced the challenge of a wave of anti-imperialism and nationalism from nearby countries such as Egypt and, later, Iraq.

After pacifying its own tribal rebels and consolidating the realm through oil revenues, Saudi Arabia began to feel the pressure of regional challenges. First Gamal Abdel Nasser in Egypt, with his version of Arab nationalism and anti-imperialism, and later the Baath Parties in Iraq and Syria began to see Saudi Arabia as a client state of the West. Many Saudis were drawn to this wave of nationalist and socialist projects and began to agitate in the oil region, where workers from different parts of Saudi Arabia intermingled with foreign, mainly Arab, workers. In the age of nationalization of state resources, Saudis engaged with the wave of protest against the ongoing Western presence in the Arab world. Saudi workers in the Aramco camp staged demonstrations and demanded the right to establish trade unions as early as the late 1940s. These became more vibrant in the 1950s, so that King Saud had to mobilize troops to end the protest and later banned demonstrations and trade unions.[16] From 1964 King

Faisal deployed even greater repression against those deemed subversive agitators.

One critical event that left its mark on Saudi consciousness was the establishment of the state of Israel in 1948 and its later annexation of Jerusalem in 1967. Saudis were confronted with the resultant refugee crisis as many Palestinians ended up fleeing to camps in Lebanon, Syria and Jordan. Nasser's radio station Sawt al-Arab showered the West's Arab allies, mainly Saudi Arabia, with accusations of being stooges of empire. Nasser presented King Saud with such a serious challenge that the king conspired to assassinate him after the short-lived Egyptian–Syrian union in the 1960s. Arab unity threatened the Saudi leadership with its rhetoric of pan-Arabism. But Saudi oil was not intended to be shared, unless given as charity to loyal Arabs.

Under Faisal, Wahhabi preachers were instructed to condemn these Arab leaders, whom they branded as secular and godless, promoting the alien concept of nationalism. After all, Saudis are Muslims. They established the realm as a Saudi Islamic state rather than as an Arab state. Nasser's propaganda had to be confronted with what mattered most to Saudis: a potent Islam and pan-Islamism. Under Faisal's rule Saudi Arabia emerged as the champion of Islamic causes, defender of the faith against subversive alien notions of nationalism, communism and socialism, and the protector of the holy places. Its location as the site of the holy cities of Mecca and Madina with their sacred centrality to all Muslims became a source of legitimacy under the guardianship of Saudi kings. New global Islamic institutions such as the Organisation of the Islamic Conference, Islamic banks, Islamic charities and global Islamic educational centres mushroomed around the globe, all sponsored by Saudi oil revenues. A new Islamic university was created in Madina in the 1960s with scholarships given to foreign Muslim students seeking Islamic studies in Saudi Arabia.[17]

Saudi Arabia still did not have enough educational cadres to fill the new Islamic bureaucracy. For its newly founded Islamic transnational networks, it initially relied on both other Arab and other Muslim immigrants. By the 1970s and 1980s, Egyptian, Palestinian and Pakistani Islamists, among many others, promoted Saudi Arabia as the most important country in the Muslim world. The kingdom began to appear as a borderless Islamic empire, devoted to stopping the tide of secularism, nationalism, communism and socialism in Muslim-majority countries and later among Muslim minorities in the West. The West itself began to construct Saudi Arabia as an important ally during the Cold War. Its oil was but one dimension of its importance. Its religious tradition was from now on deployed to defeat enemies of the monarchy, but also enemies of the West, especially those who adopted anti-imperialist agendas.

Murder in the Royal Palace

As the wave of Arab nationalism subsided after their countries' defeat in the 1967 Arab–Israeli War and the death of Nasser in 1971, Saudi Arabia breathed a sigh of relief, enjoying its growing influence in the Muslim world and its abundant and unprecedented oil wealth. Unexpectedly, however, there was murder in the royal palace, as King Faisal was assassinated by his nephew, Prince Faisal ibn Musaid, on 25 March 1975. Saudis were shocked by the daring murder of their king by one of his own kinsmen. To understand this incident, we must go back to 1965, when the assassin's brother Prince Khalid was shot by Saudi troops outside his house. Prince Khalid had remained faithful to the Wahhabi tradition that shunned all so-called innovations, including cars and the telegraph. He wanted to stick to the austere principles of a pious Islamic state, as promised by his grandfather Ibn Saud. Khalid objected to the opening of a television station in Riyadh and marched on the building with some followers. King Faisal ordered Saudi troops to eliminate this new menace, and security forces opened fire on Khalid, killing him. In the early 1970s Khalid's brother, Prince Faisal, left to study in Colorado. On his return in March 1975 he marched into the king's palace and shot him while he was receiving foreign ministers. One of the witnesses was Ahmad Zaki Yamani, a famous Saudi oil minister during the first oil boom. The king's guests were unhurt, but he was rushed to hospital, where he later died of gunshot wounds.

Conspiracy theories were rife. Rumours circulated that the USA was behind the murder, as it had never forgiven King Faisal for joining the Arab oil embargo in 1973 to support Egypt in the October War against Israel. Bizarre rumours singled out Henry Kissinger, the US Secretary of State, and claimed that he might have been behind the murder in order to eliminate Faisal, who had proved to be bold, and with great ambitions beyond Saudi Arabia. According to the rumours that were rife at the time, the CIA wanted to eliminate King Faisal, as he had become an international figure among Muslims, vowing to pray in the al-Haram al-Sharif Mosque in Jerusalem, lost to Israel after the 1967 war. The fact that the assassin had an American girlfriend while he was studying in Colorado inflamed the imagination of many Saudis searching for reasons to blame the murder on foreign agents. His girlfriend since 1968, Christina Surma, told the press that she was shocked that the prince had murdered his uncle, describing him as a gentle and educated person.[18] According to a senior Saudi civil servant who was very close to King Faisal in the 1970s, and who should remain unnamed for security reasons, a message was delivered to him weeks before the assassination from a Western intelligence source informing him that the king would be assassinated by one of his kin. He also claimed that this source had told him that the USA, together with the future

King Fahd, were plotting the assassination. However, the civil
servant refused to give me access to the document, which was
in the form of a letter he received before the murder. As such,
this version remains a rumour until hard evidence becomes
available. It claims that senior princes in the family[19] conspired
to eliminate Faisal and install the weak King Khalid as an hon-
orary monarch while Fahd assumed the most important roles
in government. This was exactly what transpired after King
Faisal's assassination.

Other rumours focused on the alleged role of the maternal kin
of the two princes Khalid and Faisal ibn Musaid, whose mother,
Watfa, was the daughter of the last Rashidi emir, Muhammad,
the ruler of Hail who was defeated by Ibn Saud in 1921. The
maternal uncle of Prince Faisal ibn Musaid, Miteb Al-Rashid,
was detained for over eighteen months, but was eventually
released as there was no evidence of his involvement in this Al
Saud family murder.

No evidence for all these rumours was presented, and sensitive
information in the US archives no doubt remains classified. In
June 1975 the Saudi authorities beheaded the assassin after investigations that concluded that he was acting on his own rather
than on behalf of foreign governments. Many Saudis simply
believed that the murder was revenge for the 1964 assassination
of his brother in Riyadh. Saudi authorities of course did not
acknowledge the connection between 1964 and 1975, but everyone knew.

Trouble in 1979

After Faisal's assassination, his brother Khalid (r. 1975–82)
became king, but he was a weak monarch and the power behind
the throne was his half-brother Crown Prince Fahd. Saudi Arabia
started to enjoy the revenues of the oil boom following the 1973

oil embargo, when its GDP suddenly shot to 99.3 billion Saudi riyals. But oil revenues masked a brewing crisis that came into the open during the siege of the Mecca Mosque by a group of Wahhabi rebels in 1979.

On 20 November, during the annual pilgrimage season, pilgrims in Mecca and the rest of the Muslim world were shocked by the news that Saudi rebels, assisted by a group of 200 armed Arabs and other Muslims, had entered the holy precinct and held pilgrims hostage. Two Saudi leaders of the siege, Juhayman al-Otaibi and Muhammad al-Qahtani, declared their objections to the moral laxity of the Saudi king and demanded the removal of the royal family. Al-Otaibi was born in the Ikhwan settlement of Sajir, one of the Ikhwan projects established by Ibn Saud. The rebels were indoctrinated in the teachings of the Wahhabi tradition and came to be known as the neo-Ikhwan.[20]

This new challenge reflected latent contradictions in Saudi state formation: how to reconcile wealth with economic modernization; how to remain faithful to the Wahhabi tradition and continue to have close ties with the West; and the vulnerability of the royal family to dissent from within the ranks of those it had supported, promoted and strengthened. Like the 1927 rebellion, the siege was triggered by the assumption that the Saudi rulers had deviated from the original project of the Islamic state that many in Saudi Arabia had contributed to establishing. Juhayman al-Otaibi wrote a famous treatise called *Rasail Juhayman*, which was circulated to explain to his followers his reservations about the monarchy, including the increasing Westernization of the country and its reliance on the West. The Saudi ruling family faced the challenge of freeing the hostages and capturing the rebels with minimum bloodshed in the Holy Mosque. As in 1927, it could not do the task on its own, so it enlisted French and Jordanian security services to help with the daunting mission. Mecca was sacred territory where no arms were permitted, but the rebels had smuggled them into the holy site in tunnels dug under the mosque. Crown Prince Fahd obtained a fatwa from loyal Wahhabi clerics justifying storming the rebels in their hiding place inside the mosque. With foreign help, and after two tense weeks, the rebellion eventually ended. Many rebels were killed and some hostages were freed. The captured rebel leaders were later beheaded as punishment for their outrageous dissent.

Although the radicalization of Saudi Arabia was an integral part of the formation of the state from the very beginning, the Mecca siege symbolized its evolution, which led to escalating terrorism across the country in the decades that followed. It is historically inaccurate to assume that before 1979 the country had followed a moderate approach to religion and politics, as claimed by Crown Prince Muhammad ibn Salman and many Saudi intellectuals opposed to Islamism. When Crown Prince Muhammad gave an interview to *The Guardian* promising that Saudi Arabia will return to its initial moderate Islam, he was delivering a political rather than a historically accurate statement.[21] He blamed radicalization in Saudi Arabia after 1979 on Iran, informing his interviewer that Saudi Arabia had previously been a peaceful country enjoying a moderate religious tradition. He specifically chose 1979 as a turning-point when radicalization in Saudi Arabia had started. Many Saudi intellectuals and state propagandists adopted this interpretation of the past, blaming the siege of the Holy Mosque and the Iranian revolution for the rise of radicalization and conservatism in their country.

In 1979 the Saudi leadership began to realize that the monster it had bred since the beginning of the twentieth century was now ready to strike back, into the heart of the sacred territory that the leadership was meant to protect and guard. To emphasize this duty, Fahd adopted the title of 'Guardian of the Two Holy Mosques' in 1986. This did little to resolve the contradictions and challenges that radical Wahhabi preachers posed to the regime that they had created and legitimized since the beginning of the twentieth century. Rebellion from within was bound to erupt under Saudi patronage of the Wahhabi movement. The movement evolved as an uncompromising totalitarian tradition that began to fragment and break up into small splinter movements, all engaged in fierce battles over religious interpretation and mission in Arabia.

Saudi Arabia and its Islamic Credentials

Saudi Arabia's susceptibility to regional turbulence had increased with the dramatic Iranian revolution in 1979 that led to the overthrow of Shah Reza Pahlavi and the establishment of the Islamic Republic. The Iranian revolution did not lead directly to radicalization in Saudi Arabia, but it pushed the Saudi regime to intensify the measures that it had already adopted to legitimize itself, namely the augmentation of its Islamic rhetoric, increased surveillance of the population, and the appearance of piety. Meanwhile the Islamic Republic adopted anti-Western rhetoric and cultivated a strong anti-Saudi position. The objective was to export the Iranian revolution abroad. This proved threatening to Saudi Arabia, as it now faced both the rising influence of its own Sunni Islamists and the agitations of its Shia communities in the Eastern Province. In 1979 the Saudi Shia declared their own *intifada* (uprising) against what they regarded as state oppression and exclusion of their community. In addition to quashing the threat of Sunni Islamism in Mecca, the Saudi ruling family mobilized its troops to suppress demonstrations in the oil-rich eastern region where most of the Shia live.

To contain the appeal of Iranian influence and the mounting Sunni Islamist threat, Saudi Arabia augmented its compliance with the demands of its Sunni malcontents. The ruling family could not afford to be seen as lax and Westernized when its Iranian Shia neighbours in the Persian Gulf overtly demonstrated their Islamic credentials, and when its country's own Islamists criticized its increasing Westernization. Saudi Arabia suppressed the 1979 Mecca rebellion, but eventually began to adopt visible measures to make it look more Islamic. It increased its patronage of the manifestations of Islam both domestically and abroad, as well as its sponsorship of Islamic education worldwide, and allowed its Islamists greater control over educational, judicial and media institutions. A re-Islamization programme was now an urgent necessity as Saudi Arabia competed with Iran over Islam and regional hegemony. Not known for his personal Islamic credentials, King Fahd became the champion of Islamic transnational links that spread Saudi religious teachings around the world. He himself started a Quran-publishing institution to export copies of the Quran worldwide. He was also responsible for establishing a network of schools and religious institutions carrying his name abroad. Saudi Arabia had to be seen as the pivotal power among Muslims and needed to displace Iran, which equally aspired to become a hub of Islamic networks under the auspices of Imam Khomeini, the supreme leader and charismatic religious authority of the revolution. Saudi Arabia also endeavoured to defeat Iran in its war with Iraq throughout the 1980s by pouring resources into the hands of Saddam Hussein, whose long, fierce war with the Iranians was fought on behalf of Saudi Arabia and the other Gulf countries, as well as asserting his own power. Saudi Arabia was not able to confront Iran directly, so it used Iraq with its million-strong army to weaken Iran immediately after its revolution.

An opportunity for Saudi Arabia to demonstrate its commitment to Islamic and Arab causes arose immediately after President Anwar Sadat of Egypt signed the Camp David Agreement that established peace with Israel in 1979. Saudi

Arabia rejected the agreement and boycotted Egypt, thus demonstrating its objection to the Egyptians' unilateral rapprochement with Israel, which had shunned Arab consensus. Saudi Arabia began to see itself as replacing Egypt in leading the Arab world, a position that Egypt had occupied since the 1950s. But soon the kingdom shifted its focus to a more urgent conflict in the Gulf. Iran represented more of a real threat than Israel in the region, as it could have easily disrupted the flow of Saudi oil to the outside world, thus depriving Saudi Arabia of its main source of wealth. Thus Saudi attention moved to the Gulf, leaving the Palestinian cause behind. From then on, Iran rather than Israel was the enemy.

Yet the kingdom continued to want to demonstrate its Islamic credentials, and the Soviet occupation of Afghanistan in 1979 offered an opportunity to mitigate the mounting Islamist threat at home. Saudi Arabia adopted the Afghan jihad and facilitated the travel of its own jihadis to assist in humanitarian and military operations. The so-called Afghan Arabs, who came from many Arab countries, included a Saudi contingent. The royal family pledged to liberate Afghanistan from the godless communists, a position that appealed to many Saudi Islamists. Throughout the 1980s Saudis travelled to many destinations in Afghanistan via Pakistan, with full Saudi financial support. This was the beginning of the formation of a global jihadi movement that came to haunt not only Saudi Arabia but also the West.

By 1990 Saudi jihadis were returning home from Afghanistan, expecting to be welcomed as Islamic heroes, but in fact faced with detention and exile. Having gained military skills, they were regarded as dangerous, but Saudi Arabia and other governments had no plans for an exit strategy to contain them. By the mid-1990s many jihadis felt betrayed and launched terrorism campaigns inside Saudi Arabia, targeting American and Saudi military compounds. Osama Bin Laden, the founder of al-Qaida, emerged in this turbulent context as an opponent of the Saudi royal family, in conjunction with the Saudis in Afghanistan. When he returned to Saudi Arabia in 1990, he was given no recognition and immediately turned against the royal family, after several years of raising the banner of jihad in Afghanistan on its behalf. According to Bin Laden, the Saudi ruling family had become the 'near enemy', but its defeat required attacking its patrons in the West, the 'far enemies'. The 9/11 attack on the Twin Towers in New York was the first manifestation of the crisis turning international in scale. Originally it had been a domestic Saudi problem, whose seeds were sown after Saudi Arabia rejected Bin Laden's offer to defend the kingdom against Saddam Hussein when he invaded Kuwait in 1990. Once again, the contradiction within the Saudi state between its pledge to protect Islam and its increasing dependence on the West for protection erupted, with consequences of a global reach. The biggest casualty was Saudi Arabia's most important Western ally and partner, the USA, held by jihadis as responsible for empowering a regime they regarded as having failed to honour its Islamic duties while remaining subservient to the West.

The jihadis returned from Afghanistan to avenge what they regarded as Saudi betrayal. Between 2003 and 2008, al-Qaida in the Arabian Peninsula was established and claimed responsibility for major terrorist attacks in Saudi cities. Its leaders, Yusif al-Ayri and Abdul Aziz al-Muqrin, among others, were prepared to die with their victims—often Saudis, but also Arab, Asian and Western expatriates.[22] Residential compounds where foreigners lived, as well as state institutions and ministries, became targets for suicide bombers. Jihadi violence in Saudi cities prompted the government and in particular the Ministry of Interior to strengthen its defences, create new anti-terrorism forces and launch an ideological campaign against jihadis. The campaign aspired to show that Saudi jihadis had been misled by foreign

Islamists, especially those who took refuge in Saudi Arabia from other Arab countries. It took a long time for the Saudi authorities to admit that jihadis were actually a home-grown phenomenon, drawing on the same religious tradition that had helped to establish the kingdom itself. Saudi Arabia was fighting its own ideology, and it was an ugly and bloody fight.

Terrorist attacks subsided after 2008, but the threat remained. Many al-Qaida operatives and ideologues were either killed or imprisoned, others fleeing to nearby Yemen. There was a moment of soul-searching to identify the source of the threat and develop defences against it. Saudi Arabia was put under international pressure that criticized its transnational Wahhabi links, its promotion of an uncompromising religious ideology and its sponsorship of radical religious education worldwide. Neither the West nor Saudi Arabia acknowledged the role they had both played in the emergence of a borderless global jihadi movement after sponsoring the Afghan jihad. Even if they privately understood their contribution, no one was willing to admit responsibility in public. Rather than being held accountable for the contribution it had made to the wave of global terrorism, the Saudi state became a partner in the War on Terror that the USA launched after 9/11.

The Arab Uprisings of 2011

Jihadi violence across the Muslim world failed to overthrow a single regime. The peaceful protest that started with the Arab uprisings, however, succeeded in toppling several Arab presidents: Husni Mubarak of Egypt, Zein al-Abdin Bin Ali of Tunisia, Muammar al-Qadafi of Libya, and Ali Abdullah Saleh of Yemen. In 2019 both Abdul Aziz Bou Tafliqa of Algeria and Omar al-Bashir of Sudan were also deposed by mass demonstrations demanding their overthrow. The jihadis employed a futile strategy of violence that led only to death and repression, as it gave governments that were riddled with pervasive corruption an excuse to suppress all dissent in the name of fighting terrorism, diverting resources away from dealing with urgent social and economic problems. Arab populations, including the Saudis, were deprived of job opportunities, decent living standards, basic human rights and social justice.

In January 2011 a truly peaceful Arab protest movement erupted, calling for the downfall of regimes in Tunisia, Egypt, Libya, Bahrain, Syria and Yemen, and leading to the overthrow of several leaders. Observers concluded that Arab republics were truly oppressive, unlike the monarchies, especially in the Gulf, where so-called social contracts bound monarchs and subjects, and where a pervasive redistribution of oil wealth through state subsidies and welfare services guaranteed better legitimacy and loyalty.

But later in 2011 demonstrations broke out in many Saudi cities—Qatif, Riyadh, Buraydah, Abha and others—demanding accountability, jobs, dignity and freedom for prisoners of conscience from prisons that were bulging after the Arab uprisings.[23] In these prisons, jihadis, peaceful intellectuals, religious reformers, civil society founders and human rights activists intermingled, all treated as security threats that undermined the durability of the monarchy. Peaceful demonstrations were regarded as an act of terrorism on a par with suicide-bombing operations. It was at this moment of the Arab uprisings that Saudi women intensified their quest for equality. They launched several campaigns demanding the right to drive, as will be discussed later in the book. Having watched the strategies of Arab protesters in public squares, Saudis staged limited demonstrations in Riyadh, Buraydah and other cities demanding the release of political prisoners. In one demonstration in Buraydah, women burnt a picture of Minister of the Interior Muhammad ibn Nayif and posted the video clip on YouTube. University students in Abha staged demonstrations against the administration. The Shia in the Eastern Province went onto the streets in huge processions demanding the release of their political prisoners. Peaceful protest became an acceptable strategy to many Saudi activists, thanks to the Arab uprisings. At this juncture, criticism of the monarch and senior princes became a red line. The Saudi leadership mobilized most loyal Wahhabis in the Council of Higher Ulama, established in the 1970s, to outlaw peaceful protest and declare it an abhorrent rebellion against the legitimate rulers. Their fatwas were distributed in mosques, and the media published them in an attempt to prevent a domino effect that would be difficult to control without the deployment of serious state violence. Fatwas insisting on the obligation to obey the rulers continue to be published until the present day. In 2017 alone, eight fatwas were issued by the Grand Mufti, Abdul Aziz Al-Sheikh.[24] The Saudi royal family worried about the wave of peaceful mass protest reaching its cities, so it tightened its control and severely punished transgression. In 2011 it also deployed its resources to absorb dissent, distributing over $130 billion on new welfare provisions, hospitals, housing and employment. It promised to send young people abroad to seek education on government scholarships and dedicated vast funds to this purpose. These measures constructed the problems in Saudi Arabia as merely economic rather than political. The problem was presented as simply one of resource distribution and provision, which the leadership promised to tackle. King Abdullah (r. 2005–15) became the champion of reform, the empowerment of women, and more lavish welfare services. He sent thousands of young Saudis abroad to seek higher education, inaugurated a new science and technology university, and promised to fight terrorism at home. A new educational curriculum was introduced, and radical preachers were sacked.

Containing and eventually eliminating the Arab regional threat by returning to the status quo ante became an urgent project for

King Abdullah. Saudi Arabia led the counter-revolution in countries deemed allies of the monarchy. Egypt was to be returned to its Arab monarchical fold under the umbrella of Saudi Arabia with lavish subsidies. Mubarak had been toppled but the regime survived as Saudi Arabia and its close ally the UAE poured in funds to consolidate the leadership of Abdel Fattah Sisi after he staged a coup against the elected Muslim Brotherhood leader Mohammad Mursi in 2013. In Bahrain, Saudi Arabia distributed lavish subsidies and deployed a military force to protect the Al Khalifa ruling family. In Yemen, Saudi Arabia and its Gulf allies undermined the overthrow of Ali Abdullah Saleh by peaceful protest and supported a Gulf agreement that guaranteed his immunity after he stepped down in 2012. A fragile peace was maintained until Saleh rebelled against his Gulf sponsors and allied himself with the Zaydi Houthis, who stormed the capital, Sanaa, and expelled the new Yemeni leader in 2015. Later that year Saudi Arabia began a controversial military intervention in Yemen under the pretext of returning the legitimate Yemeni leadership to the capital. It failed to achieve its objectives and was dragged into a military conflict that was difficult to win. This military intervention brought Saudi Arabia, under the leadership of King Salman and his son Muhammad, very bad publicity. The Saudi regime saw the uprising in Syria as an opportunity to topple Bashar al-Asad and end Iranian influence in the Levant. With other regional and international players, it supported the Syrian rebels with arms and diplomacy. But the conflict persisted without a clear victory. In 2019 al-Asad was still in power amidst the total devastation of Syria and an ongoing refugee crisis. Foreign support for various rebel groups precipitated a civil war in which sectarian conflict replaced the democratic impulse so visible at the beginning of the uprising.

The more wars raged in those Arab countries experiencing uprisings, the more the Saudi leadership felt secure. The devastation abroad gave a clear message to domestic Saudi audiences. Security is now perceived as a cherished status quo, preferable to futile protest that potentially divides countries, precipitates civil wars and undermines stability forever. The emergence of the Islamic State in Iraq and Syria (ISIS) in 2014 was beginning to be seen as the outcome of a lack of stability and security. As an alternative to the existing repressive regimes, ISIS diverted attention to itself as the new menace, thus pushing many activists to rethink their enthusiasm for real political change and democracy, especially in countries such as Saudi Arabia. ISIS itself was partly inspired by the radical Wahhabi theology that has dominated Saudi Arabia since the beginning of the twentieth century.[25] Ideologically, after its territorial consolidation in Raqqa and Mosul, ISIS began to resemble Saudi Arabia in many ways. Its punishment methods, its insistence on complete veiling for women and its religious education were inspired by Saudi Arabia's early history. This prompted an Algerian writer to claim that Saudi Arabia is an ISIS that has 'made it'.[26]

The Saudi regime felt that the message of the peaceful Arab uprisings resonated with its own population, especially the youth. But after the failure of most uprisings to establish security, prosperity and democracy, many Saudis became less willing to undermine their own economic livelihood in search of an unattainable democracy and political representation. After the establishment of the Islamic caliphate in Mosul in June 2014 many Saudis began to join its ranks, becoming the second-largest foreign cohort of ISIS jihadis after the Tunisians. As in 1979, when Saudis migrated to Afghanistan to support fellow Muslims, in 2014 they began to arrive in Syria to join the caliphate. Peaceful protest in Saudi Arabia vanished, and a new wave of sectarian terrorism began in 2015. Shia mosques were attacked by jihadis who claimed allegiance to ISIS, deploying the same sectarian killings that became a feature of the group's consolidation in Syria and Iraq.

By 2015 Saudi Arabia under the ageing King Abdullah was lacking energy and initiative. Its failure to score victory over its archenemy, Iran, and its inability to achieve its objective of ousting Bashar al-Asad in Syria, reflected a hesitant and ageing leadership. King Abdullah was unable to inject any energy into his country's foreign policy, and only repression and lavish subsidies thwarted further mobilization in Saudi Arabia. After a decade of enjoying being named *malik al-insaniyya*, the 'King of Humanity', King Abdullah died in January 2015.

After Abdullah's death a new leadership began to be consolidated, which would eventually inject both energy and controversy into Saudi politics. Abdullah's half-brother Salman, who had been governor of Riyadh, minister of defence and crown prince, became king. King Salman immediately reversed the gentle face of the monarchy. Only three months after he took the throne, he entered the war in Yemen and became known in the Saudi press as *malik al-hazm*, the 'King of Decisiveness'.

The Survival of the Regime

This chapter has set the historical scene for the contemporary state, mapping the process by which a number of different forces contributed to the unification of dispersed and autonomous regions into a single kingdom, Saudi Arabia. The history of this transformation is now being remembered in specific ways. Both local forces (the Al Saud leadership, the settled communities of the towns and oases, the religious forces and the tribal groups) and international powers (initially the British and later the USA) helped to create a state whose rationale and origins were unusual in the modern twentieth-century Arab region. But the Saudi state shares many characteristics with its Gulf emirates and sheikhdoms, as they were all consolidated by Britain's well-known policies of indirect rule in its far-flung empire and of using military and diplomatic emissaries to act as advisers to local chiefs, who were empowered by British weapons and advice. Saudi Arabia's history and the marriage between religion and politics in its formation mark it as a unique political system in the Gulf region; from its early days it promised to create a utopian Islamic state, whereas other Gulf emirates lacked this religious ambition. Perhaps only Pakistan shares similar features with Saudi Arabia, as both countries were founded by invoking Islam. While other Arab countries mobilized people on the promise of nationalism and liberation from colonial rule, the Saudi leadership worked closely with colonial powers to consolidate its rule. Its rationale was liberation from unorthodox Islamic beliefs and practices. In the process, the Al Saud restored their control over vast Arabian territories.

The chapter has also highlighted how, like other state-formation processes, the creation of Saudi Arabia was from the very beginning a violent, contested process, endorsed by many actors but strongly rejected by others. In the absence of a Saudi national unification narrative, religious mobilization brought people together to create a realm that has survived many challenges, such as the Ikhwan rebellion in the 1920s, the Arab nationalist and anti-imperialist wave in the 1950s, jihadi terrorism since 1979 and the Arab uprisings of 2011.

How the monarchy weathered many crises and survived until the present remains a question that divides observers. Was it the potency of religious discourse, the oil affluence, the wisdom and management skills of the leadership, or the traditional legitimacy they built during their unification of Arabia in the eighteenth and nineteenth centuries? Was the survival of the monarchy a function of the complacency and political inexperience of Saudis or of their inability to organize a durable challenge to Al Saud rule? Or was it the continuous foreign support for a regime whose oil resources remain crucial for the global economy and whose stability is important for the rest of the Muslim world?[27]

The survival of the monarchy is attributed to a combination of domestic and international forces.[28] The unification of Arabia under the banner of the Al Saud gave the regime a certain force—the Al Saud continue to remind their subjects that they 'took it by the sword'—but this did not rule out contestation and occasional crises, also deploying the Islamic sword of unification. So far, all challenges have been overcome by the deployment of a dual strategy: repression and containment. Oil has certainly contributed to the stability of the regime and the well-being of its subjects, as the state has provided a pervasive welfare programme. But like any redistribution and rentier economy, it was bound to include some beneficiaries and exclude others. Moreover, while religion in the form of the Wahhabi revival was a strong unifying force, it too became divisive because it excluded many people from the realm of the pious nation, especially those who rejected its practices and tenets. As a double-edged sword, religion was a unifying force while also being a language of resistance that undermined the Al Saud's rule at different historical moments.

Tribal forces have felt excluded from the political configuration, despite their historical contribution to the creation of the realm. Repression had to be deployed to bring them back within the fold. Similarly, religious minorities such as the Shia and the Ismailis have felt that the realm seriously discriminated against them and excluded them from the parameters of the pious nation. The Shia resisted this domination and have challenged the regime on various occasions. Jihadi violence too sprang from the very religious interpretations that led to the consolidation of the Al Saud's rule.

With the regime failing to create inclusive and representative political institutions, subversive forces continue to threaten it and demand a better share of the wealth and the resources, as they have done throughout the twentieth century. By the time King Salman and his son Muhammad took control of all state institutions in 2015, observers of Saudi Arabia had become tired of writing about an ageing king, only for him to be replaced by an ageing brother. Consequently, the appointment of Muhammad ibn Salman as crown prince in 2017 ushered in a new wave of optimism and wishful thinking that Saudi Arabia would finally become a modern, tolerant and open society. The next chapter explores the new foreign discourse that accompanied the rise of Crown Prince Muhammad ibn Salman, the Son King, destined to be the monarch of Saudi Arabia for a very long time.

2

APOSTLES AND APOLOGISTS

It could very well be that the Crown Prince had knowledge of this tragic event—maybe he did and maybe he didn't.

Statement of President Donald Trump following
the murder of Jamal Khashoggi, 20 November 2018

Saudi Arabia experienced a lot of bad press after 9/11, its name becoming synonymous with terrorism, radical religious teachings, persistent gender inequality, restless youth and stumbling economic development. Many outside the country were desperately awaiting the emergence of a young, charismatic, iconoclastic, energetic and preferably Western-educated reformer who would reverse this image. While King Salman hardly possessed these qualities himself, his son Crown Prince Muhammad appeared to. His swift rise to power sent Western media into a state approaching euphoria. After Muhammad ibn Salman was promoted to the highest positions in government, Western reporters could indulge the fantasy that the saviour had finally arrived, and that Saudi Arabia would quickly shed the shackles of its past, discussed in the last chapter, and in the process create the much-needed renaissance. Between 2015 and 2018, the vast majority of Western media indulged not only their own fantasies about the country and the potential of its new leader but also those of the young would-be-reformer himself, the crown prince.

Since 2015, with very few exceptions, the vast majority of news media in the USA, and indeed elsewhere, have published a succession of articles in praise of the crown prince. Their authors have included esteemed foreign reporters and analysts, such as David Ignatius of the *Washington Post* and Thomas Friedman of *The New York Times*. In order to understand the duality of reform and repression, analysis of the new seat of power in Saudi Arabia cannot be fully achieved without including its international context, as the state succeeds in enlisting global voices to justify its repression, constructed as reform.

The English-language media was one of the most powerful tools that Muhammad ibn Salman used to establish his new style of government and publicize his various projects, most of which were dependent on engaging the international political community and global financial institutions. As we shall see later, his interviews with established English media such as *The Economist* and *The New York Times* reflected his assertive drive to reach out to the constituency that really mattered for his so-called reforms. Unlike previous Saudi kings, he used these interviews to send strong messages about the transformations he envisaged for Saudi Arabia, most of which were welcomed abroad. This engagement with outside media was crucial as he endeavoured to mark his leadership as a genuine departure from previous practices, policies and initiatives. This is clear in the unprecedented decision to announce an initial public offering of 5 per cent of the oil company Aramco. This initially targeted foreign investors, in the hopes that they would rush to the project with great enthusiasm and support. These unusual announcements in the international media differed from the messaging that was adopted to reach domestic audiences, who became aware of them only after they appeared in the English-language press.

As early as 2016, David Ignatius wrote about the struggle for power within the royal family, which was resolved in favour of the crown prince. He accepted the prospect of a great transformation in Saudi Arabia under Muhammad ibn Salman, in his words a prince destined to be the future king.

Saudi Arabia was seen through the prism of a binary opposition—the uncomfortable coexistence of the modern and the pre-modern.

The fascination with the prince continued; as Ignatius wrote: 'MBS is the kind of prince that Machiavelli might conjure. He's a big, fast-talking young man who dominates a room with the raw, instinctive energy of a natural leader.'[1]

Lamenting the absence of entertainment venues in the capital and highlighting how this upset the younger generation, Ignatius predicted that the prince would provide Saudis with a leap into modernity simply by opening cinemas and theatres, which he later did. He made no mention of the stifling atmosphere in which the simplest criticism of government policies is punished by prolonged detention. In his mind, Saudi Arabia needed to be modern in a specific and limited way.

Furthermore, Ignatius was happy to praise the prince for his pledge to partially privatize the major oil company Aramco:

> The world had never seen a privatization of this size: The Saudis reckon that Saudi Aramco's valuation is between $2 trillion and $3 trillion. MBS and his advisers want to float less than 5 percent of the company to private investors, but even this tiny share could be worth more than $100 billion—which would make it far larger than any previous initial public offering.[2]

The promised privatization was postponed, and may not materialize in the near future, except in a limited way inside the country; in November 2019 the crown prince announced that the privatization had begun in the Saudi stock market.[3] The fact that the prince's original promise had been published on the pages of *The Economist* had given it the kind of credibility that investors wanted to see.[4] The announcement was meant as a vote of confidence in Saudi Arabia's economy, and, more importantly, as a harbinger of the young crown prince's visions to diversify the kingdom's economy and end its total dependence on oil revenues. But the reality that many observers preferred to ignore was that Saudi Arabia was on a path towards a rugged liberalization programme dubbed Vision 2030. This liberalization was to take place in an opaque economy, rife with cronyism and with no independent judiciary. However, the announcement in *The Economist* was enough to whet the appetites of Western investors and governments eager to have their share of the great economic opportunities on offer. But the prince underestimated the complexity of floating even 5 per cent of the Saudi oil company in international markets and the difficulty of luring risk-averse investors into the Saudi domestic economy, especially after his erratic foreign policy in Yemen and the murder of the journalist Jamal Khashoggi, discussed in full in the next chapter. The plan was stillborn despite the hype that accompanied Vision 2030. Cinemas opened and women were allowed to drive, but the great economic transformation has yet to occur.

By the time journalist Thomas Friedman got his visa to go to Riyadh and have a private audience with the crown prince in 2017, the illusions about his leadership credentials had grown even further. Friedman believed that the Arab spring had at last arrived in Saudi Arabia. The fantasy about a top-down revolution, and a prince remaking his country, gripped the journalist. Friedman described the then thirty-two-year-old prince in ways that highlight his energy and youth.[5] To Friedman, he was a born leader.

Such descriptions bring to mind the writing of an early generation of British travellers, spies and colonial officers, most notoriously St John Philby, who fell under the spell of the king-dom's founder Abdul Aziz ibn Saud. In their writings, Ibn Saud was described as a desert warrior, an imposing figure who was determined to unify the kingdom under his banner and in the name of God. He was depicted as the tall Bedouin, a saviour from the chaos of tribal warfare and even unorthodox Islam. He reignited the zeal of many Bedouin and lured them into adopting a puritanical version of Islam, Wahhabism, to launch a jihad against all those who resisted his domination. Within thirty years he had indeed transformed the kingdom, but from a land where religious diversity and pluralism prevailed to one in which radical Islam became the religion of the state. It is this Islam that the current crown prince promises to transform in his turn; one of his plans is to launch an entertainment industry to lure the youth away from radicalism and into pop culture. Underlying this strategy is the belief that entertainment is an antidote to vigorous preaching.

In the mind of many outside apostles, the crown prince became the heir of Ibn Saud, not only in his much-commented-on physique and posture but also in the grand audacity of his plans. However, Ibn Saud succeeded in unifying Arabia—with the help of British imperial power—while the crown prince is still struggling to make his visions come true.

To assure financial markets of the prospect for great profits from the opening up of the Saudi economy, the *Financial Times* announced on 8 March 2018 that:

> Mohammed bin Salman has been officially welcomed in London with all the trappings of a state visit. He has been treated to lunch with the Queen, and hosted at Chequers, the prime minister's retreat. Saudi Arabia's 32-year-old crown prince has yet to ascend to the throne, but the UK government's message is unambiguous: this is a man to do business with. ... MbS has moved fast, by Saudi standards, to liberalise the social climate, curtailing the powers of

religious police, allowing concerts and cinema, and lifting the ban on women driving. By offering a life to a young population starved of diversion he has won much support.[6]

The media was not alone in glorifying the prince: academics joined the chorus to defend the promised new transformation. Many Middle East and Islamic Studies centres and academic departments at esteemed American and British universities had already received Saudi funding. At institutions such as Harvard University and the University of Cambridge, Saudi money was important in maintaining the research and staff. Other technology institutions such as the Massachusetts Institute of Technology (MIT) had set up ventures with the prince's initiatives, for example MiSK (the Prince Mohammed bin Salman bin Abdulaziz Foundation), to empower the youth. All these universities insisted that foreign money from dictators does not compromise their academic objectivity. Their relations with the Saudi regime became difficult to defend, however, after the murder of Jamal Khashoggi.

Professor Bernard Haykel at Princeton University lamented the bad publicity that Saudi Arabia has received and endeavoured to correct stereotypes. In an interview in *Arab News*, he said that any criticism of Muhammad ibn Salman amounts to vilification of Saudi Arabia:

> It is summed up by the trilogy of excessive wealth, abuse of women and intolerance for other religions. Of course, when Westerners visit the Kingdom and see it for what it is, a place like any other with positive and negative sides, but also a very kind and welcoming people, their ideas change. There is an industry of people in the West and elsewhere who make it their business to vilify KSA and to depict the most negative image of the place.[7]

Under the crown prince, the country's excessive wealth had been plundered, women were struggling to gain equality, and religious minorities, such as the Shia, and other voices critical of

Wahhabism had all been suppressed. But Haykel took a different view despite all evidence supporting the so-called vilification of the kingdom. In doing so he admitted that the crown prince is an authoritarian ruler, implying that his power grab is inevitable if Saudi Arabia is to achieve its potential. He wrote in the *Washington Post*: 'His message is one of authoritarian nationalism, mixed with populism that seeks to displace a traditional Islamic hyper-conservatism—which the crown prince believes has choked the country and sapped its people of all dynamism and creativity.'[8]

The inevitability of authoritarian reform—or, more accurately, a type of oriental despotism—seems to be considered the only vehicle that could change a stagnating kingdom, a conservative society dependent on oil and public-sector subsidies and a fanatical religious tradition. The ills of Saudi society are seen as justifying the brutal silencing of activists, journalists and professionals, who may have had dissenting opinions with regard to the announced reforms. This analysis invited readers to conclude that Saudi Arabia has no potential without a progressive leadership, ignoring the many Saudi voices who had been calling for political reform, equality and justice. With his introduction of social reforms and policies on gender, it seems that the prince has appropriated the work and struggles of feminists and vocal activists, while holding them in detention and claiming to be the source himself of these initiatives and of progress.

Haykel concluded that 'ultimately, MBS wants to base his family's legitimacy on the economic transformation of the country and its prosperity. He is not a political liberal. Rather, he is an authoritarian, and one who sees his consolidation of power as a necessary condition for the changes he wants to make in Saudi Arabia.'[9] The inevitability of repression is here taken for granted, reminding us of earlier orientalist discourses about not only Saudi Arabia but also repressive 'Arab culture' more broadly.

Such statements were not exceptional journalistic rhetoric or informed academic policy reports. They constitute a representative sample of wishful thinking prevalent among many analysts of Saudi Arabia's prince and his reforms before October 2018, when Khashoggi was murdered. Both the physical image of the crown prince as the young reformer and his plans for transforming the kingdom into a modern nation were applauded across the board. But these images were constructed to portray hope and confidence in a regime that had repressed its people and interfered in many regional conflicts to the detriment of the impulse towards democracy that swept the Arab world from 2011. The so-called reforms of Muhammad ibn Salman were accompanied by one of the worst and most brutal waves of domestic repression and by an erratic regional policy. His apologists in the West were driven by profit, the prospect of free access to the country and its prince, or by real financial rewards. They believed that their audiences with the prince and his entourage at his opulent palace had taught them the workings of his inner mind and given them knowledge of his charismatic character. Meetings with the prince sometimes lasted through the night, shrouding these foreigners' writings with a certain mystique and consolidating the Son King's cult of personality at a global level.

Even with very few credentials and little experience in government, the crown prince knew how to manipulate the media and turned many established Western journalists and academics into apostles and apologists for his rising cult. This projection in global media came to play an important role in promoting his image as a future reformer.

In addition to print media, the crown prince was aware of how social media platforms were gradually replacing traditional outlets as strong influencers and manipulators of public opinion. He went as far as instigating Twitter employees to gather data on dissidents and critics, and also invited Instagram influencers to the kingdom to publicize tourism.[10]

APOSTLES AND APOLOGISTS

In addition to his global spy-ring, the crown prince wanted his own media initiatives that could be trusted to reach targeted Western audiences, such as policy makers. He quickly launched multimillion-dollar public-relations campaigns to cover his new Vision 2030 and National Transformation Programmes; both became cornerstones in his quest to showcase the new era of his rule to the outside world. APCO Worldwide, an American PR firm, was hired to publicize his promises and facilitate his visits to the USA in 2017. In Britain, a similar campaign was launched prior to the prince's visit to Downing Street, where the red carpet was laid and controversial aspects of his policies and detention campaigns were barely mentioned by his hosts. He hired the services of PR companies Freud's and Consulum, both of which worked hard to promote his vision and his trip to London. According to the Bureau of Investigative Journalism, such public-relations firms worked like defence lawyers: 'A former employee of one of the British PR firms likened representing a client like Saudi Arabia to being a defence lawyer. "You have to work to get the client out of trouble", the employee said, and promote "the idea that Saudi Arabia is becoming Switzerland".'[11]

The crown prince also established his own propaganda think tank in Washington, masquerading as an independent research centre. The Arabia Foundation was set up by Ali Shihabi, an ex-employee of the Saudi government, an articulate spokesman who has all the skills needed to address Western audiences. Shihabi was the director of the foundation until 2019, when he unexpectedly announced its dissolution. He endeavoured to defend the policies of the crown prince and promote him in Washington as the new face of a kingdom on the path of change, stability and prosperity. He continued in this role even after the murder of Khashoggi. Shihabi wrote:

> Political freedoms are clearly a force for good, but unleashing them in a highly polarized society in an era of considerable regional politi-

cal stress is a process fraught with great risk. What would be the cost today for a country like Saudi Arabia if its leadership were to allow its populace to thrash out their deep differences in the public arena and risk losing control of civil order as so many countries have done throughout history?[12]

In an apologetic tone, he justified the crown prince's repression and curtailment of free speech by stating that in a polarized society, these freedoms could eventually give way to instability. The alarmist approach is meant to intimidate Western partners and allies of Saudi Arabia lest they pressure the prince to relax his grip on dissenting voices or criticize his detention campaigns since 2017.

The so-called transformation of the kingdom was a typical controversial management-consultancy blueprint, the work of McKinsey. But it needed to be launched globally, simply because it depended on drawing global capital to the kingdom and contributing to the globalization of the prince's cult. Hence, the prince announced it for the first time during an interview with *The Economist*, as mentioned earlier. McKinsey's long report on the kingdom emerged in the early months of the crown prince's rule, promising a new future based on opening up the economy to foreign investment, diversification and privatization. It was posted on the firm's website, where it can be downloaded free of charge. Most controversial was its insight on social transformations, which involved entertainment for the youth and greater employment for women. Such reforms may be sound in a transparent country where the rule of law is respected and people enjoy the right to contest, debate and voice their own opinions. But in Saudi Arabia the McKinsey recommendations became a top-down initiative to make the crown prince the centre of the decision-making process with no regard for people's interest or their opinions. In the past, the Saudi regime had promised welfare in return for loyalty, which the prince's economic reforms threatened and undermined. This explains why the crown prince had to cancel many of McKinsey's recommendations, such as freezing employment in the public sector—the main source of employment, with almost 70 per cent of Saudis being government employees.

The name of young Saudi dissident Omar al-Zahrani, discussed later in this book, featured in their internal reports. McKinsey defended its work and distanced itself from accusations that it might have contributed to identifying and monitoring dissenting Saudi voices.

The prince's overt dependence on foreign management consultants was pervasive, and even the establishment of a women's ministry and the creation of a 'Saudi nationalism' became part of their mandate. Sensing how unrealistic and even counterproductive the consultants were, the king issued a royal decree forbidding the employment of foreign management consultants, apart from in exceptional cases.

The Western Press's Contested Modernity

Among foreign—mainly Western—analysts, the criteria for the new Saudi modernity were limited to the semblance of freedom for women (the right to drive and the partial loosening of the guardianship system, the ultimate symbols of liberation and modernity), restricting the religious clerics, and opening the Saudi economy to foreign investment. Modernity for many foreign journalists meant turning the kingdom into a liberal autocracy, with a cult figure ruling over it. In the past many policy makers in Western governments must have felt embarrassed by the fact that their most cherished ally and partner remained the only country in the world that did not allow women to drive. They all aspired to see an enlightened autocrat, akin to Turkey's Kemal Atatürk or the deposed Shah of Iran, ruling in Riyadh.

This narrow definition of modernity and reform excluded the basic, and fundamental, tenet of modernity: freedom to think, to debate all aspects of life, from the personal to the political and social, and to act on one's thoughts. But the crown prince was determined to silence any debate on a range of hot topics, from religious reform to social and gender issues. In 2019, feminism, homosexuality and atheism were defined as crimes punishable by imprisonment and lashing—feminism especially.[13] (After international uproar, the regime announced that criminalizing feminism had been a mistake.) The crown prince's economic plans were sacrosanct, and economists such as Abdul Aziz al-Dakhil and Isam al-Zamil, who had critical opinions on the promised privatization of Aramco, were silenced. If modernity means a flourishing debate, critical thinking and freedom to experiment with different ideas, the kingdom truly became its graveyard. Any Saudi with an alternative vision became a threat to the prince.

As for political modernity, notions of democracy, representative government and elections have been all but forgotten as fundamental markers of genuine transformation. The modern in the Saudi case was limited to women driving cars, the introduction of the cinema and popular Western culture, and the transformation of a state capitalist rentier economy into an open liberal market. Modernity was associated with a liberal economy open to foreign investment and tourism. All commentators were expected to believe in incremental reform and to abhor the thought of real revolutionary change that could lead even to restrictions of the powers of the monarch, let alone the abolition of the monarchy, the worst nightmare of Saudi Arabia's Western allies.

Saudi society is totally absent in Western reports on the crown prince, except to emphasize how popular social liberalization is among the population. When society is mentioned in passing, reporters highlight how both women and men are enjoying live concerts, sports venues (including women's boxing and wrestling shows), the cinema and the circus. The assumption is that the entertainment industry will gradually deliver the right kind of citizen, a law-abiding conformist who indulges in consumerism and is part of a global popular culture allegedly previously absent in Saudi Arabia.

Young Saudis who had engaged in global culture in the past, making the most of new communications platforms such as Twitter, Facebook, YouTube, Snapchat and others, faced arrest when they transgressed. Social media became a trap for a new generation eager to experiment with self-expression, while the crown prince used these venues to spread propaganda. Poets, comedians and critical commentators on social media were targeted by the 'technology farm' near Riyadh, a centre that employed trolls, bots and spies to monitor not only the movement of people but their thoughts too. The centre became notorious for the threatening messages it sent to dissidents, thus alerting them to the fact that they are constantly being watched by Big Brother. As tourism was launched as part of the diversification of the economy, Western women Instagram 'influencers' were brought to the kingdom, where they enjoyed arranged visits to heritage and tourist destinations, only being asked to post images on their Instagram accounts in return. Publicity for Saudi Arabia as the new tourist destination popped up on YouTube and other social media. The overuse of white foreign women as a marketing tool did not go unnoticed by Saudi women activists, who criticized Western women for falling under the spell of the crown prince while many Saudi female activists remain detained. The globalized cult of the crown prince had to be femininized, and foreign women played an important role in the process.

In March 2015, as the crown prince launched an aggressive war on Yemen, the poorest Arab country, he needed to cover up the atrocities that his US- and British-made fighter jets were causing on the ground. He always claimed that the Yemen war had international legitimacy as he had secured a UN resolution to return the government of Yemen to the capital, Sanaa, after the Houthi rebels, allegedly clients of the Iranian government, had taken it. The UN resolution became a licence to kill thousands of Yemenis and reduce almost 14 million civilians to starvation, while ensuring the silence of the international community. The crown prince sent his military spokesman, Ahmad Asiri, to Chatham House in London to defuse the crisis after many NGOs criticized Saudi atrocities in Yemen and campaigned to stop arming the regime. Protesters met him outside the building and attacked him, throwing eggs and shouting anti-Saudi slogans. He was removed from office as the Saudi-led coalition spokesman and was given a high-ranking job in the intelligence services. After the murder of Khashoggi, he went silent.

Campaign Against Arms Trade (CAAT) had already taken the British government to court over its sale of arms to Saudi Arabia and military support during the Yemen war. Britain is the second-largest provider of arms to the kingdom after the USA. According to former CIA director for Gulf and South Asia Affairs Bruce Riedel, Saudi Arabia cannot continue the war without US and British support. CAAT lost the case. Based on evidence from the British Ministry of Defence, the judge ruled that Britain is not implicated in the regime's crimes in Yemen. The case against the British government was appealed in April 2019. This time, the judge confirmed that British arms sales should come under greater scrutiny and transparency. The murder of Khashoggi might have influenced the appeal process, which took place six months after the crime was committed.[14]

By the time Khashoggi was murdered, Muhammad ibn Salman had already succeeded in winning over US president Donald Trump, with the promise of lavish investment in the American economy, most of it through purchasing arms to strengthen his weak military capabilities and enable him to continue launching airstrikes on Yemen. On 20 November 2018, just over a month after the murder of Jamal Khashoggi, the White House issued a statement clarifying its position on a crime committed by one of its partner states in the Middle East. President Trump reminded his audience:

> After my heavily negotiated trip to Saudi Arabia last year, the Kingdom agreed to spend and invest $450 billion in the United States. This is a record amount of money. It will create hundreds of thousands of jobs, tremendous economic development, and much additional wealth for the United States. Of the $450 billion, $110 billion will be spent on the purchase of military equipment from Boeing, Lockheed Martin, Raytheon and many other great U.S. defense contractors. If we foolishly cancel these contracts, Russia and China would be the enormous beneficiaries—and very happy to acquire all of this newfound business. It would be a wonderful gift to them directly from the United States![15]

After this preamble, Trump declared:

> The murder of Khashoggi was a terrible one, and one that our country does not condone. Indeed, we have taken strong action against those already known to have participated in the murder. After great independent research, we now know many details of this horrible crime. We have already sanctioned 17 Saudis known to have been involved in the murder of Mr. Khashoggi, and the disposal of his body.[16]

But even after the CIA and UN reports concluded that there was a high probability that the crown prince might have been responsible, Trump ignored the public outcry over the murder of the journalist, who had been a US resident.

American civil society and human rights organizations continued to be critical of their leader's unequivocal and unconditional support for one of the most brutal regimes in the Arab world. But the autocrat was wealthy, and he had promised to share this wealth with the US corporate world. This was not enough to silence criticism of the prince, who had made so many pledges to

Trump and enjoyed close relations with his son-in-law, Jared Kushner. Trump's complete endorsement of the Saudi crown prince, even after Khashoggi's murder, infuriated the president's many opponents, but it was instrumentalized in the US domestic political game by its media and by Democratic and Republican members of congress. The globalization of the prince's cult had reached an unexpectedly high level in Washington.

Even after Khashoggi was killed, American scholar Professor Gregory Gause III, who knows Saudi Arabia's politics well, warned US policy makers not to go as far as demanding that the crown prince step down. He advised the US administration to encourage the crown prince to change his behaviour while searching for another prince as an interlocutor with whom to engage in discussions about foreign policy: 'What the United States needs from Saudi Arabia is a change of behavior, not a change of personnel.' He regarded the murder of Khashoggi a mere setback: 'The crown prince suffered a number of setbacks that called into question both his judgment and his political capacity. The killing of Jamal Khashoggi was simply the most recent in that line.'[17] Even after brutal crimes, personality cults remain difficult to deconstruct, as they are founded on the power of the spell.

From Apologists to Reluctant Critics

Following the murder in Istanbul, it became impossible for Western journalists to continue to praise the crown prince. After all, many of them must have felt really threatened by the gruesome murder of one of their own. The tone of acclaim swiftly shifted towards condemnation of a brazen act of murder that violated all international human rights norms, freedom of speech and diplomatic conventions. After almost three years of positive reporting on the crown prince's so-called reforms in Western media, he was suddenly accused of plotting the murder of Khashoggi, of giving the order to eliminate a troubling critical voice. While the crown prince has yet to admit to being behind the treacherous murder of an innocent man, most Western media and agencies took this for granted. The magnitude of the crime and the horrific details that Turkish media slowly released to the public gave many reporters empirical evidence to condemn Muhammad ibn Salman, whose name is now closely associated with the killing. In 2019 Jonathan Rugman, a Channel Four News senior foreign correspondent, published a comprehensive and thoroughly researched book in which he expressed a belief that the crown prince must accept responsibility for the murder.[18] Unlike others, Rugman had not fallen under the prince's spell or become enchanted by his cult.

So why have many Western reporters acted like apostles and apologists for the prince? Why did many fail to see the coming storm, instead spending over two years glorifying the crown prince's so-called reforms and erratic style of government? Have reporters been misled by the prince's manipulation of domestic and global media, or have they simply succumbed uncritically to his spell and propaganda that associated limited social reforms with a top-down revolution? On several occasions, the crown prince himself told reporters of *The Economist*, *The New York Times*, the *Financial Times*, *Bloomberg* and *The Guardian* that he was not a Gandhi or a democrat. He told them that he was rich, born into a family that has ruled Saudi Arabia for generations. He was not embarrassed about his wealth, with news spreading around the world of his recent purchases, including a yacht, a French palace and a Leonardo da Vinci painting. Until Khashoggi's murder, the crown prince's sensational consumerism was entertaining but not troubling. Ostentatious consumption was actually an integral part of the celebrity cult that he wanted to project globally.

The same applies to his spectacular anti-corruption campaign against his own kin and a selected group of the Saudi elite. In November 2017 the prince ordered the detention of dozens of princes, ministers and businessmen, holding them for weeks at the Riyadh Ritz Carlton. Many thought he was serious about fighting corruption and preparing the Saudi economy for greater transparency and efficiency, but the detention campaign was highly selective. Loyal senior princes remained free, indicating that the detention campaign was a targeted purge aimed at potential rivals, such as Miteb ibn Abdullah, son of the deceased king Abdullah. Prince Miteb was in charge of the Saudi Arabia National Guard, an important military unit with a huge budget, most of which had gone to Britain since the 1960s as it was one of the most important countries that armed and trained its personnel.

While many human rights organizations pointed to the drastic, repressive measures against a wide range of Saudi activists, such reports were initially ignored and only resurfaced in the mainstream Western media after the murder of Khashoggi. Western governments might actually have been happy about the repression of Islamists, perhaps seeing the swift detentions as fulfilling the prince's pledge to reform the religious sphere in the kingdom and rid the country of radicals and terrorists. In an interview with *The Guardian*, the prince announced that he was promoting a tolerant Islam that accepts social change, allowing women to drive, watch football matches, attend rock concerts and go to the cinema.[19] Such statements went unchallenged by reporters, who simply reiterated the prince's words. Neither reporters nor the prince mentioned that Saudis had been radicalized by state programmes that had indoctrinated them in the Wahhabi tradition with its radical position on social issues since the foundation of the state in 1933. The prince told reporters that radical Islam had been exported worldwide as a strategy to

assist the USA in the Cold War when communism and nationalism threatened its hegemony in the Muslim world. He failed to
recall that radical Islam was an arm of Saudi Arabia's foreign
policy that sought to legitimize its control of the Two Holy
Mosques in Mecca and Madina in the eyes of the Muslim world
and suppress anti-regime groups.

Thanks to the prince's campaign against Islamists, feminists
and activists, Saudi Arabia is now producing exiles and asylum
seekers, as we shall see in the coming chapters. Like Khashoggi,
they are seeking asylum in cities like Washington, London,
Ottawa, Istanbul and Sydney. They do not feel safe, as the murder of Khashoggi continues to haunt them even when they are
abroad. Furthermore, not all Islamists jailed in Saudi Arabia are
terrorists or potential terrorists. Amongst them are personalities
such as Abdullah al-Hamid, Muhammad al-Qahtani and Sheikh
Salman al-Awdah, all of whom had called for real civil society
and a constitutional monarchy. None of them legitimized armed
struggle or violence to achieve their goal. In fact, al-Hamid and
al-Qahtani founded a civil and political rights association to
defend prisoners and expose torture in Saudi prisons. Al-Qahtani's
wife fled to the USA with her children while awaiting the release
of her husband. Suppressing Islamists at home has never been a
successful strategy for eliminating a religious-political movement
with a wide appeal among many Saudis. Gamal Abdel Nasser and
Husni Mubarak tried this strategy in Egypt, but both failed to
eliminate the movement. In fact, continuing repression resulted
in the emergence of violent fringe groups that launched deadly
attacks and eventually exported their violence abroad. Now the
prince is treading the same path of repression that will no doubt
lead to violence in the future. This violence is not new; Saudi
Arabia witnessed the worst wave of terrorism between 2003 and
2008, after many Islamists were released from prison in the
1990s. The crown prince has yet to understand that terrorists are

bred in prisons, where radicalization becomes inevitable. It is proven that prisons do not soften dissidents, who in fact emerge more radical and determined to continue their dissent by deploying even more violent means.

Foreign-based apologists for the regime ignored all these facts and simply publicized the prince's statements. If the crown prince got away with imprisoning Islamists, what about the women activists who had campaigned for gender equality since the 1990s? Just before granting women the right to drive, the regime in Riyadh imprisoned more than a dozen Saudi women activists. By 2019 feminism had been defined as a crime punishable by detention and corporal punishment, although the announcement was later withdrawn after a global outcry.

The modernity that both the prince and many Western apologists envisage for the country obviously excludes the critical and courageous voices who should be given all the credit for raising awareness of gender equality and acting on the many injustices inflicted on women. Thanks to the prince's failure to protect women from abusive families and patriarchal practices, Saudi Arabia now has a new social phenomenon: runaway girls who flee the country and seek asylum abroad. The private patriarchy of society is enforced by that of the government, which is always eager to please men in order to secure their long-term loyalty. But the crown prince's image remains that of the enlightened reformer.

It has to be admitted that foreign reporting on Saudi Arabia remains a difficult task, given that the government controls access to the country and restricts foreign journalists' freedom. Journalists are always watched and are allocated 'guides', who steer them to loyal voices that can be recorded. But this is not to absolve foreign correspondents of their responsibility to portray the real image and a critical awareness of the limits of Saudi Arabia's crown prince, or any other unelected leader. Falling under the spell of the young prince and having the honour of spending a couple of hours with him at his lavish palace until the early hours of the morning should not blur the journalists' vision. After all, good journalism is accountable to intelligent audiences, rather than to an autocrat who might be the most controversial ruler that Saudi Arabia will have for decades.

Saudi Arabia remains the exotic 'other' for many Western audiences to measure their own progress. It is a country unlike any other. Autocracy and dictatorship are not the inevitable forms of government there. It can benefit greatly from serious reporting that does not paint a distorted image of its alleged flourishing but selective and corrupted modernity under the rule of an absolute monarchy. After the murder of Khashoggi, real-politik prompted Trump to conclude:

> [Our] intelligence agencies continue to assess all information, but it could very well be that the Crown Prince had knowledge of this tragic event—maybe he did and maybe he didn't! That being said, we may *never* know all of the facts surrounding the murder of Jamal Khashoggi. In any case, our relationship is with the Kingdom of Saudi Arabia. They have been a great ally in our very important fight against Iran. The United States intends to remain a steadfast partner of Saudi Arabia to ensure the interests of our country, Israel and all other partners in the region. It is our paramount goal to fully eliminate the threat of terrorism throughout the world.[20]

Mr Trump added:

> I understand there are members of Congress who, for political or other reasons, would like to go in a different direction—and they are free to do so. I will consider whatever ideas are presented to me, but only if they are consistent with the absolute security and safety of America. After the United States, Saudi Arabia is the largest oil-producing nation in the world. They have worked closely with us and have been very responsive to my requests to keeping oil prices at reasonable levels—so important for the world. As President of the United States I intend to ensure that, in a very dangerous

world, America is pursuing its national interests and vigorously contesting countries that wish to do us harm. Very simply it is called America First.[21]

The USA and the West in general consider Saudi Arabia a force for stability in the Arab and Muslim worlds. But after the Arab uprisings threatened to end the status quo in the region, the Saudi regime vigorously funnelled its resources into returning to the status quo ante, selectively supporting rebellions (in Syria in 2011 and Iraq and Lebanon in 2019) while suppressing others (in Egypt, Bahrain, Yemen and Tunisia). The stark Saudi diplomatic and military interventions in the region challenged the old wisdom about its benevolent role, and the kingdom earned new enemies, from pro-democracy Arab activists to feminists to Islamists. Yet its apostles and apologists turned a blind eye, until they were confronted with the brutal murder in the consulate. Both the war in Yemen and the prevalent domestic repression that ushered a new era remained a minor embarrassment, dismissed by an aggressive public-relations campaign aided by many Western corporations, global media and partners of the regime.

Knowledge in the time of oil, and now an open economy up for grabs, proved a good foundation to build and enhance the global cult of the reformer Son King. The next chapter closely examines the sudden rise of the crown prince and his policies, one of which led to the murder of Jamal Khashoggi in the Saudi consulate in Istanbul.

3

THE SON KING AND THE
'MAN OF THE PALACE'

Author: I received a message from a common friend that you wanted my telephone number to contact me. I hope you are well.

Jamal: I am fine al-hamdullilah.

Author: Are you planning to visit London soon?

Jamal: Yes, I plan to contact you and meet you if your time permits.

Author: Inshallah, do let me know in advance, perhaps I can arrange for you to give a talk at the university or elsewhere.

Jamal: Agreed.

Author's conversation with Jamal Khashoggi on Twitter Direct Messaging, 25 September 2018.

I could not have possibly predicted that on Tuesday, 2 October 2018, only a week after I exchanged messages with Saudi journalist Jamal Khashoggi, he would enter the Saudi consulate in Istanbul at 1 p.m. and never be seen again.[1] Operatives of the Saudi regime, a rapid intervention squad that was quickly dispatched from Saudi Arabia with a secret mission, assassinated him. The rapid intervention operatives had only three days to plan his murder. On Friday, 28 September, Khashoggi unexpectedly visited the consulate to obtain a document confirming his status as a single person. The registry office in Istanbul, where he planned to marry his Turkish fiancée, Hatice Cengiz, had requested this document. Hatice told me that they walked out of the registry office perplexed and sad, as Khashoggi knew that the document could only be obtained by request from the Saudi consulate. Khashoggi's trip to the consulate was not a simple and straightforward journey. He had been in the USA since 2017, writing articles critical of the policies and repression of Crown Prince Muhammad ibn Salman in the *Washington Post*. But, after some deliberation, Khashoggi and Hatice went in a taxi to the Saudi consulate. As a Turkish citizen, Hatice was not allowed to enter the section reserved to serve Saudi citizens. She stayed outside the consulate waiting for him.

According to Hatice, staff had told Khashoggi on his first visit to the consulate to come back on 2 October to obtain the document. They were friendly, but very surprised that he had come to the consulate, Khashoggi told her. Khashoggi and Hatice were relieved that his first visit, which lasted around half an hour, went well, with the promise that he could come back three days later to collect the document. Little did he know that, after he left the consulate, the staff immediately informed their bosses in Riyadh that Khashoggi, the troublesome journalist, had visited unexpectedly and was told to come back on 2 October. It seems that whoever was informed about the visit thought that it was a great opportunity to either force him to return to Saudi Arabia or to eliminate him; the second appointment was an opportunity that couldn't be missed.[2] At that time, it was unclear what the Saudi authorities wanted to do to Khashoggi: silence him, negotiate his return to the country, kidnap him or kill him.

On Tuesday, 2 October, Khashoggi arrived in Istanbul at dawn after spending the weekend in London, where he attended and spoke at a conference on Palestine organized by Middle East Monitor, a news agency with Islamist leanings. He took a taxi from Istanbul airport to the new apartment that he had bought in a gated community. Hatice was supposed to meet him at the airport, but he called her to inform her that he had arrived very early and she should meet him at the apartment. She rushed to the apartment in a taxi, carrying some light furniture that she had bought earlier and a suitcase that Khashoggi had left with her before going to London. Hatice comes from a conservative Muslim family and, as the couple were not yet married, they preferred not to stay alone in the apartment for too long, according to Hatice. They immediately went to a nearby restaurant to have breakfast and catch up.

Khashoggi told Hatice that he had been asked to call someone at the consulate by the name of Sultan to inform him that he would be coming that day to collect the document. Khashoggi dialled Sultan's number. Sultan answered, telling him that he would get back to him in ten minutes. Khashoggi was eventually told to come at 1 p.m. Hatice asked Khashoggi if he had a friend to accompany him. Khashoggi replied that it would be difficult to find someone to go with him at such short notice. He did not directly ask Hatice to accompany him, as she had classes at the university where she was studying for her Ph.D. But he seemed relieved when she told him she would not go to the class and volunteered to accompany him instead.

After their breakfast at a nearby restaurant, they got into a taxi and arrived at the consulate. Hatice waited outside the consulate's main gate with Khashoggi's two phones, which he had left with her just before he entered the building, guarded from the outside by a Turkish policeman and in the inside courtyard by Saudi security personnel. While waiting, Hatice occupied herself by searching online on her phone for a suitable restaurant to hold their wedding reception, as the expected event finally seemed possible. Hatice told me that after an hour she started to wonder why Jamal was late, but she thought he might have been chatting to the staff and enjoying the company of his countrymen, as he must have missed being surrounded by his own people. When he failed to return after over three hours, Hatice began a series of phone calls that would eventually lead to the police, the highest level of Turkish government bureaucracy, family in Saudi Arabia, friends in Istanbul and the media. The world soon knew that Khashoggi had disappeared, as she tweeted from the pavement outside the consulate that he had not emerged from the building and the consulate was closed.

Khashoggi had met Hatice at a conference in Istanbul in the summer of 2018, and the two planned a life together, buying an apartment in Istanbul on the understanding that Jamal would occasionally go to Turkey from his exile in Washington, where he wrote opinion columns for the *Washington Post*. The exiled journalist had left Saudi Arabia in 2017 after he was suspended from *al-Hayat*, a Saudi-sponsored pan-Arab newspaper. Previously Khashoggi had been sacked from an editorial job at *al-Watan* newspaper. He was also told not to give interviews to the media and to stop using social media, especially Twitter, to express his opinions. By silencing Khashoggi and forbidding him to express his opinions, the Saudi authorities had sentenced the journalist to an early death before they actually murdered him in Istanbul.

Like the whole world, I was shocked by the assassination of Jamal Khashoggi and the brutality of his encounter with fifteen Saudi operatives inside the high walls of the Saudi consulate. Khashoggi spent the last ten or fifteen minutes of his life struggling to free himself from the grip of those operatives, according to leaked recordings by Turkish authorities, who had bugged the building. The horrific details of his murder were reported in full by the UN Council on Human Rights rapporteur Agnes Callamard.[3] While they remained in Riyadh, the fifteen agents who had been sent to Istanbul operated in a room in the consulate, from where they communicated with their bosses in the capital. Their 'boss' was none other than the new crown prince. The UN report named him on the list of persons who must be investigated in the murder case. After the murder, CCTV cameras recorded the fifteen operatives leaving Turkey with their luggage, and possibly Khashoggi's body, on private jets.

Violent, cruel, distressing, and outside the parameters of any reasonable response to a critical journalist, that consulate encounter led not only to Khashoggi's murder but also to the disposal of his body. In the summer of 2020, the body still has not been found anywhere in Turkey, because it was reportedly chopped up and disposed of, either by dissolving it or by packing it into plastic bags and transporting it back to Saudi Arabia. The journalist simply disappeared. Weeks later, after the Saudi authorities admitted that Khashoggi had been murdered in the consulate, his family in Jeddah held a funeral without a body, and many Muslims, especially in Turkey where the crime was committed, held *salat al-ghaib*, a funeral without a corpse.

Hatice continues to have nightmares about the gruesome details of her fiancé's murder. An educated thirty-six-year-old woman who expected to enjoy an uneventful life, she had clashed with her father, who was very opposed to his young daughter marrying a sixty-year-old Saudi who had already been married at least twice and had four adult children, the youngest only one year younger than Hatice. He 'could not understand what attracted his daughter to this man, whom he did not understand and who could only speak to him through an interpreter,' Hatice told me.

As she desperately waited outside the consulate for her fiancé, sharing photos online that quickly started to circulate around the globe, Hatice soon found herself the focus of an assault by Saudi electronic trolls. She was called a spy, an agent of foreign governments, a whore and a money-grabbing social climber. A CCTV image of her walking hand in hand with Khashoggi in Istanbul was enough to unleash an outpouring of insults online, attacking both her integrity and her Islamic faith. Khashoggi's family in Saudi Arabia initially denied that she was his fiancée, although his son Abdullah had met her when he came to see his father in Istanbul in the summer of 2018, when they visited tourist sites and a jewellery shop, as Khashoggi wanted to buy Hatice a wedding ring. She told me that Khashoggi mentioned that he was living on a monthly state pension of around $10,000, and that he expected this to be cut soon. He bought the apartment in Istanbul for around $300,000. Hatice continued to pay the service charge on the apartment after the murder, and later sent his son all invoices and documents relating to the apartment. Khashoggi's belongings were taken by the Turkish police, including presents that Khashoggi had bought for Hatice in London the weekend before he was assassinated. Hatice was captured on CCTV carrying the suitcase that he had left with her when they both entered the newly bought apartment very early in the morning on 2 October, just hours before the murder.

Hatice worked for various charities and had great plans to use her superb Arabic language skills to advance her country's relations with the Arab world. She published her Master's thesis on Oman, praising the country's Islamic diversity. She had spent a year in Oman doing fieldwork and had come to know it very well. Her dream was perhaps to become the Turkish ambassador there one day, but she had no experience of working in the Turkish civil service or the foreign office. By April 2019, traumatized and tired, Hatice decided to leave Turkey and start a new life as an English-language student in London. When I met her in June 2019, she was still tearful as she poured out her grief and recounted with great detail the traumas of the last ten months. But she was determined to reconstruct her life and continue her studies.

Jamal Khashoggi was murdered either deliberately or as the result of a kidnapping plan that went wrong. Premeditated murder is more likely, as full preparations for disposing of the body by a forensic expert must have been part of the plan. This was murder, by a state or the organs of a state, of an unarmed journalist, without judicial process, on diplomatic ground outside the perpetrators' home country. It is this dreadful cocktail of circumstances that explains the general outrage that the killing sparked.

For months, international outrage was sustained by the media, rightly seeking to protect their own, as Jamal Khashoggi was a writer for the *Washington Post* and a career journalist, even if he had also been a close confidant and adviser to prominent Saudi princes. The international community generally, and Turkey in particular, were understandably concerned by the abuse of diplomatic immunity, even though diplomatic missions have long been home to dubious activities. The reciprocal nature of diplomacy dictates that individual diplomats, their embassies, their consulates and even their 'bags' are inviolable. This reciprocity is under attack, as abuses exceed their tacit limits and tit-for-tat expulsions abound.

State-sponsored murder and 'targeted killing' of this kind by a state or its agents is not new. Mass killings, such as those of the 'death-squads' of Latin American dictators, were frequently tolerated by their Western sponsors, even if they were subsequently condemned. Yet targeted killings—that is to say, the state-sponsored extra-judicial murder of individuals—is on the rise, and it has become a weapon of choice of the West as much as of undemocratic regimes. The hit-squad with an ice-pick may have been replaced by high-tech drones, but this does not fundamentally change the nature of the activity.

When state-sponsored extra-judicial killing is outside that state's territory, the outrage is particularly vehement. It is one thing to murder your own people within your territory, but violating the territory of another state, especially a NATO member, by doing so abroad, is quite another. Even where the location is strictly speaking sovereign territory of the perpetrators, as with a consulate, it is considered unacceptable for a state, in this case Saudi Arabia, to do its dirty work in another country. It is the state-sponsored, extra-judicial, extra-territorial nature of the apparent murder that is the source of greatest outrage.

'Man of the Palace'

While I missed a chance to meet Khashoggi after we exchanged messages on 25 September 2018, I had met him in London in 2003–5, when he was known as a commentator on Saudi affairs, a spokesperson of the embassy, and, to many, an apologist and propagandist who always defended Saudi policies during King Abdullah's reign. Khashoggi originally came to London as adviser and media spokesperson for the Saudi ambassador, Prince Turki al-Faisal, who was later posted to Washington to work on an extensive charm offensive on behalf of the regime after 9/11, following the participation of fifteen Saudi hijackers in the attack on the Twin Towers in New York. Jamal Khashoggi followed the prince to Washington, but the post lasted for only a year— Al-Faisal was recalled to Riyadh as ex-ambassador Prince Bandar ibn Sultan continued pursuing his contacts in Washington, bypassing him.

Khashoggi's gentle manners and deep knowledge of the inside circle of several Saudi princes, including Turki al-Faisal and Walid ibn Talal, made him an asset to both the regime and Western media. Just before the launch of Walid ibn Talal's al-Arab news channel in Bahrain—an initiative that lasted only a few hours before being shut down—Khashoggi, who had been appointed as a director of the channel, declared that it would enjoy a great margin of freedom. However, he could not confirm that members of the Saudi opposition at the time such as Saad al-Faqih and Muhammad al-Massari would be invited for debates, describing them as 'not a serious opposition'.[4] In Washington, Khashoggi developed networks with a wide variety of Western journalists, policy analysts and others. He worked hard to defend and demystify Saudi Arabia at a critical moment when its reputation in the USA and globally had reached an unprecedented low. Khashoggi was known even to his Turkish fiancée as the 'Man of the Palace'.[5]

Our paths crossed in London on several occasions between 2003 and 2005, and I met Khashoggi at think-tank debates and the studios of global media. At that time, he and I debated Saudi current affairs, with media presenters framing us on opposite sides under the cherished principle of presenting 'one opinion and another opposed opinion', the kind of journalism promoted by such outlets. He defended King Abdullah's 'reforms', for example his National Dialogue Forums, and empowerment of women. I emphasized the regime's sponsorship of radical religious groups and the promotion of sectarian rhetoric denouncing religious minorities in Saudi Arabia.

Khashoggi was an ardent defender of the realm at the time. He occasionally had reservations about the shortcomings of certain Saudi policies, especially the slow progress towards gender equality, reform in the religious field and the promotion of tolerance. He always apologetically mentioned that there were several issues that needed to change. He presented himself as a strong believer in the progressive nature of the monarchy under King Abdullah, whom he always praised for starting the process of incremental and evolutionary reform. Khashoggi had an innate dislike for Salafi Islam and was reputed to be a Sufi. He therefore welcomed efforts to curb the influence of Wahhabi religious clerics and their hold over the population, especially the public sphere through the Committee for Commanding Right and

Prohibiting Vice. Like many Saudi state intellectuals and writers, Khashoggi regarded society as extremely conservative but the leadership as progressive, especially King Abdullah at the time.

As a government spokesperson, Khashoggi was always invited to speak first in media debates and give the official line. I followed immediately to debunk myths about the so-called reformist Saudi regime. I punctured the official narrative that Khashoggi always presented in an eloquent and diplomatic manner that charmed journalists and audiences, and that no doubt satisfied the quest of the regime to present its credentials to Western audiences. After these public debates, Khashoggi often quipped and accused me of wanting to return my family's dynasty to power, the emirate of Hail that Ibn Saud destroyed in 1921. I ignored the ad hominem attack and thought that Jamal Khashoggi was simply another apologist, albeit a polite, sophisticated and well-connected journalist, whose career had started when he reported on the Afghan jihad in the 1980s. His defection to Washington had no doubt deprived Saudi Arabia of a plausible and articulate defender.

As I was conducting research for my book *Contesting the Saudi State*, I came across an online photograph of Khashoggi in Afghanistan brandishing a Kalashnikov. He had reported on the hot spots of the Muslim world, from Algeria's civil war to the Gulf War in the 1990s. I had heard him praise Osama Bin Laden, the al-Qaida leader, until the latter fell out with the Saudi regime in 1991 and moved to Sudan in 1992. Khashoggi considered him 'a good guy, but in later years he became misguided'. Khashoggi changed his assessment of Bin Laden when the latter issued his famous declaration of intent to attack the USA and its Arab allies in the 1990s. As I immersed myself in more research, I came across a novel by the Islamist Muhammad al-Hodeif, in which he discusses how the regime sent spies posing as journalists to infiltrate the complex jihadi scene in Afghanistan. Was al-Hodeif alluding to Jamal Khashoggi, I wondered. Al-Hodeif has been in a Saudi jail for a long time, accused of terrorism, and Jamal Khashoggi was murdered by the very regime that he had served and defended.

Khashoggi was known to the English-speaking world through his commentary on Saudi domestic affairs, as a spokesman at embassies in London and Washington, and later through his columns in the *Washington Post*. He became an ardent defender of King Abdullah from 2005. After his murder, the Western press in general presented him in simple terms as a mere journalist who sought freedom of speech in Washington. He was also hailed as an advocate of democracy, without any qualifications for such descriptions. However, Saudis and other Arabs were familiar with his Arabic columns in various newspapers owned by Saudi princes. In his time as a journalist, Khashoggi published books in addition to his columns in newspapers.[6] His books are a mix of previously published journalistic articles, compiled and revamped, and direct policy recommendations. In both his short and lengthy publications, Khashoggi comes across as an adviser who wants his proposals to be heard by those in the high echelons of power and leadership in Saudi Arabia.

The most controversial of these books are *Ihtilal al-souq al-saudi* (The Occupation of the Saudi Market) and *Ro'yat muwatin 2030* (Citizen's Vision 2030). In the first book, Khashoggi called for complete Saudization (*tawtin*) of the labour force and the economy, even if the abrupt expulsion of foreign labour should lead to temporary chaos and a decline in certain services. He argued that Saudi markets are 'addicted' to foreign labour. The expulsion would lead to 'creative chaos, followed by affluence, prosperity and happiness'. He based his policy recommendations on statistics published by the Saudi Labour Ministry and on interviews with young Saudis, whom he described as seeking not only jobs but real participation in the prosperity of their country.

Many readers applauded his nationalistic rhetoric, as any discussion of foreign workers always produces a heightened sense of nationalism, as we shall see in the next chapter. His call for their removal carried the hope of ushering in long-lasting prosperity.

Nonetheless, many commentators criticized his book for its superficial economic recommendations and its ultra-nationalistic tone. The proposal to expel foreign labour seemed odd coming from someone whose ancestors had been Anatolian immigrants who settled in the Hijaz several decades earlier. Khashoggi's 'Turkish' roots were in fact invoked by Saudi trolls, who defended their regime's actions against him and cast doubt over his loyalty to the country, as he was a mere 'foreigner' in their eyes.

Khashoggi's last book, *Citizen's Vision 2030*, published in 2018, only months before he was murdered, is perhaps even more controversial from the point of view of the regime, and it may have contributed to his being seen increasingly as *persona non grata*. Yet, it is difficult to see the book as directly contributing to the decision to murder him. It was perhaps seen as a direct and daring competing vision to that announced by Crown Prince Muhammad ibn Salman in April 2016, also known as Vision 2030, discussed below. Khashoggi finished the manuscript in 2017 and sent it to the Ministry of Information to seek permission to publish it, a routine requirement. He hoped that the book would be ready for the annual book festival, where authors enjoy celebrity status, give lectures, sign their books, pose for 'selfies' with admirers and intermingle with potential readers and intellectuals. By 2017 Khashoggi was being denied public recognition and exposure. He wanted to be in the spotlight again, as he had always been. He had almost been confined to his house and must have felt very isolated, as he was prohibited from writing in the Saudi press. The manuscript had been sent to the Ministry of Interior, he was told. Permission to publish the book never arrived, and Khashoggi wrote that he would have preferred to publish it inside Saudi Arabia. Instead, *al-Sharq* picked up the manuscript and published it in Cairo in 2018.

To understand Khashoggi's alleged quest for democracy, one must read *Citizen's Vision 2030*, where he struggles to insert himself into a national transformation narrative that had already become the monopoly of the crown prince to the exclusion of other princes, economic advisers, intellectuals, economists, religious scholars and others. Nobody understood the shortcomings of Jamal Khashoggi like his friend Jamal Farsi, a Nasserite merchant.[7] Farsi was detained in 2018 because of his critical views on the privatization of Aramco and his objection to Al Saud-affiliated companies receiving concessions to find and develop Saud Arabia's mineral reserves. Despite his disagreement with Khashoggi on specific issues raised in the book, Farsi wrote an introduction, in which he criticized Khashoggi for not presenting any political views or quest for democratic reform. It is worth mentioning that Khashoggi was never active in the wave of demands that swept Saudi Arabia after 2001, which had led to the circulation of many petitions insisting on various reforms, above all public participation in the decision-making process. That period is often described as 'petition fever' given the daring demands that Saudis presented to the leadership. Needless to say, many signatories were detained, amongst them Matruk al-Falih, Ali al-Damini, Muhammad Said al-Taib and many others, including women. Rather than partaking in this movement, according to Farsi, in the book Khashoggi only discusses ameliorating the daily lives of Saudis. Dedicating a chapter to each, Khashoggi called for improved urban infrastructure, health, housing, education, employment, trees, pavements, football stadiums, public parks and many other services and provisions considered to be subpar for a wealthy oil-producing country. Moreover, Farsi objected to Khashoggi's infatuation with the USA and his uncritical stance toward its Middle East foreign policy, reminding us that while Khashoggi rightly objected to the Soviets killing innocent Afghans in the 1980s, he remained silent on the American devastation of the country and the killing of Afghan civilians in retaliation for 9/11. Khashoggi was suspended from writing after he wrote an article warning Saudi Arabia about the successful election of Donald Trump. However, in Farsi's view, Khashoggi was not critical of the overall US policies in the Middle East.

It is only in the last three chapters that Khashoggi hesitantly and timidly discusses, in a very evasive way, the political dimension of the book. In less than fifteen pages (out of 127), Khashoggi expresses hopes of seeing what he calls public participation in local government administration and municipalities. He insists that he is not calling for democracy, as Saudi Arabia has an exceptional system of government that establishes the 'blessing of security' (*nimat al-amn*). Having seen how the quest for democracy was thwarted in the Arab world in 2011, Khashoggi concludes that Saudis do not in fact aspire towards democracy. He ignores the Saudi activists and civil society organizations calling for democratic transition, an elected parliament, an independent judiciary and the separation of powers. This was the programme of HASM, whose founders, Abdullah al-Hamid and Muhammad al-Qahtani, among others, were all imprisoned, most of them serving between ten and fifteen years in jail. Khashoggi never signed any of the petitions that Saudis circulated after 2011 in the euphoria of the Arab uprisings. In the book he praises a new bureaucratic centre established to 'measure the performance of the public sector' which he describes as a mini accountable government sufficient for the country. He also mentions that the New Vision 2030 of the crown prince incorporates democratic concepts such as transparency, accountability and monitoring, obviating the need for an elected national assembly. Khashoggi also calls for the right of citizens to information from government sources and freedom of speech, accompanied by government legislation to protect people from slander by inexperienced or malicious media reporting. He was concerned with local government corruption, which in his view led to the deteriorating infrastructure of Jeddah where in the past flooding had resulted in many deaths. His enunciation of the right to information and criticism of officials fell short of including the princes in the category that journalists should scrutinize.

In the final chapter, Khashoggi praises what he calls Saudi heritage, the sum total of the ideological and political achievement of the Saudi state since the eighteenth century. Here he comes across as reiterating the hyper-nationalist mania that swept Saudi Arabia with the rise of Crown Prince Muhammad ibn Salman. He writes: 'We must remind the new generation of the prosperity that flourished in the first Saudi capital where gold and silver were abundant in its market so [that] they can be inspired to continue that heritage.' He refers to Diriyyah, the first Saudi capital, which is currently undergoing rebranding under the heritage-revival initiatives of the crown prince. Such comments provoked his friend Farsi to ask the author to elaborate on how the Al Saud appropriated this wealth and brought it to their capital in the first place. Although Khashoggi tries to avoid reaching 'the high ceiling in his vision and advises the readers to be realistic in their demands', he continues to play the role that he had always played so well, namely an aspiring adviser who was shunned by the very regime that he celebrates and praises. A careful reading of his articles and books certainly does cast doubt on his democratic aspirations, although they became more apparent in the columns he wrote from Washington in the last two years of his life.

In 2017 Khashoggi suddenly arrived in Washington, where he was granted residence and was enlisted by the *Washington Post* as an opinion writer. As he became more critical of the new leadership from abroad, he must have begun to be seen as a national security threat, given his insider knowledge of the Saudi regime after several decades of working in its service as a media commentator, journalist and informal adviser. Was the regime worried that Khashoggi might release information on its intrigues with radical groups, sponsorship of jihadi missions, or simply the intricate general conspiracies of the royal court? Khashoggi must have had access to sensitive information when he worked at Saudi embassies in London and Washington, and even earlier, when he was reporting on the jihad in Afghanistan and other jihadi projects around the Arab and Muslim world.

It was reported that the Saudi ambassador in Washington, Prince Khalid ibn Salman, had initiated contact with the journalist and advised him to go to Istanbul to obtain the necessary document for his marriage. It was also reported that the crown prince's aide Saud al-Qahtani had contacted Khashoggi in Washington, offering him a safe return to Saudi Arabia. These may have been attempts to persuade Khashoggi to return to Saudi Arabia, but it is difficult to know the extent of the contacts he had with the embassy in Washington before travelling to Turkey.

The Saudi authorities initially denied that he had been murdered, claiming that he had left the premises of the consulate on the afternoon of 2 October. A series of lies and denials followed—all amounting to obstructing the course of justice, according to the UN special investigation. A CCTV camera recording a man dressed in Khashoggi's clothes leaving the consulate that day was released by the regime as evidence that he had walked out alive. Several weeks later, and after many Turkish leaks to the press, the Saudis admitted that Khashoggi was murdered inside the consulate by agents who were on a mission to return him to the country. The Saudi authorities remained silent on where his body was buried or whether it had been dismembered by the Saudi death-squad that arrived in Turkey just before his appointment with the consulate staff on 2 October.

Crown Prince Muhammad ibn Salman, by then the de facto leader of Saudi Arabia, was absolved of any responsibility for the murder, which was blamed on security operatives who had been dispatched to Istanbul with a secret mission. The Saudi authorities announced that it had arrested a number of suspects in the murder of Khashoggi but failed to name them. According to Saudi sources, five of those arrested admitted to the murder. Saudi Arabia refused to cooperate with an international investigation under the auspices of the United Nations and Turkey, where the murder took place. It claimed that it was conducting its own investigation, and categorically denied that Muhammad ibn Salman was responsible for the murder or had given orders to eliminate the journalist.

In June 2019, ten months after the murder, the United Nations published a hundred-page report following its own investigation, taking into account all recorded conversations and messages between the murderers and their bosses in Riyadh that the Turkish authorities made available to them. The report concluded: 'The crown prince of Saudi Arabia should be investigated over the murder of the dissident journalist Jamal Khashoggi because there is "credible evidence" that he and other senior officials are liable for the killing.'[8] The report represents an independent investigation with important points and calls for the inclusion of the crown prince in the investigation. It also states that should the intention have been kidnapping Khashoggi, this too constitutes a violation of international law and may constitute an act of torture under the terms of the Convention against Torture. The UN report concludes that the investigations of both Turkey and Saudi Arabia failed to meet international standards regarding unlawful deaths; the Saudi investigation into the murder was not conducted in good faith and might amount to an obstruction of justice. While Saudi Arabia announced that eleven suspects were under investigation, the report called for the suspension of this investigation as it lacked credibility. The report highlighted the vulnerability of other Saudi dissidents who face covert actions by authorities of their country of origin or non-state actors associated with them.[9]

As to the whereabouts of Khashoggi's body, the report mentions a gruesome recorded conversation from outside the consulate released by the Turkish authorities, in which Khashoggi is called a sacrificial animal (*thabiha*). One Saudi official asked whether it would 'be possible to put the trunk in a bag'. Another replied: 'No. Too heavy. It is not a problem. The body is heavy. First time I cut on the ground. If we take plastic bags and cut it into pieces, it will be finished. We will wrap each of them.'[10] On the anniversary of the murder, further leaks to the Turkish press revealed Khashoggi's last words as he struggled to free himself from a plastic bag put on his head by his murderers.

A trial of the murderers, including the person ultimately responsible for the actions of the fifteen men who carried out this secret mission—namely, Muhammad ibn Salman—in an open and credible court may not take place in the near future. But the crime had to be understood in the context of a hawkish crown prince who is determined to silence all critics, encourage ultra-nationalistic rhetoric, and employ henchmen and eavesdroppers whose role has become prominent in spreading fear inside Saudi Arabia and plotting outside it in the name of protecting and defending the nation. Two of the most famous operatives, Ahmad Asiri and Saud al-Qahtani, were removed from office, but they remain free.

Like Muhammad ibn Salman, al-Qahtani was a graduate of King Saud University, where he studied law. After a short career as a law lecturer at one of Saudi Arabia's security colleges, al-Qahtani was brought into government by a senior aide of King

THE SON KING AND THE 'MAN OF THE PALACE'

Abdullah, Khalid al-Tuwaijri. He was a royal adviser before Muhammad ibn Salman made him media consultant and general supervisor for the Centre for Studies and Media Affairs.

Like Muhammad ibn Salman, Saud al-Qahtani is young, ambitious and aggressive on social media, especially Twitter. In addition, in the autumn of 2017 his name was associated with the Ritz Carlton incident, in which several senior princes and elite businessmen were detained during an alleged anti-corruption campaign. In the same year his name was also mentioned in the context of the attempt to persuade Lebanese prime minister Saad al-Hariri to read a prepared resignation letter while on a visit to Riyadh, thereby hoping to precipitate a political crisis in Lebanon and undermine Iranian-backed Hizbollah's control over the country. His harsh statements on social media prompted many dissidents and Arab critics of the regime to name him Mr Hashtag and the founder of the 'army of electronic flies', referring to his team of cyber attackers and intimidators.

Al-Qahtani is regarded as one of the crown prince's populist propagandists and cult fixers, but his actions attest to the practising of thuggery in the name of the nation. He always claimed that he wanted to rid the country of traitors and enemies of the state. On one occasion, he tweeted that the 'people should assist the government in drawing [up] a blacklist of those traitors who criticize it and tarnish its reputation'. Later, he promised to eliminate those who appeared on the list, Khashoggi's name being among them. He was the promoter of the 'citizen informer' and 'citizen policeman', demanding that all Saudis be enlisted in defending the nation in multiple ways. Adding the names of critics and dissidents abroad to the online blacklist was one. Al-Qahtani was building a data bank listing the names of random people and critics of the regime.

Al-Qahtani was responsible for projecting the image of Saudi Arabia under the new leadership as a progressive, liberal and prosperous country. For this purpose, he sought the expertise of several Western public-relations companies to rebrand Saudi Arabia. Al-Qahtani was later named by the US intelligence services as the alleged ringleader of the death-squad that eliminated Khashoggi at the consulate in Istanbul. Al-Qahtani has also been banned from entry to the USA, Britain and other European countries. His aggressive nationalist rhetoric was closely linked to security. He used the accusation of treason against all critics and mobilised ultra-nationalism to intimidate and eventually silence many dissidents, such as Khashoggi. But al-Qahtani always reiterated that he was serving his masters: the Guardian of the Two Holy Mosques—King Salman—and his Royal Highness the Crown Prince. He often thanked them for the trust they invested in him, their loyal servant. He reminded his Twitter followers that he always received orders from the crown prince.

Had Khashoggi been a revolutionary dissident, a straightforward Islamist (Muslim Brotherhood), or an 'enemy of the state', as claimed by the Saudi authorities and repeated by American president Donald Trump,[11] he would not have been recruited to write op-ed columns for the *Washington Post* in 2017. He was an insider who knew too much, rendering him useful as a weapon against one of the most secretive and treacherous regimes in the Arab world, which remains shielded from open criticism by its Western allies. He was recruited to write in the *Washington Post* as a critic who seeks reform rather than revolution. As Khashoggi praised democracy and free speech in his *Washington Post* columns, exposed the new wave of repression under Muhammad ibn Salman and criticized Trump's Middle East policies, which suited the president's critics in Washington, he increasingly became a dangerous dissident in the eyes of the Saudi regime.

Even after the masses took to the streets in 2011 in major Arab capitals, calling for democracy, justice and dignity, Jamal Khashoggi had remained a loyalist to the Saudi regime, despite being enthused by the uprisings taking place outside Saudi

Arabia. Later, in his *Washington Post* writings, he would praise the Arab impulse towards democracy and condemn the role of his country in thwarting most of the Arab uprisings. He described the wave of repression in Saudi Arabia as new, implying that previous rulers were more lenient and less brutal. While he may have applauded the Arab uprisings, he insisted—at least publicly—that Saudi Arabia itself should be saved from the kind of unpredictable and challenging upheaval that might occur should the country experience mass protest. He had known about the detention of hundreds of Saudis from January 2011, such as civil society activists who founded HASM, a civil and political association,[12] and the demonstrators who were inspired by the Arab uprisings and headed to the streets demanding the release of political prisoners in Riyadh, Buraydah and Qatif, among other places. Khashoggi justified the detention of protesters and even the beheading of a Shia cleric, Nimr al-Nimr, in December 2016. The cleric was described by state media as an Iranian-backed dissident and a separatist, who was threatening the unity of Saudi Arabia.

But by 2017 Khashoggi was beginning to feel the pressure of the heavy iron fist of the new regime in Riyadh. Several of his friends and colleagues had been detained, and he felt lonely in Jeddah, almost under house arrest and ostracized by close friends. He feared his own imminent arrest. He must also have felt guilty for not being able to publicly defend his fellow journalists, friends and acquaintances in prison, an act that would have landed him in jail. By 2017—an outcast, lonely, isolated and censored man approaching his sixtieth birthday—Khashoggi had fallen out of his ivory tower of royal patronage. He decided to leave.

In public, Khashoggi never contemplated a Saudi Arabia without the Al Saud. Yet he paid a high price for simply defecting from the Al Saud camp and joining a mass of critical voices forced into exile by new repressive measures under the leadership of Muhammad ibn Salman.

Observers who may think that the murder of Khashoggi represents an unusual turn in the history of Saudi repression are probably unaware of precedents to this heinous crime. Khashoggi himself believed that the wave of extreme repression hitting Saudi Arabia under Muhammad ibn Salman was new. Yet, he surely must have been aware of how the regime had eliminated its critics in the past. It is worth remembering that there were many previous such incidents. In 1979, for example, the Saudi regime, through its ambassador in Beirut, Ali al-Shair, and the cooperation of some Palestinian factions, used the chaos of the Lebanese civil war to kidnap Nasir al-Said, a veteran Saudi dissident who was associated with the labour movement in the 1950s. Al-Said was seized and put on a flight to Saudi Arabia. He is still missing, and his wife and children do not know what happened to him.[13] Nevertheless, the brutality of Khashoggi's murder, the online circulation of images and words globally, the Western media preoccupation with the incident, the tame and insignificant response of Western governments, and finally the damning UN investigation report have made this crime an especially unforgettable and memorable incident that will haunt the Saudi regime in general and Muhammad ibn Salman in particular for a long time to come. Its full impact on the cult of the prince is yet to be fully assessed.

How can we understand why Khashoggi moved from being a regime propagandist, some would say apologist, to becoming an enemy of state, a pariah, *persona non grata*, and a threat to a regime believed to be undergoing top-down revolutionary reform into a benevolent mighty, wealthy, secure and powerful liberal autocracy? Khashoggi's transformation cannot be understood without looking at how Saudi Arabia itself was transformed by Muhammad ibn Salman in ways that are approved of by many Saudis but also alienate many others.

THE SON KING AND THE 'MAN OF THE PALACE'

The Son King's Rise and Domestic Policy

Domestically, it is the abrupt rise of Muhammad ibn Salman and his cult that explains Khashoggi's transformation. The prince's youth; erratic leadership; ostentatious interviews in global media; unexpected speedy takeover of all power hubs in the state; detention campaign against his own kinsmen and business elite; notorious rapidly deployed death-squads; aggressive online media trolls; cyber security farm in Riyadh; Western management-consultants' reform visions; Washington- and London-based apostles and apologists; promising social transformation programme; muzzling of religious institutions and scholars; controversial entertainment industry; futuristic cities; promotion of women; relentless repressive campaign against Islamists, feminists and ordinary critics; and excessive record of executions and crucifixion of prisoners, not to mention the horrific murder of Khashoggi, all make him responsible for a real transformation in Saudi domestic politics.

On 21 June 2017 King Salman appointed one of his youngest sons, Muhammad (b. 1985) as crown prince. Since 1933 succession to the throne had been horizontal, moving from one son of the founder, Ibn Saud, to another without necessarily following seniority criteria. The succession is believed to follow the principle of eligibility, regardless of age, as in the past senior sons of Ibn Saud were occasionally overlooked in favour of a more suitable prince. This was the rationale of succession in the house of Saud until King Salman bucked tradition.[14] In 2017 neither observers of Saudi royal politics nor Saudis expected the king to skip the handful of surviving senior brothers or senior and eligible second-generation princes in favour of his own young son. Three months after becoming king in 2015, Salman sacked his half-brother Muqrin, who had been appointed crown prince by his predecessor, King Abdullah. He also completely ignored his full brother Ahmad, who had failed to secure a senior post years before Salman came to power. Other brothers such as the once-ambitious Talal were too old and ill to be considered as heirs to the throne. The dwindling number of eligible senior brothers worked to Salman's advantage as he moved the succession swiftly to his own son.

King Salman promoted his nephew Muhammad ibn Nayif to the position of crown prince in April 2015 and upgraded his son Muhammad to deputy crown prince. Rumours about rivalry between the crown prince and the young son of the king became rife. Saudis and observers expected this rivalry between the two princes to erupt into open conflict, but as an absolute monarch and one of the eldest surviving sons of Ibn Saud, Salman used his royal prerogative and sacked Muhammad ibn Nayif by royal decree who received the Central Intelligence Agency's George Tenet Medal on 10 February 2017 for his efforts in fighting terrorism. Saudi online propaganda circulated the story that Muhammad ibn Nayif was addicted to painkillers following an attempted assassination by al-Qaida operatives almost a decade previously.

King Salman promoted his son Muhammad to crown prince and has not appointed a deputy,[15] thus setting up young Muhammad, still in his thirties, to be the monarch for a very long time. Muhammad ibn Salman is the future king, but he is also the de facto ruler of the kingdom, waiting to become de jure monarch after his ageing father passes away. By June 2017 the king had ended speculations and rumours about the future of leadership and ensured that Saudi Arabia can now be truly referred to as *al-mamlaka al-salmaniyya*, Salman's kingdom. This is what it has been dubbed by observers and critics who were astonished at the speed by which the king shifted the succession in favour of his own son. It is now expected to remain in the hands of the latter's descendants after him. As of 2020, Muhammad ibn Salman has four children. It remains to be seen who will become crown prince when Muhammad succeeds his father as king.

THE SON KING AND THE 'MAN OF THE PALACE'

Within months of his appointment as crown prince, functionaries loyal to Muhammad ibn Salman detained several senior
princes in the Riyadh Ritz Carlton hotel, amongst them the
powerful Miteb ibn Abdullah, son of the late King Abdullah,
who was in charge of the Saudi Arabia National Guard, and
Walid ibn Talal, entrepreneur and wealthy businessman. A dozen
members of the commercial elite were also imprisoned. The
crown prince presented this drastic measure and unprecedented
humiliation of senior princes as part of a campaign against corruption. Not many observers were convinced; the prince suspected that his relatives had felt sidelined with his sudden promotion to the highest positions in government, and he may have
wanted to show that he was capable of drastic measures should
senior princes challenge his newly acquired powers. In the process, he appropriated huge amounts of money—reportedly over
$100 billion—from the detainees, both senior princes and suc-
cessful private-sector businessmen. At a time when oil revenues
were dwindling, the crown prince increased his wealth, and in
specific cases was able to become a partner in the businesses of
other commercial elites. It is worth mentioning that none of the
prince's other cousins, for example the sons of Nayif (with the
exception of the humiliation of Muhammad, who was sacked as
crown prince), Sultan, and Fahd (with the exception of Abd al-
Aziz ibn Fahd, who was reportedly put under house arrest) were
detained in the anti-corruption campaign. The selective nature
of this purge made its credentials as a genuine anti-corruption
measure look weak. None of the detainees appeared in open
court; the issue was settled privately between them and the
crown prince and his private aides and secretaries. The princes
and the commercial elite were gradually released one after the
other, but only after they paid ransom money. In addition to
Miteb, other sons of King Abdullah were also detained, possibly
because the crown prince wanted to punish them as their father

had sidelined the erratic Prince Muhammad from the royal court during his kingship. The billions of dollars that were appropriated from the princes and the elite thus demonstrated the new style of governance and zero tolerance for the wealth and prestige of other princes. In addition to conveying a chilling warning to potential rival princes, Muhammad ibn Salman also sent a troubling message to Saudis, who were intimidated and frightened by how far the young prince was prepared to go to pursue his leadership goals of becoming the undisputed Son King.

In addition to his appointment as crown prince, Muhammad became second deputy prime minister, minister of defence, chief of the royal court, chair of the Council of Political and Security Affairs, and chair of the Council of Economic Development Affairs. He also presided over newly created foundations and a network of organizations intended to serve specific interests, such as the promotion of art, entrepreneurial skills and youth empowerment. Through the restructuring of the Saudi bureaucracy the crown prince is now in charge of domestic political decisions, regional policies, international relations, and security, intelligence and financial matters. As minor princes were appointed within various key ministries, governorships of the provinces, and military institutions that had lost their leadership in the crown prince's detention campaign, Muhammad ibn Salman became the face of Saudi Arabia and the main state actor and military commander. No other prince has ever held as many positions at such a young age.

Muhammad ruled while his elderly father, rumoured to suffer from Alzheimer's, took a back seat. The king occasionally appeared at big state events and banquets when foreign visitors arrived in the kingdom and during international conferences held domestically and abroad. Salman increased his orchestrated and televised appearances during times of crisis. Immediately after the murder of Khashoggi, he and his son toured the kingdom, pretending that it was a routine visit by the monarch and the royal court. It was undoubtedly an attempt to restore faith in a monarchy whose name had become associated with not one but two international scandals: the murder of Khashoggi and the ongoing war in Yemen, in which the Son King took the lead as minister of defence. During the heightened tension with Iran in the spring of 2019, when three terrorist attacks targeted oil tankers in the Gulf and Saudi pipelines, followed by an Iranian attack on a US drone in the Persian Gulf, the king called for three summits in Mecca, attended by senior Gulf, Arab and Muslim guests. Under the king's umbrella, the future king could operate without any sign of being restrained or reprimanded by his father. In fact, the father stood by the side of his son and protected him from attempts to erode his future legitimacy and popularity, all attributed to outside conspiracies against the king-dom by Western media, Saudi traitors and agents of Qatar.

From 2015 Saudi Arabia began to be seen as undergoing a top-down revolution and religious, social and economic transforma-tions. It is seen as being on the verge of leaping forward into new horizons of modernity, all attributed to the energies of the crown prince and his many visions. The Saudi press was given unprece-dented access to the young prince, who was filmed in 'fun' situa-tions such as festivals and concerts. This contributed to building his reputation as the young, enlightened and energetic monarch of the future, ushering in a great revolution in his country.

The dominant narrative of this top-down revolutionary trans-formation is embedded in Vision 2030, which Muhammad ibn Salman, at the time deputy crown prince, announced on 25 April 2016 on the Saudi-owned al-Arabiyya television channel[16] two months after he had announced it during an interview with *The Economist* and Bloomberg.[17] It is this vision that Khashoggi responded to in his book. It is telling that the interview with *The Economist* took place only days after a mass execution of forty-seven prisoners convicted of terrorism on 2 January 2016, amongst them Shia cleric and activist al-Nimr.[18] After criticism online about the choice of *The Economist* to announce such an important and controversial vision—and in English—the prince appeared on al-Arabiyya and was interviewed by Turki al-Dakhil, who was later appointed ambassador to the UAE.[19] The owner of al-Arabiyya was among those detained in the Ritz Carlton.

The prince justified one of the most controversial aspects of Vision 2030—the expected privatisation of 5 per cent of the Saudi oil company Aramco and the downgrading of government welfare and subsidies—to a sceptical Saudi audience, as many economists and intellectuals criticized the announcement. Jamal Farsi, Isam al-Zamil and Abdul Aziz al-Dakhil were among many economists who voiced their criticism online and in lectures attended by Saudi intellectuals. In 2019 both al-Zamil and Farsi were still in prison. The prince claimed that Saudi Arabia had been able to defy British colonialism at a time when there was no oil, implying that it could survive the sharp drop in oil prices since 2014, as his plan for the economy is to increase diversification. He criticized the opaqueness of Aramco and suggested that its privatization would increase transparency, leading Saudi income to be derived from investment rather than oil as a commodity. He predicted that most of Aramco will be privatized at a later stage.

In his Arabic media interviews, the prince identified the country's three major strengths. First, its Arab and Islamic heritage, which can be used to benefit the economy. Second, Saudi Arabia has great investment power worldwide; the Public Investment Fund (PIF) is the largest in the world. The prince forecast that the PIF, which was established with $320 billion under his personal control as chairman, responsible for development, diversification and privatization, will be a world leader. Muhammad ibn Salman took control of this important financial institution and transformed it to serve his own purposes, thus completing his control over Saudi financial policies. He praised Saudi business-men, describing their mentality as grounded in commercial investment, and hinted that it is their efforts that will make Vision 2030 materialize.

Third, the prince highlighted the country's distinct geographi-cal location: 'We sit in between three straits (Hormuz, Bab el-Mandab and Tiran), with all global trade between Asia, Africa, Europe, and beyond passing through them.' He plans to provide logistical services for global aviation, business hubs for invest-ment, and connections to create a bridge between countries. He promised to create growth not only in Saudi Arabia but also throughout the world.

The decrease in oil prices since 2014 was not a driver of Vision 2030, according to the prince. He insisted that it will not be affected by future rises in oil prices, as it will not be dropped, but will continue to guide the Saudi economy for years to come. He confidently announced that 'we will not need oil in 2020'.

Regarding society, the prince's vision emphasizes the role of the 'citizen', who must work to develop its multiple programmes. Government bureaucracy, the private sector, and everyone else needs to contribute to create *mujtama hayawi* (a vibrant and organic society):

> We need to serve more pilgrims; we need their numbers to rise to 15 million annually. The airports of Jeddah and the infrastructure of Mecca, with its new metro, in addition to land development near the Grand Mosque, will accommodate and serve pilgrims. For all this to happen, the Saudi bureaucracy should regulate work with speed. The executive branch is already shaken, for example the Council of Ministers. We need to be efficient.

Other bureaucracies will be created to monitor public-sector performance in order to have greater accountability, according to the prince.

The prince introduced yet another controversial aspect of his vision: that relating to culture, entertainment and tourism. These amount to a cultural revolution in disguise, with all the elements of a top-down eradication of previous practices to introduce a new way of thinking, seeing and acting. The prince promised to turn the country into a hub for global tourism, in addition to the traditional religious tourism associated with the annual pilgrimage and the minor visit to Mecca and Madina. The first step is to create an Islamic museum, as he declared himself appalled by the absence of such an important foundation in the land of Islam. He also said:

> We have a barren landscape. Our history is short because we trace it only as far as Islam. But we have a hub of ancient civilizations and archaeological sites before Islam. We are part of the civilization of Europe, the Arab world and other civilizations. We will enlist many sites as UNESCO heritage sites and open the country for tourism, according to our values.

The prince also mentioned schemes to attract wealthy foreigners to reside in Saudi Arabia as permanent residents. The scheme was approved by the Council of Ministers in 2019: for 800,000 Saudi riyals foreigners can start a business, import labour, purchase transport vehicles, and apply for their relatives to come to Saudi Arabia. Green Card residence for foreigners is dependent on high income, investment potential and non-oil-based initiatives. Foreigners must also bring capital and promote investment inside the country. Those who had been in Saudi Arabia all their lives could now apply for a Green Card, a fast-track residence permit with all these benefits, if they meet the conditions. The prince expects profits to remain in the country and reduce foreign remittances by expatriate labour. Wealthy foreigners no longer need a Saudi sponsor. He also organized several investment conferences attended by global consultants, bankers, government officials, investors and developers. However, the last conference in 2018, dubbed Davos in the Desert, took place only weeks after the murder of Khashoggi, which led to several important investors cancelling their attendance.

The prince predicted controversial cuts in government subsidies and spending, especially in the energy, water and services sectors. Such a move worries a population that is expected to consume most of the energy produced in the country in the near future. The prince spoke of 'restructuring of the economy' and avoided elaborating on the controversial cuts and the anticipated reduced government spending on welfare and services. He identified an important aspect related to energy and water subsidies: in his view they benefit the rich, who consume more water and energy than the rest of society. In a populist move, the prince promised to avoid hardship for low-income Saudis. He wants to restructure the economy in such a way as to take from the rich and give to the poor. Improvement in housing, health and employment are high on the prince's agenda during his populist-style interviews with Saudi media. There is also a promise to increase home ownership from its current 47 per cent to 52 per cent. In addition, unemployment will decrease from 11 per cent to 7 per cent as a result of partnership with the private sector. These promises present the crown prince as a champion of the people, and in particular the youth.

New economic sectors such as mineralization and military industry will be created, according to Vision 2030. The reservations that Jamal Farsi expressed about giving Al Saud-owned companies the right to launch the mineralization industry led to his imprisonment. The prince claims that the huge funds Saudi Arabia spends on weapons could remain in the country, as he envisages manufacturing weapons at home. He insists that 'we have great demand for arms and we should produce them here to create new jobs. We will create a 100 per cent [Saudi-]owned company to oversee arms production.' The promise to create a military industry may be far-fetched, but the crown prince has truly shifted Saudi Arabia from its historical status as one of the greatest spenders on armaments to one that actually uses its military arsenal. There is nothing new in the urge to buy an excessive amount of highly modern military equipment. What is new is the beginning of the direct deployment of these weapons in regional conflicts, especially in Yemen since 2009, culminating in the ongoing 2015 war.

With a growing young population and fluctuating oil prices, rulers such as the crown prince can no longer continue to distribute largesse to the people. Since 2016 the prince has been forced to draw on the country's foreign reserves, estimated at $654.5 billion before the 2014 oil crisis.[20] He has had to borrow more than $10 billion annually to cover the budget deficit, and was forced to cut state spending leading to the erosion of government budgets. Borrowing is done through issuing government bonds, whereas in the past the government borrowed from local banks during oil crises. The fiscal vulnerability of Saudi Arabia has begun to show after several decades of having the reserves that protected it from exposure to global market hazards.

Vision 2030 combined old promises and new aspirations. The familiar elements included moves to replace foreign workers with Saudi citizens (*tawtin* or Saudization); the privatization of some state assets; and promises to curb budgets and expand the non-oil sectors of the economy. Since the 1970s Saudi Arabia's policy has been expressed in a string of five-year plans, each promising variations on these themes.

But there are also genuinely novel aspects, including the development of a $2 trillion sovereign wealth fund, paid for by oil revenues. Most surprising was the decision to float 5 per cent of Aramco, the huge Saudi Arabian state oil company, which provides around 10 per cent of the world's oil. It is a highly secretive company—but that will have to change if its shares are to be sold in global stock markets. Investors will want to know how much oil is still in the ground, and who ultimately controls the company. At present, the answers to these questions are state secrets. By 2019 the promised privatization of Aramco had been postponed, and many observers think that it will not happen, simply because of the requirement for greater transparency.

After Vision 2030, the prince introduced the National Transformation Programme (NTP),[21] incorporating the cooperation of several ministries such as health, communication, finance and tourism. The objective of the NTP is to identify strategic objectives and targets for the participating entities, translate strategic objectives into initiatives, promote joint action, create jobs, strengthen partnerships with the private sector, maximize local content, and contribute to digital transformation.[22] However, only a year after its launch, the original NTP was followed by NTP 2.0, a redrafted version to replace the original plan, which was described as too aggressive and ambitious. Core elements of the original plan included privatizing state assets, creating 1.2 million private-sector jobs, and reducing unemployment from 11.6 per cent to 9 per cent by 2020.[23]

On social reform, the prince announced a pledge to return Saudi Arabia to its original moderate Islam, which had allegedly been corrupted by Saudi Islamists, known as the Sahwa movement, since 1979. The king ordered restrictions on the infamous Committee for Commanding Right and Prohibiting Vice, known as the religious police. He also lifted the ban on women driving, and by 2018 almost 40,000 women were able to obtain driving licences. Gender equality became high on the prince's agenda, promoting a reformed face and greater visibility for women in public- and private-sector employment. A relaxation of the guardianship system, discussed later in this book, started with women being able to take jobs without the permission of their guardians. But in marriage and travel abroad the restrictions remain in place. In 2019 Saudi official newspapers announced that a committee had been formed to study the possibility of abolishing the need for the guardianship system for non-minors.

While a succession of royal decrees led to greater openness of the public sphere, where men and women began to intermingle freely, the crown prince led an unprecedented detention campaign against intellectuals, economists, university professors, journalists, feminists and above all Islamists of all shades. Any criticism of his social, economic and religious policies, in addition to his regional strategies, such as the war on Yemen, rift with Qatar, and close ties with Israel, became taboo. Hundreds of detainees languished in prison in successive waves of arrests from 2017.

To contain the youth and foster creativity, the prince co-opted the arts. He founded the Prince Mohammed bin Salman bin Abdulaziz Foundation (MiSK)—an initiative, according to its website, 'devoted to cultivating learning and leadership for the Saudi Arabia of tomorrow'. Or, in the words of its founder and chairman, 'Allah Almighty has bestowed humans with power, money and knowledge to be utilised in the right direction. Not only that, humans should ensure the sustainability of these blessings as we may consider sustainability one of the most vital factors in prolonging the timespan of any given civilisation.'[24] The prince appointed Bader al-Asaker as head of his private office and chairman of the MiSK Initiative Centre.

The most controversial aspects of the prince's social reform that came from Vision 2030 is al-Haya al-Ama lil Tarfih, the General Entertainment Authority.[25] It was headed by another close aide to the crown prince, Turki al-Sheikh, who moved from being in charge of sport to become the director of the Entertainment Authority. He immediately launched a pervasive entertainment programme that brought many Arab and Western performers to the kingdom. Pop stars, circuses, and shows were staged, bringing thousands of youth deprived of such entertainment to newly constructed stadiums and concert halls. However, not all Western pop stars honoured their contracts to perform in Saudi Arabia after the murder of Jamal Khashoggi. Many global activists and human rights professionals urged them to boycott the events in Saudi Arabia because of its bad record on human rights. A global campaign to name and shame those who accepted invitations to perform in Saudi Arabia proved to be successful and led to several artists and singers cancelling their performances. The last one to cancel was the rapper and singer Nicki Minaj, who was due to hold a concert at the Jeddah Festival in the summer of 2019. Only days before the festival, she announced on Twitter that after 'educating herself about Saudi Arabia's record on human rights and LGBTQ rights, she decided to pull out'.[26] While Saudis can only voice criticism of such events anonymously online, they nevertheless condemned the overtly provocative shows that the Entertainment Authority organized. In an attempt to absorb contentious opinions, the Authority announced that it had organized a Quran and call for prayer recitation competition open to all Muslims, with a generous prize of 12,000,000 Saudi riyals. While the Authority is a state-owned establishment, it invites the private sector to apply for licences to hold concerts, plays, circuses and other cultural events.

The Regime, the Exiled Saudi Opposition and Khashoggi

The crown prince undoubtedly regarded Jamal Khashoggi as an enemy of state. Both the appeal and danger of Khashoggi stem from the fact that he was neither overtly Islamist nor liberal. He looked and behaved like a liberal in the West; he also looked and talked like an Islamist in Muslim countries—like Turkey, where he was killed. According to Jonathan Rugman's book on the murder, where he cites one of Khashoggi's friends in Washington, we are told that a long time before Khashoggi settled in Washington, he would enjoy a glass of wine while he discussed Saudi matters with journalists. CCTV pictures of him with his fiancée in Istanbul show a modern Muslim couple holding hands even before signing the required marriage documents that would render such a public display of intimacy *halal* (legitimate). But both in his youth and old age, Khashoggi was fond of Islamic causes, and according to many observers he was a member of the Muslim Brotherhood. It is noteworthy that all political parties are banned in Saudi Arabia, and the Muslim Brotherhood was criminalized in 2014. Whether he was a member or a sympathizer, Khashoggi wrote that Islamists (meaning those like the Muslim Brotherhood who participate in elections) should be included in any future governments.

When Khashoggi became a Washington-based exile, he found himself in a difficult situation. The regime began to see him as an enemy, while the Saudi opposition abroad looked at him with suspicion, simply because he had worked for the regime and defended it throughout his career as a journalist. He began to receive hate messages from both, which saddened him deeply. He was perhaps unprepared for the mistrust of opposition figures and expected them to embrace him as soon as he announced his reservations about the regime and its policies under the crown prince. But Khashoggi had friends across the world, especially among Arab and Muslim activists and intellectuals in exile, and among Islamists in Turkey and Qatar. With time, he began to build bridges with members of the Saudi opposition in Washington and London, in addition to Turkey.

There had been Saudi dissidents and exiles abroad since the creation of the Saudi state. In the 1950s and 1960s the novelist Abdulrahman Munif, the labour activist Nasir al-Said, the oil minister Abdullah al-Turaiqi, and a handful of Free Princes, among many others, fled Saudi Arabia and settled in Beirut,

THE SON KING AND THE 'MAN OF THE PALACE'

Cairo, Europe, the USA and other places. In the 1990s Saudi Islamists Saad al-Faqih and Muhammad al-Massari, with others, fled to London, where they launched a media campaign against the regime. They joined an early cohort of Shia activists in exile such as Hamza al-Hassan, Sheikh Hasan al-Safar, Tawfiq al-Saif and Fuad Ibrahim. However, several decades later the Saudi Islamist opposition in exile looked aged and exhausted. It had failed to transform and reinvent itself to appeal to a new generation of Saudi millennials. The discourse of the Islamist opposition in exile remained static, while Saudi society was changing at an unprecedented rate.

Recently uprooted, well connected to several countries deemed hostile to Saudi Arabia—such as Qatar and Turkey—and well positioned in Washington, Khashoggi promised to inject fresh blood into the stagnating discourse and strategies of an ageing opposition movement and appeal to the new generation, despite his own age. Opposition figures such as al-Faqih and al-Massari welcomed his defection, and they both condemned the brutality of his murder, although they may not have trusted him fully.

Khashoggi was expected to be among those impressed by the crown prince's reforms. But his defection punctured the narrative about the Saudi transformation and drew attention to the mounting repression. He initiated contact with young exiles and promised to mobilize resources to support freedom of speech from outside the kingdom. He started appearing on Al-Jazeera television and other media as an opposition figure who had lost faith in the ability of the regime to contain dissent. He participated in think-tank debates and conferences and presented speeches critical of the new era of repression that had begun with the rise of Muhammad ibn Salman. He was murdered because he promised to bridge wide gaps between Saudi Sunni and Shia opposition groups, young and old activists, and men and women. The regime felt threatened by the international platforms that Khashoggi was invited to, and quickly decided to silence him—even if this required eliminating him at the earliest opportunity.

The new repression ensured the acquiescence of many, but not all, Saudis at home. But the regime must have realized that excessive coercion alone may become counterproductive in the long term. The crown prince searched for other means to extract loyalty from sceptical and aspirational subjects, especially the youth, whom he hopes to contain and enlist in his multiple projects. There remained the difficult task of how to convince Saudis of the authenticity and ground-breaking nature of the prince's reforms and enlist them as disciples in his personality cult. Like all absolute monarchs before him, Muhammad ibn Salman invoked the Saudi nation and deployed populist nationalism to cover up his divisive policies against his own kin, dissidents, Islamists and feminists. Populist nationalism became a weapon deployed to extract consent over his domestic policies and enforce loyalty to himself rather than belonging to an inclusive Saudi nation. The next chapter traces the process whereby Saudi Arabia moved from religious nationalism and pan-Islamism to populist nationalism to mobilize the loyalty of citizens to the future Son King.

4

THE NEW POPULIST NATIONALISM

Saudi Arabia for Saudis; Saudi Arabia is Great; Saudi Arabia First.
Hashtag slogans of the new Saudi nationalism

Under Muhammad ibn Salman, the kingdom continues to call itself Saudi Arabia, a name that does not invoke a national identity or people but refers to the Al Saud family, who brought it together. State building evolved over time, and various state institutions were created, proliferating along with the country's increasing oil wealth. The other, more difficult, project—that of building a nation or a national identity—was equally fluid, evolving over time, in most cases dictated by state consolidation, and above all its legitimacy. Consequently, the project of nation building was troubled from its first days as the Al Saud struggled to construct a nation out of fragments, mainly the pervasive subnational identities that dominated Arabia or the supra-national Islamic identity that the regime promoted. Even after almost a century of state formation, according to anthropologist Nadav Samin, 'Saudi national identity remains deeply in flux'.[1] In 2019 the content of this identity was still ambiguous: 'National iden-

139

tity remains a contested and complex issue. When I posed the question "what is Saudi?" to my focus groups I was frequently provided with vague definitions or answers with varying degrees of disagreement amongst group members as to what actually constitutes "Saudi"'.[2] This is so because of 'the personalized and seemingly arbitrary exercise of power that obscures the process by which Saudi national identity has come into being'.[3] In a recent assessment, 'Saudi Arabia is the opposite of a "melting pot" in which a new national identity can be built and it is possible to determine the status of Saudi national identity located as it is between regionalism and globalization'.[4] Muhammad ibn Salman is determined to change this and create a Saudi nation. But many Saudis still consider the Al Saud to have created a state rather than a nation.

Nations are held together by historical and structural factors; they need, above all, a national narrative to justify their inclusion in one political entity: a state. Moreover, nations need special institutions—especially education, print and visual media, and the military—to homogenize newly conquered people. Ardent advocates of nationalism always insist that their nations are ancient, constant and unchanging, but their narratives about what constitutes the nation often do change over time, as certain of these 'constant' and 'ancient' characteristics of the nation are dropped, forgotten, or replaced by new rhetoric. However, unlike most post-colonial states, the Saudi polity did not consolidate itself on the premise that there had been an ancient Saudi nation aspiring to be freed from foreign domination to eventually become included in one state. The Al Saud's justification for the creation of the state was occasionally depicted as a return to possess by the sword what had originally belonged to them but had been lost over time. In addition, they presented their conquest of Arabia as an urgent religious mission to return its population to a pristine Islam and correct the allegedly un-Islamic malpractices of the Arabian population. These narratives specifically distinguish so-called Saudi nationalism from other manifestations of nationalism in the Arab world and beyond. Perhaps only the creation of Pakistan in the mid-twentieth century as a nation for Indian Muslims or Israel as a home for the Jewish diaspora offer parallels with the Saudi project.

Like all national narratives, Saudi Arabia has changed its focus since the creation of the state, and various elements have been added to it; but three phases can be identified over time. First, religious nationalism dominated the country immediately after the creation of the state. Second, a pan-Islamic transnational identity was promoted in the context of the Cold War from the 1960s. And third, we notice now under the leadership of Muhammad ibn Salman a retreat into a narrow definition of Saudi Arabia summed up in developing a strong local Saudi national identity, represented in online campaigns and hashtags such as 'Saudi Arabia for Saudis' and 'Saudi Arabia is Great'. Such recent imagining of the nation is at odds with the prince's other project of turning Saudi Arabia into a global centre for economic prosperity that could benefit the whole world, a new capitalist liberal economy in which state assets are sold and floated in international markets. Equally, the prince's urgent and incessant quest to tempt both international capital and high-profile investors to make Saudi Arabia their home seems to undermine the rhetoric claiming Saudi Arabia is exclusively for Saudis.

These three phases of nation building have occasionally coincided, and sometimes overlapped, but are distinguished by their specific focus and rhetoric. Before exploring the current nation-building project of the crown prince, it is important to examine how in a previous era constructing and narrating the nation overlooked the focus on a narrow domestic project such as the current 'Saudi Arabia for Saudis' campaign. The invention of

Saudi nationalism today appears to seek a departure from the previous two projects, religious nationalism and pan-Islamism, and replace them with a nationalism that is intimately tied to expressions of loyalty to the crown prince.

Religious Nationalism

The first state-building project was conducted under a religious umbrella rather than with a national agenda. Unlike many post-colonial states in which national liberation struggles determined the character of the new nation and underpinned nation-building projects, Saudi Arabia came together as a result of a religious narrative that focused on salvation, purification of faith and the correction of religious practice. The project of creating a pious nation, a central Islamic hub where an Islamizing project could be launched to return the Arabian population to a pristine Islam, was paramount, and was the only narrative justifying the creation of the state—at least, in the eyes of the populace. The Al Saud narrative 'we took it by the sword' was meant to enforce their mighty leadership, but of course it did not encourage or nourish the development of a Saudi national consciousness. It was the Al Saud's Islamizing rhetoric and associated project that gave their conquest of Arabia a meaningful mission that encouraged groups to identify with it.

Much has been written about the centrality of the Wahhabi tradition in the creation of the state,[5] but less about how the tradition was transformed into a national religious project whose objective was to homogenize the fragments that gradually became part of the state, thus becoming central to the project of nation building. In the first chapter I highlighted the central role of religious revival as a mechanism to justify the conquest of Arabia by Ibn Saud's jihadi warriors. He promised them that he would create an Islamic utopia[6] in which strict adherence to Islam would be respected in all aspects of life. The religious scholars of Najd played a critical role similar to a 'national intelligentsia', theorizing the contours of the pious nation, delineating its parameters, defining its norms, values and moral boundaries, excluding those fragments that did not belong, and assigning to the nation certain roles such as obedience to its legitimate rulers, applying sharia, spreading Islam, and policing the population to ensure its conformity to the right Islamic path. Applying Islamic law as interpreted by this religious intelligentsia while eradicating other interpretations was meant to homogenize the legal framework within which the population was governed. Furthermore, this intelligentsia was entrusted with the role of educating and indoctrinating the population in the right Islamic conduct, belief and rituals.

Wahhabism, the religion of the state, was turned into a quasi-national narrative that enabled many to imagine the new Islamic utopia. The religious intelligentsia and their followers did not imagine themselves as part of a 'Saudi nation', but rather of an Islamic nation. They saw themselves in Islamic rather than secular and cultural terms. The narratives of this religious nation were based on divine sources interpreted by a small circle of religious scholars rather than contemporary and modern intellectuals of national identity. Both the leadership and the religious intelligentsia missed no opportunity to congratulate themselves on creating this pious, moral and authentic Muslim community, the 'Saudi' dimension of which was neither emphasized nor cherished except in highlighting the pivotal role of the Al Saud leadership. The 'Saudi' element of the nation referred only to Ibn Saud and his descendants. Najd, the region from which most Wahhabi scholars came in the state's early years, was elevated to the status of the core region of the envisaged Islamic nation, thus excluding the Hijaz, where Islam had emerged in the seventh century, and where Mecca and Madina, sites of the Two Holy

Mosques, were situated. Many Najdi religious scholars considered themselves to be in the vanguard of a mission to save the whole of Arabia, including the blasphemous Hijazis, from their descent into unorthodox Islam. They elevated their own specific interpretations of Islam to the level of the only authentic Islam, and regarded other Muslims as following a corrupted tradition. In later years the Wahhabi scholars became more vocal in asserting that true Islam was only manifest in the central province of Arabia, Najd, their homeland. Instead of the vision of belonging to one Saudi nation, religious scholars promised the population an Islamic utopia, guided by themselves and the Al Saud leaders of Najd.

This religious nationalism left its impact on certain features of the country. Before 2015 visitors to Saudi Arabia were surprised that shops closed during prayer time. Members of a notorious religious vigilante force, known as the Committee for Commanding Right and Prohibiting Vice, roamed the shopping centres and the streets in search of immoral behaviour. They imposed a dress code on men and women, conducted searches for the prohibited manufacture and consumption of alcoholic drinks, punished illicit encounters between men and women, and arrested those who failed to heed the call to prayer. Public squares in cities were turned into spectacular platforms where beheadings and crucifixions took place. Such features were regarded as manifestations of the application of Islamic law and of a robust commitment to Islam—but to a specific interpretation of the tradition closely associated with the Wahhabi movement and its interpreters.

When a king died, the crown prince was declared the new king. Society and its multiple constituencies, such as other princes, religious scholars, tribal chiefs, the economic elite, military commanders and notables, were invited to give the oath of allegiance (*bay'a*). Subjects pledged allegiance to God, king and homeland (*watan*). This anchored the Saudi political succession in Islam, even though it had always been the prerogative of the king, a small circle of princes, and an ill-defined group referred to as *ahl al-hal wa al-aqd* (people who matter in running the affairs of the pious community). This was regarded as Saudi compliance with another ill-defined Islamic concept: *shura*, or consultation, used by the Al Saud to mask the exclusionary practices of the absolute monarchy. There was no constitution that regulated the process of succession; the Saudi Law of Governance issued by King Fahd as late as the 1990s stipulated that the country's leadership rests solely within the Al Saud family and their descendants. But by invoking the Islamic concepts of *bay'a* and *shura*, the regime ensured that its succession was sanctioned by ancient and authentic Islamic tradition. This bestowed on the absolute hereditary monarchy the veneer of Islamic legitimacy.

The requirement of the *bay'a*, and the spectacle in the royal palace where it was offered to the new king by well-wishers, demonstrated the religious nationalism of the country. More importantly, it rendered political dissent a religious sin rather than merely a political position. Opposition to the king or his policies became an illegitimate rebellion against the legitimate Muslim ruler, on whose obedience rested the survival of Islam, the security of the pious Muslim realm, and the security of the Islamic nation. Undermining the king's authority by openly criticizing him amounted to a crime punishable by several years in prison, or even execution. This remains the case, as in 2016 and 2019 King Salman approved the beheading of several detainees on the basis of judgments passed by Wahhabi judges who applied *hadd al-hiraba*, an Islamic punishment for those rebels who take arms against the legitimate ruler who has received the *bay'a*. But in Saudi Arabia even peaceful protest is put on the same footing as the abhorrent crime of armed rebellion in Sunni Islam. Amongst the beheaded were peaceful protesters who were as young as sixteen when they engaged in peaceful resistance and demonstrations during the 2011 Arab uprisings. The list also included al-Qaida ideologues, terrorists, murderers and others who were accused of crimes punishable by the death penalty, such as sorcery.

The religious nationalism of Saudi Arabia stipulated that Islam can only flourish under the authority of the king and that, regardless of his mistakes and shortcomings, the king should not be undermined by public criticism, demonstrations, or civil disobedience, all banned in the country by fatwas from Wahhabi scholars. The nation's commitment to Islam depended on obedience to the ruler, whereas openly challenging him and criticizing his policies would lead to the decline of the religious nation, and of Islam itself. In theory, there was one specific condition that might justify rebellion against the king, whether peaceful or armed. If the king undermined Islam—for example, if he issued royal decrees closing all mosques in the country, obstructed the performance of Islamic rituals, or suspended Islamic law—then rebellion against him could be justified, in the eyes of religious scholars. This injunction was merely theoretical, as Saudi kings, both past and present, have deviated from aspects of Islam in their legislation and policies, which Wahhabi scholars criticized—but in secrecy, lest they undermine the legitimacy of the king. Deviation from true Islam was considered grounds for rebellion by their own Wahhabi constituency, such as jihadis, who challenged their teachers' preaching on this important point at several moments in history, as discussed earlier.

Beyond appearances, if one digs deeper into the institutions of the state, one finds that the country upheld Islamic principles in its legal system in ways that exceeded what was common in other Arab countries. The latter maintained Islamic law in personal matters, for example marriage, divorce and inheritance. But in addition to these areas, Saudi Arabia claimed to apply sharia in all aspects of life, including private and public law. While this claim implies that its laws derive from a sacred or divine source, the king can also be the source of legislation, often referred to as royal decrees, *marsoum malaki*. He can also hire and fire senior princes, governors and ministers by the same royal prerogative. The removal of the ban on women driving in 2017 and the curbing of pervasive powers of the Committee for Commanding Right and Prohibiting Vice were implemented by royal decree, and in 2019, allowing adult women to obtain passports and travel abroad was accomplished by royal decree after a century of upholding the guardianship system.

In compliance with religious nationalism, the country's education curriculum was dominated by excessive emphasis on Islamic studies, often amounting to dozens of lessons per week. Students were introduced to Quranic recitations and interpretations, Islamic jurisprudence, knowledge in Islamic rituals of prayer, purification, fasting, pilgrimage and understanding of the prophetic tradition. In the education curriculum there was also great emphasis on Islamic history, including the rise of Islam, the Islamic caliphates, and the establishment of the Saudi state from the eighteenth century to the present. As religious nationalism infiltrated education, it depicted the rise of the Saudi state as a continuation of the great Islamic tradition and linked it to past glories of the Muslim conquest of Arabia and beyond.

Gender relations clearly demonstrated the commitment of Saudi Arabia to religious nationalism. Religious nationalism aspired to create 'godly women', whose role was determined by God's design for this world. The education of girls was introduced in the 1960s to inculcate in them their domestic role under the guidance of religious scholars.[7] While Muslim women elsewhere were able to enjoy freedom of movement at least from the legal perspective and drove cars without any controversy or heated debate, Saudi women were denied the right to drive until 2017.

So why did Saudi women have to wait until 2017 to be given the right to drive? To explain this enigma, we must see the ban on driving as part of keeping the public sphere Islamized in ways that conform to the Wahhabi tradition and its insistence on pre-emptive legislation to avoid potentially sinful situations. More importantly, the Saudi leadership's need for the loyalty of men compelled it to uphold private patriarchy and institutionalize it in legislation and policy. The state gave men the power to control the women in their families and supported them in law. Furthermore, Saudi women were held responsible for maintaining the piety of the religious nation, and as such they had to be confined to traditional roles and kept under the control of their men. They also had to respect the obligation to veil in public; those whose veiling fell short of compliance with the expected norm were reprimanded by the religious police.

Religious nationalism sought to control women in the pursuit of grand political designs and communal identities. The state became the agency responsible for upholding the piety of the nation, which was increasingly defined in terms of excluding women, restricting their citizenship rights, allowing them only selective employment in education and health services, and minimizing their appearance in the public sphere. We shall see how the third wave of nationalism, symbolized by 'Saudi Arabia for Saudis', discussed later in this chapter, came to depend above all on reversing old gender policies, thus increasing the visibility of women, empowering them, and promoting them to high positions in government. As religious nationalism gave way to modern constructions of 'Saudi' nationalism, it became an urgent matter to alter the status of women from the repository of the nation's piety to the icons of its modernity.

The centrality of religious identity for Saudis is illustrated in the discourse of many Islamists and jihadis.[8] Several Saudi jihadis who participated in the worst wave of terrorism between 2003 and 2008 recorded themselves tearing up their ID cards in order to show their rejection of their Saudi identity. The ID card of course has 'Kingdom of Saudi Arabia' on the front page, with two swords crossed over a palm tree. In their YouTube videos they often invoked their long tribal names, listing their tribal genealogies and ancestors in ways that establish continuity between the early Islamic era of the seventh century and the present. They boasted about their tribes which had played central roles in spreading Islam and defending its frontiers beyond Arabia. They also rejected the name Saudi Arabia, promoting other names reflecting the religious nationalism they had internalized during their education, in which they were subjected to the rhetoric of its religious scholars. They all called the country *bilad al-haramayin* (the Land of the Two Holy Mosques) or *jazirat al-arab* (the Arabian Peninsula). They considered this region the central province (*wilaya*) of the Muslim community. By rejecting the name Saudi Arabia, they asserted their belonging to a wider Muslim entity rather than a Saudi nation.

These were among the many features that distinguished Saudi Arabia from other countries in the Arab and Muslim world. They all represent a commitment to define the Islamic nation according to the tenets of Wahhabism rather than the 'Saudi' nation. In the opinion of many advocates of religious nationalism, unless such Islamic features and practices were displayed and upheld in the public sphere, the country's commitment to Islam would weaken, and eventually vanish. Saudi Arabia defined itself as a nation committed to Islamizing its own public sphere. This project gave it a sense of identity and a destiny like any national narrative developed by secular intelligentsia elsewhere in the world. Its religious nationalism connected a past to a present and projected it to the future.

Throughout the rule of Ibn Saud and his son Saud, there were no serious official attempts to export Saudi Arabia's religious mission abroad. But in later years, when the project of Islamizing Arabia appeared to have been accomplished, the country turned its attention to initiating transnational religious networks, reaching many countries beyond the Arabian Peninsula. This was associated with new regional Arab and international political contexts.

Pan-Islamism

By the 1960s the Saudi regime was beginning to export its Islamic utopia abroad, helping to incorporate a transnational, pan-Islamic and supra-national narrative that justified its control over the holy cities of Mecca and Madina in the eyes of both its own citizens and the rest of the Muslim world. The state encouraged Saudis to identify as Muslims, belonging to an imagined supra-national and non-territorial Muslim *umma*, larger than Saudi Arabia, while thinking of their own role and territory as central to the world of Islam. The state and its religious and educational institutions began to indoctrinate Saudis with the idea that they had a responsibility to export their own Islamic utopia abroad, a concept that was endorsed by both the leadership and many Saudis. In this process, many Saudis adopted and celebrated a pan-Islamic outlook and worked to fulfil their religious responsibility to educate other Muslims in the right path of Islam and defend them against real and imagined enemies, including Western allies and partners of the Saudi regime.

Pan-Islamism became particularly appealing to Islamists from the 1960s. Like other Arab and Muslim countries, Saudi Arabia had its own Islamists who aspired to create an Islamic realm at home and abroad. The previous religious nationalism incorporated a duty to Islamize Saudi society first. During that phase it was not possible to export the religious mission, owing to Saudi Arabia's limited resources and a shortage of religious scholars who could be dispatched abroad. Saudi Arabia's drive to implement a pan-Islamic orientation was in great part assisted by other Arabs and Muslims, including Islamists, who came to Saudi Arabia as teachers, administrators, economic immigrants and exiles. Together with Saudis, they contributed to a religious and political movement that came to be known as the Sahwa, the Islamic awakening. The Sahwa became extremely influential in the 1990s and began to have its own outspoken leaders and advocates, such as Sheikhs Safar al-Hawali, Salman al-Awdah, Aidh al-Qarni, Awadh al Qarni, and many others. Most of the Sahwa advocates had a strong commitment to pan-Islamism, which 'shares a number of structural similarities with nationalistic-type ideologies, notably the focus on the liberation of territory, the primacy placed on the fight against external enemy and the emphasis on internal unity in the face of outside threats'.[9]

By the 1960s Saudi Arabia had become truly 'Islamic', and from that time on the Islamic utopia had to be spread abroad. This pan-Islamism developed out of several challenges and international situations that pushed the state to become the champion of transnational religious networks, promoting its own domestic religious nationalism as a blueprint for other Muslims to endorse.

Why did Saudi Arabia adopt pan-Islamism, spend enormous wealth on championing Muslim causes, and create Saudi-sponsored pan-Islamic institutions, financial services, educational organizations, schools, universities and cultural centres abroad? Why did the regime distribute free Qurans and fatwas of its own parochial religious scholars, initially across the Islamic world and later among Muslim minorities in the West?[10] It is not sufficient to argue that the sacred geography of Mecca and Madina was the sole pillar of Saudi pan-Islamism that prompted the Saudi leadership to endorse a pan-Islamic national narrative from the 1960s. Nor it is sufficient to claim that the leadership simply wanted to promote its own legitimacy among Muslims by endorsing a pan-Islamic outlook, justifying its own control over the Holy Mosques of Mecca and Madina.

To inaugurate the promotion of pan-Islamism, in 1961 King Faisal established the first Islamic university in Madina[11] as a hub for the education of Muslims by Saudi and pan-Islamic staff, who were recruited from all over the Muslim world. Students came from Africa, Asia and the Arab world. In later years Muslims from Western countries were given Saudi scholarships to study in Madina. After examining the curriculum of this institution, Farquhar concludes that 'Saudi funded missionary work has relied upon multivalent flows of persons, ideas, practices and resources—outward from the kingdom of course, but also inwards, from locations around the world'.[12]

In 1962, immediately after opening the university, King Faisal created the Muslim World League. He hoped that 'by championing Islamic causes abroad, he could persuade conservative Muslim governments and activists to ally themselves with the kingdom rather than with nationalist leaders like Egypt's Gamal Abdel Naser. Pan-Islamism would be the answer to pan-Arabism'.[13] Projecting its localized religious tradition abroad became a pre-emptive mechanism to shield the country from the threat of subversive forces associated with Arab post-colonial nationalism. This threat came not only from outside the Saudi borders; it had substantial advocates at home too.[14]

The Saudi commitment to pan-Islamism must be situated within the global Cold War. The West—above all, the USA—began to construct Saudi Arabia as the centre of the Muslim world, and its religious tradition became instrumental in luring Muslim youth away from radical socialist and communist trends, in addition to what was defined as subversive Arab nationalism with its anti-imperialist rhetoric. Islam was seen as a powerful anti-communist belief system.[15] Saudi cooperation in the Cold

War culminated in its sponsorship of the jihad in Afghanistan against the Soviet Union's occupation of the country. The Saudis 'famously matched US funding, channelled through the CIA, "dollar by dollar"'.[16] While Saudi funding was important, another substantial Saudi contribution was its potent ideology inspiring young Muslims to participate in the jihad. Now a champion of pan-Islamism, the Saudi regime mobilized its own religious clerics, for example its Grand Mufti, Abdul Aziz ibn Baz, to support the Afghan jihad. Young Saudi men, including Osama Bin Laden, enthusiastically responded to the call and travelled to Afghanistan in the 1980s. Bin Laden became central to creating a hub for not only Saudis but also Arabs seeking to honour a pledge to support Muslims worldwide and die for their faith. This was the seed that led to the creation of al-Qaida, a global umbrella under which jihadis operated. The cohort of recruits became known as the Afghan Arabs. The Reagan administration authorized covert aid to the rebels, while Saudi Arabia was entrusted with presenting the liberation of Afghanistan from godless communists as a stage in the pursuit of freeing a Muslim country from evil. Its initial commitment to pan-Islamism was now translated into action in support of other Muslims.

Pan-Islamism was a crucial ideological weapon in the Cold War. King Salman, at the time the powerful governor of the capital, where more than 5 million people lived, was an enthusiastic sponsor of the migration of young Saudis to Peshawar in Pakistan, near the Afghan border, and his charitable foundation provided much-needed financial help to make their travel cheap and possible.

Muhammad ibn Salman reminded his US audiences when he visited in March 2018:

> Saudi Arabia's Western allies urged the country to invest in mosques and madrasas overseas during the Cold War, in an effort to prevent encroachment in Muslim countries by the Soviet Union. ... But

over the years, Saudi governments lost track of such funding. Funding comes mostly from Saudi foundations rather than from the government.[17]

The crown prince was aware of how Saudi pan-Islamic missionary endeavours have become controversial, especially after 9/11, as fifteen of the nineteen hijackers who hit New York's Twin Towers were Saudi nationals. Since this terrorism crisis, Saudi Arabia has struggled to roll back its pan-Islamism and reverse its reputation as a hub for radical ideology. According to the crown prince, government funding to radical groups and projects has stopped. However, pan-Islamism was mainly an attempt first to make Saudi Arabia relevant to its Western allies during the Cold War, and second to instrumentalize Islam in the pursuit of domestic national security and regime legitimacy.

While it was clear that several factors contributed to transnationalizing Saudi Islam, pushing the regime to adopt pan-Islamism as an antidote to all ideologies deemed subversive, the trend set in motion by this deliberate strategy became difficult to stop, and had a life of its own. Above all, global jihad that drew on Saudi religious interpretations, among others, was like a snowball: the more it rolled, with the support of oil wealth, the more it gathered multiple Muslim voices and activists from around the globe. The monster that Saudi Arabia and its Western allies created began to have its own agency, as an ideology capable of mobilizing Muslims around the world who sought to die for their faith.

The New Nationalism and its Discontents

After 9/11, as Saudi Arabia came under increased pressure to roll back its commitment to export its Islamic interpretations abroad, and when it became the target of al-Qaida terrorism between 2003 and 2008 and the Islamic State group in 2014–15, the regime began serious reconsideration of its pan-Islamism. Many Saudis blamed the weak and ill-defined Saudi national identity on the pervasiveness of the previous commitment to a transnational pan-Islamic identity. However, a conscious decision to reduce the pan-Islamic outlook needed to be accompanied by a new national narrative to fill the void. As mentioned earlier, pan-Islamism was closely associated with both the regime's efforts and society's enthusiasm, especially among those Islamists who belonged to the Sahwa movement. Therefore, to create a new Saudi national identity, the old religious nationalism and pan-Islamism had to be criminalized, and eventually destroyed. By the time Muhammad ibn Salman became crown prince, the Sahwa was being blamed for all Saudi problems, especially radicalization, terrorism, corruption of faith, intolerance of minorities, discrimination against women, unemployment, weak national identity, lack of commitment to the national interest, and preoccupation with wider Muslim issues at the expense of local concerns. The Sahwa was now viewed as the cause of Saudi backwardness and the country's lack of initiative and prosperity. Islamism became a criminal offence under new anti-terrorism laws.

To mark the end of the era of both religious nationalism and pan-Islamism, a pervasive detention campaign targeting Islamists was launched in 2017. This followed the implementation of new laws in 2014 that criminalized Islamist movements such as the Sahwis and the Muslim Brotherhood. Any member of or sympathizer with these groups faced imprisonment after closed trials in terrorism courts. The government lumped together violent jihadis, radical ideologues and peaceful Islamist reformers under the wide umbrella of terrorism. This new wave of arrests followed the one that started in 2009 when the regime under King Abdullah launched a campaign against both Islamist and non-Islamist civil society and human rights organizations and activists. Reformers such as the founders of the Saudi Civil and Political Rights Association were sentenced to between ten and fifteen years in prison. Amongst them were Abdullah al-Hamid, Muhammad al-Qahtani, Muhammad al-Bijadi and Walid Abu al-Khayr. Founders of a political party, Hizb al-Ummah, were also detained on the grounds that political parties are banned in the country. In the Hijaz, reformist Islamists who gathered with the intention of establishing a political party were arrested, amongst them Isam Basrawi and Mousa al-Qarni. They were referred to as the Jeddah Cell.

The Arab uprisings in 2011 pushed the regime to tighten its control over all dissent. This came with yet another new wave of arrests, of activists who either mobilized Saudis to demonstrate or simply used social media to criticize government policies. Shia activists in the Eastern Province mobilized their own community to demonstrate peacefully, but confrontation with the security forces have led to the deaths of many activists since 2011.

When Muhammad ibn Salman became crown prince in 2017, he continued the campaign against the Islamists and jailed many others, such as Sheikhs Safar al-Hawali, Salman al-Awdah and Awadh al-Qarni. With tension rising between Saudi Arabia and Qatar over the latter's support for Islamist groups since 2014, the regime in Riyadh accused the detainees of links to Qatar, now described by the Saudi leadership as the main sponsor of terrorism. Others were detained for allegedly belonging to terrorist organizations and failing to support the government against Qatar.

Those Islamists who escaped detention were forced to publicly denounce the Sahwa and apologize for the radicalization its advocates had spread in Saudi Arabia since the 1990s. In May 2018 Sheikh Aidh al-Qarni, an outspoken member of the Sahwa, was summoned to appear on the al-Khalijiyya television channel to discuss the ills of the Sahwa, especially its overtly pan-Islamic outlook and contribution to radicalization. On behalf of the

Sahwa, he apologized to Saudi society for promoting intolerance and denying Saudis an opportunity to modernize. He acknowledged that the Sahwa was a misguided movement, saying that after travelling around the world and exposing himself to other ways of peaceful coexistence between people, he had come to the conclusion that tolerance is better than radicalization and rejection of others. The Saudi regime is now eager to write the obituary of the Sahwa in an attempt to absolve itself of any responsibility both as a promoter of jihadi groups, starting in Afghanistan, and as a sponsor of the export of Wahhabi interpretations around the globe. The Sahwa became the scapegoat to be sacrificed in pursuit of the birth of a new Saudi nation.

In the twenty-first century, a new trend resembling an ill-defined Saudi nationalism began to be seen as an alternative to the Islamism that had underpinned the previous two phases, religious nationalism and pan-Islamism. In the 1980s Prince Khalid al-Faisal was perhaps the first prince to articulate a vigorous Saudi identity in a vernacular poem entitled 'Raise your head, you are Saudi'. As expected in a nationalist poem, al-Faisal celebrates Saudiness by drawing on glorious symbolic characteristics and undermining others, as he tells his audience that 'you are elevated while others are of lesser significance'. Heroism, chauvinism, generosity and manly qualities are celebrated as national characteristics of Saudi men. Such a national narrative is overtly masculine and mighty, as it reminds people of their ancestors' chivalry and courage, which led to Saudi guardianship over Mecca. As expected, the sword is present in the poetic display of strength, as is Islam, as Saudi Arabia shows overt hospitality and generosity to the millions of pilgrims who arrive each year, referred to as 'God's Guests'. Such poetry invokes the leadership as the top of the Saudi national pyramid, and al-Faisal reminds his audiences of the centrality of Fahd, the king at the time, in the national narrative about the greatness of the Saudi nation.

The new narratives about state-sponsored Saudi nationalism
began to appear early on, but after years of scattered delibera-
tions, Crown Prince Muhammad ibn Salman openly adopted a
fresh brand of Saudi nationalism, partly inspired by non-religious
elements. While many observers dubbed this new redrawing of
Saudi Arabia's identity as secular, it is probably better to avoid
such a label, which does not fully capture the shift in constructing the national narrative that characterizes the new realm, ushered in by King Salman and his son Muhammad. Al-Faisal's
nationalistic poem does not abandon Islam altogether as a foundation of Saudi identity. A Saudi national identity means that
new elements are added to the repertoire of imagined national
characteristics rather than simply reducing the national narrative
to a single religious dimension.

Since Muhammad ibn Salman's appointment as crown prince,
the country is believed to have been undergoing 'aggressive
nationalist rebranding', witnessing a 'national revival' and even
singing a 'nationalist tune'.[18] This revival 'has also inspired a
patriotic zeal among some citizens who attempt to define national
identity in increasingly confrontational terms'.[19] This amounts to
a mix of boasting about an eternal Saudi national identity, the
promise of 'greatness', the prospect of national rejuvenation and
new economic projects and technological innovations in a post-
oil era. The state-controlled media publicize what is dubbed by
critics as hyper-nationalism.[20] While the centrality of the crown
prince is obvious in this new trend, the national narrative celebrates the new Saudi citizen, who is committed to the development of his country economically, rather than the previously
cherished pious Saudi who memorized the Quran, spread Islam
around the globe and supported Muslim causes. He is also the
citizen informer, or the citizen policeman, who helps the regime
and its security agencies identify 'traitors', 'transgressors' and
'subversive persons', critics of the new policies domestically,

regionally and internationally. The newly celebrated citizen is no longer the one who obeys the religious clerics and is rewarded by the distribution of state-sponsored prizes for religious observance and zeal, but the eclectic and creative young entrepreneur and propagandist for the regime.

National glory now resides in reinvented geographies, other than, or perhaps in addition to, the historical Islamic Mecca and Madina. The ancient archaeological sites that had been ignored and neglected as they were considered icons of blasphemy in a pre-Islamic era, such as Madain Salih and Al-Ula, are now sources of national pride. Their importance in the new national narrative is reflected in the establishment of the Royal Commission for Al-Ula in 2017, which aims to develop the site for local and global tourism. The development of tourism in the sites of ancient civilizations across the country is now seen as part and parcel of the new Saudi national project. At the times when religious nationalism or pan-Islamism were dominant, this rich archaeological heritage was not only disregarded but condemned as a reminder of an ancient age of paganism. With the exception of Diriyyah, the first Saudi capital in the eighteenth century, which was restored and glorified under the patronage of King Salman, other historical sites were simply ignored. Now Saudis are expected to be proud of their pre-Islamic heritage, which is incorporated in their new national narrative about themselves. They take pride in the listing of some of these ancient sites as UNESCO world heritage sites.

The crown prince is now the champion of the construction of a new kingdom and a new Saudi nation. Western companies were enlisted to help create a modern Saudi nationalism, despite their lack of experience in such political endeavours, which go far beyond their financial and economic expertise.[21] While tourism may bring revenues much needed under the pressure of decreasing oil prices, the development of tourism and the promotion of archaeological sites can also be a pillar of national narratives and pride. The crown prince is gradually abandoning previous Saudi rhetoric about the state's commitment to promote Wahhabi Islam at home and export it abroad, as his ancestors had done throughout the twentieth century. He preaches a new, populist national narrative, overtly focused on domestic interests, and projected abroad to be consumed by global audiences, especially investors, financial groups and foreign tourists. The previously promised Islamic utopia at home and abroad is now gradually giving way to the promotion of a local Saudi entrepreneurial utopia.

The imagined Saudi utopia is guided by an allegedly original, tolerant Saudi Islam, to be achieved by royal decree: Muhammad ibn Salman declared his intention to revive this Islamic tradition and reclaim Saudi Arabia's original Islamic heritage before it was hijacked and corrupted by Islamists and countries such as Iran. In an interview in the Western press, he announced his plan to root out radicalism and replace it with Saudi moderation. He propagated the myth that Saudi Arabia was an island of tolerance before 1979, the year of the Iranian revolution and the siege of the Mecca Mosque, which he claimed were the causes of Saudi radicalism. Whatever the historical and sociological accuracy of such a claim, the crown prince was absolving Saudi Arabia of any responsibility for radicalism, the export of which was regarded as the responsibility of the West, as discussed earlier in this chapter. However, its previous religious nationalism and pan-Islamism both show up the country as a long-time active propagator of radical interpretations of Islam. Furthermore, its history attests to how these radical interpretations were at the heart of the foundation of the kingdom. But the prince was not interested in historical accuracy or sociological facts. His main objective is a demagogy that ushers in the rebirth of the Saudi nation, an act of restoration to an original glory and tolerance that supposedly existed before the 1979 onset of radicalism. This includes a determination to uproot terrorism and promote a moderate Islam. Like all constructed national narratives, the new Saudi version is not concerned with accurate historical facts; its main objective is to remember and forget at the same time.

The prince is determined to turn young Saudis into champions of this new nationalism. Its slogans are represented in Twitter hashtags such as 'Saudi Arabia for Saudis', 'Make Saudi Arabia Great' and 'Saudi Arabia First'. The state communication officers are directly responsible for its online campaigns. It is clear that they represent an official endorsement of the themes embodied in such propaganda slogans, which echo a global phenomenon associated with far-right nationalist and populist politics, in the West and elsewhere in the world. But in Saudi Arabia the new national narrative is closely linked to the increasing atmosphere of securitization. All these slogans have been prominent in the discourse of writers enlisted in the state-owned press and social media. The new nationalist narrative is not a spontaneous grass-roots movement, but a state-led initiative under the auspices of the crown prince, with obvious controversial undertones and mixed outcomes.

For the crown prince, the Saudi nation is mainly the under-twenty-fives, almost 51 per cent of the population. Constantly reminding his audience of the youth of his subjects, he presents himself as a role model to be emulated if Saudis are to be counted among the modern nations. His 'youthfulness' is symbolized by a carefree presentation of himself and his body, and his excessive use of media and modern communication gadgets. This came to the forefront when he appeared as a champion of car races on camera, sending a message that the youth and modernity of the prince should be emulated by the new young nation. He plays on the needs and aspirations of young Saudis to foster a new sense of belonging to the nation and to consolidate his cult as the future monarch. As the youth are his priority, he expects them to make Saudi Arabia theirs and to pledge undisputed loyalty to him personally. In return, he promises them greater employment opportunities, a flourishing national heritage industry, new global popular cultural entertainment, an increasing connectedness with the outside world, and the illusion of future liberal modernization. In short, the crown prince offers the Saudi nation 'bread and circuses'.[22] But the remaining 49 per cent of the population seem to be forgotten. This cohort must include all Saudis above the age of twenty-five, amongst them many old government employees awaiting retirement or already retired while living on meagre pensions and insufficient benefits to sustain the promised new lifestyle and enjoy the new entertainment utopia.

By constructing the youth as a homogeneous national category, the crown prince defines their needs, dissolves their differences, and promises to provide opportunities for their rising aspirations. The new so-called nationalism offers the youth a break from past economic stagnation, religious zeal and social conservatism. It is only after the destruction of the old ways of doing things that the new nation will be born. The first step in rooting out and destroying the old forces, held responsible for immersing Saudi Arabia in religious fanaticism and social conservatism, is to launch a repressive detention campaign against religious scholars and Islamist activists, who are considered a potential subversive force against the crown prince's social reforms. While not many detainees would have objected to, for example, granting women the right to drive or the introduction of the entertainment industry, many religious scholars and Islamist intellectuals were detained in 2017 on the pretext that they are radicals and many amongst them are terrorists. Other religious scholars who have so far escaped detention exercise self-censorship, while others reverse their opinions and fatwas to embrace the new social changes, especially members of the official religious scholars' council. Fear of detention after criticizing any regime policy is paramount. The crown prince wants to purge Saudi Arabia of the Sahwa, hoping that this will eventually lead to endorsement of the new Saudi nationalism. Veteran pillars of this movement remain in prison at the time of writing this book.

The new Saudi nationalism is a top-down initiative that has already enlisted ideologues to define and defend it. The trend is beginning to create a social base and embed itself as a new discourse filling the void after the 'death of ideologies of Arab nationalism and Islamism'. Its purpose is to create a new nation divorced from its recent radical Islamic past and Arab roots. In a recent defence of the new nationalism, online writer Mansour al-Blushi tweeted that the 'Prophet was Saudi', a statement that created fierce debates and controversies. In a later podcast interview with Muhammad Nakhlan al-Shammari, he elaborates on how the failure of both Arab nationalism and transnational Islamism led to the Saudi nationalist trend, which, he argues, is a welcome evolution that will free the country from previous failed ideologies. He defends the social basis of Saudi nationalism and considers those who defend their homeland to be the true nationalists (*watani*). According to al-Blushi, the development of *watani* identity is a welcome reaction to the failure of Arab nationalists and the Islamists who followed them. He argues that Saudi Arabia suffered from the transnational Islamist trend, which led to attacks by al-Qaida and the Muslim Brotherhood. The Saudi nationalists are shocked that 'the Islamists whom Saudis had defended and supported are now attacking the country'. Moreover:

> The nationalists who claim that we are Arabs because we speak Arabic are misguided as nationalism should not be linked to language. Arabs have their own *amsar* (countries). There are people in Arabic-speaking countries who are not Arabs. Egyptians, Iraqis and

others are not all Arabs. There is an attempt to terrorize their identities by Arab nationalists. In these countries there are ethnic minorities who refuse to be called Arabs, for example the Berbers and the Assyrians. *Amsar* is not pejorative; it simply reflects the fact that they were simply countries not nations. Those are outside the Arabian Peninsula and they were historically referred to as *mawali*, which is a negative way of referring to the inhabitants of those countries. The nationalists are identity entrepreneurs who sell identities to people.[23]

He defends Saudi nationalism by undermining an overall Arab identity in which Saudi Arabia and other countries can be merged. He also points to how the liberation of Palestine should be a Palestinian rather than an Arab project. He argues:

Palestinians trade in their cause like the Turks and other Arabs. We Saudis are committed to the Palestinian cause as our king allows one thousand Palestinians to perform the pilgrimage on his own account. We are surprised that the Palestinians insult us and they launch hate speech against us. I refuse that they insult our kings who had helped them most.[24]

Al-Blushi has a troubled relationship with Twitter, as Twitter MENA administration discontinued his account for violating certain rules and conditions of free speech and for his tendency to 'insult other nations'. After nine years of using Twitter and engaging in heated debates on nationalism, al-Blushi explains that his Twitter account was suspended because of 'those *amsar* employees of Twitter in Dubai who apply their own culture and heritage to an American company without supervision from their managers'.[25]

Like all newly launched nationalisms, this new Saudi nationalism needs intellectuals, entrepreneurs and young advocates to spread it at grassroots level among the youth using social media. Being 'Saudi' rather than 'Arab' or 'Muslim' is now key to the crown prince's plans for his own consolidation of power, the future outlook of Saudi Arabia and the success of his economic transformation—the three goals that underpin most of his new so-called nationalist agenda and policies. Furthermore, Saudi nationalism is a justification for abandoning regional Arab projects and pan-Islamic causes.

As this new nationalism is launched as a coherent and promising project on diverse platforms and embodied in the mission statement of newly created institutions, it is debated and promoted in the local state-sponsored press. One hot issue underpins the Twitter hashtag campaign 'Saudi Arabia for Saudis', namely the role of foreign labour and the need to decrease the number of immigrants in order to allow Saudis greater employment opportunities. Journalists like Muhammad al-Mutairi commented that those who adopt the mantra 'Saudi Arabia for Saudis' are right, but warned against xenophobia, as the slogan might become a pretext for aggression against foreign labour. Al-Mutairi advises young Saudis to channel their anger over their own unemployment towards those private companies that exclude them from jobs by overlooking government Saudization initiatives and laws. The writer avoids criticizing regime policies and instead focuses on the uncooperative role of the private sector, accused of not fulfilling its promise to employ more Saudis, replacing foreign workers.

Another writer comments on the hashtag 'Saudi Arabia for Saudis' by supporting the slogan, which he believes is a just call to end what he believes is foreigners' monopoly over high-ranking jobs in the kingdom. Muhammad Qashqari points to how foreigners in Jeddah evolved in business like a mafia. He claims that 'they usually employ people who belong to their own countries and exclude Saudis and other nationalities'.

On al-Khalijiya television channel, a discussion of the hashtag was aired as the campaign generated two opposing views: one considered that the slogan reflected how many young Saudis truly feel, while the other deemed it racist. Supporters of the campaign depict both foreign workers and the remittances they send to their home countries as having a negative impact on the country. This was the position adopted by Jamal Khashoggi in one of his books, mentioned earlier. Remittances by foreigners undermine the campaign to 'Make Saudi Arabia Great', in their opinion. They argue that the *watan* (homeland) is naturally for Saudis, but that this does not necessarily imply racism. A defender of the campaign argues that 'we have a rentier economy and we bring hundreds of nationalities to work here. We have to find Saudis to replace the foreigners. All private sector employees earning 7000 SR are foreigners. Why don't we impose special taxes on them? The Ministry of Labour is not planning well as it does not start Saudizing the private sector.'

On the other hand, those who object to the campaign see it as a racist slogan that goes against what Islam calls for, namely peaceful coexistence between different nationalities. Moreover, those who are against the campaign to Saudize claim that chaotic Saudization might lead to economic decline, as there is still a shortage of qualified Saudis to take the jobs that foreigners currently do. For those against haphazard Saudization, the real campaign should focus on the development of Saudis rather than chaotic *tawtin* (Saudization) of jobs. Al-Mutairi and Qashqari among many others warn against racism, which is already finding a platform online.

The Twitter account @ksaforsaudis popularizes the idea that only pure Saudis are the real members of the nation. The account occasionally promotes xenophobic rhetoric by claiming that foreigners (*ajanib*) are responsible for crime, theft and immoral activities. Such claims echo debates about migration in the USA and Europe, among others, where social ills, economic hardship and moral degeneration are blamed on immigrants and asylum seekers. However, on this Saudi online account, *ajanib* does not only refer to immigrants who came to Saudi Arabia in the second half of the twentieth century with the oil boom. In fact, *ajanib* are also Arabs, such as Yemenis and Hadramis; Muslim Caucasians from Tsarist Russia; Turkic-speaking Muslims; Central Asians known as Bukharis; Africans; Indonesians; Thais; and Burmese Asians known as Burmawis who came to live in the Hijaz as early as the late nineteenth century. Most but not all of these early immigrants are now naturalized, but there is still a cohort who are denied Saudi nationality. They are treated as outside the pure Saudi nation on ultra-nationalist social media accounts. Many Hadramis are well-known traders and successful merchants, bankers and businesspeople.[26] Amongst the Yemenis was the father of Osama Bin Laden, who came to the Hijaz in the 1930s and worked as a construction labourer, later becoming one of the wealthiest people in Saudi Arabia. Nowadays ultra-nationalist Twitter accounts such as @ksaforsaudis claim that there was a conspiracy early in the twentieth century among the Hadrami community and their diaspora in Singapore[27] to turn the Hijaz into a *watan badil* (alternative homeland) for them.[28] The category 'foreigner' is extended to include a wide range of people who are mainly resident in the Hijaz and its cities Mecca, Madina and Jeddah. The diversity of this region prompts ultra-nationalists to call the population of the region *tarsh al-bahr*: rejects from the sea.

Contradictions of the New National Narrative

The crown prince is a latecomer to the game of ultra-nationalism. But his narrative about who Saudis are or should be—their destiny, responsibility and national characteristics—suffers from the common and inherent contradictions of nationalism that currently flourish elsewhere throughout the world, especially in those highly and intensely connected societies with heterogeneous groups.

In the new Saudi national narrative, there is a celebration of nationalist hyper-masculinity in the context of the Saudi military intervention in Yemen and the conflict with Iran. Since 2015, when the Saudi war on Yemen started, there has been a conscious effort to celebrate the bravery of the men defending the nation's borders in the south-west. 'Protecting the nation' from the danger of an expansionist Iran and its proxies, mainly the Yemeni Houthis, became a dominant narrative in the new nationalism. The crown prince often visits hospitals where injured Saudi soldiers are treated and publicizes the material rewards given to families of martyred soldiers. These televised appearances demonstrate the bravery of soldiers and their willingness to die for the nation while celebrating the generosity of the leadership in its compensation for loss of life in defence of the nation.

The national narrative about the war in Yemen totally failed to divorce itself from the sectarian dimension of the Saudi state's religious tradition. When the war was initially launched, in March 2015, the regime drew on its loyal religious clerics such as Muhammad al-Arifi to travel to the border and enthuse the soldiers with a narrative about how this war is a jihad against the Zaydi Houthis and their Shia backers in Tehran, long considered to be outside the realm of true Islam. The war was initially portrayed as defence not only of the Saudi nation and the Arabian Peninsula, but also of Mecca, a central destination for all Muslims. The Houthis are accused of wanting to destroy Mecca, the *qibla* (reference point for prayer) of all true Muslims. On several occasions when Houthi missiles were launched into Saudi territory, above all the environs of Jeddah, state media claimed that they were targeting Mecca before they were intercepted. 'Storming Mecca' is invoked as a reminder of how only pagans and non-Muslims can contemplate such an abhorrent destruction of the sacred site, reminiscent of Abraha al-Ashram, the

Abyssinian king of southern Arabia who rode on elephants in 571 AD to attack the city, a famous story in Surat al-Fil (the Chapter of the Elephant) in the Quran.

Notwithstanding the hyper-masculine and sectarian discourse that infuses the Saudi national narrative, the young nation is also being feminized to include women as avant-garde economic contributors to its prosperity, and even as important participants in the effort to protect it against Houthi aggression. Women are drawn to become spectators at football matches, but they are also skilled workers, whose expertise is needed to fulfil the promise of a post-oil economy, and journalists who report on the success of the Yemen war. According to Nora Doaiji, one journalist was coopted into the war in Yemen, where she appeared dressed in military uniform to support Saudi soldiers and report on their progress.[29] Such unprecedented acts in a society in which women were always told to honour their natural roles as obedient wives and daughters, performing a limited number of suitable jobs, are part of the new militarized nationalism sponsored by the crown prince.

But the inflated national masculinities that are infused with feminine elements refuse to naturalize children of Saudi women married to foreigners, or even to recognize their marriages if conducted outside Saudi Arabia without the permission of the Ministry of Interior. Their children remain non-Saudis, and the Saudi mothers may lose their citizenship as a result of marrying a foreigner without permission. When a Saudi wants to marry a foreigner, the Ministry of Interior has to issue a licence. Men are easily granted such licences, but women have to seek permission from their guardians to marry at all, let alone a foreigner, thus incurring a double burden as a result of simply being Saudi women. In 2019, for example, Ghada al-Fadl, who had had two unsuccessful marriages with Saudi men that had ended in divorce, left the country and married a Syrian man. But, when she went to the Saudi embassy in Beirut to renew her passport (she was pregnant at the time), the embassy staff refused to renew her passport and ejected her from the embassy, according to her YouTube video recordings. Her crime was marrying a Syrian Arab. She then went to Turkey, and on to Greece, where she was stranded with her husband and children in a detention centre for refugees.[30]

Women can now go to football matches in stadiums, attend concerts and watch circuses with men, but if a woman dances in a provocative way or runs up to embrace a music icon, she will certainly be arrested for violating the masculine honour of the youth cohort that the crown prince needs to keep obedient and under control. The crown prince occasionally avoids provoking the ultra-masculine egos of the male nation while at the same time enlisting women into his new nationalist project of building a non-state service-centred liberal economy in the post-oil era. Women journalists and writers are expected to glorify the prince and assert their membership in his personality cult, praise his war in Yemen, and defend all his domestic, regional and international policies. The national project involves branding the new nation as young and hyper-modern, with gender equality as a powerful promised symbol.

The new orchestrated nationalism is seen as integral to creating the new Saudi *homo economicus*. This person is no longer the pious Muslim eager to defend the faith of devout co-religionists, the lazy recipient of lavish welfare benefits, or the idle Bedouin who in the past spent most of his time either herding camels or composing heroic poetry. He is now expected to be the bearer of the knowledge economy, a pioneer of neoliberal services, the consumer of a wide range of products, and a risk-taking creative entrepreneur. Like the crown prince, he is the connected global ideal Saudi man, dressed in a long white robe (*thowb*), but with a smartphone rather than a now-defunct old Nokia. Women are no longer required to be strictly draped in a black *abaya* but can instead dress in colourful veils and drive to the shopping malls, developments that are symbolic of their modernity, cosmopolitanism and new sophistication. They can also travel abroad without the consent of their guardians. Saudis are now asked to be both proud nationalists and internationalists, ready to consume products and gadgets of modernity, with the inevitable apparent contradictions surfacing even in regime propaganda.

No doubt the crown prince appeals to the youth by opening new social and cultural forums and venues, but young Saudis perhaps need more than football matches, art exhibitions, or rock concerts to turn them into modern, entrepreneurial citizens. The crown prince cannot just sell them slogans, symbols and promises. He needs to make nationalism yield concrete benefits such as jobs, low inflation and freedom from surveillance and detention. He cannot be at the head of all decisions and expect everyone simply to obey his orders. With dissent appearing at multiple levels, he increasingly relies on a coterie of companions, advisers and aides, most of whom engage in aggressive construction of the nation online. Amongst those aides were the special security operatives who murdered journalist Jamal Khashoggi.

Under the new nationalism, the charge that a detained person had maintained contact or communication with foreign agents or governments is now extremely common. Dissidents criticizing Saudi policies and foreign relations from abroad are accused of treason and of undermining the new Saudi Arabia. Talking to foreign media without authorization is also a crime that can lead to imprisonment. Most of the detainees are labelled traitors against the *watan*, and the likes of Saud al-Qahtani and his team of cyber-trolls always contrast the *khain*s (traitors) with the real nationalists (*watani*s).

The prominent discourse about *khain*s and *watani*s prompted many Saudis to launch a counter-discourse that undermines the overuse of binary opposites in ways that silence criticism and dissent, and in some cases can lead to murdering critics, as the Khashoggi crisis demonstrated. Abdullah al-Awdah, son of detained cleric Salman al-Awdah, highlights how nationalist language has been deployed to justify detentions, and even murder. He points to the rise of a radical Saudi nationalist cohort, allied to the regime and willing to fight its battles with society by deploying labels such as 'traitor'. This cohort is far from being correctly described as *watani*s. Instead, al-Awdah introduces a rather pejorative name, *watanji*, to describe those who easily invoke treason—a crime punishable by beheading—against critics of the state, and who flaunt their loyalty to the nation in aggressive and threatening ways. In his view, the *watanji*s are a far-right group that believes in force rather than negotiation, debate and discussion. In foreign affairs, they tend to applaud military conflict: for example, they uncritically support Saudi airstrikes on Yemen, describing the war as a cherished aspect of King Salman, known as the 'king of decisiveness' (*malik al-hazm*). The *watanji*s are always confrontational and are willing to use force to eliminate dissenting voices. They do not cherish the soft power of persuasion. Rather, they always support aggression in the name of glorifying the nation and insist that force should be deployed to eliminate its internal and external enemies. The *watanji*s are more likely to blame all problems on foreign enemies of the state than to examine the record of the government and its success or failure. They are devoted to the 'hero', presented as faultless, strong and trustworthy. They accept nothing from society but total loyalty to the state and its hero, and they are ardent supporters of the cult of the Son King.

The language of treason may not be the only troubling aspect of the new nationalism. This new phase of aggressive nationalism was accompanied by 'death squads', trained and armed by Western experts and technology, and deployed to rid the regime of critics and dissident voices. The fifteen operatives dispatched to Istanbul to kill Khashoggi are believed to be part of a fifty-officer force known as the Tigers Squad, a new extra-judicial security force under the leadership of the crown prince that only came to public attention after the murder of Khashoggi. It includes a consortium of intelligence, policing and torture operatives, in addition to doctors, who may be helpful in drugging victims and dismembering and disposing of their bodies.

The cyber-troll farm outside Riyadh, where employees used Twitter accounts to precipitate an atmosphere of fear and apprehension, became notorious.[31] Under the pretext of defending the nation, the government's infamous cyber-army intimidates activists both inside and outside Saudi Arabia. They send Twitter messages to exiled Saudis and threaten them with kidnapping and assassination. They are also experienced in hacking dissidents' online accounts and implementing a pervasive surveillance regime, using the latest imported technology from the USA, Europe, China and Israel.

Ultra-nationalism is also associated with group punishment inside Saudi Arabia. The family members of prisoners of conscience are either detained or banned from travel. This practice is used to put pressure on Saudi exiles or to precipitate a rift between them and their families, who eventually are held liable in Saudi Arabia for the 'irresponsible' actions of their sons and daughters. Family members of Saudi exiles Abdullah al-Ghamdi, Omar al-Zahrani, Said ibn Nasir al-Ghamdi and Abdullah al-Juraywi, among others, are banned from travel. The parents of detainee Lujain al-Hathloul are under the same ban. The four-year-old son of exiled Sheikh Said ibn Nasir al-Ghamdi was prevented from travelling to join his father in London. His young daughter died in Saudi Arabia while he was in exile. Brothers and relatives of the religious clerics Salman al-Awdah, Safar al-Hawali and many others are either in detention or banned from leaving the country. Families of exiles who remain in Saudi Arabia are expected to demonstrate total loyalty to the regime by denouncing or disowning their detained or exiled relatives. But even denouncing exiled family members does not seem to be enough to allow their families to visit, communicate with, or send money to them if they are students abroad. Such severe measures are a by-product of the so-called new Saudi nationalism.

The crown prince's hasty promotion of Saudi nationalism remains a controversial step coming after several decades of indoctrination in specific narratives about state and society, their past, present and future. Sultan al-Abdali, a recent asylum seeker in London with a history of commitment to the Sahwa, explains that Muhammad ibn Salman's promotion of 'Saudi Arabia is Great' and other hyper-nationalist slogans comes at a time when he lacks legitimacy, first among his own family, and second in society at large. According to al-Abdali:

> The crown prince wants to fill a vacuum in national sentiment to consolidate his rule. Unlike other Arab countries, Saudi Arabia does not have a strong national identity. The crown prince also wants to legitimate his monopoly over power after he failed to secure the consent of his own cousins and relatives. To distinguish his new regime from previous eras, he amplifies his achievements and conceals his failures under empty nationalist slogans. The nationalism that we see during the National Day celebrations absorbs young people's frustration and disappointments. They rush to attend concerts and celebrate by raising flags in the streets, but most of these festivities are directed from above.

Women are also included in the nationalist festivals: 'The crown prince promotes women as participants in development after the regime ignored them and even marginalized them.' Some aspects of the new nationalism are directed outward, as they are meant to be for external consumption. Al-Abdali explains that:

THE NEW POPULIST NATIONALISM

The crown prince wants to show that he is also capable of serving the West by making himself the champion of peace with Israel. For this he needs to make sure that Saudis lose their solidarity with the Palestinians, which they had expressed for years. The prince also wants this new Saudi nationalism to be directed against the millions of foreign workers to absorb citizens' frustration with the economy and unemployment. The foreigners came because Saudi princes and businessmen profit from their visas and employment. Of course, foreign labour depresses the local labour market, but we Saudis did not ask them to come. When things go wrong, the prince wants Saudis to blame foreigners as part of this national project and forget the real cause of their unemployment. This is like blaming the Sahwa for all problems. It is a strategy to direct people's anger towards a local Islamist enemy or foreigners. The prince gives people limited but visible personal freedom but he denies them [the chance] to be partners in the nation.

Al-Abdali rejects the new wave of nationalism. He says:

I am not a partner in the nation if I am not allowed to have my representatives in an elected parliament. Even my Hijazi heritage is denied, and I am expected to celebrate the Najdi dance that the regime chooses to represent me. I have my own cultural tradition, which is totally absent from state festivities. The National Day is not my national day. It is the Al Saud day. Our society is a rich mosaic of cultures from the Hijaz, Najd, south and west, but we are expected to be one Al Saud nation. How can I celebrate the construction boom of the regime? This does not correspond to building my national consciousness. Walls and buildings are not my national heritage. Society does not have a place in the new nationalism because citizens are denied a say over festivals, entertainment and major changes under the crown prince. We are forced to adopt his slogans, but we did not contribute to making them. This is not how nations are built.

When I see people celebrating the National Day, I think they are simply enjoying a moment of limited freedom after they were denied real political rights. Most people want to let some steam off. The

more the regime celebrates, the more I conclude that there is a deficit in our national belonging. Stable and secure nations don't overdo
celebrations unless they are divided, broken and frustrated. This is
our current situation under Muhammad ibn Salman. The crown
prince failed domestically and regionally. He cannot even protect our
oilfields. He bombed Yemen without victory. He wants to cover up
all his plunders and he thinks slogans such as 'Saudi Arabia is Great'
will solve his problems.[32]

Another London-based exile, Ahmad ibn Said, professor of
political communication at King Saud University in Riyadh,
questions the quick transition from pan-Islamism to 'Saudi
Arabia First'. He remembers his childhood in the late 1960s
when regime media under King Faisal propagated a pan-Islamic
identity in the public sphere. From religious *anashid* (songs) to
radio and television programmes, Saudis were expected and
forced to embrace a pan-Islamic identity. Ibn Said explains:

As a child, I used to recite the official songs that we listened to on
the radio. All public culture was deeply Islamic, asking us Saudis to
engage with many Muslim and Arab causes, especially the Palestinian
crisis. I lived this atmosphere and endorsed the *umami* (internation-
alist) discourse of the regime. The Palestinian cause was the primary
occupation of my generation because state television kept us engaged
in it. So now we are expected to abandon this outlook and focus on
Saudi Arabia first. We are not machines that can be switched on and
off, whenever the leadership wants. Also, I am against the racist and
chauvinistic undertones of the new nationalism. Notice how Saudis
are now talking about *arab al-shamal*, 'northern Arabs' of Lebanon,
Syria, Iraq and Palestine, in very pejorative ways. Also, Saudi so-
called intellectuals are promoting the idea that Palestinians sold their
land to the Jews.

The crown prince promotes this hyper-nationalism for two reasons.
First, he wants Saudis to dissociate themselves from Arab and
Muslim causes to establish peace with Israel. Second, this national-
ism covers up the failure of the economic, social and regional policies

of the crown prince. The regime strengthens tribal and racist feelings as people start boasting about their worth but without achieving greatness. They nevertheless repeat his slogan 'Saudi Arabia is Great'. These are myths that spread illusions of greatness. Great nations do not need to overdo their national celebration because they know they are great. But Saudis under the crown prince entertain themselves with these slogans.[33]

As many young Saudis flock to attend concerts and participate in national entertainment and festivals, Ahmad ibn Said explains that society has had enough of the religious restrictions that the regime used to impose on them, enforced by the religious police. People have had enough of the religious police interfering in their personal lives and scrutinizing their private affairs. The religious police never respected people's privacy. At the same time, the regime allowed its media to undermine the religious police and criticize their many mistakes. This made it easy to abolish this state institution that played a negative role and gave Islam a bad name. Saudi society was suffering from repression in the name of religion. When an opportunity to celebrate national days came up, the people quickly went out to the street to enjoy a kind of limited freedom with the regime's backing. The Saudi regime is a radical regime, which operates by shifting its policies from one extreme to another.

Both al-Abdali and ibn Said strongly defend their belief in the centrality of Arab and Islamic identity, rejecting the current Saudi nationalism as chauvinistic and racist. Other younger Saudis defend the Arab identity of the country and see no contradiction between being Arab and being Saudi. As Saudi national identity is promoted under many slogans, its Arab dimension remains, but it is played down in regime propaganda on social media and in the traditional press. As mentioned by the two Saudi exiles in London, criticism of *arab al-shamal* in ways that express hostility and even racism are pervasive in the Saudi public sphere under Muhammad ibn Salman.

An advocate of neo-Arabism, Ph.D. student Sultan al-Amer, who is currently studying at George Washington University, contributes to the debate about the old Arab nationalism, its mistakes, failures and future revival.[34] Al-Amer is an avid critic of the current chauvinistic nationalism that highlights Saudi exceptionalism and imbues it with fascist and jingoistic under-tones.[35] His critique focuses primarily on how a marginal hyper-nationalist discourse became central in the public sphere, espe-cially in the media, with advocates such as Muhammad al-Sheikh propagating it on the pages of the local press.[36] In 2016 al-Amer started writing on two independent online news sites, *Ewan24* and *al-Taqrir*. Both sites were launched by young modernist intellectuals Abdullah al-Maliki and Sultan al-Jamri, who are currently in detention.[37] Al-Amer highlights the flawed underly-ing assumptions of those Saudis who endorse anti-Arab senti-ments in discussions of employment in Saudi Arabia, for example about the so-called *arab al-shamal*. For him, those Arab immi-grants cannot be blamed for the unemployment of the Saudi youth, the real problem being the dysfunctional labour market where merchants and government businesses favour cheap labour. He promotes the idea that the current fascism of the Saudi nationalist discourse is truly 'the opium of the unemployed', as it diverts attention from serious structural problems in the local labour market.[38] Al-Amer draws on the fiction of Abdulrahman Munif, borrowing the fictional names the latter gave to imagi-nary countries in his famous novel *Now, Here*, in order to alle-gorically criticize the Saudi airstrikes on Yemen. Al-Amer rhe-torically askes what moral position one should adopt if Moran (the name of a fictional country) attacks another, Amoriyyah, with whom people share history, religion and culture. He excludes 'national interest' as a legitimate justification for sup-porting Moran's aggression. Instead, he proposes rejecting aggression and racism within the Arab world for both moral and political reasons. This racism is built on glorifying the purity of one group of aggressors while demonizing its victims.

Above all, al-Amer attacks the essentialist origins of the discourse on so-called Saudi exceptionalism, which depicts the country as possessing a unique past and present not shared by other Arab countries. He argues that in order to talk about 'us and our interests' as Saudis, we must above all define who we are. In a debate that circulated on a podcast,[39] he argues that Saudis have to disentangle our Arab identity from the twentieth-century ideologies of Arab nationalism such as Nasserism and Baathism. We have a shared history, language and culture with other Arabs. While ideologies may become defunct, our Arab identity stays with us. Our religion, Islam, is the second largest in the world, and our Arabic language is the fifth-most spoken by people around the globe. We can have an Arab union like the European community to complement each other as Arab countries. We can share economic resources, human labour and influence without one country imposing its domination the way Egypt or Iraq wanted to do in the 1950s and 1960s. Our Arab *hawiyya* (identity) must acknowledge the diversity of each *watan*. Our task is to find a way to live with two identities, the wider Arab nation and our local *watani* (national) identity. This has been the most difficult task, and many attempts to unify Arabs failed because they did not get the balance right. The failure was threefold. First, those who invented the ideologies of Arab nationalism wanted to dominate other countries. Second, there is no serious political will invested in the project of unifying Arabs. Third, Arab nationalism emerged when the region was under foreign domination and consequently, it was resisted by 'outside colonial forces'.[40]

Sultan al-Amer resists the current drive to distance Saudi Arabia from Arab national causes, for example the right of the Palestinians to have their own state and homeland, especially at a time when

Saudi nationalism is turning against expressing any concern or solidarity with their problems. He insists that 'a local national identity does not necessarily negate belonging to an Arab nation'.

Together with like-minded young writers, in 2016 al-Amer published a revisionist edited volume that deals with assessing the history of *ourouba* (Arabism).[41] He proposes offering young writers an opportunity to express their views on a topic that attracted a lot of attention in the past. He argues that 'the history of Arabism was written from the perspective of the regimes who either promoted it or opposed it. The new generation of writers proposes to revisit this history. In my view, any solution to Arab problems must be grounded in a general solution to the problems of the region as a whole.' Al-Amer's volume brings the Arabian Peninsula from the 'the margin of that history to the centre'. He chooses to focus on Saudis who contributed to the Palestinian cause, and who even fought in the 1948 war as part of the Arab volunteer force.[42] His objective is to highlight the early awareness among Saudis of their Arabism, which led to supporting regional causes. According to al-Amer, Saudis had always been marginalized in the grand Arab narrative about nationalism. This is allegedly used to prove a kind of 'Saudi exceptionalism' and to justify Saudi exclusion from Arab nationalist projects. Saudi Arabia is 'depicted in the literature of Arabists as an isolated region despite the fact that socially, its people had historical and social connections with the rest of the region. Moreover, domestically, Saudi Arabia's public sphere is Arab and Islamic, and Saudis engaged with the problems of the Arab region even before the rise of Arab national ideologies.'[43] Al-Amer concludes his revisionist history by asserting that *watani* (Saudi) and *qawmi* (Arab) nationalism are interconnected in the modern history of the Arabian Peninsula.

* * *

THE NEW POPULIST NATIONALISM

The Saudi regime's three stages of constructing the nation were attempts to homogenize its fragments, but by their own nature they all failed to be inclusive in a true sense, and were in effect divisive instead. From its early days the religious national narrative excluded religious minorities and those whose Islam differed from the version imposed by the clerics of the Al Saud family, mainly those originating from the central Najd province. The pan-Islamic transnational identity excluded those Muslims who either were opposed to Saudi political projects, for example the Iranian Shia, or subscribed to a different Islamic tradition, for example the Sunni Sufi Turks. The prosperity and security narrative associated with the new Saudi Arabia excluded peripheral regions. The narrative undoubtedly led to xenophobia and populism, justifying the targeting of critics of state policies, Saudis of foreign origin and immigrants.

The trend that many media reporters and analysts are referring to as a new Saudi nationalism may not be nationalism after all. What we are witnessing in Saudi Arabia is the systematic and aggressive efforts of a prince who was elevated to the highest position in the state, with no history of experience in government and at the expense of other more senior princes, to consolidate his power. A true nationalist movement would require more than rhetoric, thuggery, murder and readily available treason charges against critics. There are no outstanding ideologues in this nationalism who can construct a plausible new national narrative, one that is anchored in an imagined new Saudi identity that partly relies on a pre-Islamic heritage, Islam and current promises of a prosperous future. The likes of Saud al-Qahtani, whose online presence and statements may have succeeded in intimidating many dissidents, may not be capable of creating a durable vision of a nation with the characteristics that the crown prince desires.

It has rightly been pointed out that nationalism in the Gulf remains a highly contested notion in general, liable to promote national divisions as much as conceal them.[44] The surge in a Saudi national identity so firmly anchored in Najd, where the royal family originated, belies that: 'Places like Shiite-dominated Qatif in the Eastern province, Asir in the southwest and the Hejaz, which hosts the holy cities of Mecca and Medina, all have local identities that may be empowered by nationalism and may bristle against the state's imposition of Najdi symbols, rituals and culture.'[45] The new Saudi nationalism may unleash counter-regional nationalisms that threaten the domination of both the Al Saud and their loyal supporters in Najd itself. Even Islamists in exile are openly and critically beginning to associate Najd with Wahhabism and to distance themselves from its theological domination. They may have reluctantly endorsed the Wahhabi tradition as they moved towards Islamism inside the country, but now in exile, many voices are condemning Wahhabism and its patrons.

If national narratives are meant to homogenize and merge the fragments in one nation, the statements and actions of the new nationalist cyber-trolls fail to unify Saudis in a tangible way beyond the cheering of crowds at football matches and the heroic songs and poetry on National Day celebrations and during festivals celebrating the first Saudi capital, Diriyyah. The new nationalist discourse also has both regional and global implications, as it problematizes the engagement of Saudi Arabia as a country in other conflicts and invites its adherents to look inwards rather than outwards. This reorientation is a necessary condition for 'making Saudi Arabia great', and its greatness must be felt domestically and globally. In the following chapter, I examine the fragments of the nation and the current divides in a society that struggles with diversity and suffers from exclusion.

5

THE SUB-NATIONALS

DIVERSITY AND EXCLUSION

I am proud of my Hijazi identity, but I am a Muslim.

Saudi exile in the USA

In an absolute monarchy, the role of Saudi royalty as head of the imagined nation is paramount. Kings and princes occupy the highest positions in government and shape social, economic and foreign policies. The monarch is always constructed as a unifying force ruling over a diverse and fragmented society, without serious consideration of his potential role as the agent of an ancient divide-and-rule policy. The Saudi king rules over a population consisting of tribes, non-tribals, religious minorities and immigrants, all living in regions with their own distinct historical identities. In the past, the Hijaz, Najd, the northern territories, the Eastern Province, and the southern province of Najran had distinguishable characteristics; but now they are part of the Saudi kingdom. While the population is predominantly Sunni, other Muslim minorities such as Shia and Ismailis coexist with the majority, in a troubled relationship. Since the discovery of oil, immigrants from Arab, Asian and African countries have contributed to the Saudi economy in ways that have so far been neglected except in statistical handbooks and demographic profiles of the population, which amplify their remittances in order to demonstrate their negative impact. American, British and other European expatriates sit at the top of the hierarchy of foreign residents in Saudi Arabia. Saudi Arabia, rather than being a homogeneous nation, is a mosaic, held together but also divided by a centralized absolute monarchy.

This chapter explores the tribal, ethnic, regional and religious diversity of an increasingly urban population. This diversity poses challenges that are masked by the rhetoric of national inclusion, while many members of these sub-national groups continue to suffer from the obstacles and disadvantages of exclusion. While diversity is a fact to be reckoned with, the exclusion of minority groups is a political act that the monarchy perpetuates. A divided population obsessed with its essentialized and primordial identities is perfect for an absolute monarchy that denies its subjects any form of national political representation and punishes the emergence of national politics that cut across the imaginary divides. In fact, the monarch governs by fragmenting the nation, as the mere appearance of national unity threatens the very foundation of his absolute rule.

Yet the semblance of an ethnically, religiously and racially homogeneous population is maintained, and is disguised by the rhetoric of *muwatin* and *muwatana*, citizen and citizenship. This illusory homogeneity manifests itself in uniform dress codes for men and women, especially in the public sphere, and above all in government bureaucracy, where almost 70 per cent of the population is employed. The public manifestations of state Islam and piety conceal the distinctive rituals and practices of religious minorities. The written classical Arabic language and its diluted spoken equivalent among intellectuals in the media unsuccessfully

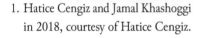

1. Hatice Cengiz and Jamal Khashoggi in 2018, courtesy of Hatice Cengiz.

2. Author's correspondence with Jamal Khashoggi on Twitter Direct Messages.

3. Exiled Omar al-Zahrani, Canada, 2019, courtesy of Omar al-Zahrani.

4. *I Am My Own Guardian*, by Saudi artist Ms Saffaa, courtesy of Ms Saffaa.

5. Exiled Muhammad al-Massari, Muhammad al-Omari and Sahar al-Fifi in discussion, 2019, courtesy of Diwan London.

6. Exiled Abdullah al-Juraywi and journalist Safa al-Ahmad attending the Diaspora Conference, December 2019, courtesy of Diwan London.

7. Saudi exiles hold a demonstration outside the Saudi embassy in support of detained activists, December 2019, courtesy of Diwan London.

8. Outside the Saudi embassy in London, December 2019, courtesy of Diwan London.

9. Yahya Assiri, director of Diwan London, at the centre of a demonstration outside the Saudi embassy in London, December 2019, courtesy of Diwan London.

conceal different regional and tribal vernacular accents. These linguistic variations coexist with broken Arabic spoken by Pakistani, Thai, Indonesian, Bangladeshi and Filipino immigrants who have lived in Saudi Arabia for decades. In addition, Arabized communities from Central Asia, the Far East and Africa settled in the kingdom, especially the Hijaz, before the establishment of the Saudi state. A new generation of young Saudis converse in English among themselves, thus adding to the cosmopolitanism of the workplace and the modern shopping malls where they congregate for leisure, shopping, courting and entertainment.

Tribes and Their Ethos

Tribes and their ethos remain important in the kingdom.[1] In fact, according to anthropologist Nadav Samin, there is a compulsion to affirm tribal belonging in modern Saudi Arabia. This may seem odd 'in a country so overwhelmingly saturated with public religiosity—its symbols, its laws, and its functionaries'.[2] However, one should not imagine that there were or are distinct tribal communities, fixed in time and space, with well-defined boundaries and distinct cultures. Tribes have always been fluid social categories and organizations, despite the fact that early colonial catalogues of Saudi Arabia and contemporary genealogists such as Hamad al-Jasir, studied by Samin, consider the 'tribes' as clearly distinctive communities with genealogies that can be traced in the present with precision. In the twenty-first century many Saudis take pride in their tribal (*qabili*) origin, believed to be a superior category associated with noble descent from well-known ancestors that people can trace, which children learn at a very young age. In fact, the learning process of a child starts with memorizing at least five ancestors, then moving swiftly to the tribal name. A small minority of *qabili*s can recite their tribal ancestors as far back as their epic ancestor. While many observers of Saudi Arabia think that central Arabia—Najd—is the homeland of the tribes, most of the regions have their own *qabili*s.

Although there is an egalitarian ethos in Islam, Saudi tribal genealogies continue to be debated and fetishized. Discussions of genealogies are often accompanied by controversy and heated arguments. In popular entertainment, tribal Bedouin accents and regional dialects are rich material for comic television serials. When fictionalized stereotypes dominate popular television programmes, such as the Ramadan series *Tash ma Tash*, they are immediately condemned for encouraging national division and animosity. Ridiculing someone's tribe in a comedy show often results in the show being suspended and the producer punished for tarnishing a tribal reputation and undermining its honour.

The diversity of the Saudi tribal groups who claim descent from identifiable tribes does not mean that these are seen as equal entities, even though they remain fluid. A hierarchy of tribes is still apparent, a legacy from the pre-state era. Groups that exercised power over others and imposed levies on them occupied the highest positions on the tribal ladder. Those who coerced others, such as camel herders, were the tribal nobility, while the tribes subjected to coercion, such as sheep and goat herders, were held in lower esteem.[3] At the bottom of this hierarchy were the non-tribals.

However, in contemporary Saudi Arabia, loyalty to the regime can elevate certain members of a tribe to the top of the hierarchy. In addition, tribes, and specific lineages within them, who had become maternal kin of Saudi princes are also held in esteem by the princes and are given monthly salaries from the state as court 'nobility'. They also receive annual *sharha* (gift of money by a superior person to someone of a lower status), and many other privileges and gifts such as land, houses, cars, jewellery, watches, free first-class travel and other consumer goods.

THE SUB-NATIONALS

Careful attention to and concern with tribal genealogies and noble Arabian origin seem to have become increasingly important following the social and political changes that swept Arabia, above all the increasing urbanization and the marginalization of the tribes within the higher political apparatus of the state. Many Saudis belonged to fluid tribes whose genealogies provided topics for discussion, storytelling and oral entertainment. Those belonging to tribal aristocracies, often tribal chiefs of important tribal confederations, enjoyed the prestige that comes with noble origin and held written documents lavishly portraying tribal trees and pedigrees. But the rest of the tribals know their origins in less pronounced and documented ways, reverting to oral culture to seek identification and authenticity. In fact, the tribal world of pre-state Arabia was fluid, constantly in the process of construction and reconstruction. It was only with the shift to textuality that many tribal entrepreneurs, genealogists and storytellers started the project of fixing the tribes in solid documents and tracing the ancestry of individuals and groups on demand by resorting to quasi-scientific methods. Tribal belonging and authentication were also requested by the state bureaucracy to grant someone benefits, citizenship and other privileges confined to 'nationals' and denied to 'foreigners'.

The increasing importance of tribal belonging in modern Saudi Arabia has to be understood in the context of modern state formation, governance and consolidation, all of which had marginalized the tribes.[4] In addition, social change, sudden affluence and the shift towards new forms of urban anonymity, almost all products of a recently urbanized population, are factors that contribute to the reinvocation of tribal origins in modern-day Saudi Arabia. The marginalization of tribal forces that brought the Al Saud to power and consolidated the state was discussed in Chapter 1. Many observers of the country conclude that tribes were forced to accept central authority after they 'fought alongside the Saudi government and opposed it, but ultimately, they all were relegated to positions of lesser influence'.[5]

Consequently, the state is correctly described as a *hadari* (sedentary) state that overlooked the tribal forces, especially the Bedouin communities, after they had played a central role in its formation and expansion.[6] While tribals were important as a military force, they were immediately excluded from the administrative and bureaucratic apparatus of the state. When trusted tribes were integrated, only a few groups whose loyalty is guaranteed were fully incorporated in the state and its mushrooming military and civil institutions. This resulted in marginalization and a quest to assert noble tribal origin at a time when the modern state ignored and even suppressed the tribes. Using Islam and the Wahhabi clerics, the state promoted an egalitarian ethos that dissolved tribal specificity to mask the marginalization and exclusion of tribal groups. Many Saudi intellectuals regard the tribes as a divisive force, rife with nepotism, blind solidarity and bigotry. Tribes are often considered reminders of a savage past that was tamed only by the efforts of the Al Saud to unify the country and rid it of its fragmentation and weakness. Such essentialist and orientalist views of the tribes among intellectuals are so common that when the municipal elections were first introduced in 2005, many observers predicted that Saudis would vote along tribal lines, favouring their own kin. These predictions were proven wrong, as many Islamist candidates won seats in municipalities as a result of well-managed and organized campaigns rather than simply on the basis of tribal origin or mobilization.[7]

Negative depictions of the tribes always drew on the Islamic egalitarian ethos, which insists on equality based on religious brotherhood. But many commentators also drew on Islam to highlight how the religious tradition did not completely negate the importance of genealogies but did in fact recognize the signifiçance of *ansab* (genealogies). Sunni Islam glorifies the Quraysh, the Prophet Muhammad's tribe, whose descendants, known as Ashraf, are regarded as the legitimate heirs to rule over Muslims. However, the Wahhabi tradition, among other interpretations of Islam, does not fully subscribe to such a doctrine, as it accepts that in the absence of a legitimate Qurayshi any Muslim can become the ruler. In fact, the Saudi Wahhabi *ulama* accept conquest as a legitimate mechanism to install someone in office. In Shia Islam, the Twelvers and the Zaydis, the descendants of the Prophet and his cousin Ali, are the revered Imams of the Muslim community.

The current obsession with tribal genealogies and lineages in Saudi Arabia is attributed to social change and rural–urban migration rather than a relic or survival from a distant past. In the pre-state era, the people most concerned with their tribal genealogies were members of the tribal aristocracy, historically known for commissioning elaborate drawings of their tribal trees. However, they never carry the name of the tribe as part of their names, as everyone knows the chiefs of a particular tribe and as such they need not remind others that they are Qahtanis, Ajmis, Shammaris, Otaybis, etc. More recently, those 'government clerks and middle managers, teachers and engineers, small and large businessmen, and newspaper and journal readers— newly literate strivers' are concerned with their tribal names and genealogies.[8] As the tribals are only given lip-service deference in the new state apparatus, they cling to constructed genealogies marking their ancient and authentic noble origins. Others who benefited from social mobility as a result of government employment feel that they lack authenticity despite their recently acquired wealth. Consequently, they search for their *ansab*, thus adding symbolic capital to their new material gains. With sudden oil wealth since the 1970s, and mainly concentrated in big cities, Saudis began to look for new signifiers and distinctions. They found in the art of inventing and fixing genealogies a symbolic resource that they can draw on to plot themselves onto the map of prestige and significance. Both Saud al-Qahtani and Ahmad Asiri, mentioned earlier, close aides of the crown prince, continue to use the names of their tribes (Qahtan and Assiri) to signify their tribal ancestry and belonging. In the past, the chiefs of Qahtan and Assiri tribes would not have added such tribal titles to their names.

Against this background history, tribes in present-day Saudi Arabia value their genealogies especially where the marriage of women is concerned. While a man may marry a woman of lesser tribal origin, or even of no tribe at all, the marriage of women is highly regulated by social norms that are supported by the state judiciary. The regulation and strict rules governing the marriage of women is in line with other patrilineal and patriarchal societies where women inherit wealth. In such societies, tribal endogamy is the preferred matrimonial union. In 2007, the case of the Saudi couple Mansour and Fatima was widely covered by the media as a judge annulled their marriage, invoking an Islamic principle known as *takafu al-nasab* (tribal compatibility) in marriage.[9] Fatima belonged to a tribe, while her husband was described as *khadiri*, a pejorative name for non-tribals. She had therefore demeaned herself by marrying the less noble Mansour, considered unsuitable for a woman of her tribe. When the marriage was declared void on the grounds of genealogical incompatibility, Fatima's family accused her of *khilwa* (being with a man outside wedlock). She moved to a state-run shelter with her two children as she refused to be returned to her family, who had taken her to court to annul the marriage.

On another occasion, the police intervened to prevent a wedding from taking place in Khobar because the bride and her groom were deemed genealogically incompatible. In 2016 a court in Uyayna annulled a marriage for the same reason, even after the Justice Ministry issued a clarification statement to the effect that in Islam compatibility between husband and wife in marriage refers to respect for religious observance rather than tribal ancestry.

Such cases are common in present-day Saudi Arabia, where the tradition of tribal endogamy for women persists and is given support by judges who mould their interpretation of the principle of genealogical compatibility to suit social norms and values. According to one source, in ten months in 2015 around sixteen requests to annul marriages were presented to the courts on the basis that the husband and wife were genealogically incompatible. Nine of these cases were in Riyadh, five in the Eastern Province, one in Madina, and one in Jeddah.[10] The increase in these cases reflects both the persistence of tribal endogamy and the changing norms of many young Saudis who do not object to exogamous marriages. These marriages are on the rise as young Saudi men and women live in urban centres where multiple tribals, non-tribals and even foreigners live and work. As the tribal ethos is weakened by education and the notion of the love match, the younger generation of Saudi men and women are challenging genealogical compatibility as a precondition for marriage. Families resist the change, provoking girls to run away when presented with no choice or an arranged marriage, as will be discussed in the next chapter.

Discussion of tribal compatibility as a requirement for marriage is now common in state media. Recently, an anonymous woman called the Saudi-owned MBC television channel, which was airing a programme on the subject, to expose her dilemma. The woman is an orphan whose brother is now her guardian. The brother refused to give his permission for her to marry a man he considered to be genealogically inferior. The woman described herself as educated and as managing several employees in her office. Yet, she was denied the right to marry the man of her choice because his non-tribal status renders him inferior. Her brother suggested a candidate who fulfilled the tribal compatibility criteria, but he was much older and already married with six children. She refused to marry her brother's candidate. The woman expressed her frustration that the court is yet to resolve the dispute with her brother in her favour. She is still waiting for the judge to accept her request to be removed from the control of her guardian. She eventually sought justice from the king on television: 'I call upon my father King Salman and his son Muhammad to solve my problem. I want to be free from the control of my brother. I am *maadhula* [a woman denied marriage by my guardian]. I fully support the crown prince's vision and want him to rescue me.'[11]

Such televised cases are part of subtle state propaganda. First, the appeal focuses on the supposed progressive nature of the monarch, King Salman, and Crown Prince Muhammad, who rule over a nation plagued by divisive tribalism and persistent chauvinism to the detriment of its own citizens. In Saudi media, these cases emphasize the centrality of the monarch, who can save the country from the nation's abusive tribal fragments, especially those who refuse to become part of the one nation and who continue to flaunt and boast about their tribal genealogies. The woman voices a plea to be removed from the tribal patriarchy and be placed instead under the patriarchy of the monarch, the father of the nation. Second, in such televised programmes, the backwardness of Saudi society, its conservatism and its resistance to change are all highlighted. Salvation of the nation from the negative aspects of its ancient and persistent tribal heritage is the responsibility of the monarch. It is he who protects the realm from returning to the status quo ante, when tribes occasionally raided and massacred their rivals while oppressing their own members. The centrality of the monarchy is then asserted above all as a force responsible for maintaining social harmony and family stability, able to save women from the excesses of the tribal past and the bigotry of their own men.

With the advent of the internet, it is hard to find a tribal group without its own websites, forums, Facebook pages, YouTube channels and Twitter, Snapchat and Instagram accounts. Online tribalism is now an important feature of the Saudi cyber-sphere.[12] It is also common to find multiple virtual sites for one tribe, thus reflecting the fragmentation of tribal confederations. Administrators of the tribal sites always emphasize that their webpage is *rasmi*, the 'official' tribal window in the virtual world. As a social organization and a source of identity, the tribe is alive in both the imagination of the past and the concerns of the present. Much of the content of these websites celebrates a heroic age of chivalry and courage. Each tribe provides pages of pedigrees, family trees, oral histories, old pictures of important tribal chiefs, heroic poetry, praise for tribal deeds, current images of banquets held during wedding celebrations, and commentaries on the past glory of its own members. Most such tribal websites also affirm their loyalty to the ruling family and register stories that chronicle their own contribution to creating the Saudi state. Such loyalty statements are necessary to prevent these websites from being blocked by central censorship agencies. Those who flaunt their tribal credentials without praising the leadership of the country will immediately be accused of entertaining separatist tendencies, disloyalty to the monarch and racism against other members of Saudi society. Urban intellectuals often condemn the overt and excessive tribal celebrations and camel pageants in which tribes take pride in their camel pedigrees. Such loud tribal festivals are described as tribal *hiyat* (noise).

Judgments for murder in Saudi courts allow the payment of *diyya* (blood-money), which can save a murderer from beheading if the victim's family agrees to receive a payment instead of punishment. In the case of *diyya*, tribal websites and Twitter accounts often serve as platforms to raise donations and contributions towards the payment to save a member of the tribe from execution in such circumstances. *Diyya* payments are colossal and can amount to hundreds of thousands of Saudi riyals. A tribal murderer can count on his kinsmen to appeal to tribal solidarity online and invite others to save his life. In addition to online calls to donate money, banquets are held to encourage donations in solidarity with the family of the murderer, enabling them to pay the victim's family an acceptable amount as *diyya*. In cases where a tribe is distributed across several Gulf countries, calls to donate become transnational, with online forums reaching out to a wide network. The Saudi tribals join their counterparts in Kuwait, Qatar and other GCC states to celebrate their sub-national identities and seek solidarity. The online forums enforce a sense of belonging to a wider tribal confederation in which solidarity is maintained by occasional visits, poetry recitations and festivals.

Gulf regimes often consider the transnational links of their tribal population to be very suspicious, warranting intervention to stop or undermine the tribal solidarities of groups scattered across the borders of the Gulf nation-states. Moreover, tribals who hold two Gulf nationalities are viewed with mistrust and are often accused of claiming benefits from these countries on the basis of their dual citizenship. In May 2018, twenty-nine-year-old Nawaf al-Rasheed, a descendent of the Rashids of the Shammar tribe who ruled in Hail until 1921 when their capital fell into the hands of Ibn Saud, arrived in Kuwait to attend a poetry banquet organized by a famous poet, Abdul Karim al-Jubari, a Kuwaiti Shammar.[13] Nawaf holds both Saudi and Qatari passports. He is the son of the famous poet Talal al-Rasheed, who was assassinated in Algeria in 2003 while on a hunting trip. The identity of the murderers was never revealed, and Algerian investigators concluded that jihadis in Algeria may have mistaken the poet for a Saudi prince and assassinated him. But such allegations were never proven in a court, and no one was charged with the murder.

Rumours were rife that the Saudi regime organized the murder to punish Talal, who had become very popular across the Gulf because of his vernacular poetry celebrating courage, love, hospitality and occasionally the past glory of his Rashidi ancestors. By a remarkable coincidence, in 2017 Saud al-Qahtani tweeted that 'we can make one funeral into two, one in Rawdat Muhanna and one in Algeria', in the context of boasting about how the Al Saud killed Amir Abd al-Aziz ibn Rashid (known by his nickname al-Jinaza, which also means funeral) in the battle of Rawdat Muhanna in 1906, with the comment about doubling the funeral implying that the regime was behind the murder of Talal in Algeria. Al-Qahtani denied that he wrote the tweet and claimed that it had been fabricated by Qatar.[14] The past continues to haunt the Saudi regime and its aides and can erupt unexpectedly online.

Talal had a troubled relationship with the Saudi authorities, although he was occasionally honoured as someone who appealed to many audiences both inside and outside Saudi Arabia. His son Nawaf lived in Qatar with his Qatari mother after his father's assassination in Algeria. In 2014, as the Saudi–Qatari crisis became heated and citizens of both countries were prevented from visiting their kinsmen across the borders, a tense situation emerged whereby dual nationals, especially members of tribes, felt the pressure to side with one or the other country. Saudi Arabia used the tribal card against Qatar and started promoting individual Qatari emirs in its media as alternatives to the leadership of Tamim ibn Hamad al-Thani, current emir of Qatar. As will be discussed below, the Saudi regime and its clerics launched a genealogical war on the Al Thani to deprive them of the prestige of their ancestry.

In this heated regional conflict, Nawaf was received with lavish hospitality in Kuwait by members of the Shammar tribe and others, who gathered for a spectacular dinner organized by al-Jubari. After spending three days in Kuwait, and on his way to the airport, where he was expected to take a flight back to Doha, Nawaf was kidnapped and deported to Saudi Arabia, where he was detained for over a year. The Kuwaiti authorities cooperated with the Saudis in this forced repatriation. According to Kuwait's Ministry of Interior, Nawaf was repatriated to Saudi Arabia in accordance with a bilateral security agreement. Both Saudi Arabia and Kuwait may have resented the hospitality and lavish reception offered to Nawaf. He was honoured as the son of a famous poet whose ancestors had fought battles with both the Kuwaitis and the Saudis. This overt display of tribal solidarity across nations was regarded as provocative, and so Nawaf was forcibly sent to Riyadh at the request of the Saudi regime. The Saudi regime may have worried that Qatar would promote Nawaf and use the symbolism of his noble ancestry to undermine Saudi rule, as the Saudis had done themselves after the outbreak of hostilities between the two countries. A tribal poetry festival in honour of an Al Rashid member revived a portion of history that the Saudi regime preferred to remain buried rather than be celebrated across the border. While tribalism is occasionally dismissed as a relic of the past, it remains a potential threat to regimes with weak national identities and exclusionary policies that are inadequately compensated for by propaganda and the celebration of national belonging.

However, while the regime remains apprehensive about the public display of overt tribalism both inside Saudi Arabia and across the border, it also selectively highlights aspects of Saudi tribalism that boost its legitimacy and promote it as a repository of tribal heritage and authenticity. The project of 'tribes as heritage' started with King Abdullah when he was the commander of the Saudi Arabian National Guard, a military force composed of tribal Bedouins. Their forebears were the Ikhwan, created in the early twentieth century to conquer Arabia, as mentioned in Chapter 1. The leader of the Mecca Mosque siege in 1979, Juhayman al-Otaibi, had been in the National Guard. After the consolidation of the state and the rooting out of troublesome tribal leaders of the Ikhwan, the regime decided that the rest of the tribal force should be incorporated into a special military unit, separate from the main Saudi army. The National Guard was thus developed into a large institution to contain and control tribes. In addition to being a military force, it became a vehicle to distribute benefits such as health services, housing and salaries. Furthermore, its creation was designed to balance the emergence of a unified strong Saudi army whose generals might challenge the regime and stage a coup d'état, as had happened in other parts of the Arab world in the 1950s and 1960s. From 1962 the National Guard became King Abdullah's fiefdom, which developed patronage networks among various tribes.

Given the tribal composition of this military force, Abdullah invented the Janadiriyyah Festival in the 1980s to celebrate the tribal culture of his military force and recognize the contribution of the tribes to the establishment and consolidation of the Saudi state. It is reported that his close aide Khalid al-Tuwaijiri was behind the idea of the tribal festival. It was also considered a good antidote to the increasing strength of Islamism in Saudi Arabia, which by its nature created a movement that cut across tribal belonging and promised a transnational identity in which solidarity with other Muslims was paramount.

Similar to celebration of the true and authentic Islam of Wahhabism in state religious and educational institutions, which excluded those outside its traditions, the Bedouin and tribal heritage industry of the festival was initially equally narrow. Many Saudis were neither tribal nor Bedouin and were thus left outside the realm of these festivities, which flourished around the tent, the camel, the coffee pot and vernacular poetry celebrating and praising the Al Saud family. Whole regions of the country were initially excluded from the festivals, for example the Hijaz, Asir and the Eastern Province. Their material culture was later incorporated in the festivities. While the festivals were meant to celebrate the tribal heritage, they quickly became an opportunity to promote the Al Saud family and extract loyalty from the tribes on an annual basis.

In the 1990s the festivals were expanded to include celebrations of the diversity of local regional cultures across the kingdom. Important foreign guests from Western and Muslim countries were invited every year to witness the celebrations and engage in wider intellectual and Islamic discussions about modernity and development. Now Saudis look forward to the annual festivals, where they enjoy the displays of local material culture, art and music. At more recent festivals, men and women wave the Saudi flag and dance in specially designated areas to nationalistic music specifically composed for the event. The festival's tribal origin is gradually giving way to the promotion of a diverse cultural tradition beyond tribes and tribalism. But its origin as a tribal festival, associated with the militarized Bedouins, has never totally disappeared. Like all state-sponsored festivities, the Janadiriyyah is also a controversial occasion debated by Saudis.

Saudi Arabia's persistent tribalism, fascination with genealogies and celebration of tribal purity and authenticity are a function of state governance. In fact, all these reinvented concerns reflect how genealogies are part of state governmentality, and concern with tribal authenticity has been institutionalized by the Al Saud rulers. According to Nadav Samin, identification of individuals is done by *muarrif*, Bedouin employees of the Ministry of Interior, whose job was invented in the 1990s to authenticate the tribal pedigrees of Saudi citizens. These authenticators 'came to play important roles in the new Saudi economy, from the validation of citizenship claims to the distribution of state subsidies, to the facilitation of foreign labour imports schemes—they could even influence the composition of the royal family itself'.[15] One can just imagine how the system was open to abuse, especially by influential royal family members who were able to import foreign labour on the basis of false claims about ownership of farms that needed expat labourers. After being granted licences to import labour, they would release the labourers into the economy while receiving a fee from them or their new employers. According to Samin, this abuse was responsible for the surge in foreign labour since the 1990s.

Genealogies are also important for the Al Saud themselves. When Prince Salman was governor of Riyadh (until 2015), he surprised the television audiences of al-Mustaqilla channel, a partly Saudi-sponsored media company based in London at the time and run by Tunisian Muhammad al-Hashimi, when he phoned in to contribute to a heated debate about the Al Saud *nasab*, or genealogy. In 2012 he had offered his own narrative in a letter about the royal family's *nasab*, hoping to establish their origins and gain the authenticity that comes with tribal origin. The special television programme was dedicated to discussion of the multiple versions of the origins of the Al Saud. According to al-Hashimi, many viewers had asked for such a discussion to put an end to an old controversy. The reality may have been that Prince Salman demanded the airing of the programme to end the debate, which had become heated, as the topic was discussed many times on a Saudi dissident channel, al-Islah, under the directorship of Saad al-Faqih. Its Saudi callers ridiculed the Al Saud *nasab* and claimed that the sheer fact that there is ambiguity about who they belong to attests to their lack of tribal origin. Callers denied the Al Saud the right to rule, on the basis of a lack of noble origin or, more importantly, of not belonging to Quraysh tribe of the Prophet Muhammad and the Ashraf, who ruled in the Hijaz until 1925. It was often mentioned on al-Islah that one criterion for the legitimate ruler of the Muslim community is descent from the Prophet's Quraysh tribe. Such statements echoed one of the main criticisms of Juhayman al-Otaibi in 1979, when he occupied the Mecca Mosque and denounced the Al Saud, rejecting their leadership on the basis that they are not descendants of Quraysh. This controversy over the Al Saud's *nasab* is revealing. In a previous publication, I argued that the Al Saud's lack of association with an obvious large tribal confederation is perhaps one of the main reasons that their authority was accepted, albeit with the sword, as they may have been seen as outside the tribal world of Arabia. Consequently, they could play the role of mediators between various tribes, without being overtly associated with one.[16]

Prince Salman, who already had his own interest in the matter with his 2012 statement, entered the debate in the hope of ending the controversy. During his intervention he mentioned two versions of the family's genealogy, claiming that one version states that the Al Saud belonged to the Anayza tribal confederation, while the other narrative says that their ancestors belonged to the Banu Hanifa in central Arabia. He ended the discussion by asserting that the Al Saud are more likely to have been descendants of Banu Hanifa.[17] This went against earlier official publications under his own patronage and sponsorship that favoured the former version, according to Samin.[18] The shift towards the second narrative reflects how tribal genealogies are charters about the past created and manipulated in the present, rather than fixed and unchanging historically accurate statements about identity and belonging. Nevertheless, the ongoing debate reflects the salience of tribal identities and genealogies in the contemporary state.

Notwithstanding the exclusion of the tribes from the apparatus of the state, the tribal ethos is occasionally deployed to score political gains. Recently, the regime resorted to using tribalism in regional conflicts. This surfaced most clearly during the latest dispute with Qatar in 2017 when Saudi Arabia mobilized Saudi tribal groups to compose derogatory Bedouin poetry that not only denounced the Qatari emir but also emphasized his allegedly inauthentic genealogy. Tribal poetry of this kind was recited in special tribal ceremonies, organized for the purpose of condemning Qatar and its emir, Tamim ibn Hamad al-Thani. The Wahhabi Mufti of Saudi Arabia, Abdul Aziz Al-Sheikh, together with 200 members of his family, issued a statement claiming that the Al Thani emir of Qatar does not belong to their family. The statement was published in *Okaz*, an official Saudi newspaper. Both the emir of Qatar and the Al-Sheikh family claim descent from the central Arabian Banu Tamim tribe who populate large settlements in central Arabia and beyond. This is the tribe that produced the founder of the Wahhabi tradition, Muhammad ibn Abd al-Wahhab, whose eighteenth-century alliance with the Al Saud created the kingdom. To negate the tribal origins of the Qatari emir amounts to a serious insult in Arabia, whose population and royalty are proud to flaunt their nobility and tribal ancestry. Tribal festivals mocking the Qatari emir were held within the Saudi border, especially among tribes that had members living in both Saudi Arabia and Qatar, such as the al-Murrah. Tribal vernacular poetry was composed to denounce the origins and achievements of the Qatari enemies. Such poetry quickly degenerates into serious insults and is circulated widely on social media. Denying the Qatari emir a tribal ancestry is insulting in a world that still cherishes imagined genealogies.

This strategy exposes the contradictions of the all-encompassing nationalistic agenda of creating new Saudi citizens out of tribal fragments that are increasingly deployed to fight a media war with Qatar. In the effervescence of tribal wars and poetry, both nationalism and diplomacy sink into oblivion. A mild form of patriotism is acceptable to mobilize citizens, but xenophobia, neo-tribalism and superficial cosmopolitanism are hardly consistent with a neoliberal project to transform Saudi Arabia into a productive cosmopolitan economy, a tolerant, diverse country and an open society, in line with the crown prince's Vision 2030.

The exclusion of tribals from integration in the state apparatus and bureaucracy did not pass without comment and has been the subject of scholarly studies inside the kingdom. Academic Muhammad al-Sunaytan, member of the Hijazi Harb tribe, conducted a survey of top government jobs such as ministers and members of the Consultative Council. He found that the regime excluded the tribals and promoted the sedentary people of the central province, Najd. In his study of beneficiaries of government education scholarships, he found that only sixty-eight tribals obtained such scholarships in one year, compared to hundreds granted to others. In terms of obtaining government licences to launch industrial and financial projects, he also found that tribals had very low success rates, and that the region that obtained most licences was Najd, followed by the Hijaz. State ministers from Najdi families occupied 78 per cent of ministerial jobs, and no tribal was ever promoted to this position.[19] Such conclusions point to the contradictions in Saudi state propaganda, especially the glorification of tribal heritage, which masks a reality where the exclusion of tribes from key state institutions was a constant feature accompanying state consolidation.

People Without Genealogy

The cases of Saudi women whose marriages were annulled by courts for genealogical incompatibility draw attention to how many Saudi citizens are held in low esteem for not having tribal ancestry. The non-tribals are a large category of Arabian society, locally known as *khadiris*. They are people who cannot trace their origins to a major or minor Bedouin tribe, or to sedentary communities such as the Banu Hanifa and Banu Tamim, mentioned earlier. Historically, in the pre-state era, such persons inhabited the oases and towns of Arabia, and may have worked in farming, building and small-scale industries that such settlements needed. They may have also been attached to large tribal confederations, but without forging kinship links with them.

Like all Saudis, *khadiri*s now live in big cities, working in government offices and the private sector, but benefiting largely from expansion in state employment. They may be aware of how tribal groups hold them in low esteem, especially when divorce cases on the basis of incompatible genealogies become hotly debated in the media. Many amongst them denounce the esteem that a tribal identity and genealogy bestow on its holder and call for a return to an egalitarian Islamic ethos in which tribal identity is unimportant compared to Islamic observance and piety. Others invoke equality in citizenship to undermine claims to tribal superiority. Such calls are often not very successful in weakening tribal prestige, as they rely on weak national identity and are less likely to convince tribals that other Saudis are their equals, especially when the state itself encourages tribalism in the administration of the political realm. A non-tribal man still faces humiliation and rejection if he seeks marriage to a tribal woman, whose father and brothers may not give the required permission.

The apparent disadvantage to marriage prospects of not having a tribal origin may not be felt in certain government positions. Being non-tribal can be an asset in certain professions, for example those jobs that the regime does not want to be occupied by tribals because of their sensitivity. The state does not trust a tribal with certain jobs that may become an opportunity to strengthen tribal belonging and empower one tribal group over others. In such situations, a *khadiri* or a member of a loyal sedentary family that has served the Al Saud for generations is often a better choice to counter the empowerment of large tribal groups through employment in government or high positions in the military. In general, the Saudi regime prefers members of the settled Najdi communities, whose tribal origin is very distant and whose ancestors have been settled for centuries, to the extent of partially losing their tribal memory, as trustworthy bureaucrats and military personnel.

Other people in the category of non-tribals include racialized groups such as ex-slaves, often but not always black Africans, whose ancestors were freed in 1962. Those people of colour have often been under-studied in Saudi society. Since ancient times, slave markets flourished in Mecca, Riyadh and Hasa, and many people, both black and white, were traded in Arabia for centuries. Poor Muslim pilgrims from as far as Indonesia often remained in Mecca and Madina after performing the pilgrimage if they could not pay for their journeys home. They were held in bondage locally until they paid their debts, but those who could not do so were sold as slaves in the markets of the Hijaz, while distinguished religious scholars amongst them were integrated in the religious schools of Mecca and Madina.

In the pre-state period, slaves were mainly used as warriors in the households of tribal chiefs, oasis emirs, settled nobility and wealthy merchants. They were the trusted security forces of tribal chiefs, while their women became domestic workers, concubines and milk mothers, nursing children of wealthy families. When slavery was abolished in 1962, slaves of large families were given the option to leave the households of their masters or stay on as wage labourers. Many ex-slaves chose to remain in the service of their masters as they had nowhere to go—at least in the years immediately following the abolition of slavery. Their children benefited from mass education and joined the government bureaucracy in later years, while their elderly parents worked as peddlers in local markets.

The Al Saud princes had a large number of slaves, many of whom have remained in their service. In 2010 the murder of a black man by an Al Saud prince in a five-star London hotel shocked observers, as not many people know the history of slavery in Arabia and the harsh treatment some of them experienced even after they became legally free. Prince Saud Abd al-Aziz ibn Naser al-Saud beat and strangled his servant, Bandar Abd al-Aziz, to death at the culmination of a campaign of 'sadistic' abuse, facing a life sentence after being convicted of murder.[20] After serving several months in prison, the prince was exchanged for several British citizens held in prison in Saudi Arabia according to a prisoner-exchange treaty. The prince was thereafter believed to be serving his life prison sentence in the kingdom, but no confirmation is available. The punishment for murder in Saudi Arabia is execution, but as the crime was committed in London this did not apply. Moreover, it is rare for a Saudi prince to be executed for murder, with most of the known cases being settled by payment of *diyya* to the family of the victim.

It is often reported that many ex-slaves work in prisons as guards and security personnel, and some may have been involved in the torture of detained activists. They are highly visible as private entourage and travel companions of both senior and young princes abroad. The latter surround themselves with their own servants, often descendants of slaves. Poverty levels among those who are not in the service of princes are no doubt higher among people of colour, especially women, who beg in the streets of Mecca, Madina, Jeddah and Riyadh. In the past many such women worked as household servants, coffee makers and cooks, in addition to being singers, dancers at weddings and peddlers. But as most of these professions are now taken by cheap foreign labour, many Saudi ex-slave women find themselves without employment opportunities. In government statements on poverty, it is often reported that beggars are foreign Africans and Asians who stay behind after coming to Mecca to perform the pilgrimage. But many amongst them are local Saudi ex-slave women who in the past would have worked as street traders and household maids. Such deprived persons, together with recently settled Bedouins in the shanty towns and slums of Jeddah, Mecca and Riyadh, resort to charities and social-relief centres to survive. They are often seen joining long queues in Ramadan outside palaces where Islamic *sadaqa* (charitable donations) are often distributed.

Discrimination against people of colour is rife. Sami al-Shaibani, in charge of Snapchat for government security, was filming an award ceremony held for orphaned children of security personnel. He allegedly overlooked black girls standing in line to receive the award, and instead focused the camera on the fair-skinned girls. The video clip went viral online and was hotly debated, with many Saudi commentators condemning al-Shaibani.[21] Such incidents are now publicized on social media where many Saudis engage in heated debates about racism, exclusion and poverty.

This racism is even more prevalent when it comes to marriage. Children born to mixed marriages with slave women are considered less worthy of respect, as they have 'contaminated' genealogies. Prince Bandar ibn Sultan is believed to be such a case, as he was born to a slave mother. He was sent to Washington as the Saudi ambassador, where he developed his career and strengthened the Saudi–US partnership for over two decades. However, his 'half-caste' status remained a contentious aspect of his identity, often mentioned by his critics and rivals to discredit him. Nevertheless, he was trusted by King Fahd and later kings to play a key role in promoting Saudi–US relations. He thrived abroad and became important; neither would have been possible had he remained in Saudi Arabia among other princes claiming a purer descent. Similarly, Prince Muqrin ibn Abd al-Aziz was appointed deputy crown prince by King Abdullah. His rivals always reminded others of his mother's slave origin—she was a Yemeni concubine. In 2015 King Salman sacked Muqrin and appointed Muhammad ibn Nayif as crown prince. Ibn Nayif was then replaced as crown prince by Salman's son Muhammad in 2017. However, Muqrin was not sacked because of his mixed ancestry, although this may have contributed to excluding him as a potential monarch. The main reason behind his marginalization was the fact that King Salman wanted to promote his own son to inherit the throne. The throne is now secured in the hands of a second-generation prince whose ancestry on the side of both his father and his mother, Fahda bint ibn Huthlayn, a descendant of the chief of the al-Ajman tribe, is believed to be noble.

Religious Minorities

As the foundation of the Saudi state was legitimized by Wahhabi discourse on the basis of returning the Arabian population to true Islam, the religious beliefs and practices of many Arabian Muslims inevitably became controversial. Different religious practices were denounced, and even banned, across the territories that became Saudi Arabia. The intolerance towards mainstream Sunni Muslims and minorities was embedded in the theology of the Wahhabi movement and enforced by the policing agencies of the Saudi state. In addition to other Sunni Muslims, two religious minorities, the Shia and the Ismailis, were most affected by sectarian and exclusionary Wahhabi theology. While Sunni Muslims, with the exception of Sufis, were incorporated within the realm of Wahhabi Islam, religious sects such as the Shia developed outside its reach and in opposition to its domination over the religious field in Arabia, thus leading to sectarian tensions over the last century.

Among the Shia, a political movement emerged and consolidated itself by demanding both religious freedom and political equality. The fact that most of the Shia lived in the oil-rich Eastern Province gave their opposition to the regime a regional focus. However, sectarianism in Saudi Arabia is not a simple product of historical animosities, obvious exclusion or persistent discrimination, although these experiences augmented confrontations with the state and its religious clerics. As argued by Sultan al-Amer, both sectarianism and regionalism are nourished by state policies that divided Saudi Arabia into clear administrative provinces. The protest and collective action that had been consistent in the Eastern Province among the Shia, and for that matter the central Qasim region among the Sunnis, is a function of the mobilization of intellectuals in both areas who engage in defining their communities and fixing their regional identities. The protest of the Shia took the politics of identity to its logical conclusion, by demanding rights on the basis of a history of discrimination against them, all articulated by intellectuals in Awamiyya, Qatif and other small towns. In both Qatif in the east and Buraydah in the centre of the country, regional identities played an important role in mobilization.[22] However, while the Shia were truly excluded and discriminated against, the Qasim region, where Buraydah is, has provided both religious and bureaucratic services to the state of the Al Saud since its foundation. As a result, it is perhaps inaccurate to compare the two regions, except in terms of their potential for generating well-organized protest against the Saudi state, with the understanding that they share few characteristics in other areas of political life and engagement with the state.

From its very beginning, the project of Wahhabism was to correct the religious practices of Sunnis, especially those deemed blasphemous, and to convert those Muslim minorities deemed non-Muslims to the right path. Wahhabism considered folkloric Sunni Bedouin religious practices a manifestation of their ignorance and lack of commitment to Islam. Its religious scholars condemned tribal Bedouin religiosity and endeavoured to eradicate sacred sites, trees and tombs, in addition to fertility and healing practices associated with ancient unorthodox religious beliefs.

In the Hijaz, a clash with Sufism and Sunni schools of Islamic jurisprudence other than the Hanbali school favoured by the Wahhabis became inevitable from the moment the region was incorporated in the Saudi realm. Tomb visiting and intercession were banned by the new religious clerics who came with the expansion of the state into the Hijaz. Manifestations of Sufi *tariqa*s, or paths associated with known Sufi traditions; the annual celebration of the Prophet's birth; *dhikr*, or recitations accompanied by chants and music; and many other rituals were rejected and banned by the new religious overlords of the Hijaz. Such harsh bans on religious diversity in the Hijaz, which had absorbed many sects, nationalities and ethnic and racial groups, failed to eradicate what the Wahhabis regarded as unorthodoxy. Nevertheless, Wahhabism succeeded in eliminating the public display of religious diversity. According to Hijazi anthropologist Mai Yamani, the overt expression of identity and religious rituals of the old Hijazi families in Mecca and Madina were suppressed, and a uniform dress code was imposed on those in public civil service.[23] Religious differences simply went underground and, if discovered, were often severely punished.

Sheikh Muhammad Alawi al-Maliki (1944–2004) was a prominent Hijazi Sufi of the Shathiliyya Sufi *tariqa* (order). In 1979 a fatwa circulated declaring him a non-believer. The regime sacked him from his teaching position:

> [He was] banned from giving lessons at the Grand Mosque, where both his father and grandfather had taught, and interrogated by the religious police and the Interior Ministry. Maliki was later attacked by a throng of radicals incensed at his presence in the mosque, he could pray there only under armed guard. Meanwhile, thousands of cassettes and booklets circulated calling Sufis 'grave-lovers' and dangerous infidels who had to be stopped before they made a comeback.[24]

The sheikh was released from prison in 2003, but he died in 2004. It was reported that Crown Prince Abdullah came to offer his condolences at his funeral in an attempt to honour the Sufi leader in front of his mourning followers. Their spiritual leader had received harsh treatment simply because he was the leader of a Sufi order.

Punishment for religious differences and folkloric Islam among the diverse indigenous population of Arabia and the immigrants who had settled in it for decades, dubbed deviations from true Islam or *bida* (innovations), can be extremely harsh, in some cases resulting in execution. From its early days the Wahhabi movement showed no tolerance towards culturally infused Islamic practices, especially those healing traditions practised by women in Arabia for centuries.[25] In recent times the intolerance and severe punishment of religious difference is reflected in the Saudi record on the beheading of people, often African and Asian immigrants, charged with sorcery, witchcraft and healing practices that do not conform to the Wahhabi definition of true and pure Islam or Prophet-inspired healing practices.

Theological diversity within Sunni Islam was also regarded as a threat and an aberration of true faith at a higher level. The Hijaz was known for the diversity of its Sunni schools of jurisprudence, where Malikis, Shafi'is, Hanafis and Hanbalis coexisted in Mecca. Their special *madrasas* taught their doctrines and theology, but after 1925 it was difficult to acknowledge this diversity, as the imposition of one *madhhab* (school of jurisprudence) in the legal system became the norm. The Wahhabis rejected the other *madhhabs* and prioritized Islamic texts such as the Quran, the Prophetic tradition and the sayings of the righteous *salaf* (early Muslims). Non-Wahhabi religious scholars were marginalized in favour of the new religious elite, preachers, imams and judges originating from the central province of Arabia. In 1971, when King Faisal established the Council of Higher Ulama, headed by Grand Mufti Muhammad ibn Ibrahim, hardly any non-Najdi or non-Hanbali religious scholars were appointed. Between 1971 and 2010 the Council of Higher Ulama consisted of 73 per cent Najdis, 9 per cent Hijazis, 6 per cent Asiris and Jizanis, 4 per cent Ahsais, and 7 per cent naturalized foreigners.[26] The predominance of Najdi scholars, a reflection of the regional homeland of the Wahhabi movement, continued until very recently. The regime had always resisted the inclusion of Shia clerics, and there is no representation of the Shia Jaafari school of jurisprudence at this high level of religious bureaucracy.

The Shia

The Shia of Saudi Arabia are the largest religious minority, estimated at around 2 million. Their main regional presence is in the Eastern Province, with a small group, known as Nakhawla, living in Madina. As mentioned in Chapter 1, Ibn Saud expanded in the eastern region as early as 1913, and since then the community has felt the pressure of Saudi–Wahhabi domination. Although they benefited from the expansion of the oil industry in their own region and employment opportunities in the Saudi oil company Aramco, the community has been the most politically active in modern Saudi history, a reflection of a deep sense of exclusion and discrimination.

The oil industry brought foreigners, both Arabs and others, to the Eastern Province, where the fertilization of political ideas, movements and people started as early as the 1940s. The Shia became very active in the Arab nationalist, socialist and communist movements that spread among Aramco workers in the 1950s and 1960s.[27] They were responsive to such political ideas because of a certain level of awareness, prompted by their marginalization as a religious sect in Saudi Arabia and the constant anti-Shia rhetoric of Wahhabi scholars.

Fatwas by Wahhabi scholars dissuading true Muslims from eating meat butchered by Shia butchers and prohibiting marrying into the community were notorious.[28] In anthologies of Wahhabi fatwas, the clerics outlaw marriage to a Shia, and if such a marriage takes place it should be annulled, lest the person commit great *shirk* (blasphemy). The religious purity of the pious Sunni nation needed to be guarded against contamination by the Shia, thus keeping the boundaries between faith and blasphemy well demarcated.[29] Harsh condemnation of the Shia in the Saudi religious curriculum creates hostility and animosity, not to mention the development of strong feelings of being excluded from, initially, the religious nation, the Muslim transnational *umma*, and now the new Saudi nation under the auspices of Crown Prince Muhammad ibn Salman. The slight easing of sectarian tension during King Abdullah's time—when Shia clerics were invited to participate in National Dialogue Forums, scholarships were granted to many Shia youth to study abroad, and rhetoric about religious tolerance was promoted—is now a thing of the past.

A turning-point in the regime's relations with the Shia was the execution in 2016 of Shia cleric Nimr al-Nimr, who led peaceful demonstrations against the regime's exclusionary policies during the Arab uprisings in 2011. The execution followed several years of confrontation between the regime forces and young Shia activists, who had been inspired by the Arab uprisings and expressed overt solidarity with their Shia brethren across the causeway in Bahrain. The clashes led to several deaths in Awamiyya and Qatif, two main towns where mobilization and demonstrations occurred regularly. As Saudi relations with Iran became very tense from 2011, the return of the regime's confrontational policies amounted to imposing a state of siege on these towns and the presence of heavily armed military and police forces around them on a permanent basis. The ongoing demonstrations prompted the regime to demolish old neighbourhoods in 2017–18 and construct new development projects, as the old parts of the Shia areas were believed to be hotbeds of subversive activities and youth agitations.

In 2019 a further thirty-three Shia activists, amongst them religious scholars, intellectuals and young persons, were executed, supporting the narrative about the regime's discrimination against the Shia and their exclusion from the boundaries of the nation. Saudi–Iranian relations had deteriorated further after the execution of Sheikh Nimr; the Iranians retaliated by attacking the Saudi embassy in Tehran. The Shia remain a 'suspect' community in Saudi Arabia, whose loyalty to the country is always doubted. The politicization of sectarian identities is destined to continue as long as full citizenship is lacking in Saudi Arabia. The Shia region consequently continues to produce intellectuals and writers[30] whose work promotes identity politics and calls for equality in response to decades of exclusion and discrimination.[31]

Discrimination on religious grounds meant that for a long time the community was not allowed to build its own mosques and *husayniyya*, where the Shia mourning rituals of Ashura in memory of the Shia Imams are held, and could not obtain land from municipalities for Shia burial. Until the 1990s there was a ban on public mourning rituals outside designated areas. While discrimination on religious grounds was scaled down and a kind of recognition of discrete religious practices has been allowed in Shia residential areas since the 1990s, many Shia intellectuals and activists still feel marginalized and discriminated against. Their leaders in exile, such as Hamza al-Hassan, Ali al-Ahmad and Fuad Ibrahim, constantly remind audiences of how the Shia cannot reach high positions in government bureaucracy, educational institutions and the military. The Shia are also overrepresented in the large number of executions by the regime.

A young generation of Shia activists find refuge in exile, where they focus on human rights issues and document serious and systematic abuse by the Saudi authorities. They include Hani Abandi, Taha al-Hijji and Ali Dubaisi, among many others scattered in the USA, Europe and the Middle East. This has coincided with a new phase in Saudi–Shia relations. The decision of Crown Prince Muhammad ibn Salman to curb the powers of the religious police and the Wahhabi clerics was welcomed. According to Taha al-Hijji, a Hasawi lawyer in exile in Germany since 2016:

The Shia welcomed the cessation of hate speech by clerics and of the harassment of the religious police in Shia areas. The Shia wanted to give the crown prince the benefit of doubt. They also welcomed the change in the education curriculum in which the Shia had always been denounced as outside Islam. Yet the reality of the situation on the ground in Shia areas remained bad and tense with security forces raiding Awamiyya, Qatif and other Shia towns. Many Shia clerics, intellectuals and ex-activists thought they could engage with the regime to improve the situation, but now they face the reality as the regime continues to blame the Shia for all sorts of problems. We are always blamed for trouble and regarded as clients of Iran. We are Saudis and Iran may not care too much about us. During every crisis with Iran, we hear Saudi voices accusing us of being followers of Iran and even accusing us of destabilizing Saudi Arabia on its behalf. We pay the price for the rivalry between the two countries. All we want is equality and inclusion. The regime created 'Shia notables' to co-opt them and show that it is inclusive. As a lawyer I defended members of the so-called spying cell, accused of spying for Iran. I initially agreed to defend them when no lawyer would dare take the cases, but later I realized that working as a lawyer on their behalf legitimized the regime, its courts and judiciary. I left the country in 2016 as it was evident that I would be arrested with my clients. I established Adala, a human rights forum, and the application to license it was rejected by the Ministry of Interior. In April 2019 the regime executed all the accused. Their execution was simply carried out to spread fear and intimidation. In all situations, we are used as a card to blame for Saudi security problems.[32]

Under Muhammad ibn Salman, Ashura mourning rituals are now allowed in Shia towns, but according to a dissident in exile:

> The ritual is emptied of its most important message, namely rejection of repression and injustice. Every year, Shia notables are summoned to the municipalities to be told to keep Ashura as a low-key ceremony and [that] any transgression will be severely punished. We obey the orders, but I don't see improvement in our economic situation, and the regime continues to execute young activists. It does not even return their bodies to their relatives so that they can bury them according to our own tradition.[33]

Since the 1970s, and in response to Shia mobilization and activism, Western scholarly work on the Shia of the Eastern Province has grown steadily. This literature was driven by concern over the security and stability of the Eastern Province region, where there are oil reserves, and where the majority of the Shia live. After 1979, literature on the Shia increased in depth and magnitude as the region witnessed an uprising, dubbed *intifadat al-mintaqa al-sharqiyya* (the uprising of the Eastern Province). Many in the West feared that the Iranian revolution had precipitated increased Shia agitation and mobilization. While the Shia were politically active before the Iranian revolution, Western allies of the regime failed to acknowledge that the Eastern Province had been the first in Saudi Arabia to develop the modern political awareness lacking in other regions. Nevertheless, a persistent narrative about the impact of the Iranian revolution on the Shia continues to be held both outside and inside Saudi Arabia.

Intellectuals, religious scholars and activists in the Eastern Province produced abundant literature on themselves even before the Iranian revolution. Amongst the Shia were Arab nationalists, such as the Baathist Ali Ghannam, the leftist Ali al-Awami, and Islamists Tawfiq al-Saif, Hamza al-Hassan and Sheikh Hasan al-Safar. A certain concern with Shia identity, religious discrimination and political marginalization led to a focus on Shia heritage and Arab identity, history, culture and religious rituals for over half a century. Consequently, the Shia have greater visibility not only in Western literature on Saudi Arabia but also in the work of their own intellectuals and scholars.

The Makrami Ismailis

While the Shia of Saudi Arabia have been highly visible and very active for several decades as an organized opposition to the regime, another Shia sect, the Makrami Ismailis of the Yam and Hamadan tribes of Najran on the southern border with Yemen, remained quiet until very recently and have attracted almost no scholarly attention. The Makrami Ismailis of Najran Province are barely studied by outsiders or local intellectuals. Their agricultural region is truly the remotest southern backyard of Saudi Arabia. It was and is still geographically, economically, socially and politically peripheral. It is almost 1,000 kilometres southwest of Riyadh, with a population of 400,000 people. The region suffers from underdevelopment and lack of services. In 2019 it was reported that lengthy power cuts threatened the lives of patients in local hospitals. The province's significance arises only in the context of discussion of Saudi–Yemeni relations, contested Saudi borders, the deportation of Ismailis to other regions away from the Saudi–Yemeni border, populating the province with recently naturalized Sunni Yemenis to render the Ismailis a minority in their own region, and as an example of general acute discrimination against minorities in the kingdom.

The Saudi regime always wanted to empty this region of its ancient Ismaili inhabitants, especially those regarded as remote from the true beliefs of Saudi Islam and close to the Zaydi Yemenis on the other side of the border. Deportations are accompanied by systematic and successful campaigns to fragment the community into four groups, each with its own religious leadership, thus undermining the consolidation of a unified religious minority group. According to Abu Hadi al-Yami, an Ismaili activist abroad:

> The Ministry of Interior created hatred and animosity between the four Makrami groups to the extent that the community is turned against its own members, who are threatened with elimination and violence. As Najran is considered a security zone, the ministry rushed to build hundreds of mosques, Quran recitation houses, charitable foundations and religious competitions in order to facilitate conversion to Wahhabi Islam. The objective is to create a popular army from the Yam tribe to be the first line of defence against any Yemeni intrusions and threats. There is also a campaign to confiscate agricultural land to build Wahhabi mosques where constant insults against the Ismailis are announced after each prayer.[34]

The University of Najran is described as a hotbed of radical Salafism. Abu Hadi claims that 'the state is absent and al-Qaida is present in Najran', listing several individuals and religious institutions set up in the region to host radical Salafi preachers:

> The government brought a large cohort of the most radical Salafis and *takfiris* to teach at Najran University. So while the government claims to fight al-Qaida and ISIS elsewhere, Najran University is a hotbed for their ideas. The university ignores other academic subjects and instead focuses on sharia and creed studies. The university and the region have become a Qandahar under the fragmentation of the Yam tribe, which cannot stage resistance against the government Wahhabization policy.

According to Abu Hadi, radicals born in Najran and indoctrinated in the Wahhabi religious and charitable centres set up in the region are overrepresented among Salafi Fath al-Islam radicals in Lebanon. He names several Najran-born recruits; amongst them are Muhammad Yahya Shayba (b. 1983), Talal al-Saiyari (b. 1984), Mubarak al-Kurbi (b. 1986) and Ali al-Hmami (b. 1984).

Ismailis always complain that they are forced to migrate to the north, as government jobs in Najran are predominantly given to non-Ismailis. This indicates a systematic policy of forced migration, where Ismailis must move in search of jobs away from their historical home and spiritual centre, the Khushaiwa, where their supreme religious and spiritual leader, *al-daiyya al-mutlaq*, resides. If the Saudi Shia are considered 'the Other Saudis',[35] then the Ismailis qualify as 'the other other', far beyond the parameters of true Muslims.

Sectarianism prevails in Saudi religious discourse about the Ismailis of Najran, as they are considered a secret cult belonging to the Batiniyya, a sub-branch of the so-called *rafida* (rejectors), as the Shia are pejoratively known. Fatwas by senior Saudi clerics such as al-Lohaydan, denouncing them as infidels, are notorious. But with the advent of internet forums, religious rulings against the Ismailis find a new accessible niche for all others to read and 'benefit' from.

Muntada Hawamer al-Boursa al-Saoudiyya, an internet forum concerned with economic and financial issues, published the most bigoted interpretation of Ismaili beliefs and history. It posted the opinion of Sheikh Mamdouh al-Harbi:

> [To] enlighten the people of *sunna wa al-jamaa* (Sunnis), of their [Ismaili] secret beliefs and books that only their religious scholars are allowed to read. The people cannot examine their creed books because they contain a lot of *kufr bawah* (utter blasphemy). To enlighten Sunnis about these secret beliefs, we refer you to the lecture of Sheikh Mamdouh al-Harbi, entitled 'al-Rafidah al-Ismailiyya al-batiniyya: Makarimat Najran'.[36]

Intense 'conversion' campaigns are constant features of how Saudi authorities and their religious scholars deal with the Ismailis. Wahhabi clerics regularly hold lectures in Najran with the objective of demonstrating the *dhalal* (corruption) of the Ismaili creed, hoping to lead them to the right path of true Islam. This intense

Wahhabi campaign in Najran Province prompted a member of the community to tweet that converting the Ismailis is futile, as '*dhalal* is truly what they, the Wahhabis, believe in'.[37]

While current conversion campaigns may not lead Ismailis to abandon their faith in great numbers and convert to Wahhabi Islam, Sheikh al-Harbi mentions that some members of the Yam tribe had responded to the call for monotheism (*tawhid*) by the Saudi leadership. He reminds his audiences that during the Saudi expansion into Najran early in the twentieth century, Majhud, leader of the al-Arja lineage of the Ismaili Yam tribe, was captured in battle and taken to Riyadh. He was subjected to intensive preaching and, perhaps under duress, eventually converted to Sunni Islam. Later, he was able to convert three further lineages of the Yam tribe.

A general denunciation of Ismaili beliefs is in line with the Wahhabi sectarian outlook, in which other Muslims are regarded as outside the realm of true Islam. They are considered corrupt in their creed, believers in sorcery and as seeking *tawasul* (intercession) from jinn and the devil. The Ismailis cannot be trusted as they, like all other Shia, practise *taqiyya* (dissimulation), in Sheikh al-Harbi's view. There are restrictions on the building of their own mosques, often referred to as temples rather than mosques, thus emphasizing their existence outside the true Muslim *umma*.

In April 2000, a military confrontation between armed Ismailis and security forces outside the Najran Holiday Inn hotel, where province governor Prince Mishal ibn Saud al-Saud was staying, brought attention to this community and the systematic discrimination to which it had been subjected. As early as 1999, Ismailis became aware of the Ministry of Interior's plan to close down their main mosque and another twenty mosques on the day they celebrate Id al-Fitr, which normally does not correspond to the official Saudi date for the same celebration. According to a Human Rights Watch report in 2008:

Ismaili men erected defenses around Khushaiwa, the seat of the Ismaili religious leader, *al-Da'i al-Mutlaq* (Absolute Guide), and the spiritual capital of Sulaimani Ismailis, a community with followers in India and Pakistan as well as Saudi Arabia and Yemen. Khushaiwa, which is an area of Najran city, includes the Mansura mosque complex. The army surrounded the Ismaili positions and placed the city under its control. The standoff ended later the same day without further bloodshed.[38]

When security forces came to arrest Muhammad al-Khayat, a religious cleric of Yemeni origin, clashes with the students in his *madrasa* erupted, resulting in injuries but no fatalities. Crowds of demonstrators headed towards the Holiday Inn to meet with the governor, but he refused to grant them an audience. Others joined the demonstration, which prompted army units stationed nearby to intervene. This was followed by around 500 arrests (including of Ismailis working in the police force and civil service), torture during interrogation, secret trials and death sentences.[39]

Many Ismaili prisoners were later pardoned by King Abdullah, and the governor was sacked. After these dramatic events, which represented an unexpected eruption of Ismaili grievances against systematic Saudi discrimination, many Ismaili employees, especially policemen, border guards and intelligence officers, were transferred to other cities, some as far as Tabuk in the north. Following this move, many Ismailis resigned from their jobs in government bureaucracy. It was estimated that 1,000 employees lost their jobs in a region with one of the highest unemployment rates in Saudi Arabia, amounting to 40 per cent.[40] Tribal sheikhs who spoke to the media after the riots were arrested, including Sheikh Ahmad bin Turki al-S'ab. He was released after his health deteriorated in detention.

When Saudi Arabia started its airstrikes on Yemen in 2015, the situation in Najran worsened as the province became increasingly securitized. According to Abu Hadi:

The community is caught between two fires: on one side there is the repression of the Al Saud. On the other side there are the Salafi radicals imported by the regime and settled in the region. So the government wants us to submit to its control as we become fearful of the alternative, namely al-Qaida and ISIS.

Government intelligence reports accuse us of being sympathetic to the Yemenis and [say that] this is why the war has not succeeded in the southern province. But the main reason is the failure of the Saudi army, not us. The war affected us badly. Education stopped and was later resumed electronically. Stagnation of the local economy is so bad. People living on the most southern border in Saqam, al-Sharfa, Khabash, Nahouka, al-Zur and al-Humr fled to the north, but they found no appropriate shelter and camps. Another reason for leaving the region is the constant harassment of women and children by soldiers and mercenaries stationed in our area. The Saudi army considers Ismailis as *rafida*, loyal to the Houthis in Yemen. People hear that it is permissible to take our women as *sabaya*, captives, as they consider us non-Muslims. Anybody who calls for our rights disappears in prison. Some families went to live with their relatives in Jeddah and the Eastern Province, but they returned as they cannot stay there forever. They have no money to rent houses elsewhere. The government put tanks, rocket launchers and military equipment in residential areas. Its foreign mercenaries are hosted in schools since the beginning of the war.[41]

Abu Hadi's account of how the war in Yemen is fought as a jihadi project, with Wahhabi preachers mobilizing soldiers on the basis of the duty to fight the *rafida* Zaydi Houthis, is confirmed by a 2019 Carnegie report:

The Ministry of Islamic Affairs organized a training course for imams near the border on how to counter Houthi 'doctrine', promote the 'doctrine of monotheism', and advance the 'features of Sheikh Mohammed Ibn Abdul Wahab's proselytism'. Saudi soldiers have been designated nationally as Al-Murabitoun (Sentinels), a religious reference to the high status and rewarding of soldiers protecting borders against breaches (*thoghour*) by infiltrators. Protection of the kingdom is regularly equated with 'jihad' in defense of the 'doctrine', 'Muslims', and the 'the land of the two holy mosques'. Zaydi Houthis are identified as 'majus', the term for Zoroastrians, therefore non-Muslims. They are also called 'moushrikin', or polytheists, with historical and religious ties to the 'safawis', in reference to the Persian Safavids, and 'rafidah' meaning rejectionists, a reference to the Twelver Shi'a.[42]

The contradiction between the regime's promise to promote moderate Islam as part of the crown prince's National Transformation Programme and the jihadi mobilization of Saudi soldiers and the population in the south shows up clearly on the border with Yemen, with the Ismailis caught between the two, as described by Abu Hadi.

The shadow of the 2015 Yemen war on the border and in Ismaili territories led to further tight security measures and deportations under the pretext of creating safe zones for residents. Houthi missiles launched from the other side of the border or as a result of occasional penetration of the porous Saudi–Yemeni frontier aggravated the situation in this already deprived province. But the new governor of Najran, Abdul Aziz ibn Juluwi, and his deputy, Turki ibn Huthloul, have tried to reach out to the Yam tribal chiefs, showing willingness to meet with them on a regular basis. According to Abu Hadi:

> Meetings with sheikhs like Ibn Munif, Ibn Nasib and Abu Saq became common; the government realized how weak it is in the war on Yemen so it started to bribe the tribal chiefs, giving them donations and royal gifts. These visits resulted in creating military units, *fawj*, as the first Saudi line of ground defence against the Houthis. The government used the chiefs to its own advantage. Also, it used the poverty and unemployment of the *shabab*, the youth, to recruit them.[43]

Like tribal groups, religious minorities are subject to the regime's policy of divide and rule. Selected tribal chiefs and minority religious leaders are often promoted to jobs that make them visible to both their own community and others. They become mediators between their own group and the state in a personalized manner and in the absence of institutional means to deal with grievances and demands for better living conditions, respect for human rights and full integration into the country. Such appointed leaders are meant to control their tribe's behaviour and their religious community, in most cases both serving the interest of the state and enriching themselves. When demonstrations erupt in Shia areas and among Ismailis, such appointed mediators are quickly summoned by local governors or the Ministry of Interior to calm the situation. The regime uses them to convey messages and denounce the behaviour of their own members, should the latter go into the streets and demonstrate. When a member of their group criticizes the regime or mobilizes people to stage demonstrations, these appointed leaders are put under pressure to issue a declaration that the whole tribe or the religious minority group must dissociate themselves from such defiant acts by their own members. In the long term, such leaders fail in most cases to improve relations between local government and central state agencies and their own communities. The examples of local Shia leaders who are promoted as members of municipal councils and religious leaders attest to the limitations of the regime's policy of reaching out to selected members of these diverse and excluded communities, who continue to feel that they are not full members of the Saudi nation.

Non-Nationals: Foreign Labour and Expats

In 2017 Saudi Arabia had over 12 million non-national residents, rendering it the second-highest remittance-sending country and among the top five migrant destination countries worldwide.[44] The story of migration to Saudi Arabia had been told by both demographers and political economists. In the late 2010s, the plight of immigrants became a hotly debated topic among human rights activists and organizations, as many face serious abuse, especially those who work in the domestic sphere.[45] Others, such as construction workers, stage minor demonstrations when their salaries have not been paid for several months—for example, the workers of the Binladin construction company after 2014 when oil prices collapsed, resulting in government projects being put on hold or cancelled altogether. However, it is a mistake to lump together all foreign labour under one category of non-nationals. The foreign cohort must be divided into sub-categories to understand the experience of being an expat or a manual worker in Saudi Arabia, a status that many aspire to but others loathe and cannot wait to escape.

John (pseudonym) was a young and creative British employee of a British firm of architects. He was posted to Saudi Arabia during King Abdullah's time to help with designing an important complex of government buildings. He lived and worked in Saudi Arabia for eight years, during which he fell in love with Jawahir (pseudonym), an educated Saudi girl belonging to one of the major tribes of the country. John and Jawahir had an intimate relationship for several years and intended to marry after he converted to Islam. Jawahir planned to go to London with him and continue her education at one of the British universities. She had already secured a place on a course in preparation for starting a new life with John away from Saudi Arabia.

News about this 'forbidden love' reached her father, who vehemently objected to the relationship and the proposed marriage. The father was uncompromising and, after several abusive encounters with him, she escaped to a state-run shelter, where she remained, as she feared that her father might kill her. In the meantime, John's contract with his employer finished, and he was expected to leave the country immediately after his visa expired. He had to fly back to London without his lover, whom

he described as 'an amazing woman, so intelligent, and so lov-
ing of life and what it has to offer'. For several months John
lost contact with Jawahir, but he never gave up on finding a
way for her to leave the country and join him in Britain. This
proved to be more complicated than he had anticipated. With
her passport confiscated by her father, Jawahir was not able to
leave the shelter, let alone travel outside the country. After
spending a long time isolated in the shelter, she was finally
allowed to leave without her father coming to sign the required
forms for her release. With great difficulty, she rented a flat in
Riyadh, where she found a job. In the meantime, John set up
an online campaign to draw attention to her case. He started a
Twitter account and relayed information on the plight of
Jawahir, who kept in contact with him after she left the shelter.
In 2019, Jawahir was still trying to leave Saudi Arabia and
marry John, but without success.[46]

The story of John and Jawahir's forbidden love moves us away
from a discussion of expatriates in Saudi Arabia that generally
focuses on labour markets, economic outlook, the *kafala* (sponsorship) system, Saudization programmes (*tawtin*), loss of remittances, and the isolated and opulent Western expat lifestyle
behind the high walls and security barriers of luxury compounds
in major Saudi cities. In 2003–8 several compounds were targeted
by al-Qaida operatives, who killed many Westerners, Arabs and
Saudis. Their motto at the time was 'remove infidels from the
Arabian Peninsula', and they launched a terror campaign with
bombs and beheadings, images of which were posted online at
the height of the crisis.[47] The presence of Westerners in the
country had always been controversial. Saudis resent foreigners
allegedly taking their jobs, while the government regards them
as a necessary evil in the absence of a qualified Saudi labour force.

While the current ultra-nationalist discourse depicts foreigners as responsible for all economic ills, and even for corrupting

the morality of the nation, and considers Saudis of foreign ancestry as a mafia controlling the economy, the forbidden love of
John and Jawahir shows how some Saudis cross these boundaries
at a very high risk to their own lives. It points to how difficult it
is to maintain the boundaries between Saudis and *ajanib* (foreigners), a high percentage of whom work inside Saudi homes as
maids, drivers and estate keepers. As more and more Saudi
women work in mixed offices where expatriate men are present,
cases of forbidden love are bound to become common.

John was lucky to belong to that category of expats that the
Saudi regime would think twice about severely punishing for
crossing the social and religious boundaries.[48] He was also lucky
not to be at the receiving end of the wrath of Jawahir's father and
brothers, who might have been tempted to take the law into their
own hands and punish him for violating the reputation and honour of their tribal daughter. When Westerners transgress, they
are likely to be put in prison and tortured, but, unlike poor
African, Asian and Arab immigrants, beheading is not so readily
inflicted on them. The case of six Westerners who were arrested
and accused of starting a bombing campaign in 2000 as part of
alleged in-fighting between various gangs, who made alcohol and
sold it to Western residential compounds, reveals how the Saudi
authorities deal with crimes by Westerners.[49] The expats were
held at the infamous al-Hair prison in Riyadh, where they were,
according to their own testimony, subjected to torture. After
over two years in prison, they received clemency. The allegations
against them were dropped, as the bombing campaign might in
fact have been part of al-Qaida's intensive terrorism attacks on
Western compounds. It took several bombing campaigns for the
Saudi authorities to admit that it had a terrorist problem on its
doorstep. Blaming foreigners is always a readily available way of
avoiding admitting responsibility for indigenous terrorists.

Western expatriates constitute the top hierarchy of foreign
labour in Saudi Arabia. They include US, Canadian, Australian

and European citizens who work in military, oil, medical, financial and educational institutions, in addition to construction and the recently launched creative industries such as entertainment, heritage foundations, tourism and the state-sponsored English media. Many Westerners are seen as 'experts', held in esteem and raised above local Saudis, who are believed to be unable to engage in creative strategic thinking. As in other Gulf countries, Crown Prince Muhammad ibn Salman relies heavily on Western consultants, who open franchises in the country or run Saudi projects from nearby Dubai. The prince's Vision 2030 was the product of an expensive project run by a prestigious and controversial management-consultancy firm.[50] It is often believed that Western expertise and strategic advice are more valued than the opinions of local civil servants. Since 2017 Saudi Arabia has dramatically increased its spending on Western consultancy firms, who not only advise on economic and financial matters but are also enlisted to provide consultations on social and cultural projects, such as building national consciousness, creating entrepreneurial culture and launching women's social services ministries. While management-consultancy firms are often associated with advice related to privatization, diversification and cutting welfare subsidies, in Saudi Arabia their mandate goes far beyond these traditional areas of restructuring the economy in the post-oil era.

The post of Western 'expert' is a lucrative job enjoyed by a large number of expatriates who are paid high, untaxed salaries and compensated with lavish services and benefits. They are part of a Western global elite, including oil men educated at esteemed US and European business schools and universities who are shipped off to Saudi Arabia or Dubai to lead projects they are not always competent to manage. Their local knowledge tends to be shallow, and they rely on ready-made blueprints for economic restructuring without serious consideration of the complex local contexts in which civil servants, bureaucrats and royalty coexist in an opaque economy and in very unequal relationships. In 2017 the crown prince was advised by consultants to cut fuel and energy subsidies and freeze employment in the public sector, among other restructuring initiatives. He later backtracked when serious opposition from society, most of it expressed on social media, intensified, leading his popularity to decrease in the eyes of the youth whom he wants to empower. He did not want his name to be associated with austerity programmes.[51]

In 2019 the government passed a new *iqama* (residency) law—the Green Card scheme for wealthy foreigners who are willing to bring investment to Saudi Arabia—in an attempt to attract foreign capital. The law was approved by the Consultative Council in May 2019. The Green Card allows foreign nationals, mainly investors and entrepreneurs, to obtain special residence status without the obligation to have a Saudi sponsor, and to own property and businesses if they meet special criteria. The holder of such a privileged card will have 'family status, can recruit workers, own property and transport in the kingdom. He can also obtain visit visas to relatives, can freely enter and exit the country and will also have the use of designated queues at airports.'[52] However, if the financial and economic reasons for residing in Saudi Arabia lead to more intimate encounters with Saudi women, the consequences can be serious, as the case of John and Jawahir demonstrates. A Saudi man, by contrast, would not be subjected to punishment should he fall in love with a Western woman and marry her in Saudi Arabia.

Many Western expat women married to Saudi men become cheerleaders for the new reforms of Muhammad ibn Salman, as do many foreign academics teaching at Saudi universities. They applaud the reforms, and many have taken it upon themselves to promote tourism in Saudi Arabia by visiting and photographing heritage and archaeological sites, then posting images on social media. In 2018 Laura Alho, a Finnish woman living in

Saudi Arabia, engaged in intensive online promotion of Saudi tourism, outraging many Saudi women in exile, as many women activists were still detained.[53] Amani al-Ahmadi, a Saudi woman living in exile, criticized Alho's tourist promotion of the kingdom on Twitter, saying that Alho, whose blog is called Blue Abaya, 'is a blogger dedicated to boosting tourism in #SaudiArabia, while also promoting #MBS's efforts. So why is a Finnish woman doing what a native Saudi woman can do? Because #MBS is more concerned with his global image and privileged women like Laura profit from this.'[54] The heated debate about Blue Abaya infuriated many Saudi women for a variety of reasons. Above all, Saudi women in exile objected to how the new crown prince is so concerned with his image in the West as a great visionary reformer. He promotes himself by relying on Western expat women, who try to appeal to citizens of their own countries by tweeting about the 'new kingdom' in very positive ways, thus masking the reality of life in Saudi Arabia, especially the subjugation of women.

The inclusion and integration of wealthy foreigners in the Saudi financial and economic spheres is, however, unmatched by similar settlement schemes targeting less-skilled, non-Western foreign labour. In fact, since 2013 many illegal immigrants have been deported after the government announced deadlines for returning them to their countries. Many foreign embassies struggled to deal with the massive flux of workers who demanded that their governments facilitate their repatriation by issuing travel documents and contributing to the cost of the journey home. A combination of compulsory Saudization programmes—popular among the youth but not among owners of private businesses, who are reluctant to incur the high cost of employing Saudis—and forced deportations of illegal immigrants accelerated the exodus.

The expulsion of poor illegal workers peaked between 2012 and 2014, when Ethiopians in Saudi Arabia staged massive demonstrations against their forced repatriation. At the time, the Saudi government enlisted citizens to report undocumented residents to the police, who raided poor neighbourhoods in Jeddah, Riyadh and the highlands of Asir, where Ethiopians worked and lived. Many were accused of promoting prostitution, alcohol and other illegal activities, thus directing Saudi anger over declining incomes and opportunities during the months before the 2014 crash in oil prices towards foreign 'enemies of the people'. Immigrants circulated images of demonstrations and confrontations between workers and the Saudi police online. At the same time, the Saudi press and online accounts boasted about the heroic acts of Saudi citizens who assisted the police to find illegal and undocumented immigrants who contaminated the nation with their unlawful presence and immoral and clandestine economic enterprises. It was estimated that during this phase of deportations, over 160,000 Ethiopians, including women and children, were forced to leave the country, precipitating a humanitarian and political crisis in Ethiopia. Many had to be hosted in special refugee camps in Ethiopia. The Saudi decision to expel them was accompanied by a 'xenophobic campaign led by the police and civilians that went together with the return of foreigners in 2013–2014. ... It is an extreme example of the harsh treatment Saudi Arabia reserves to foreign workers.'[55] The expulsion of foreign labour is not new; in the 1990s, during Saddam's invasion of Kuwait, over a million Yemenis were expelled from Saudi Arabia because Yemeni president Ali Abdullah Saleh sided with Iraq against the Gulf countries.

Under Muhammad ibn Salman's leadership, 1.1 million out of around 12 million foreigners have left Saudi Arabia, according to government statistics.[56] Newly introduced high visa and residence-permit fees for manual workers and their dependants, amounting to $54–60 per month, mean that the kingdom is no longer a lucrative place to work for the majority of poorly paid

Asian and African workers, who sought help from their own embassies for repatriation. Almost 5,000 Muslim Thai immigrants, known locally as Jawis, some of whom had lived in Saudi Arabia for forty years, asked their embassy to repatriate them to Pattani, one of the most deprived regions in the south of Thailand, where they originally came from.[57] Some of them had been in the country for several generations, and not many had been able to obtain Saudi citizenship. They live in Mecca, where they work in the pilgrimage industry, providing religious and tourist services for pilgrims. Many of their children do not speak Thai, and only know Arabic, which made their repatriation to Thailand difficult. Some have ended up working in the tourist hub known as 'Little Arabia' in Bangkok as cooks in restaurants, tailors, tourist agents and merchants.

Being a non-national resident in Saudi Arabia can be a rewarding experience that comes with a lucrative untaxed salary and many other benefits. But it can also be a journey into racism and exclusion. Many workers can face long prison sentences passed in state courts for minor offences, and eventually deportation. The execution rate among African and Asian workers tends to be high.

While all fragments of the nation and the non-nationals coexist in a troubled relationship with the state and with each other, there is one category of persons who have become extremely vocal over their historical exclusion: Saudi women, to whom I turn in the next chapter.

6

WOMEN AND RIGHTS

I Am My Own Guardian.

Twitter hashtag by Saudi women in support of abolishing
the guardianship system

Arguably, Saudi women have been excluded from the nation both as citizens and in ways specific to their gender identity. In recent times, many observers have expressed doubt over whether the country actually has a feminist movement. In the 2010s, however, a diverse, complex and evolving independent feminist movement began to define itself and represent its hopes to society in academic work, lectures, art, literature and films. Central to this is the context of historical, systematic and ongoing exclusion of women. Unfortunately, the movement quickly came to be defined as a threat to national security simply because it operated outside state-controlled feminism. Women activists engaged in successful mobilization that bypassed the state and the entrenched tribal, sectarian and regional cleavages described in the last chapter. The struggle for women's rights not only united women across those divides but also enlisted men in the struggle for equality. This important aspect of the Saudi feminist movement alerted the authoritarian regime to its potential to threaten the very foundation of Saudi rule. The regime feared that the new feminism would undermine its deliberate policy to segment the population along ancient primordial divides and ideological schisms, for example between Islamists and liberals. The most threatening crime of feminism from the perspective of the state is to engage in national politics in the pursuit of legitimate rights.

The movement now has its own named activists, cherished by some but despised by many others. Women who mobilize not only on Twitter, Facebook and other social media but also in person are increasingly considered by the government and its security agencies as a menace. They are subjected to harsh repression, slander and detention. In official traditional and new media, women who are believed to have gone too far in criticizing the status quo are named and accused of being agents of foreign governments, serving Western agendas, and undermining the reputation of the new kingdom under the rule of Crown Prince Muhammad ibn Salman. Those women who voice reservations about the current social openness are labelled sympathizers with terrorism.

Since 2017 a contradictory situation has emerged in Saudi Arabia: specific women are honoured and 'empowered' while others are imprisoned. In general, the social reforms of the crown prince have raised the threshold of aspirations among women. But both Saudis and the rest of the world are left trying to understand the contradiction between empowering women and detaining them at the same time. There are no easy and convincing answers as to why several women campaigners have been jailed since 2018 while many other women are enjoying unprecedented visibility and new opportunities. The struggle of some Saudi women and their ability to mobilize others, uniting them by a simple message—gender equality for women—astonished both outside observers and Saudis themselves.

While many women are appointed to high positions in the political, social and economic apparatus of the state, others— writers, artists, academics and professionals—have been detained. In 2019 the latest high-profile appointment was that of Princess Rima bint Bandar, the new ambassador to Washington. At the same time, more women are pushed into leaving the country and seeking asylum abroad, for both economic and political reasons, while others inside Saudi Arabia remain silent to avoid repression. But why do so many young women choose to flee at a time when the government is committed to their empowerment? What kind of rights do women struggle to achieve even at a time when the leadership pledges to endorse their aspirations, widen their employment opportunities and increase their visibility in public spaces? This chapter introduces vocal activists belonging to diverse backgrounds and orientations, discusses the problem of the runaway girls, and finally explores the multiple layers of what has become known as the 'guardianship system', a controversial but central focus for women's mobilization, and, some would argue, the cause of many social problems such as the flight of young women abroad.

From University to Prison

I came to know Hatoon al-Fassi when she was a Ph.D. student at Manchester University in the 1990s. She was studying archaeology, focusing her research on Nabatean inscriptions in Madain Salih, an area of great beauty and historical significance in the north-west of Saudi Arabia. Madain Salih was the southernmost frontier of the Nabatean kingdom, whose capital was in Petra in present-day Jordan. The site is now a prime location for the tourism industry that Crown Prince Muhammad ibn Salman wants to develop to attract local and global tourists as part of his Vision 2030. Hatoon was interested in a gender-inspired reading of the inscriptions of this ancient civilization.

After finishing her Ph.D., Hatoon returned to Saudi Arabia and was appointed lecturer at King Saud University, where she had obtained her Bachelor's degree.[1] She continued to write about the ancient civilization she admired and studied, but also began to be more involved in contemporary issues that occupied the minds of many Saudi women. She resented women being excluded as voters and candidates in the first municipal elections in 2005, blaming Saudi Arabia's conservative society and narrow interpretations of Islamic texts for its gender gap. She started campaigning for greater inclusion policies and launched a campaign, named Baladi, to train women to participate in the promised municipal elections of 2015. She also organized a weekly literary salon, al-Ahadiyya, where women met and discussed literature and social issues with a special focus on women's empowerment.

After leaving King Saud University, Hatoon taught at Qatar University for nine years. She gave lectures on women and Islam. She continued to write on various gender issues, publishing her research in Arabic and English journals. Her main focus was to find ways from within the Islamic tradition to counter current misinterpretations of religious texts that maintain and justify gender inequality. She believed in the diversity of the Islamic tradition and wore a special Hijazi veil different from the common black *abaya* that many Saudi women were obliged to wear in public, especially in Najd, the central province of Saudi Arabia. Hatoon's family, al-Fasi, originated in Fes in Morocco, and included amongst its members a woman who married the senior Saudi prince Turki ibn Abd al-Aziz, and Abdullah al-Fasi, Hatoon's uncle, an Arab nationalist who was detained in the 1960s.

In response to one of her lectures on gender and Islam in Qatar, conservative students who objected to what she called Islamic feminism launched an online campaign against her, demanding her expulsion from the university. Hatoon was eventually suspended from teaching. This coincided with the Saudi–Qatari crisis in 2014, when Saudi Arabia recalled its citizens from Qatar and forbade travel to the country. Hatoon returned to Riyadh, where she lived with her husband and two children. She always framed her campaign for women's rights within the parameters of the state. In the past she had praised King Abdullah's reforms and criticized conservative elements in society, such as religious scholars, for perpetuating gender inequality in Saudi Arabia. But this short-lived period of openness by the regime had evaporated by 2015.

Crown Prince Muhammad ibn Salman introduced new social reforms that allowed women to drive cars and be more visible in public places. Hatoon gave interviews to global media celebrating the achievements and success of the women's mobilization that in her opinion had led to the lifting of the ban on women driving in 2017–18. This came at a time when the Saudi authorities issued a warning to several women activists, forbidding them to talk to foreign media unless they were authorized to do so by the government. The authorities wanted to claim all credit for lifting the ban on driving and did not want to be seen as succumbing to pressure from women activists. Hatoon's praise for the nascent feminist movement for raising awareness of gender issues and campaigning for gender equality was viewed by the regime as undermining its new image. Her short-lived career in Qatar may also have become a contentious issue after 2014, when Saudi Arabia imposed sanctions on the Gulf state and accused many detained Saudis of forming secret cells on behalf of foreign governments, of belonging to the banned Muslim Brotherhood, or simply of being outspoken critics of the current economic and social reforms of Muhammad ibn Salman.

A respected academic in Saudi Arabia and abroad, Hatoon found power in Saudi women and their resilience, attributing the crown prince's reforms to their courage and perseverance. This must have angered the regime, which wanted to be seen as the only source of reform and social change. Together with almost a dozen women activists, Hatoon was detained in the summer of 2018. For the first time, the official press published the names and photos of the detained women activists, portraying them as traitors.

Hatoon's academic contributions to the study of gender and modernity in Saudi Arabia point to a concern with equality and the documentation of the feminist movement. In one study she explores the work of four Saudi women writers whose intellectual positions reflect diverse paths to emancipation.[2] Women writers with views ranging from conservative to liberal contribute to the emergence of a feminist consciousness, according to Hatoon. She acknowledges that many observers of Saudi Arabia deny the existence of an independent feminist movement, but through an analysis of women's literature and essays, she gives evidence of the new consciousness that underpins the emergence of a feminist movement regardless of the political inclination of the writers— and, more importantly, independent of the state.

While Hatoon stayed in Saudi Arabia and faced detention, fifty-six-year-old Hissa al-Madhi decided to leave and seek asylum in Sweden, where she is currently learning Swedish and waiting for her application to be granted. Like Hatoon, who was working at the university in Riyadh, Hissa was director of one of the units for academic learning at the Ministry of Education. She was active on social media, posting critical opinions on the general political situation and the status of women:

All my Twitter and Facebook accounts were hacked. I also used to receive threatening phone calls, and my house was always watched. I started writing online using an anonymous name, but I was found out and warned about voicing critical opinions. I wanted to leave before I got detained. I convinced my father that I needed general medical examinations and arranged to travel to Switzerland. I had to take my nephew with me as my *mahram*, or guardian. After I finished my medical tests, I asked my nephew to come with me to Sweden for a holiday. He accepted. A few days after arriving in Sweden, I told him that I would not go back with him to Saudi Arabia as I intended to apply for asylum. He was furious, but he eventually returned to Saudi Arabia and I started the long process of becoming an asylum seeker.[3]

Hissa explains that her opposition to the Saudi regime centres on several issues:

> I object to how the royal family monopolizes power and wealth. We have no civil society or political parties. We have no separation of powers. We have no freedom of speech or assembly, no transparency, and no accountability of the government. The situation of women's rights is abysmal. I do not accept the guardianship system over me as applied by the Saudi regime. This is different from guardianship in Islam. Sharia is not represented in Saudi Arabia in this area. The only acceptable *wilaya*, guardianship, in Islam is in marriage, as women need to seek permission of their fathers or guardians when they marry. The Saudi regime controls women by applying a pervasive *wilaya* over them. *Al-wilaya al-shariyya* is only invoked in marriage.

From the time of her arrival in Stockholm, Hissa became active in campaigning for human rights. She became a member of ALQST, a London-based Saudi human rights organization. She participates in drafting statements and publicizing the plight of political prisoners and women detainees. She is also active in support of the campaign to abolish the guardianship system as applied by the Saudi regime. She says, 'I do not accept the way the guardianship is interpreted and applied. It is the law of the regime, not the law that is recommended in Islam.' As she cannot travel outside Sweden while she is in the process of applying for asylum, Hissa connects with other opposition figures and activists via Skype. In December 2018 she joined a group of Saudi activists, human rights campaigners and dissidents at a conference in London entitled 'Saudis Abroad'. Like many other activists in the diaspora, she presented her ideas to the participants via Skype. She is open about calling for the downfall of the regime as 'it is corrupt to the extent that it is impossible to reform it'.

Saudi women activists such as Hatoon are remembered and honoured in the West, but in their own country many face arbitrary detention, even at a time when women are allowed to drive cars and attend football matches, cinemas and concerts. Knowing how dangerous it is to be outspoken like Hissa, Hatoon nevertheless retuned to Saudi Arabia, confident that her activism, encouragement and praise of the slow reforms under King Abdullah (2005–15) would allow her some leeway to pursue her goal—the real empowerment of women. But the limited space she had enjoyed began to shrink after 2015 when King Salman and his son took control of the kingdom. It was at this point that Hissa decided to fight the regime from abroad. By 2017, when Muhammad ibn Salman became crown prince, the limited measure of freedom had completely vanished, and many Saudi women activists who had been reluctantly tolerated, like Hatoon, became aware of a new and mounting pressure to silence them. Hissa remained silent for three years prior to her flight to Sweden, where she is now enjoying the freedom to pursue her objective, namely the fall of the regime.

With the increasingly repressive climate, many Saudi women decided to leave the country in search of refuge abroad, despite the real social changes under the new leadership. But Hatoon stayed in Saudi Arabia, as she had faith in the new leadership to honour its pledge to empower women in more substantial ways, beyond granting them the right to drive. Little did she know that she would be arrested in 2018. The increasing visibility of women in today's Saudi Arabia conceals a persistent campaign to silence and tarnish the reputations of many activists and feminists. Both Hatoon and Hissa belong to an older generation of women activists that included a cohort of women who have campaigned for the right to drive since the 1990s.[4]

The New Activists

Today there is a younger generation of Saudi women who are challenging the patriarchal system in novel, controversial and unexpected ways. The millennial generation grew up in Saudi cities in an age of increasing interconnectedness. They consume news on satellite television and the internet, and they regularly travel abroad for study, tourism and even work. A small group of young women have lived abroad with their parents when the latter were pursuing higher education. Some of them became hybrids, even having another passport in addition to their Saudi one. But the majority of this generation of Saudi women were born and bred in Saudi Arabia, living through rapid social change, benefiting from new opportunities, however limited, working in education, business, the media, the legal profession, and health and welfare services. Some women experiment with alternative careers as artists, filmmakers, actresses and fashion designers.

Many women of this generation want to be heard and feel a strong sense of civic responsibility. They are great campaigners and mobilizers, with a commitment to charitable work and voluntary service. Organizing relief for victims of flooding in major cities, launching breast-cancer awareness campaigns, highlighting environmental concerns, exposing injustices in employment, and challenging administrative rigidity in universities, young women have proved to be active and engaged citizens. In addition to being on the ground raising awareness and organizing others, their main strength has been to use the internet as a medium for resistance, protest, support and mobilization. Their blogs, images, art, video clips and Twitter hashtags have become notorious, reaching audiences beyond Saudi Arabia, and thus exposing cracks in the official narrative about the current government policy to empower women. They captured the excessive surveillance practices of the religious police on camera (before King Salman curbed their powers), the negligence of uncooperative state bureaucrats, the persistent physical and sexual violence against women in the confines of the family home, the plight of young women held in state rehabilitation centres, and the rigidity of the guardianship system. Suddenly, from the perspective of these women, Saudi Arabia had become too small to contain their ambitions, aspirations and quest for equal citizenship, rights and freedom. They are of the same generation as Saudi Arabia's crown prince, and some are even younger. Since 2011 they have been specifically known for two major campaigns, among many others: for the right to drive cars,[5] and the ongoing campaign to abolish the guardianship system.[6]

In 2017 King Salman gave women the right to drive by royal decree.[7] Young women activists celebrated their victory, especially those who launched the Campaign2Drive and October26Drive campaigns. The campaign to lift the ban on driving led to the submission of a petition to the king, drawing attention to the increasing number of Saudi women who had been educated abroad and had returned to the country to seek jobs. The ability to drive is considered a precondition for women's economic participation.[8]

But, according to Abdullah Al-Awdah, son of detained cleric Salman al-Awdah:

> For more than thirty years, state-sponsored fatwas released by the General Presidency of Scholarly Research and Ifta, a subcommittee of the Council of Senior Scholars, warned women against driving cars, mixing with men, or uncovering their faces. Sheikh Saleh al-Fawzan, an influential member of the Council of Senior Scholars, did

not just warn against women driving cars, but also against women driving motorcycles, and the council's Grand Mufti, Abdul-Aziz Al ash-Sheikh, had also said the disadvantages of women driving far outweighed the advantages. The state specifically managed to overcome entrenched opposition to women driving by giving the impression they had a change of heart rather than following the state's own varying stance. The decree was careful not to reference non-state actors and, more importantly, not to credit the civil activists and feminists who struggled for decades for women's rights. By referencing the Council of Senior Scholars and their fatwa, the state gave the decree more religious legitimacy and allowed it to present the change as royal largesse.[9]

Allowing women to drive was depicted as a royal gift, but the right to drive would not have been granted without the mobilization of Saudi women since the early 1990s, a movement that remains unrecognized, and even criminalized, in Saudi Arabia to the present day.

Thirty-year-old Lujain al-Hathloul is one of this new generation of women. She was very active in the Campaign2Drive, launched around the time of the 2011 Arab uprisings by a young generation that continued the struggle for women's freedom of movement. Lujain was one of the leaders of the campaign to drive, together with many other key and well-known activists, including Iman Nafjan,[10] now detained in Saudi Arabia, and Manal al-Sharif, who currently lives in Australia.[11] In 2011 Manal drove a car in al-Khobar, together with activist Wajiha al-Howaiyder and her own brother. She recorded the journey, posted the video clip online, and was arrested. In 2014 Lujain followed the same courageous path, and she too ended up in jail. Having obtained a UAE driving licence, Lujain drove her car from the UAE to the Saudi border, where she was arrested and spent several weeks in prison. Her crime was violating the ban on driving at the time. During the municipal elections in 2015, she presented herself as a candidate, but was denied registration because of her earlier detention. She remained in Saudi Arabia and was able to witness the new changes that have swept gender relations since 2015. But like Hatoon, Lujain's activism did not stop at the right to drive. Her ambition and courage pushed her to demand more fundamental rights, such as the abolition of the guardianship system, which restricts women's choices and puts them under the control of male relatives. In 2016 she presented a petition to King Salman with 14,000 signatures, asking him to abolish the guardianship system. But on 15 May 2018, Lujain was detained, along with Aziza Yousif, Iman Nafjan, Hatoon al-Fasi and many other activist leaders of the new campaign against the guardianship system. Among the charges against her was contact with foreign agents, and that she was reportedly in the process of applying for an internship with UN agencies when she was arrested.

In detention since 2018, Lujain was reportedly tortured. Both Alya, her sister in Belgium, and Walid, her brother, broke their silence and informed the world about the harsh conditions and serious abuse to which their sister had been subjected in detention. They became regular guests in global media, commenting on the plight of detained women activists in ways that are bound to shift public opinion against the regime. Walid and Alya have both continued to campaign for Lujain's release, informing the media about how she was tortured and gravely abused.[12] They both knew the inevitable negative consequences of their open activism abroad on behalf of their detained sister. Yet they chose to talk openly about what goes on inside prisons, perhaps after they lost hope that Lujain would soon be released. The Saudi authorities denied that Lujain and other activists had been subjected to physical and sexual abuse. They also refused to allow independent observers to assess the situation of the women activists in prison. A campaign against Lujain's relatives was launched online, especially on Twitter, where they are regularly insulted and humiliated. Their sister is described as a traitor and an immoral woman, who appeared in the media without a veil.

Women in the Diaspora

Nobody represents the I Am My Own Guardian campaign in art like forty-two-year-old Saffaa Hassanein, known globally and online simply as Ms Saffaa, a Saudi visual artist living in Australia since 2008.[13] Ms Saffaa lived in Mecca until the age of six, ben-efiting from the love and support of her family—above all, her liberal father.[14] She then moved to Jeddah, where she lived until the age of nineteen. She studied graphic design in the USA. Then she returned to Saudi Arabia briefly, and in 2003 she moved to Dubai, where she worked. She married a non-Saudi Arab whose father had been an employee of the oil company Aramco. However, the marriage ended after her husband sub-jected her to physical violence that resulted in a broken hand. With her father's support, she quickly divorced her husband. In 2008 she moved to Sydney, where she enrolled in further studies. She finished her Master's degree in 2014, and is now preparing her Ph.D. thesis in visual art.[15]

It was in Australia that Ms Saffaa became aware of the strict controls imposed on Saudi women seeking education abroad. In Australia, her application for a Saudi scholarship was initially rejected on the grounds that she was not accompanied by a *mah-ram* (male guardian). She had to ask for her brother to travel from Saudi Arabia to Canberra to testify at the Saudi embassy that he was her guardian. Her brother eventually returned to Saudi Arabia, as it would have been inconvenient for him to stay with her during her long study period. She comments on this incident: 'Having to fly my brother to Australia to prove he is my guardian is what brought to my attention the restrictions of the

laws. It is in fact what propelled me to create the artistic I Am
My Own Guardian series,' a set of images that became integral
to the campaign to end the guardianship system.

On another occasion in 2017, a year before journalist Jamal
Khashoggi was murdered at the Saudi consulate in Istanbul in
October 2018, Ms Saffaa went to the Saudi embassy in Canberra
to renew her passport. She asked her mother, who was visiting
her at the time, to accompany her. In her own words, 'the meeting with embassy staff amounted to interrogation', and after
three hours she had failed to obtain a new Saudi passport. The
problem of the guardian had arisen again, as no male *mahram*
was with her to support her application; her mother did not
count. Her Saudi passport expired, but this did not affect her stay
in Australia, as she had already obtained residency rights there.
Like many Saudi women abroad, she has not applied for asylum
while she is in Australia, as she hopes to obtain Australian citizenship after she meets the residency requirements.

Ms Saffaa told me that when she lived in Saudi Arabia, she
was not aware of the magnitude of the problem of the guardianship system. She thought of it as simply an administrative
requirement. In the past, and on many occasions, she had presented papers to her father to sign in his capacity as her guardian, considering the whole process to be 'something that fathers
need to do'. She unquestioningly accepted the requirement as a
bureaucratic procedure. In Saudi Arabia, 'fathers sign forms when
their daughters apply for jobs, demand the issuing of passports,
travel abroad, and many other activities that they may embark
on'. Ms Saffaa considers her father a supportive man, someone
who willingly signed these administrative forms, which made her
unaware of the consequences for other women whose male
guardians refuse to put their signature on a job application or
passport renewal form. Ms Saffaa commented that the plight of
young Saudi women who leave the country without the permis-

sion of their guardians made her realise the restrictions that deprive women of free movement and choice under the guardianship system. Together with the inconvenience of bringing her brother to Australia as a precondition for her Saudi scholarship, the so-called runaway girls, discussed later in this chapter, raised Ms Saffaa's awareness of the problem, and she began to represent in her art a quest to abolish the guardianship system and campaign for greater equality for women.

Ms Saffaa represents in her visual screen printing and street art what many women campaigners strive for, mainly the abolition of the guardianship system. Her daring visual representations of the quest to be free from male domination prompted her to represent women wearing *shimagh*, the Saudi male headgear, always a symbol of masculinity and eminence, with the slogan 'I Am My Own Guardian'. She describes her iconic art pieces:

> In November 2012 I published in a photo-essay a body of artworks titled I Am My Own Guardian to criticize the discriminatory laws requiring male guardianship of adult women in Saudi Arabia (Muftah 2012). This series consists of four images, each of a single, larger-than-life woman's head wearing a headdress typically donned by Saudi men. The figure in each print uses rich black ink that strongly contrasts against vividly white paper. Two of the portrait visages look at the viewer (in black and white) and two look away (printed over a colorful, free-flowing cloud-like mist). I first exhibited the four portraits as large screen prints in November 2012 at Sydney College of the Arts as part of my honors degree. A small version of my artwork was included in a January 2015 Saudi exhibition in Jeddah titled Fast Forward: Inner Voices. Interestingly enough, when state representatives came to inspect the exhibit they showed no interest and raised no objections. This deeply personal project was born of frustration with a system that favors men over women. After posting my images on my Tumblr account in 2012, users shared them on additional social media platforms like Instagram, Facebook, and Twitter, without credit or attribution. The

most widely circulated image was of a young woman wearing the Saudi male headdress (shumagh) with Arabic and English words across her face saying, 'I am my own guardian'.[16]

Ms Saffaa's vivid and courageous visual artworks, such as the pieces she mentions above, are bound to exclude her from the flourishing new Saudi art scene, which is patronized by the crown prince in special institutions created to promote loyal Saudi artists.[17] Ms Saffaa acknowledges that there was a vibrant art scene in Saudi Arabia, but 'when the state co-opted and institutionalized art, it became difficult for me to be part of it. My art talks to all people.' Her eclectic reversal of gender roles, appropriation of male dress symbols and daring images of unsilenced women all make her a controversial artist. She has documented responses to her art, especially the piece in which a woman appears dressed in male attire, which caused heated controversy online. Although the image of a woman dressed in male headgear became an icon for the struggle to end the male guardianship system, many Saudi feminists reprimanded her for appropriating the male attire. She defends her decision as she insists that 'the male headgear is only a symbol and making women wear it in art does not mean that I want women to be like men. I simply want women to be equal to men.' Ms Saffaa regularly receives abusive emails and Twitter messages, but she is not deterred from expressing her activism in controversial art. She has found a niche for her art in Australia and beyond, with many Saudi feminists appropriating her images, sometimes without acknowledging the source. She refuses to be silenced, even by the harshest criticisms of her provocative work. She says, 'I make art for the general public and my work is not elitist. Once it is done, my art is exhibited in public places and it has its own agency.'

Ms Saffaa is one Saudi woman who chose to remain abroad. She does not envisage returning to Saudi Arabia soon, as she says: 'I cannot return under the rule of this royal family who uses women to achieve political goals,' pointing to a recent government decision to empower women through high-profile appointments. She is sceptical: 'The right to drive may not be empowering; after all, if I don't have money to buy a car, I will not feel empowered by lifting the ban on driving. If I don't have money to buy a ticket for a concert, I will be excluded from the entertainment industry. ... But if I am not restricted by the guardianship laws, I will be able to leave an abusive home and study and get a job.'

Her criticism of the government centres on her conviction that the so-called reforms are 'introduced by the privileged to benefit the privileged'. Unlike many other Saudi feminists who think that religion and society are to be blamed for gender discrimination and inequality, Ms Saffaa believes that 'the state empowers fathers, husbands and brothers; many abuse this power and impose a strict regime on women. I was lucky my father didn't abuse the power that the state gave him over me.'

Women like Ms Saffaa represent an educated cohort with great stamina and creativity. Although it is difficult to estimate the size of this female diaspora with accuracy, they have become a small but growing minority abroad. They refuse to be silent as Saudi propaganda announces the birth of a new Saudi Arabia under the leadership of Crown Prince Muhammad ibn Salman.

Women in the diaspora are numerous, but amongst them are Hala al-Dosari, Amani al-Issa, Amani al-Ahmadi, Umayma al-Najjar, Insaf Haidar, Maha al-Qahtani, Sahar al-Fifi, Sarah al-Otaibi, Manal al-Sharif, Safa al-Ahmad and others who continue to register their presence online. They create a virtual community of women activists who use the freedom of being abroad to highlight continuous discrimination. They all puncture the state narrative about the emancipation of women and the recent efforts of the state to grant a select cohort of women orchestrated visibility. Their life stories and activism represent only a small glimpse into the struggle of Saudi women. While these women have settled abroad and started new lives, others leave the country in dramatic ways, such as the young *haribat* (runaways).[18] These are Saudi millennial women who choose to escape the country without the permission of their guardians. In the following section, I will turn my focus to the young runaway girls.

The Millennial Runaway Girls

In April 2017, thousands of miles away from Saudi Arabia, Dina Ali, a twenty-four-year-old woman in transit to Sydney, was kidnapped at Ninoy Aquino International Airport in Manila by two of her uncles, who had come to return her to Saudi Arabia. She screamed and kicked as they forced her aboard Saudia Airlines flight SV871 to Jeddah. The Philippines government, a signatory to the 1951 United Nations Convention on Refugees, denied that it had cooperated with the Saudis in this case. But forcing an adult to enter an aeroplane against her will is not easily accomplished without the cooperation of the police and airport immigration officers. In Dina's case, airline security officials and two men secured her forced repatriation to Saudi Arabia, according to eyewitness accounts.

While at the airport transit hall, and just before she was kidnapped, Dina had borrowed the phone of Meagan Khan, a Canadian traveller whom she befriended while waiting for her flight to Sydney. She used the borrowed phone to record and post her final words online before she was forced to board the Saudia flight. She may have realized that she was being followed and that her journey to Sydney would be cut short, and so she found a way at least to tell her story, knowing that if she was arrested, her own phone would be immediately confiscated. Dina said that she had left Saudi Arabia to escape a forced marriage, and confessed that, should she be forced to return, she would face death for leaving the country without the permission of her male guardian.

Social media played an important role in publicizing Dina's case. Within hours of her recording and sharing the video, friends and sympathizers on Facebook and Twitter posted it across continents. Meagan Khan helped Dina at the airport and played an important role in making the short recording available. Saudi women activists and others immediately set up a hashtag on Twitter, #SaveDinaAli. Online hashtag mobilization was the only means to publicize abuse, seek help and enlist other women and men in the fight against domestic violence in Saudi Arabia. It is not known what has happened to Dina.

In the same month, this time inside Saudi Arabia, anti-guardianship campaigner Maryam al-Otaibi left her abusive family in Ras, a small town in the central region of Qasim, and moved to Riyadh to work as a cashier. On Monday, 17 April 2017, two officials and a woman approached her while she was working. After verifying her identity, the officials informed her that she was to be arrested. She was told that her family had filed a 'runaway report' with the authorities, because she had left the family home in Ras and been absent without the consent of her father. They told her, in front of eyewitnesses, that they were acting on behalf of her family and were at the Riyadh supermarket to arrest her and take her back to them.

Maryam's father and brother were the principal actors in this domestic drama that went global. Saudi state agencies cooperated with the family to enforce their control over their runaway daughter. In Ras, Maryam had been subjected to abuse by her younger brother, who had encouraged another brother to go to Syria and join ISIS in 2013. He became more abusive as videos of the brother's death flooded social media only weeks after he made the journey to Syria. The brother who had remained in Saudi Arabia wanted to 'purify the family home of sins', imposing strict rules on all members of the family, including Maryam. According to one source, he had always put pressure on their father to restrict Maryam's movements in order to protect the family honour and demonstrate its commitment to Islam and tradition. After the 'martyrdom' of the younger brother, he became more disturbed. He told the family that they should all purify the 'house of the martyr'.

In the past, Maryam had occasionally confronted her brother and reminded him that their father was her guardian (*wali al-amr*), implying that her brother had no authority over her. The brother became more aggressive and abusive. He started threatening the father, telling him that if he did not honour his responsibility as the legal guardian of the girls in the family, he too would migrate to Syria and join ISIS. The father, afraid at the prospect of losing another son to the jihad in Syria, succumbed to this blackmail and filed a complaint about his daughter, who had already left Ras to work in Riyadh.

After her arrest, Maryam languished in al-Malaz prison in Riyadh. The brother continued to put pressure on their father to return her to the family home. He also told his father to take her to court and accuse her of *uquq*, disobeying her parents, including her male guardian, and *hurub*, absconding from the family home—two serious accusations for a twenty-nine-year-old single woman in Saudi Arabia.

Informal local women's groups and government human rights organizations initially declined to take on Maryam's case while she was in prison. But a group of women activists found her a lawyer to represent her in court after her story went viral on social media. However, after reading the details of the story, the lawyer too declined to take the case and eventually disappeared. The activists contacted other social and welfare organizations for help, but all were reluctant to intervene in 'a family matter' in which the state had already acted.

Maryam's case became famous thanks to social media, as activists had no way of reaching out to the public except through Facebook and Twitter. Several Twitter hashtags such as 'we are all Maryam al-Otaibi' were created both inside and outside Saudi Arabia. Of course, such hashtags are picked up both by supporters and by those who condemn the girl for defying her family. However, the case became notorious and earned publicity.

In May 2017, only a month after the above two cases erupted and became hotly debated in the Saudi press and globally, two sisters, Ashwaq and Areej, fled to Turkey to seek asylum, according to several brief videos they recorded on their mobile phones. They posted the videos online and claimed that their family had abused them physically and forced them to live as prisoners in their own home. According to one report, the Turkish authorities detained the runaway sisters, aged eighteen and nineteen, after their family put out a request through the Saudi embassy to bring them back.

After the girls' videos were circulated, Sahar Nassif, an activist and Areej's literature professor, recognized the girls and admitted on Twitter that she had listened to Areej talking about her abusive family in her university office: 'Areej was my student. I can't forget her innocent eyes as she was sitting in my office relating her dad's continuous abuse. ... Every other day there are girls escaping for their lives, or dying or suffering greatly. ... Why would a girl escape to a foreign country at a great risk without knowing anyone unless her conditions are so dire?' she asked.

In 2019, the last girls to run away at the time of writing this book were Rahaf al-Qunun and sisters Maha and Wafa al-Subaiyi. Eighteen-year-old Rahaf was stranded at Bangkok airport on her way to Australia. After blockading herself in a hotel room and broadcasting her plight online and her fear of being forcibly returned to Saudi Arabia, she was put under UN custody as a potential asylum seeker. She finally reached Canada, where she was granted asylum. Maha and Wafa spent some time in Georgia, before receiving asylum in an undisclosed third country.[19]

Many Saudi 'runaways' are brought back to their families by the Saudi government and foreign agencies in countries where they seek asylum or refuge—the Philippines and Turkey in the above cases—thus demonstrating the high level of cooperation between Saudi authorities and foreign governments. In the case of Turkey, cooperation took place before the murder of Jamal Khashoggi. In Saudi discourse about its women nationals, words such as 'queens', 'jewels', 'privileged' and 'protected' mask a social problem that is compounded by the cooperation of the state. The plight of the runaway girls exposes the emptiness of state narratives about its role in providing for women and protecting them from abuse.

Statistics from within the kingdom are usually inaccurate, but according to one sociologist the number of 'runaways' is rising.[20] In 2018 it was reported that over a thousand women flee the kingdom every year, while more leave Riyadh for Jeddah, the kingdom's more liberal coastal metropolis.[21] Others escape from rural areas to Riyadh. Running away from an abusive family to an overseas destination seems to be a final, desperate solution, but other women find ways to 'escape' Saudi Arabia in less dramatic and more convoluted ways.

Young women have deployed many strategies to avoid returning to Saudi Arabia, including marrying a Saudi who lives abroad, prolonging overseas study time, or seeking jobs in cities in neighbouring Gulf states, for example Dubai, after completing their education. An increasing number of Saudi women students seek asylum in countries where they have been studying, on the grounds of conversion to another religion, a relationship with a non-Muslim man, or pregnancy outside wedlock, each of which constitutes a serious crime in Saudi Arabia that is punishable by death. Canadian, British and American immigration lawyers, among others, deal with such cases and seek expert reports from professionals, academics and Islamic law experts to ensure that such women are not deported back to Saudi Arabia. Of course, there are no reliable Saudi statistics on Saudi women asylum seekers, as they would be a serious embarrassment in a country where state legitimacy is now built on generous welfare given to women and on the appearance of promoting modernity. The reputation of women asylum seekers abroad is deliberately tarnished, as they are often accused of dishonouring their families and running away from punishment, even if they have not committed a crime. They are often described as immoral women who seek sexual freedom abroad.

Other women choose to leave Saudi Arabia and work abroad, especially after becoming active in calling for the right to drive or to abolish the guardianship system, or simply for being different. Among others, Manal al-Sharif, a divorced thirty-three-year-old mother, established computer engineer at the Saudi oil company Aramco, and activist, encouraged women to drive, posting videos of herself driving with her brother in al-Khobar. She was arrested, humiliated and treated like a criminal by the police, intelligence services and her employer. She spent nine days in a prison infested with cockroaches. She was eventually released and later left the country to work in Dubai. Manal eventually married an Australian man and moved to Sydney, where she wrote her memoir, *Daring to Drive*,[22] a book full of pain, psychological trauma and real scars of abuse, including a horrific circumcision episode when she was eight years old in Mecca. Exhausted, humiliated and scarred, in the end she chose flight over fight. She remained active online, mobilizing from abroad and documenting the stories of other abused women. However, after the murder Jamal Khashoggi, Manal al-Sharif announced that she had stopped her Twitter account and would not go back to being an active campaigner. She has a son in

Saudi Arabia from her previous marriage and may have been worried about the prospect of not seeing him again. In 2019 she returned to activism, driving 3,000 miles across the USA to raise awareness of the plight of detained women activists in Saudi Arabia.

The Guardianship System

The struggle of women under the slogan 'I Am My Own Guardian' generates campaigns, controversies and debates both locally and at the global level.[23] So what is this guardianship system that baffles outside observers, is rejected by many Saudi women, and is still upheld by the state and many Saudis, despite having been relaxed in some areas affecting women's lives?

Religion, State and Society

The guardianship system (*wilaya* or *wisaya*) is one of the most misunderstood legal requirements in Saudi Arabia. According to Human Rights Watch, it is not legally codified but is enacted through a series of informal and formal bureaucratic arrangements that stipulate that a father, husband, brother or even son has complete authority to approve matters that dictate the daily lives of women.[24] In Saudi courts, judges often side with male relatives and uphold the *wilaya* system, according to the HRW report. State institutions (hospitals, schools, universities, embassy staff, immigration officers, employers, etc.) continue to demand the permission of male guardians before they deal with women. Education, health, travel, employment and marriage, among other domains, all require the approval of the guardian. The report's global vision of the guardianship requirement, based on international norms about gender discrimination, does not fully address its diverse Islamic meanings, political contexts and multilayered evolution in states that uphold Islam as the source of law in personal matters, such as Saudi Arabia.

In fact, the guardianship system is controversial even from an Islamic point of view. Issa al-Gaith, a judge and writer and a member of the appointed Shura Consultative Council, articulated the official Saudi view in June 2019. He stated that the guardianship system is upheld only in marriage, citing the Prophetic saying '*la nikah illa bi wali*', no marriage without a guardian. Beyond marriage, guardianship should be understood as a man's duty of protection, responsibility and obligation, rather than an absolute right.[25] This official Islamic view comes from someone who studied at Cairo's al-Azhar Islamic University and Saudi institutions. However, it does not translate into practice in Saudi Arabia. Al-Ghaith volunteered his opinion after many women campaigners launched their online campaign. He engaged in clarifying the issues related to the guardianship system using the same means that women activists use: Twitter.

According to another Saudi source,[26] there are differences among religious scholars over the meaning of *wilaya* or *wisaya*. *Wilaya* as a judicial concept means the ability to have control over body and money. It also includes guardianship over a minor until he or she reaches adulthood. Male relatives can also have guardianship over a mentally incapacitated person. This interpretation leads to the conclusion that *wilaya* is not legitimate over an adult woman who has full mental capacities. Therefore, in his opinion, sharia does not justify guardianship over a woman who seeks health services, for example. Moreover, a woman has full control over how she deals with her own wealth, according to a general understanding of the concept.

In Saudi Arabia, guardianship is specifically invoked when women marry. With the exception of the Hanafi school of Islamic jurisprudence, a woman is obliged to seek the approval of her *wali* (guardian or agent), understood to be her representative, before she marries. The approval of the *wali* is a precondition for *nikah* (marriage) in Islam. This corresponds to *al-wilaya al-shariyya*, mentioned earlier by Hissa al-Madhi. However, if the guardian refuses to grant the woman this permission, his guardianship is annulled and she can take him to court for *adhl* (obstructing marriage). In this case, the judge can marry the woman without the father's approval or any other guardian's permission.

Another related Islamic concept is the *qawama*, the right of men over women in marriage only. It cannot be extended to other areas of social or public life, according to a Saudi religious scholar. As the concept is mentioned in the Quran, it has been interpreted to mean that it is the right of a man to manage the household and family affairs, with the understanding that he is responsible for supporting the family financially. But even then, the husband is not entitled to control a woman's wealth, which remains separate from that of her husband. A woman can challenge the *qawama* of the man when he fails to honour his responsibility to provide for her, or when he abuses her physically or sexually.

Women are also expected to demonstrate *ta'a*, obedience to men in marriage. This obedience is limited and is annulled when a man forces a woman to perform tasks that are regarded as un-Islamic, such as disobedience to God. Both *wilaya* and *qawama* become redundant when the father or the husband dies; therefore, a brother has no right to assume the role of guardian. The woman becomes her own guardian, according to a Saudi scholar who provides a modernist interpretation of these concepts and prefers to remain anonymous.

These fluid religious interpretations are different from what is required by the Saudi legal system, which has expanded the meaning of these Islamic concepts to include a specific legal requirement imposed on women. If the above interpretations had remained as unfixed without being turned into uncodified legal requirements, Saudi women would not have been under the requirement to have a *wali* or a *wasi* when they engage in commercial activities, seek medical services, take employment, enrol in higher education, demand the issuing of travel documents, or travel abroad.

Permission to travel abroad has become one of the most controversial requirements. From the sharia perspective, there is no obligation to seek permission to travel, although there is an obligation to be accompanied by *mahram* (male guardian), for 'protection', according to a reformist religious scholar who now hesitates to speak openly about the issue. The obligation to have a *mahram* is not, however, absolute, as there are situations when this requirement can be dropped, for example when visiting family or travel for urgent matters. Needing to have a *mahram* is not the same as requiring permission to travel. But in Saudi Arabia's legal system, the two are conflated.

The controversial role the Saudi state plays in enforcing specific meanings of these fluid Islamic concepts may not have historical precedence in previous Muslim states. According to one source, who prefers to remain anonymous, 'many laws in Saudi Arabia are not sharia-based but are *wad'i*, promulgated laws by royal decrees, and often there is no apparent and explicit religious text to support them'. In fact, their application depends on what the religious scholars depict as a requirement to prevent or mitigate sin, or their implementation is justified by drawing on a specific understanding of the 'public interest'. The guardianship system as applied in Saudi Arabia can be seen as an amalgamation and endorsement of social and cultural norms, rather than a strict application of a clear sharia ruling. According to one Saudi Islamist:

> There is nothing in Islam that requires these concepts to become law applied and enforced by the state. I have never read that Islamic scholars in the past asked the state to interfere and apply a law in this

regard. Some Islamic scholars in Saudi Arabia have asked the state to drop the guardianship system, but many families and tribal groups resist losing control over their women if the system is abolished.[27]

To understand women's increasing and visible feminist struggles in Saudi Arabia, as well as their persistent deprivation of fundamental rights, we must examine the intersection of several important contributing factors. At the heart of this problem, which is symptomatic of wider and pervasive gender inequality, is the way that politics, society and religion work together to impose the most oppressive interpretations on women. Restrictions on movement, the guardianship system, disenfranchisement, forced marriages and unfavourable divorce laws are but varied manifestations of general discrimination against women.

In its official narratives the Saudi state portrays itself as a benevolent, paternalistic agent, supporting women via extensive welfare provisions (in health, education, social benefits and employment). The state enforces a type of patriarchy that is neither entirely private nor public, existing where the two spheres complement and reinforce each other. This patriarchy easily and comfortably moves from the family domain to the public sphere, where state agencies monitor its contours and reproduce both the dominant ideology—for example, in the schools' religious study curriculum and various official *ulama* fatwas—and the practices that keep it intact.

Discrimination and marginalization are perpetuated in Saudi Arabia because the state, society and religious institutions cooperate to restrict women's choices and perpetuate their dependency. Often this starts within the confines of the household. If a woman experiences abuse and restrictions within her own family, she has no recourse. In the cases of the runaways mentioned above, state agencies inside Saudi Arabia and outside it (i.e. embassies) promptly became accomplices in the crimes perpetrated by family members. This happened despite the fact that in

2013, the Saudi Council of Ministers passed a draft law to criminalize domestic abuse; it was not clear, however, which state agency is to enforce the law, thus making it ineffective and ambiguous. The Islamic judiciary is usually expected to cooperate and issue legal rulings to return such girls to their abusive families. The courts invoke concepts such as *uquq* (disobedience to family) and *hurub* (running away from the family home) to justify intervening on behalf of guardians. Running away from an abusive family is a crime, punishable by detention, enforced by state agencies and sanctioned by strict religious interpretations of Islamic law. State, society and religion thus work together to maintain gender inequality.

The state provides prison-like shelters that most abused women prefer not to be taken to. Poor conditions and restrictions on their freedom inside the shelters, combined with the stigma attached to these places, make women hesitate to seek help from such badly run institutions. While many remain silent, a few have gone public with their cases of abuse. Almost a decade after the famous television presenter Rania al-Baz was badly abused by her alcoholic husband and struggled to free herself from him, many younger women now see no alternative but to flee. Al-Baz's case was taken up by a charitable organization under the patronage of a princess. Only when the presenter was seriously disfigured was she saved and treated in hospital. This happened only after a 'crime of passion' became, in her own words, a 'state affair'. She then went to France, where her memoir was published in 2005. Despite her injuries, her prompt flight to France gave her an opportunity to register her presence as an abused Saudi woman: in her book, she described how her journey to France lifted her morale, but the prospect of exposing herself in public brought her abruptly back to reality: 'Am I presentable?'[28]

Under the new leadership of Muhammad ibn Salman, the state combined its commitment to Islam with a truncated hyper-modernity in which success is measured by the incorporation in the public sphere of the latest technology, some of which is used to restrict women. Recently, Abshir, a Google app that allows guardians to monitor the movement of their dependent women, even across borders, was promoted as a great technological e-government service innovation. Operated by the Ministry of Interior, the app violates women's rights and makes it even harder for them to flee violence. Saudi women activists raised their concern over this technological innovation, which was destined to empower men even more, widens their surveillance of women, and can lead to further restriction of women's movement and rights in general.

In 2017 the government waived the need for a guardian's approval for a woman to work as a shop assistant, cook or attendant. Seeking health care is also now exempt from the guardianship requirement. This proves that the state is the main arbiter of what had always been described as compliance with religious requirements, and that it can alter the guardianship requirement in a selective way. But the majority of women still cannot marry or travel outside the country without the approval of their guardians. Enlightened fathers sometimes give their approval, as Ms Saffaa explained, but they receive text messages from immigration officers at airports every time their daughters or wives leave the country. As well as impeding on women's rights, the system fails to take into account abusive male relatives who should not be entrusted with the responsibility of being the first arbiters in a woman's life.

The technological aspect of modernity is double-edged in Saudi Arabia. At one level, technology helps to enforce an archaic system and perpetuates the denial of women's freedom of movement. But at another, the same technology empowers women, intensifies their mobilization and exposes injustices inflicted on them.

This is a truncated modernity in which technological innovations such as smartphones, surveillance cameras, apps and video recordings can work in contradictory ways both against and for women. Women can publicize their plight and mobilize others to help them using the internet and social media; yet they can also be controlled by the same enabling technology. A wealthy government obsessed with controlling its population can invest heavily in modern technology in the interests of general surveillance, including for the maintenance of patriarchy. The state supports private patriarchy within the confines of the family in order not to lose the loyalty of men, empowering men over women in the process. While not all men use this power in subversive and cruel ways, many do, as demonstrated in the cases of the runaway girls.

It seems that the role of the state cannot be ignored—especially its project of nation building and the centrality of gender in this project. Gender is fundamental to managing the image of the state domestically and globally. Women have become important for the realization of a liberal, market-based economy struggling to overcome its dependence on declining oil revenues. The Islamic legitimacy narrative, development projects and, more recently, the state's drive to move into a neoliberal technology-based market economy have all shaped the way in which women are constructed and treated. The state now wants to shrink welfare benefits and increase its global outreach through capital transfer and investment. For all these projects, women are the cornerstones of state identity and the vision of building a non-oil-based liberal economy.

While Saudi Arabia is not exceptional in instrumentalizing women and gender relations, in the past it has nevertheless granted a privileged place to strict religious interpretations and the cultural norms of its citizens in its legal system, discourses, policy and practices. Women can potentially either threaten state integrity, promote its piety, or, under Muhammad ibn Salman, demonstrate its modernist transformation.

As a result of the increasing promotion of women in state narratives and the expansion of their role in the labour force under the new leadership, the employment of women rose to 21 per cent by 2017.[29] Since the reign of King Abdullah, specific programmes have been introduced to boost women's employment, such as the feminization of lingerie shops and cashier jobs in supermarkets. The gradual shift from a state-centred capitalist economy to open, liberal trade culminated in the appointment of several women to high-ranking positions in both government bureaucracy and the Consultative Council (Majlis al-Shura), in addition to their election to chambers of commerce and public- and private-sector institutions and businesses.

The only women who get into trouble and may face detention are those who incite other women to engage in collective action and mobilize against some existing restrictions, for example the ban on driving, detention and mistreatment of political prisoners and the guardianship system. Hatoon al-Fassi, Hissa al-Madhi, Manal al-Sharif and Lujain al-Hathloul were among the activists who were inspired by the 2011 Arab uprisings and mobilized against the ban on driving. They were behind the Campaign2Drive and built a strong presence online calling on other women to drive. But women who violated the ban on driving and drove their cars with male relatives as passengers, such as Manal al-Sharif and Lujain al-Hathloul, ended up in prison.

Yet specific elite women—for example Hind al-Sudaiyri, a comparative literature professor at a women's university in Riyadh and a member of the privileged Sudaiyri family, maternal kin of several kings, including King Salman—celebrate the achievement of the state in empowering women. In her book *Modern Woman in the Kingdom of Saudi Arabia*, al-Sudaiyri highlights the achievements of several Saudi women in government, sport, literature and medicine.[30] While she acknowledges that there are still challenges and obstacles to full emancipation, she regards the state as the most important agent in women's empowerment. She invokes a nativist approach, stipulating that only an insider Saudi woman like herself can understand the complexity of gender in Saudi Arabia. The life stories of Hatoon, Ms Saffaa and Lujain, among others, demonstrate that women have agency outside the state, but this is not fully acknowledged in al-Sudaiyri's work. As we have seen in this chapter, many women drive change independently of the state and refuse to be co-opted by it.

The current shift of the state towards paying greater attention to women's needs began after 2014, when the Saudi regime wanted to distance itself from ISIS and anchor the country by ushering a seismic economic change, the success of which is bound to be tangled up with real social transformation.[31] A combination of low oil prices and greater international media interest in the similarity between the treatment of women by ISIS and in Saudi Arabia led to new shifts in the kingdom. In these comparative contexts, gender issues are as central in Saudi Arabia as they are in Western capitals, among ISIS recruiters and supporters, and elsewhere.

To push for a new Saudi image, Salman reappointed thirty women to the Consultative Council immediately after becoming king, thus honouring the pledge of his predecessor to empower women through appointment. He also issued a royal decree to restrict the powers of the Committee for Commanding Right and Prohibiting Vice, known as al-Haya. This committee had harassed women as much as men, and there had been well-publicized cases of young men and women challenging its members in public and resisting arrest. Women celebrated their defiance in the face of al-Haya by posting videos on YouTube in which they appear to be chasing al-Haya men from shopping centres, rather than al-Haya succeeding in controlling women there. As restrictions on Saudi women began to appear similar to those practised in the cities of Raqqa and Mosul where IS militants controlled the public domain, the Saudi regime desperately tried to alter perceptions of the status of women inside the kingdom.

The new reforms associated with Vision 2030 and the Social Transformation Programme promise women greater opportunities. But US-based Saudi activist Dr Hala al-Dosari is sceptical. She posed a legitimate question: how, in a national workforce largely composed of Saudi men and male foreign workers, can economic reform ensure women's participation? Would legal restrictions on women's autonomy be considered in the reform plans?[32] She argues that neither religion nor conservative culture inhibit women's participation in the workforce. Rather, it is the problem of transport, together with the ban on driving, that deters women from seeking employment outside the house. Transport is under the control of the state; hence while the state wants to promote women's employment, it assists in restricting the possibilities for its realization. The neoliberal transformation may stumble and prove to be limited in increasing women's participation in society if the social controls remain in place, with women unable to secure their own freedom of movement. While freedom of movement became possible after 2017, when women were granted the right to drive, Dr al-Dosari does not think that the problems of Saudi women are now resolved.

Like the detained women activists, amongst them Aziza al-Yousif, Iman Nafjan, and many others, Dr al-Dosari's activism goes beyond gender issues, which she considers an integral part of a general struggle for government accountability. 'I do not think that monarchies are good models for government. I want to see constitutional change in Saudi Arabia that guarantees people's participation in decision making. ... There is no place in my thinking and aspirations for a monarchy,' she said.[33] She decided in 2015 to remain in the USA, as she became aware that her name is on the radar in Saudi Arabia. On one occasion she was contacted by an anonymous—possibly Saudi—person, warning her against attending a conference in the USA in which several Saudi activists would be participating in a discussion about domestic Saudi issues. She is very sceptical about the current Saudi propaganda about the improved position of women and their empowerment:

> The regime promotes a specific woman and a specific religious scholar, mainly those women who do not challenge its overall centrality in development and those religious scholars who keep reiterating their loyalty to the regime and have no reform agenda outside that dictated by the state. Reformist religious scholars and thinkers such as those who try to reinterpret Islam in ways that precipitate a political renaissance are all in prison.

In her opinion, women activists were detained not simply because they campaigned for women's rights, but because their leadership skills and engagement with wider political issues, such as the plight of political prisoners, torture in prison, regional Arab issues, the quest for democracy, and domestic politics in general, are threatening to a regime that wants to suffocate civil society.

Al-Dosari is a participant in the I Am My Own Guardian campaign, which she now describes as an impossible activity inside Saudi Arabia. Given pervasive repression, she comments that mobilization has now stopped in Saudi Arabia. She told me: 'It is we in the diaspora who have the freedom to continue the struggle for a constitutional government, separation of powers, accountability and justice.' She acknowledges that the campaign was transnational, pointing to her role in the revamping of the 2008 Human Rights Watch report on the guardianship system, which was later upgraded and republished in 2016. With other women, she organized several interviews with men and women inside Saudi Arabia to discuss the restrictions that the system imposed on women. The 'global dimension of women's situation in Saudi Arabia is as important as the work of local activists, who are now in prison', she argues. In addition to enlisting global human rights organizations, al-Dosari insists that Saudi men were also a great asset in the campaign, as many provided support, religious opinions and advice on how the guardianship system can cease to restrict women, especially their marriage choices and travel. During our conversation, al-Dosari informed me that women activists even obtained a fatwa from an eminent Saudi scholar in support of abolishing the guardianship system.

Depriving women of basic rights is a reflection of how much the state fears the language of rights in an authoritarian and undemocratic context like that of Saudi Arabia. While both men and women are disenfranchised and deprived of political and civil rights, women tend to suffer double discrimination. As women, they are subjected to the strictest legal constraints that deprive them even of the right to move freely in their own country or marry the person of their choice. As citizens, they share with men their marginalization and disenfranchisement in the absence of meaningful political participation. Both men and women remain unrepresented in an elected national assembly in Saudi Arabia. Despite the surge in propaganda highlighting the achievements of super-heroic Saudi women and the celebration of their educational achievements and contribution to society, women in general remain hostage to both their own male guardians and evolving state projects, which serve only those who design them.

The grand state narrative about the emancipation and modernity of Saudi women aims to draw them into changing state agendas and the project of nation building, which has gone through several transformations. While there is no single factor that explains why Saudi women continue to live under the strictest codes, this chapter has shown that interconnected factors perpetuate the situation. This indicates that women's rights are unlikely to be granted under an undemocratic and authoritarian regime.

In the past, the state promoted women as guardians of the nation's morality, piety and modernity. However, the majority of Saudi women are oblivious to such grand designs, and a minority choose flight as a final solution to their trauma, as this chapter has shown. As oil revenues decline, new taxes are introduced, employment in the public sector is frozen, the welfare state shrinks and salaries are cut, women will find themselves the most negatively affected by Vision 2030 and the Transformation Programme. The welfare state that they had depended on is gradually but steadily being eroded by austerity measures that will be detrimental to the most vulnerable amongst them: young women, widows, divorcées and the unmarried. In a neoliberal economy, prioritizing the protection of women against abuse in the workplace, family home and elsewhere is paramount. Without adequate legal mechanisms, Saudi women will be drawn further into dangerous spaces and, in the case of the diaspora, will suffer the trauma of displacement, uprootedness, loneliness and the loss of home and family. The I Am My Own Guardian campaign demonstrates the central importance of removing legal restrictions, but of course it is no guarantee that the current discrimination will vanish. Nevertheless, the campaign is a step in the right direction.

By July 2019 both Saudi women's activism and the support of the international community had put sufficient pressure on the Saudi government for it to announce that it had set up a committee to study the loosening of the guardianship system in ways that allow both adult men and women to travel abroad without the need to seek permission from their guardians. By August 2019 women were given the right to obtain a passport, travel abroad, and register marriages, deaths and births without the permission of their guardians. However, women still cannot give their nationality to their children if they marry a foreigner. They are also not allowed to leave prison after serving a sentence without their guardians. Abused women who seek refuge in shelters run by the state cannot be released without their guardians' approval and signatures. Women cannot marry without the approval of their guardians.

The negative publicity of the runaway girls has truly pushed the government to seek solutions that allow young women to leave the country without creating a scandalous situation for the regime, which now claims to promote women's rights.[34] As the guardianship requirement is lifted as a prerequisite for travel abroad, many Saudi women may now voluntarily leave the country in search of jobs and better living conditions without being labelled as immoral runaways, refugees or asylum seekers. However, there are no signs that the new committee studying the guardianship system will recommend that women can leave shelters or prisons, or marry without the permission of their guardians. While the reforms to guardianship are hailed as great steps towards gender equality, many women activists remain in prison or are banned from travel. The freedom of their relatives is curtailed too, as many fathers, mothers and relatives are unable to leave Saudi Arabia while their daughters are in arbitrary detention. Lujain al-Hathloul's struggle for equality, her torture and the hardship under which her parents have lived since 2018 attest to the contradictions of Saudi projects to empower women while silencing the most active amongst them. Saudi women succeeded in gaining the solidarity of men, and it is to these men that I turn my attention in the next chapter.

7

YOUNG AND RESTLESS

If common national interest does not unite us, injustice will unite us soon.

Walid Abu al-Khayr, lawyer and head of Monitor of Human Rights
in Saudi Arabia, arrested 15 April 2014

Unlike its Middle Eastern neighbours, Saudi Arabia has not been a significant source of exiles and asylum seekers. Nor has it accepted refugees in large numbers, not being a signatory to the 1952 UN Convention on Refugees;[1] rather, it is a recipient of economic migrants, despite successive attempts to Saudize the labour force. But today the number of Saudi asylum seekers is on the rise. In 2017, the United Nations High Commission for Refugees (UNHCR) showed that there had been a 318 per cent rise in Saudi asylum seekers since 2012—815 applicants, compared with a mere 200 in 2012.[2] Most of the recent exiles applied for asylum in the USA (280), Canada (212), Germany (68), Australia (60) and Britain (59). These figures almost certainly understate the level of de facto exiles, as they exclude those who have not applied for asylum but have delayed their return for fear of repression. Many Saudis seek residence abroad in a state of

271

forced self-exile without applying for asylum. Nevertheless, self-exile may be a misnomer, as those who stay abroad are often pushed to choose exile for political reasons. Jamal Khashoggi was one of them. It is only when passports expire and Saudi embassies refuse to renew them that people might feel the pressure to apply for asylum, if they have reason to do so.

The growing number of asylum seekers does not worry the regime, as it is still very small. Rather, it is their increasingly effective activism abroad that causes offence. Since the killing of Khashoggi, dissidents abroad have been successfully engaged in lobbying at the UN, the EU and Congress in the USA. By working in unprecedented ways, they have played a central role in the backlash against Saudi Arabia in recent months. If they had remained silent the international community would have '[forgotten] the killing of Khashoggi and moved on'.[3] The government has pursued multiple strategies to silence them—the silencing of Khashoggi was one. But after the silencing, a softer, less confrontational approach towards dissidents was recommended by an internal government study. Government emissaries often call dissidents and inform them that the crown prince wants a rapprochement, inviting them to return. So far, dissidents have not moved back to Saudi Arabia in great numbers. If they had returned, the government would have made announcements to encourage other exiles to follow suit. In fact, the silencing of Khashoggi precipitated a new exodus. The crown prince has commissioned a study to assess this troubling new phenomenon. An internal government report, which is not publicly available, predicted that by 2030 the number of Saudi exiles would rise to 50,000.[4]

Even if this level of forced migration may appear modest compared with the likes of Syria, Iraq, Iran and Afghanistan, it is highly significant for one of the largest oil economies in the world, purporting to pursue a modernizing agenda. The rise in the number of asylum seekers raises many questions and challenges for the kingdom itself as well as the governments of receiving states such as the USA, Canada, Britain and Australia. Unlike other exiles in the past, Saudis today in general prefer not to seek asylum in countries with troubled relations with Saudi Arabia, such as Qatar, Turkey and Iran, but rather flee to countries deemed close partners and allies of the regime in Riyadh. In the 1980s many Saudi Shia fled to Iran and Syria in addition to London and the USA, but Iran is no longer a desirable destination, and many Shia prefer to seek refuge in the West.

There are challenging consequences for this statistically insignificant but politically important new development. Saudi Arabia cannot afford to lose its highly educated young citizens after spending millions of dollars on scholarships, especially when it has pledged to lessen dependence on foreign labour and Saudize employment opportunities. The activism of this diaspora presents an embarrassment abroad and threatens to alter global public perceptions of the country, not least now that reforms are being announced as a great top-down revolutionary measure to serve the youth. Furthermore, as the crown prince is determined to attract both foreign capital and wealthy foreigners to Saudi Arabia, the heightened dissident mobilization abroad detracts from achieving his objectives.

Behind every young exile fleeing Saudi Arabia and abandoning the supposed economic opportunities and social reforms on offer, there is a personal story of injustice and repression. These stories puncture the official narrative about Muhammad ibn Salman's modern new Saudi Arabia, envisaged as liberal, with a new and vibrant entertainment industry, tourism and the promise of job opportunities outside the old oil sector. Regime entrepreneurial and artistic initiatives have targeted the youth (*shabab*), who are meant to be the main beneficiaries of the new forums established by the crown prince to honour his pledge to open the economy and reward young creativity and talent. In the words of Muhammad ibn Salman, on behalf of the MiSK Foundation, 'we take initiatives, encourage innovation and in turn ensure sustainability and growth to achieve the higher goal: developing the human mind'.[5]

The young target market of MiSK and other initiatives is precisely the one that produces asylum seekers. Many students who had obtained government scholarships during King Abdullah's reign (2005–15) and had studied in the West failed to return and build the new Saudi Arabia after completing their higher education. By 2017, when Muhammad ibn Salman consolidated his power and became the new face of Saudi Arabia, many of the students had become sceptical about the promise of creativity, opportunity and prosperity. They feared repression, especially those who had enjoyed the freedom abroad to criticize the regime and expose its shortcomings during the 2011 Arab uprisings.

It is easy to provoke the Saudi regime. A tweet, a WhatsApp message or participation in an academic or policy event deemed hostile to the regime can be enough to put someone on the suspect list. The regime maintains tight control over its citizens abroad, watching every move with developed surveillance technology. As Saudi students were sent abroad to study, they were expected to become ambassadors promoting their country and enhancing its reputation. Cultural attachés and embassy staff keep a close eye on students abroad, commissioning reports on them from security agents, as we shall see in this chapter. In 2019 it was reported that there were over 60,000 Saudi students in the USA alone, most of them studying on government scholarships. This cohort of students is the prime target for infiltration and spying.[6] While many students voluntarily became 'ambassadors' for the regime, either out of conviction or for fear of losing their scholarships, a small minority simply refuse to pay back their debt to the regime in propaganda. However, there are no official statistics that capture the number of scholarship students who fail to return or who seek asylum abroad after completing their studies.

If young, educated asylum seekers undermine Saudi propaganda about the new opportunities that come hand in hand with repression, recently exiled Saudi princes further erode the regime's power base. They pose yet another challenge,[7] this time to the myth about the solidarity and cohesion of the Saudi royal family, especially after the Ritz Carlton purge in 2017 that led to the detention of several high-ranking princes. Moreover, the exodus points to a departure from the old style of managing disgruntled princes. Previously the regime deployed its purchasing power to buy their loyalty, but now the norm has become to inflict detention and the straightforward humiliation that comes with it. In 2019 it was reported that the crown prince bullied the princes who had been detained in the Ritz Carlton and other wealthy elites to invest in the new initiative to float part of the oil company Aramco—promised in 2016 by the crown prince, but partially materialized only in the local stock market in December 2019.[8]

From his exile in Germany, Prince Khalid ibn Farhan al-Saud announced his defection and started a media campaign to cast doubt on Muhammad ibn Salman's many promises. He did not hesitate to give media interviews to the BBC and other media outlets that the regime deems hostile to Saudi Arabia, such as London-based Al-Hiwar TV and Lebanese Al-Mayadin. One of Prince Khalid's criticisms of the crown prince was his corruption and marginalization of other princes. He was also sceptical about the new entertainment industry. While he did not object to pop culture and inviting Western singers to concerts in the kingdom, he lamented Muhammad ibn Salman's hypocrisy, pointing out that society was not consulted about the new *infitah* (openness).

He told his audience that the royal family enjoyed all the prohibited pleasures in the privacy of their palaces, but that ordinary Saudis were denied such fun. He called King Salman a Machiavellian monarch, a pragmatic man with a dark side to his personality, citing how he had dealt with both princes and commoners in the past.[9] According to the exiled prince, the king had contacts with both Islamists and liberals and deliberately set them against each other, like any pragmatic ruler who practises the strategy of divide and rule. This is done in the pursuit of *al-dawla al-salmaniyya* (Salman's state), pointing to how the kingdom is now the fiefdom of King Salman and his son to the exclusion of other princes.

After the murder of Khashoggi, Prince Khalid announced that there had been an attempt to kidnap him in Germany, but that he had managed to avoid the trap designed to bring him back to the kingdom. In September 2019 he announced the formation of an umbrella political forum, Tajamu Ahrar al-Jazira al-Arabiyya (the Association of Free Arabians), to seek change in the kingdom and push the regime to become a constitutional monarchy. Prince Khalid believes in reform from above and envisages replacing the crown prince with a reformer prince, thus saving Saudi Arabia from the chaos and turmoil of revolution. He considers the Al Saud central to the stability of the kingdom and argues that the country is important to all Muslims and to the global economy.[10] He has documented his vision for Saudi Arabia in a book in which he discusses its history, including the opposition and relations between various branches of the Al Saud. He sees no future for the country unless the royal family stages a coup against Muhammad ibn Salman, who has antagonized many influential people inside the kingdom and throughout the Arab world.[11]

The exiled princes may not belong to the core Al Saud lineage that has ruled the kingdom since 1933, but in a family dynasty in which the king is supposed to be *primus inter pares*, even the defection of a minor prince challenges the foundation of dynastic rule. Now that it has become clear that Muhammad ibn Salman is above them all and is willing to punish and humiliate critics and defectors, exile seems to be the only solution for disgruntled princes. Prince Khalid was lucky, but others such as Saif al-Islam al-Saud and Abdulaziz ibn Turki al-Saud were kidnapped in Europe and taken back to Saudi Arabia. They have not reappeared.[12] In 2020, Muhammad ibn Salman continues to detain princes who are potential rivals, such as his uncle Prince Ahmad, the brother of the king, and Muhammad ibn Nayif, the once powerful minister of interior and crown prince, before he was sacked by King Salman in 2018.

The new Saudi diaspora is extremely diverse in its political orientations. It consists of liberal-minded young men and women, Islamists fleeing the current wave of repression, Shia activists, and feminists based in the USA, Australia, Canada and Europe. It may be difficult to unite them under one umbrella, as proposed by the exiled prince. Yet all are critical of freedom of speech restrictions, corruption, marginalization and abuse of human rights. The latter concern has gradually united them and encouraged them to participate in joint diaspora conferences.

One organization that has held such conferences is Diwan London,[13] a forum headed by human rights activist Yahya Assiri, who had trained with Amnesty International and established the ALQST human rights organization.[14] Before seeking asylum in London, Assiri had been a captain in the Saudi Royal Airforce for fourteen years. He visited London in 2009 and 2010, but in 2013 he resigned from his job in the military and applied for asylum in Britain. He objected to the imminent war in Yemen, which was launched in 2015, and began to work as a human rights activist.[15] Diwan London hosted its first conference in December 2018, attracting many voices in the diaspora.

In London, newly exiled Islamists Sultan al-Abdali, Muhammad al-Omari, Ahmad ibn Rashid al-Said and Muhammad al-Qahtani, as well as Shia activist Fuad Ibrahim, were present in person at the diaspora conference. Other dissidents joined via Skype, as many were still waiting to be granted asylum and travel documents in the countries where they had applied. Among them were Washington-based activist Hala al-Dosari, now Jamal Khashoggi Fellow at the *Washington Post*, Abdullah al-Awdah, Amani al-Ahmadi and Amani al-Issa. All presented their ideas and visions of a different Saudi Arabia. Many activists demanded practical measures to stop repression and secure the immediate release of prisoners of conscience. Others called for the overthrow of the regime as the solution. Recent émigrés were joined by old exiles who had fled the kingdom in the 1990s, like physics professor Muhammad al-Massari.[16] Young participants as far away as Australia and Canada condemned the murder of Khashoggi and the controversial role Muhammad ibn Salman had played in what they believed to be a treacherous and brutal operation.

Dissidents at the conference had different agendas and aspirations, but the recent brutality of the regime united them all. Their joint efforts may come to haunt the regime, as they form a national front determined to challenge the current repression and lobby the international community. Their efforts so far may not be taken seriously by their host governments, all of whom are allies of Saudi Arabia. But, as the number of exiles increases and their voices become louder at Saudi embassies, the EU, the UN and the US Congress, they are bound to become more of an embarrassment for the regime and its allies. They are a counterpoint to the propaganda about a new and modern Saudi Arabia and help to change the image of the country abroad.

In the past Saudi Arabia leant on its allies to deport its exiled citizens. In 1996 it put pressure on British prime minister John

Major to reject Muhammad al-Massari's asylum application and deport him to the Dominican Republic. Al-Massari took the British government to court and won the right to stay in Britain. He still lives in London. Another exile, Saad al-Faqih, had been running a media channel since the 1990s, and on many occasions the Saudis reprimanded British diplomats for allowing him residence in Britain. The Saudi regime considers the granting of asylum to its citizens an unfriendly act that encourages more dissidents to leave the country. The fact is that for most people, fleeing the country is very difficult, and many undertake arduous journeys into exile. From the regime's perspective, the worst-case scenario is to have a critical mass of dissidents abroad, especially if they are high-profile, articulate and serious. Although he was not an asylum seeker in the USA—he was resident in Washington, DC—Jamal Khashoggi's elimination attests to the policy of zero tolerance for such critical voices abroad. They are not simply a nuisance; they are viewed by the regime as a national security threat and enemies of the state.

Despite their small numbers at present, Saudi exiles pose a serious challenge to the kingdom. The regime is intolerant of their voices to the extent that it was willing to silence one of them through a brutal murder. Not all exiles are politically active, but a sufficient number of them could become a nightmare for the regime. The new regime of Muhammad ibn Salman obviously cannot eliminate, buy off or intimidate them all with what occurred in the consulate in Istanbul. The more they arrive in the countries of his own closest allies and partners, the more these hosts will feel pressure from the Saudi regime to reduce their numbers and deny them refuge.

The new Saudi diaspora is destined to grow, as there are no signs that repression was eased even momentarily in response to the damning global response to the the Khashoggi murder. Muhammad ibn Salman may release some activists who have been in prison without trial, as he did on 28 March 2019, when Aziza al-Yousif, Hatoon al-Fassi, Iman Nafjan and Ruqayya al-Muharib were freed after several months in jail. But a ban on travel always follows. For the regime, keeping your friends close and your enemies closer is perhaps one strategy that may slow the exodus.

A New Vision for the Youth

In discussions about the future of Saudi Arabia, Muhammad ibn Salman highlights that his Vision 2030 and Social Transformation Programme both address a major demographic fact about the country: the large cohort of youth (*shabab*). He presents himself as the embodiment of their dreams and aspirations, capitalizing on his own youth—he celebrated his thirty-fifth birthday in August 2020. Realizing that the youth are avid users of the internet and social media, he has posed for photographs and ditched his defunct Nokia phone in favour of an iPhone. He tries to connect with the youth through the same medium that they use to voice their aspirations. In this way, the crown prince has endeavoured to establish his own cyber outreach programme, appointing his confidants and aides, amongst them Saud al-Qahtani, and the head of his private office and chairman of MiSK Initiative Centre, Badr al-Asaker, both mentioned earlier in the book, to launch a propaganda campaign publicizing his reforms and spreading a hyper-nationalist narrative. Yet, while the king and other senior princes continuously resort to Twitter messaging to register their presence, the prince has preferred to remain remote online, guarding an aura and mystique fit for a future monarch. His mouthpieces have proved to be sufficient for publicizing his plans and inviting Saudis to applaud and congratulate him for the success stories.

Burdened by an economy overwhelmingly dependent on oil and budgets subject to fluctuations in oil prices since the creation of the state, the crown prince has pledged to meet the needs of the youth. He promised to create a post-oil economy, undermine the religious and social conservatism that allegedly stifles modernity, and introduce popular entertainment and tourism industries. He also wants to provide much-needed new job opportunities, beyond those offered by the oil industry and the traditional public sector, where in the past a whole generation of Saudis found secure employment, generous social benefits, free education, health services and scholarships to study abroad.

In the age of internet connectivity and social media, the youth themselves were active in articulating their own hopes and ambitions before the crown prince appeared on the public stage. Connected by Twitter, Facebook, Instagram, Viber, Telegram, Snapchat and other digital technology, and with university degrees obtained at home and abroad, they have been avid consumers of global trends, engaging with aspirations such as being able to contribute to the development of their country and participating in its future. Many of the country's youth continue to seek public-sector jobs with salaries and other benefits that allow them to have housing, get married, establish stable family lives, and partake in the conspicuous consumerism so enjoyed in the country.

Since the 2011 Arab uprisings, many young Saudis have endorsed the global discourse on human rights, democracy, justice and empowerment. They have become vocal critics of the corruption of officials, which often leads to sub-standard infrastructure in urban areas and inadequate health and education services. Under the new repression prevalent since 2015, expression of these ideas is risky. Those who volunteer critical commentaries on their society and its leadership may find themselves jeopardizing their future by prolonged spells in detention centres, where they linger without open and fair trials. Journalists and professionals who express the mildest criticism of the crown prince's policies are sacked, and many amongst them end up in prison. Others flee the country in search of secure exile abroad, leaving family members behind. Their families face an uncertain future, as imprisonment and bans on leaving the country are common punishments for those related to dissidents.

Many Saudi youth express their individual and collective aspirations and critical opinions in art, comedy, theatre and films—the very spaces created and patronized by the crown prince and the institutions he established.[17] Those who criticize the conservatism of the country's religious and social elites escape punishment, as this is now permissible in the press, government-sponsored conferences, the arts, television series and films. In fact, Saudi youth are expected by the regime to join in the condemnation of previous Islamist and conservative trends and to celebrate the new social reforms, such as the opening of cinemas, theatres and circuses. They are meant to be the vanguards of the new drive to promote hyper-nationalism. But if they voice any criticism of the political elite, particularly the top leadership of the country such as the king and his son, they are seen as crossing a red line and are quickly punished and sent to jail.

Saudi Arabia under the leadership of Muhammad ibn Salman offers greater openness in the public sphere, where there are now ample opportunities to be enjoyed by those who can afford them. But there are also multiple risks for transgression. The youth are seizing new opportunities, navigating an ambiguous moment in which the old and the new coexist in a state of tension, contradiction and bewilderment. The main focus in this chapter is the plight of the youth persecuted by the regime in the pursuit of its reform agenda. Many amongst them practise self-censorship, or seek to leave a country that so far has not been known to produce asylum seekers or to generate a diaspora with sufficient critical mass to make an international impact.

YOUNG AND RESTLESS

Fathers and Sons

Among the older generation of men were socialists, communists, Arab nationalists, Nasserites and Baathists of the 1950s and 1960s. Many amongst them became liberals, especially during King Abdullah's reign in 2005–15, but others remained loyal to their previous ideologies and embarked on writing their memoirs, describing their imprisonment in the 1960s, freedom after amnesty, and current accommodation with the regime. Matruk al-Falih, Muhammad Said al-Taib, Ali al-Damini, Ali al-Awami and Aql al-Bahli, among others, continue to live in Saudi Arabia, avoiding open confrontation with the government.

Another group celebrated the regime's elimination of Islamists since Muhammad ibn Salman came to power, becoming propagandists for his policies. Amongst them is the famous novelist and political scientist Turki al-Hamad, who declared that, as King Abdullah gave him his pen as a gift, he writes in the name of the regime. During Salman's reign, al-Hamad became totally loyal to the crown prince and defended all his policies, from curbing the influence of the religious clerics to promoting gender equality and propagating a nationalist agenda. Al-Hamad is active on Twitter, where he vocally supports the regime.[18] His writings antagonized the Islamists, who considered his novels offensive.

Other Saudi liberals are journalists who work in the media empire of the princes, above all newspapers such as *al-Sharq al-Awsat* and television stations Rotana, Al-Arabiyya, MBC and others. Intellectuals such as Abdullah al-Ghathami were instrumental in defeating Islamism and undermining its rhetoric in the 1990s, when he devoted his time to deconstructing and criticizing Sahwa Islamist thought. Like al-Hamad, he was targeted by Islamists. He is now a defender of the regime who congratulates it for its suppression of all forms of Islamism. Throughout the 1990s, Islamists regarded both al-Hamad and al-Ghathami as pillars of secularization and Westernization.

Few of the aspirations of the fathers of Saudi dissidence in the second half of the twentieth century were fulfilled, but now the old guards of secular, nationalist and leftist protest choose self-censorship lest they return to the familiar prisons where they were incarcerated decades ago. They are the retired fathers of a non-Islamist opposition that emerged in Saudi Arabia but failed to attract enough attention and grassroots support. With few exceptions, most scholars of the country ignored the history and struggles of this generation of non-Islamists. Only recently do we find that their struggles are the subject of serious academic research, especially after members of this old opposition started publishing their memoirs, documenting a bygone era of protest and rebellion.[19] According to Mohammed Turki al-Sudairi, research has often highlighted the foreign influences that prompted Saudis to engage with secularist ideas to challenge the state, but one must not ignore the local agency of those who chose to adopt secular ideologies in their struggles of the 1950s and 1960s.[20]

The strongest opposition to the regime, however, sprang from the Islamic tradition, namely Wahhabism. Its adherents have challenged the Al Saud's rule since 1927, and they continue to do so under the broad umbrella of contemporary Islamism, which includes radical Wahhabis, al-Qaida, Islamic State jihadis and reformist Islamists. Each Islamist trend draws on its own interpretation of Islam to challenge the regime from within.

In general, religious-political dissidence is broadly divided into diverse orientations. A strong trend aspires to keep the kingdom faithful to the dominant Wahhabi tradition with its emphasis on displaying an overall Islamic character and Islamic policies. This Salafi Wahhabi trend has shown that it can be both loyal and disloyal to the regime. The official Saudi religious establishment belongs to those who adopt peaceful means, such as advice to the rulers, known as *nasiha*, to ensure that the regime's Islamic character is upheld. In contrast, Salafi jihadis, who come from the same Wahhabi tradition, believe that the Al Saud deviate so much from the original eighteenth-century message of Wahhabism that they deserve to be overthrown by violence.

Another prominent Islamic opposition trend stems from a genuine attempt to reform the regime and divorce it from its original Wahhabi ideology while remaining faithful to Islam. Islamist reformists engage with Muslim Brotherhood ideology, modern Islamic political thought, and the Islamic awakening, the Sahwa, to articulate a vision of Saudi Arabia steeped in adherence to Islam but also ready to explore democratic government and political representation. The Saudi Association for Civil and Political Rights, known as HASM, founded by Abdullah al-Hamid and his comrades in 2009, seeks to reform the regime and move it towards a constitutional monarchy in which the Al Saud become symbolic figures and the people rule themselves.[21] HASM followers call for elected representative government, an independent judiciary and the separation of powers. They strongly believe in peaceful collective civil action to pursue justice, equality and political representation.

Like the early dissidents of the 1960s, the Islamist generation consists of ageing fathers who have struggled either to restore the regime to its original eighteenth-century Islamic state or to push it forward towards becoming a modern Islamic democracy.

Neither jihadi violence nor peaceful Islamist protest by the older generation has yielded the desired outcome. The Saudi regime today is neither an Islamic state nor a fully fledged Islamic democracy. It remains a hybrid authoritarian and absolute monarchy that recently embarked on promoting Saudi nationalism to ensure loyalty to the leadership. The fathers of the diverse brands of the Islamist opposition are dead, are detained, or have fled the country to safe havens in the West and elsewhere. Loyal Salafi Wahhabis practise self-censorship when they see their country gradually abandoning its commitment to a strict interpretation of Islam and opening social spaces for women and men to enjoy entertainment, popular culture and greater personal freedoms. Their pragmatism proves useful for maintaining their privileges and keeping out of trouble.

In the 1990s only a few Islamist opposition figures fled the country. The most famous of them was no doubt Osama Bin Laden, who went to Afghanistan and established al-Qaida. Muhammad al-Massari, who espouses the ideology of Hizb al-Tahrir, and Saad al-Faqih, who is a Salafi Islamist, both on the Sunni opposition side, found refuge in London. On the Shia side, Hamza al-Hassan, Sheikh Hasan al-Safar, Tawfiq al-Saif and Fuad Ibrahim were among those who fled the country after the 1979 Shia uprising. By 2015 many Islamists who had stayed behind were in prison. The most famous are Sheikhs Safar al-Hawali, Salman al-Awdah and Nimr al-Nimr, among many other younger Islamists, preachers, religious scholars and professionals.

Jihadis who engaged in terrorism in Saudi Arabia from the late 1980s died in shootouts with the regime's security forces between 2003 and 2008, languished in prison, or fled to neighbouring countries. Many of them took part in the global jihad in the 1980s–90s in Afghanistan, Bosnia, Chechnya and the Philippines, among many other destinations. Since 2003 they have appeared in Iraq, Yemen, Syria, Lebanon and beyond the Arab world.

The sons, and even grandsons, of both the early Islamists and the non-Islamists are now the millennial population that the crown prince wants to serve, control, change and promote, lest they continue the struggles of their fathers and challenge his rule. Whether he succeeds remains to be seen. But not all sons have followed their own rebel fathers and engaged in dissent. Many amongst them are now employed in the public sector, seizing the new opportunities that Muhammad ibn Salman promises. By contrast, a few millennial sons today rebel against

their retired fathers who remained loyal to the regime throughout their lives, many of whom worked in the security, military
and intelligence services, as we shall see later in this chapter. And
a few remain faithful to the Islamism of their fathers.

New hybrid political trends are currently emerging among the
millennial sons. Many young men hesitate to wholeheartedly and
uncritically endorse the old ideologies of Islamism, socialism,
communism and Arab nationalism adopted by a previous generation. The new millennial youth of the country, born since the
1980s, are engaging in hybrid and mutated dissent that combines
what appear to be contradictory projects, which nonetheless sit
comfortably together in the minds of the youth. They pursue
selective causes and join with others who share their hybrid outlook. Above all, they cherish their own personal freedom of
speech and conscience, engaging with Islam in novel ways, either
by rejecting it altogether or by following new and liberating
interpretations from within the tradition. They all criticize the
Saudi leadership for its excessive repression and corruption. They
call for social justice and fair distribution of wealth.

As much as they are intolerant of the regime's monopoly over
power, the economy, religion and society, these Saudi millennials
are equally intolerant of members of the old opposition who
claim to speak on behalf of society. They see these figures as
self-appointed dissidents deemed unworthy of their uncritical
loyalty or respect. Yet, despite their diverse views, they are united
by perceived injustice, exactly as predicted by a young lawyer who
is a member of this new generation.

Walid Abu al-Khayr, quoted at the beginning of this chapter,
was a young and aspiring lawyer whose main passion was to
defend human rights and support prisoners of conscience. He
represented the HASM founders, who were all imprisoned for
establishing an unlicensed civil and political association. Abu
al-Khayr soon joined the defendants in prison, and in 2014 he

was sentenced to fifteen years by a specialized terrorism court. He was aware of how common national interest had failed to generate a coherent national opposition that could agree on basic demands. But as injustices became prevalent and the regime widened the circle of detainees, it is exactly this new repression and injustice inflicted on a cross-section of society that promises to unite young Saudis. Saudis are suffering as a result of restrictions on their political and civil rights, despite being able to enjoy greater freedoms to go to the cinema, theatre and circus, and to travel abroad, without the permission of their fathers.

By adopting hybrid political discourses and mastering new communication platforms, the young generation is very active online, exactly like the trolls and bots of the crown prince who operate from his so-called Twitter farm in Riyadh. Young men create YouTube shows and act as media presenters, discussants, comedians and satirists. The most famous and popular satirist is London-based Ghanim al-Dosari, who produces YouTube shows called Fadfada and Natter, in which he mocks the king, the crown prince and other senior princes.[22] With over 400,000 subscribers to his channel and Twitter account, he appeals to the youth and sends strong political messages that undermine the legitimacy of the king and his son.

Many dissidents organize online protest, promote narratives that counter regime propaganda, volunteer for charitable and civil society initiatives, assist others who seek asylum outside the country and campaign in support of prisoners of conscience. Articulate dissidents present assessments of the Saudi human rights record in forums in Brussels, Geneva and Washington, DC. Many amongst them want the complete downfall of the regime; others are willing to accept the Al Saud as rulers but ask for greater representation and power for society, with its diverse ideological outlooks. They are specifically active in supporting freedom of speech, human rights, social justice, gender equality, the rights of prisoners of conscience and respect for diversity and inclusion. Above all, they are the most internet-engaged cohort population, not only in Saudi Arabia but worldwide. Their engagement makes them the masterminds of Twitter hashtag activism, defined as discursive protest on social media united through a hashtag word, phrase or sentence.[23] The women discussed in Chapter 6 are pioneers in raising awareness of their plight using hashtags. Men too are now active in this domain of digital activism, but after 2015 they tended to congregate abroad, as Twitter became a platform for the regime to intimidate its critics.

The Jeddah-based sons of Jamal Khashoggi—Salah and Abdullah—publicly accepted the king's condolences and issued a statement warning against public discussion of the case, as they consider themselves the only persons entitled to discuss the murder. They stated that they have faith that the regime will punish those responsible. So far, Khashoggi's family have kept silent and remain in Saudi Arabia, possibly under a travel ban. His sons were allowed to travel to the USA immediately after the regime admitted that Khashoggi had been murdered. They were interviewed by US media, appearing shocked, sad and bewildered; they reiterated that they await justice from the Saudi authorities. Since their return to Saudi Arabia they have kept a low profile after holding a funeral for their father without being able to bury his body, which remains missing in the summer of 2020. While Khashoggi's daughters live quietly in the USA, his sons were already estranged from their father before he was murdered. Perhaps they objected to his new activism, which was bound to affect them in Saudi Arabia. Khashoggi's wife demanded a divorce when he moved to Washington.

But many detained fathers are missed and remembered by their sons, who, if they are in the diaspora, feel compelled to engage in activism to secure their release. Thirty-six-year-old Abdullah, legal scholar and senior fellow at Georgetown University and son of Sheikh Salman al-Awdah, became very outspoken from his exile in Washington, where he began to write opinion essays in international media. In detention since September 2017, Abdullah's father faces thirty-seven charges. The public prosecutor demanded his execution. As a child Abdullah witnessed the first arrest of his father in 1994. He remembers:

> The security forces came to our house and broke our small computer. They even urinated in my father's office. I participated in *intifadat Buraydah*, the demonstration that was staged to protest the arrest of my father in 1994. I was probably the youngest demonstrator. These events made me what I am now. I started writing articles in several Saudi newspapers like *al-Sharq al-Awsat, al-Jazirah, al-Hayat* and *al-Madinah*. Later I wrote articles for web-based newspapers like *al-Maqal* and *al-Taqrir*; both promoted a modernist Islamist agenda and were shut down under regime pressure. Then I began to write messages on Twitter.[24]

As an adult, Abdullah came to Pittsburgh University to do a Master's degree in 2010, later beginning a Ph.D. in 2013. He describes his journey from student to asylum seeker:

> I was on a scholarship. But in 2014 my scholarship was revoked. I asked the embassy for reasons behind their decision and they told me there are social issues, a euphemism for political problems. They often commission informers to write reports on students abroad, and the report must have informed them about my student activities. They perhaps wrote about my objections to sending troops to Bahrain during the 2011 Arab uprisings. I gave power of attorney to someone in Saudi Arabia to take the Ministry of Higher Education to court and compensate me for the loss of my scholarship. After several months, I won the case. When Salman became king in 2015, the embassy informed me that there had been a mistake, and they reinstated my scholarship. I felt that perhaps there was a new era under Salman. But my optimism was short-lived. After finishing my

Ph.D. I returned to Saudi Arabia in 2017 to rest and visit my family. During my stay, my father was informed that he was banned from travel. It was the moment of the rise of the crown prince and his aide Saud al-Qahtani. I cut my visit short and left the country within days. I knew that I would be banned from travel too. I had a one-year post-doctoral fellowship at Yale Law School. I thought that I would return to Saudi Arabia after my fellowship expires, or that I might stay for another year in the USA. I did not want to miss a great opportunity to be at such a prestigious university. I left Saudi Arabia in July 2017. By September, my father had been jailed and the real new face of the regime became clear.

Abdullah describes the conditions his father is enduring in detention:

Since his arrest he has been held in solitary confinement, where he remains today. He has been mistreated, handcuffed, blindfolded and chained inside his cell, and deprived of sleep and medication—so much so that after five months he had to be taken to hospital. Seventeen members of my family have been banned from travelling; my uncle Khalid was arrested because he tweeted about my father; and I was asked by the Saudi embassy in Washington to go back to Saudi Arabia to 'renew my passport', which has been frozen.[25]

Saudi embassies refuse to renew the passports of people abroad who they suspect are critical of the regime, always asking them to return to Saudi Arabia. This becomes a mechanism to either control citizens abroad or trap them into returning, where they face prison or, if they are lucky, a travel ban. When Abdullah's passport expired in 2017, he went in person to the Saudi embassy in Washington to renew it. He explains:

The embassy staff told me that there has been a decision to 'suspend all services' put on my file. This means that the passport cannot be renewed abroad, and I should go back to Saudi Arabia to renew it. I tried again at the consulate in New York without success. The third time I applied online when the crown prince visited Washington. I thought the embassy might renew the passport to show good will. But I was wrong. They asked me to go back to Saudi Arabia. I did not return to Saudi Arabia as my father was still in prison. My uncle and other relatives were banned from travel. My passport expired and I decided to apply for asylum in the USA in July 2018. By December, I was granted asylum.[26]

Abdullah believes that the real reason his father was detained is that

he represents an independent religious source of authority. Even though my father's approach is peaceful, the regime fears alternative visions and reformist agendas. The regime knows that my father is a popular preacher and scholar. He has the potential to mobilize people if he chooses to. He has an alternative national agenda with a political and social vision. He is a *tanwiri* Islamist, a modernist, who seeks reform within an Islamic framework. This is why my father is still in jail and may face the death penalty.

In exile, Abdullah continues to follow the news about his father's health and regular court hearings. He tries to use his legal training to formulate responses to the charges that his father faces in court.

While Sheikh Salman al-Awdah's thinking was deeply rooted in Islamism, initially influenced by the Sahwa movement, and later by the modernist Muslim Brotherhood, albeit without belonging to their *tanthim* (organization), Abdullah does not describe himself as an Islamist. He says:

I am a practising Muslim and a scholar of Islam. This does not make me an Islamist. Equally I am neither a secular nor a liberal. I am best described as someone who defends the rights of people, their *huquq*. I also support the transformation of the Saudi regime into a constitutional monarchy in which we have an elected house of representatives and an elected government.

Abdullah crosses many divides, as he cooperates with both men and women in exile, not all of whom are steeped in

Islamism. He celebrates the scene during the Diwan London Saudi Diaspora Conference in 2018: 'I was amazed at how Saudis in the diaspora overlooked their ideological divides. Islamists, secularists, men and women all came together under one roof, which was unthought of a decade ago when the regime exaggerated the divides to break the solidarity of people and their unity to fight repression.' Abdullah became very active on social media, relaying information about the trials of various detainees, including his father. In his view, the explosion in social media activism is a positive development, which spreads awareness of the repression that people are subjected to.

It may not be easy to measure the success of this new youth-based digital protest in the near future. But through hashtag activism, Saudi youth, especially those abroad, and to a lesser extent those who can mask their real digital identity inside the country and escape repression and censorship, try to insert their voices in the narrative about their country and its future. They seek to achieve many things.

The Hashtag Generation

Members of the hashtag generation often select a hot topic and gather supporters and contributors to its hashtag. They measure their own success by seeing how much their statements and messages are trending. They quickly abandon a successful hashtag campaign to move to another. Before the crown prince came to power in 2017, Saudis had already practised launching campaigns such as 'The Salary Is Not Enough', and 'Free Political Prisoners'. Among the most successful examples of digital activism were the 2008–9 and 2014 viral campaigns that followed flooding in Jeddah after heavy rain, when bridges and infrastructure collapsed, all attributed to the corruption of officials in municipalities and urban development projects.

But after 2017 the plight of prisoners of conscience of all per-suasions—Islamists, feminists and others—became a dominant theme. Young men participated in and amplified the campaign to free Lujain al-Hathloul, showed support for the runaway girls, and in September 2019 launched a campaign to mark two years since a number of citizens had been detained, named Sanatayn ala Itiqalat September. They countered the hashtag celebrating the crown prince's birthday and undermined the official euphoria associated with this virtual celebration. They also mocked official hashtags such as 'Saudi Arabia is Great', 'Saudi Arabia for Saudis', and 'Saudi Arabia First', all launched to promote fidelity to the crown prince and spread a hyper-nationalist discourse. As the regime produces new hashtags to enforce loyalty and securitize the online sphere, young dissidents bash the effort with subver-sive messaging. For example, Kuluna Amn (We Are All Security Agents), tweeted by the chair of the MiSK foundation, Bader al-Asaker, during the National Day celebrations in 2019, was meant to mobilize ordinary Saudis to involve themselves in domestic security. However, dissidents are quick to mock such slogans in their counter-messaging. The satire reaches a high level with Ghanim al-Dosari's online shows, in which he uses simple language interspersed with piercing humour and cartoon-like images. As the regime hashtag 'Saudi Arabia is Great' reached trending levels, Saudis abroad appropriated it and launched their own Twitter account with the same name, in order to articulate a different perspective on how the country can be great. The activists emphasized the centrality of justice as the foundation for real greatness.

Young Saudi online activists aspire to achieve many individual and collective goals. By choosing a subject for their hashtags, they seek to publicize a problem by making it trend domestically and globally. They accompany their hashtag with messages, inserting their own narratives outside the traditional, heavily censored public sphere, such as state print, visual, and online media, university clubs, literary private salons, public forums and book fairs, all extremely hostile to alternative opinions, let alone criticism of regime policies. They also seek to achieve solidarity with others in support of specific causes. They reach out to like-minded people and create a virtual community of peers who share their concerns. Their messages and hashtags reach a critical mass among a diasporic young population with no historical memory or prior experience of exile, dislocation and alienation. Those abroad embark on learning and training themselves in advocacy and contentious digital politics in order to mobilize others.

Those who have been forced to flee repression at home, as well as the prospect of prison for simply expressing contentious opinions, register their presence online in the hopes of remaining relevant to their country and its youth. As young people concerned with public good and change, they see themselves as contributing to efforts that may lead to the release of political prisoners and the exposure of corruption cases and failing social services. They also aim to raise awareness of the Saudi regime's intrigues in the Arab world and its many military and diplomatic interventions to derail the impulse towards democracy in 2011. Saudi youth in exile seek to reach a global audience for support and sympathy, while naming and shaming their regime and other governments that are considered Saudi Arabia's partners and allies. They try to demonstrate solidarity with their compatriots across tribal, regional and sectarian divides, an objective that is not always easy to achieve either at home or abroad.

By shaming the crown prince and naming senior officials, and by highlighting contradictions and scandals, the active youth counter official propaganda about the well-being and prosperity of the Saudi nation. They focus particularly on the regime's new hyper-nationalism, especially that expressed online, and offer a nuanced interpretation of what it is like to be a nationalist (*watani*). They insist that real citizenship is based on inclusion rather than exclusion and repression. They call for equal opportunities, and above all for respect for the citizens' freedom of conscience. They specifically criticize regime policies in whose formulation and implementation they have played no part, thus rejecting the so-called top down revolution of the crown prince.

The question of whether specific youth-led activist campaigns can really lead to general political change is complicated and may not be easily and conclusively answered. In the last decade, hashtag activism has had mixed outcomes. In some rare cases it has promoted the changing or even reversal of certain government policies. Increases to the salaries of public-sector employees, termination of fuel subsidies and threatened cuts in social benefits were all partially abandoned by the crown prince after hashtag campaigns flooded the Twittersphere and alerted the regime to how unpopular certain austerity measures could be— and how they might damage the image of the crown prince himself.[27] Having spent several years and $3 billion dollars on foreign management consultants,[28] who organised Vision 2030 and the National Transformation Programme, the king issued a decree banning the use of such firms by ministries except in exceptional cases. This followed digital denunciation of the use of foreign experts who have no deep knowledge of local social and political contexts and may not care about the lives of those Saudis affected by privatization, restructuring of the economy, cuts in subsidies and shrinking public-sector employment.

Because of the youth's digital activism, the regime is always on alert to cover up cases of corruption and mismanagement, regional and foreign policy blunders, and other scandals such as the abrupt detention and sacking of senior princes by the crown prince. As online rumours—mostly by Mujtahid,[29] an anonymous Twitter account that specializes in leaking stories about royal rivalries and intrigues—pointed to a rift between Muhammad ibn Nayif and Muhammad ibn Salman, the Saudi news agency was quick to circulate an image of the young Muhammad kissing the hand of his sacked cousin. Ibn Nayif was immediately reported to have given the oath of allegiance to Muhammad ibn Salman following the latter's promotion. The opinions that Saudi dissident voices spread around the globe force the regime to counter critical messages by emphasizing the solidarity of the royal family.

Youth activism occasionally forces the regime to moderate its enthusiasm for unrealistic and overambitious projects and initiatives, especially when they are mocked online, such as the famous Social Transformation Programme (STP), which was followed by STP 2, a less ambitious plan. For example, in 2019, after days of viral hashtags criticizing the Entertainment Authority for planning to open a nightclub in Jeddah, it was officially announced that the venue would not open. The Entertainment Authority immediately posted details of the upcoming Quran recitation competition on its website, inviting potential candidates to register for the big prize.[30]

Saudi youth in the diaspora practise hashtag hijacking, or what is known online as bashtag, to create a counter-public to that of the regime. As the crown prince promoted the hashtag 'Saudi Arabia First', which trended on Twitter, dissidents used the same hashtag to undermine a slogan that in their opinion embodies racism, bigotry, and counterproductive and unwarranted nationalism. The official news agency and individual regime accounts on Twitter quickly dismiss bad news circulating online as fake news and rumours. They deem counter-hashtags that undermine the regime's own messaging as subversive and threatening to stability and national security. Through its cyber-trolls the regime popularizes the idea that such messages are the work of exiled Saudi traitors who act as agents of hostile foreign governments.

*The Crown Prince and Youth Activism: A Crisis of his
Own Making*

Muhammad ibn Salman's entrenched repression at home and the
ongoing Yemen war both eventually precipitated serious reputa-
tional damage, not only globally but also domestically. The murder of Khashoggi pushed global media to seek the opinions of
dissidents abroad, as few Saudis were authorized to comment on
the incident. After 2 October 2018, many activists abroad were
overwhelmed by media attention. Many amongst them were
unknown exiles who kept a low profile, but global media soon
began to incorporate their opinions in reporting on the crisis.
Since then, no foreign opinion essay, documentary film, or report
on Saudi Arabia was able to ignore these voices abroad. Young
students such as Abdullah al-Awdah, activist Omar al-Zahrani
and human rights defender Yahya Assiri were among those who
exposed the new wave of repression that had been sweeping the
country since 2015. Their voices joined those of women activists
in the diaspora, who highlighted the emptiness of reforms, especially those that targeted women, as most of the women activists
had already been in jail for several months before Khashoggi's
murder. In the words of one exile, Muhammad ibn Salman rendered a great service to the opposition, as his erratic and harsh
decisions brought their united voices to the forefront. In response
to the greater visibility of their voices, the dissidents themselves
began to be increasingly targeted by cyber-trolls and bots.

Western journalists based in Riyadh struggled to find a single
person brave enough to express scepticism about the regime's
strategy to cover up the murder and absolve the crown prince of
any responsibility. By the time Khashoggi was murdered, many
women had already paid a high price for celebrating the pressure
the feminist movement had put on the leadership to lift the ban
on driving. Hatoon al-Fassi, mentioned in Chapter 6, was per-

haps the last female academic interviewed by foreign media on social reforms who did not sufficiently applaud the crown prince's initiatives. She was arrested for speaking to *The New York Times* and celebrating the achievements of Saudi women who led the campaign to drive. Nicolas Pelham of *The Economist* recorded an interview with Lujain al-Hathloul and her husband, both of whom demanded more rights. The recording went viral, and she too was imprisoned for offering critical opinions and failing to praise the crown prince. Local Saudi journalists who criticized the regime on television or YouTube, such as Saleh al-Shihi, simply disappeared. Academic Anas al-Mazrou gave a lecture at Riyadh's book fair and reminded his audience of the plight of prisoners of conscience. He was not seen again. In such a climate of fear, foreign media turned its attention to Saudi exiles, students and older opposition figures abroad. By his own short-sighted repression, the crown prince created an active opposition among the very youth he wants to empower. Repression amplified and united the scattered opposition voices.

Dissidents abroad resist the current drive towards individualism and the abandonment of collective responsibility and action, all promoted by the regime. The depoliticization of Saudi youth under the crown prince involves disengagement, promoted by the entertainment industry and the introduction of pop culture controlled from above. The same applies to the arts patronized under the prince's umbrella, so that dissent and transgression are not only excluded but also severely punished. In the new entertainment industry, there is no room for politically subversive voices or messages. A government agency was created to control how to entertain the youth and their families. The circus in a very repressive context like Saudi Arabia offers an escape, a magical forum akin to *Alice in Wonderland*. The invited foreign performers barely know the local context, and their performances do not touch the contentious issues in the lives of Saudi families and young people. As such, they represent carefully selected and detached Western entertainment, affordable by the privileged. From the 75 SR cinema tickets to 150 SR live concert tickets, a large family of eight individuals with a father in medium-level public-sector employment can hardly access the new entertainment venues. The entertainment is described as 'organized by the privileged to serve the privileged' in Ms Saffaa's opinion, as mentioned in Chapter 6.

Despite the drive towards depoliticization, apathy and disengagement from public life, except in ways made legitimate by the regime, the youth, especially those abroad, have made their voices louder in recent years.

Easy to Organize, Hard to Win

The limited success of the counter-campaign of digital activism, mainly launched by Saudis in exile as those in the country face increasing surveillance and repression, may not automatically and swiftly translate into changing the structures of power, or even loosening the tight fist that the crown prince wields. But Saudis who launch such campaigns insist that they raise the level of awareness among their peers and in the long run they may achieve their desired objectives—the fall of the regime, the formation of a constitutional monarchy, or simply the introduction of limited but serious political reforms that undermine the absolute monarchy and the one-man rule of the crown prince.

Jamal Khashoggi realized that under the crown prince the narrow space for freedom of speech in Saudi Arabia had totally vanished. While in Washington, Khashoggi not only wrote critical columns in the *Washington Post*; he also had plans to allow Saudis inside the country to voice their opinions. He discussed a project with a young asylum seeker in Canada, Omar al-Zahrani, on WhatsApp. The objective was to set up virtual counter-platforms to allow Saudis to express themselves without censorship. Al-Zahrani, a twenty-eight-year-old journalist, planned to purchase telephone SIM cards and send them to Saudi activists inside the country to escape the surveillance technology of the regime. But Saudi authorities intercepted Khashoggi's conversations with al-Zahrani.

Al-Zahrani had always suspected that his telephone and messages were hacked by the regime, so he sought advice from a Toronto University–based centre, the Citizen Lab,[31] which specializes among other things in investigating cyber surveillance, hacking, and targeting of dissidents and civil society activists by repressive regimes. The investigation concluded that al-Zahrani's phone had been hacked by the Saudi authorities using a programme purchased from an Israeli company called NSO. Al-Zahrani appeared on CNN together with Citizen Lab staff and announced that his phone had been hacked. He claimed that he had suspected that the regime was listening to his conversation with Khashoggi as the two were planning to work together on several projects.[32] Khashoggi had plans to set up a research centre or an academy for the promotion of democracy in the Arab world. Within two years of settling abroad, Khashoggi had gone from being a mild critic of the regime to becoming an activist, drawing on the internet-savvy youth in exile. The Saudi authorities feared that he would become a focal point around which opposition voices could coalesce to launch a systematic and persistent campaign undermining regime propaganda. Longer-term dissidents abroad were initially suspicious and apprehensive of Khashoggi, but within months of taking up residence in Washington, he was able to build trust and engage with young activists.

Only after the murder of Khashoggi did it emerge that he had been in correspondence with al-Zahrani. Al-Zahrani broke his silence and announced that he had received $5,000 from

Khashoggi to help set up a specific project. Khashoggi and al-Zahrani were determined to counter the regime's online harrassment. Al-Zahrani suggested creating a Twitter account called 'the Electronic Bees', to debunk the regime's propaganda and spread information about how to engage in digital activism securely and without fear of arrest. After Khashoggi was killed, the project was put on hold for several months. But by the summer of 2019 the Electronic Bees had taken shape, thanks to efforts by al-Zahrani and other young Saudi exiles such as Abdullah al-Juraywi in London and Abdulaziz al-Muayyid in Dublin.

Omar al-Zahrani grew up in Jeddah, where his father was an employee of the intelligence services. He confesses to having been influenced by his education and regular attendance at the summer camps where young Saudis had extra lessons in Islamic education and were exposed to an Islamist agenda. At one point he felt attracted to the Sahwa, especially the Sururi trend, a mix of Muslim Brotherhood ideology and Salafi thinking, that dominated the Islamist scene at the time. He was socialized into 'Islamic morality and an awareness of Muslim causes from Afghanistan to Iraq'.

Al-Zahrani reflects on his childhood:

My father was *multazm* [conservative Muslim who shuns excesses in life]. He did not eat meat and abhorred excessive indulgence. He believed that his work for the intelligence services helps the stability of the regime. But he also believed that the regime can be reformed from within, and as such he remained loyal to the Al Saud. However, he took early retirement at the age of forty-four. He then moved to the private sector, establishing schools and motels while also starting to study for a Ph.D. degree. He always loved teaching and education. We then were able to see our father more regularly and play with him as he became free from public employment. It was the best period in my life, as I was able to spend time with my father, which I didn't have an opportunity to do before. Our financial situation improved a lot and we were able to enjoy a good and comfortable life.[33]

In Saudi Arabia, al-Zahrani was already aware of the Islamist trend, and supported HASM when its founders were arrested and put on trial in 2009. His concern with public affairs coincided with an awareness of scandals, corruption and mismanagement, all discussed at home with his father, who had an insider's knowledge of these issues given his work with the intelligence services. His introduction to activism was during the Jeddah floods in 2009, when he began to express critical opinions of officials:

> I began to connect with other like-minded young men to discuss the abysmal infrastructure of the city and got introduced to new vocabulary such as constitutional monarchy, human rights and representative government. I felt attracted to such concepts. I began to use Facebook to write my ideas. The most critical moment in my activism came with the Arab uprisings in 2011. I felt thrilled by the prospect of democracy and change. I began to tweet in support of the Arab uprisings and hoped mobilization would start in Saudi Arabia.

At the age of eighteen al-Zahrani received a scholarship to study in Montreal, where he was when the Arab uprisings started. He first enrolled in an English-language school and later moved to Bishops University, where he is still studying sociology and political science. With the Arab uprisings, al-Zahrani began to

> raise the ceiling when demanding political change. I was convinced that constitutional monarchy would deliver the required change and deal with the crisis of repression. I built strong connections with Abdullah al-Hamid, Walid Abu al-Khayr and many others, all online and without meeting any of them. I returned to Saudi Arabia abruptly as my father had a car crash and almost died. I stayed until my father received a call commonly known as *istid'a* to appear at the intelligence services headquarters. They told him that I would end up in prison if I continued to be so vocal against the regime. My

father returned and told me that I would languish in prison and nobody would know about me or defend me, as I was a young, insignificant activist. I decided to return to Canada.

When I arrived in Canada, I realized that my scholarship had already been suspended. I then started working in restaurants to support myself and continue my studies. Then came the Saudi-led coup in Egypt in 2013, which augmented my activism, as I was against the coup and hated how the Saudi regime derailed democracy in the Arab world. This coup was *sadma* [shock] as far as I was concerned. I was told by the Saudi consulate to go back to Saudi Arabia to renew my passport after they refused to do this in Canada. I thought this was a trap, so at this point I applied for asylum and got it in 2014. I immediately started a YouTube series called Fitna[34] [discord], explaining how the regime labels any criticism as discord to dissuade us from engaging with dissent. The show was immediately a success among the youth and suddenly I had many followers and subscribers to my YouTube channel. I began to build my reputation as a dissident, calling for the end of unemployment, corruption, illegal confiscation of land, the well-known *shubuk* [plots of land enclosed by barbed wire given to princes as gifts], arbitrary detentions, and Saudi regional policies that supported coups against democracy. I want a constitutional monarchy, transitional justice, freedom for prisoners of conscience, and many other demands. This is just the beginning, and I adopt these slogans so that I don't frighten followers who might think I am a radical calling for the downfall of the regime. I want political parties, civil society and an elected government.

Al-Zahrani reflects on the Saudi opposition in general and laments the absence of unity. He praises the recently founded forum Diwan London, where Yahya Assiri brought together several dissidents to discuss issues relevant to political change despite their ideological differences. Al-Zahrani is aware of differences among dissidents:

> I don't want to force people to accept my political ideas. I should respect their different paths. But we should all have a document,

mithaq sharaf [an honoured statement], to respect each other as critics of the regime, and work together. We should overcome our individualism and seek collective action. We don't want sectarianism to divide the Sunnis and the Shia, or ideological divides between liberals and Islamists, or between men and feminists. We need to unite against the injustice inflicted on all of us.

A life in exile may not be smooth and easy, but al-Zahrani insists that he wants to send a message to other young Saudis that choosing activism and inevitable exile do not automatically lead to misery, poverty and dislocation:

I make sure that in my shows I appear well dressed and composed so that the regime doesn't succeed in painting a dark picture about us in the diaspora to intimidate and dissuade the youth from activism. My only regret is the hardship that my brothers experienced after my activism, as I can count around twenty members of my family and friends who were arrested because of me. Other members of my family are banned from travel. This was a great shock, but I reached a state of *sakina* [peace of mind], and I turned more aggressive in my attack on the regime. I wasn't intimidated by this group punishment.

The murder of Khashoggi was yet another incentive to continue the struggle, according to al-Zahrani. This resulted in his reputation reaching an unprecedentedly high level, especially when he announced that he was corresponding with the slain journalist:

I suddenly became the focus of CNN, the NYT and many other media. I have never experienced such attention. Many people offered to support me with funds to continue Khashoggi's unfinished projects, and now there are two anonymous donors who support the Twitter Electronic Bees initiative. I want to expose the myth that the youth are unhappy abroad. We are prospering away from the repression under the rule of the crown prince. I highlight youth problems such as the high suicide rate, unemployment, drug addiction, apathy, and inability to establish their own families. Many sons still live off the salaries of their fathers. I don't want to reprimand young men and humiliate them. I want to empower them and make them believe they are strong and capable of changing their miserable and repressed life. I want to give them hope. I want to counter the regime narratives which stress that if we mobilize against it, we will share the fate of Arabs who rebelled against their regimes in 2011, like Syrians, Egyptians and Yemenis.

Al-Zahrani realizes that the real awakening and inevitable change could take several years. He argues:

> This is like the excavation of stones. We need to expose the regime, and we are not immoral young men seeking fun and freedom in the West, or renegades and traitors in exile, as the regime describes us. We have intellectuals, human rights activists, professionals, students and lawyers in exile, and together we will succeed in sending a coherent message.

To pursue his objective of introducing the many diverse dissident faces and voices in exile, al-Zahrani launched a new show named Fi al-Khaliyya (In the Cell)[35] during the fasting month of Ramadan in 2019. The show was accompanied by a hashtag of the same title, under which audiences could send comments and engage in discussion. Ramadan television series have become notorious on official Saudi-owned satellite channels such as MBC and others, where the television and film industry serve the state agenda of either showing how conservative Saudi society is or attacking the regime's opponents in dramatized ways. Fi al-Khaliyya plays on the regime's accusations that activists found dormant cells to undermine the security of the kingdom, adapting this to portray the multiple peaceful voices calling for political change. Al-Zahrani's show consisted of evening interviews with known opposition figures, both Saudi men and women, but also a few non-Saudi Arabs, to discuss history, politics and society. The show was interactive, as followers posted their questions and comments on the interview and evaluated the discussion with messages, some praising the content of the interview and others condemning it. Al-Zahrani offered biographies of the interviewees and let them describe their journey into the world of opposition, so that the younger generation of dissidents could get to know the previous one. He hopes that the youth will follow the steps of the dissident fathers and mothers whose lives were affected by repression and struggle for a better future. Al-Zahrani is determined to continue the struggle himself. He informed me when I interviewed him in September 2019 that his new project is to establish an online academy, along the lines that Khashoggi envisaged, and to invite Saudi and other academics to give lectures about Saudi Arabia, the Arab world, democracy and political change.

The popularity of al-Zahrani among young Saudis turned his platform into a digital hub for many critical voices. His chitchat style, casual conversation and spontaneity all made him an attractive focus for many young men and women to listen to an alternative discourse. His shows differ from the very formal and ideologically saturated media activities of the old Islamist opposition and regime propaganda, as he appeals to young Saudis by talking their language. His effort to continue the projects of Khashoggi materialized, thanks to his perseverance following the shock that he experienced after the journalist was murdered.

Al-Zahrani is currently working on the Electronic Bees project with other exiles. This work is divided into a branch that deals with human rights and another covert electronic operation that undermines the regime's propaganda. Since launching the project, he has sought help from many young Saudis, including Abdullah al-Juraywi in London, Abdulaziz al-Muayyid in Dublin and Bader al-Hamid in Canada. Their work depends on reaching out to Saudis inside the country using relatively safe and protected internet technology.

Twenty-two-year-old Abdullah al-Juraywi left Riyadh in January 2019, only two months after Khashoggi was murdered.[36] His journey into exile started after a relative and blogger, Nouf Abdulaziz, was arrested for critical tweets. In his words, she belongs to *al-jamaa*, his family group of Banu Khalid. He believes that harming women is a red line that should not be crossed by the regime. Her crime was to defend detained prisoners of conscience and demand their release. After her arrest, al-Juraywi wanted to participate in the Electronic Bees project, but realized that doing so from inside the country would be very risky:

> I began to work with al-Zahrani for three months while inside Saudi Arabia and provide secure communication among activists so that they are protected from the regime. But I received many threats on Twitter from regime trolls. Exile became an unavoidable option as I expected to be arrested. My objective is to exercise pressure on the regime to change and to release political prisoners. We are peaceful young activists. When I arrived in London, the regime began to call on my family and interrogate them. They want to know who my friends are and who I communicate with. Now I cannot call my parents as this might subject them to threats and even detention.

A life in exile is not easy. Al-Juraywi describes it as *ghurba*, estrangement and alienation:

> I belong to the middle class and my father is now retired from his job in the military. My mother is a housewife. When I arrived in London, my life suddenly stopped. It is almost like death. But I am slowly embarking on a new life as a dissident in exile. Since I arrived in London, I work openly. I don't need to erase my name and myself. I will not stop my activism like our fathers and grandfathers did. I want freedom of speech and if I don't express myself, I will die again. Freedom is so important to me. The murder of Khashoggi was followed by many lies in the media. How can the regime lie so much in its propaganda? If I had stayed in Riyadh, I would have disappeared, but unlike Khashoggi nobody would know about me, as I am

young and not so famous. It is great that dissidents are grouping in London where we have regular discussions and debate at Diwan London. I am an independent person and do not follow any political trend, whether Islamist or secular. But I am willing to cooperate with all Saudi opposition figures as long as they don't ask me to follow a specific group and leader.

Al-Juraywi describes how he abandoned his relatively uneventful life in Riyadh:

> When I was in Saudi Arabia, I was studying at university and in my free time I used to volunteer for charities. I have no problem with the new entertainment and even worked for the Entertainment Authority as a temporary organizer of events and exhibitions. The youth need entertainment, but the cost is too high even for the middle classes. Society needs better shows than the ones available now. We need to respect our heritage, but the regime only respects its own history and promotes Diriyyah, the first capital of the Saudi state. The regime ignored other heritage and destroyed our diverse *hawiyya* [identity]. They want us to adopt *hawiyya Saudiyya* [Saudi identity], but we have our own identity. The regime succeeded in trivializing the concerns of *shabab* [youth] who are suffering from unemployment, debts and housing shortages. I want to send a message to the *shabab* so they understand that if you have all these things, there are others who don't, and we should think about them. I want them to overcome their selfishness and think about all of us.

Al-Juraywi is studying English and plans to continue his university education and obtain a degree in Sociology. He is focused on reading about democracy and human rights to help him with his online media activities, together with Omar al-Zahrani and others in exile. He admits that 'there isn't an Arab model of government that I can follow. They are all bad. But I accept people's choices and if there is an election in Saudi Arabia and people vote for the Islamists or others, I am happy to support them.' On the first anniversary of Khashoggi's murder, al-Juraywi demonstrated outside the Saudi embassy in London together with other activists.

The proliferation of youth digital activism seems to spread around clusters that overlap and cooperate. Sometimes activists coordinate their activities, but most of the time there is no over-all joint strategy apart from deconstructing regime narratives. Canada emerged as a centre for Saudi activism, based around al-Zahrani, as many students on scholarships became asylum seekers. Dublin is also developing into a forum for Saudi youth under the media initiatives of Abdulaziz al-Muayyid, a human rights activist. Both draw on the efforts of other exiles scattered around Europe, in Australia and in other countries. Since many young Saudi girls have sought asylum in Australia, a new human rights forum was founded in September 2019 under the name Sawa. In Germany, exiled prince Khalid al-Farhan and other asylum seekers engage in conversations over Skype, YouTube and other online networks.

In Berlin, thirty-four-year-old Ali Dubaisi is the director of the European–Saudi Organization for Human Rights, funded by Reprieve and other private donors.[37] He documents human rights abuses, arbitrary detention and cases involving the death penalty. He mobilizes international and UN human rights organizations in support of Saudi detainees. It is illuminating to understand Dubaisi's journey, which led to seeking refuge in Germany. A Shia from Awamiyya and owner of a computer and smartphone shop, he travelled to other nearby towns to deliver goods to his clients.[38] In May 2011, at the height of the Arab uprisings and during the demonstrations in Qatif, Dubaisi was stopped at a checkpoint between Awamiyya and Safwa, searched, and taken to the police station for interrogation:

> I was stopped and asked first by the officer for my Saudi ID and then he began to search my car without showing a proper warrant. He found some articles printed from websites that include various topics

such as culture, economy, politics and society, and he decided to take them. Then they put me into the police car and sent me to the police station in Safwa, where I was put into a prison cell (2m x 2m), and was not allowed to make any contact, including with my family or a lawyer. I was interrogated twice, and then it became clear to the detective that there was no reason to keep me since they found no problem. As a result, I was released after three days spent in an individual prison cell.

In September 2011, Dubaisi was detained again

in the same place, for the same reasons, by the same officer and after nearly four months (exactly 124 days) from the release date of the first arrest. During that time, I was preparing to move into another apartment and I was cleaning my office, so I had a couple old books and printed articles in my car that I was planning to recycle. On the same day I had to deliver a number of orders, since my business is computer and smartphone sale and repair. During one of the delivery journeys from Awamiyya to Safwa, I passed by the checkpoint which is located between the two cities after delivering the order, and I was arrested on my way back. At the checkpoint, the same officer who searched my car and arrested me the first time asked me for my Saudi ID. So again, he began searching my car and found a number of ordered smartphones that I was planning to deliver plus boxes of old books and articles. Then he asked me to get out of the car to go to the police station. I explained to him at that moment that 'you arrested me four months ago for the same reason and I was released after three days, so there is no reason to arrest me again,' but he did not respond. All he did was handcuff and leg-cuff me, and I was sent immediately to the main police station in Qatif, where they put me in a dark solitary confinement cell for seven days. During that time, I was sent for interrogation once, and I wasn't allowed to make any contact with the outside world at all. On the Sunday morning they threw me blindfolded, handcuffed, and leg-cuffed into the rear compartment of the police car and sent me to an unknown destination; it dawned on me later that this was the General Intelligence Prison in Dammam, where authorities usually hold prisoners of conscience. During my time there for forty-eight days, I was exposed to many types of violations and torture (ethical, racial and sectarian degrading and insults, beatings with hands, slapping, punching, kicking of the legs, beatings with hoses, standing for hours with hands up and blindfolded, denial of medical treatment, reduction and raising of the temperature of the cell ...). Also, I was only allowed once to make a phone call which was on Monday 10/10/2010, fifteen days after my second arrest, and the phone call's duration was only for seven minutes, mostly spent hearing my mother crying.

Once in the hands of the Intelligence Services, Dubaisi underwent

five sessions of interrogation; the detective found no justification for the arrest. The detective told me they would release me from the General Intelligence Prison back to the police again but did not tell me the release time. I spent dozens of days in solitary confinement not knowing my fate. After forty-eight days spent in the General Intelligence Prison in solitary confinement, I arrived at the police and was sent back into a dark solitary confinement. On the second day the detective told me I would be released during the next few days, and he told me that I could call my family and tell them, so I called my wife and my mother and I told them that, but without specifying a time. This was the first contact with my wife for fifty-seven days. Contrary to what I was promised by the detective, I was transferred to the Dhahran police station on Monday 21/11/2011 into solitary confinement and then handcuffed and leg-cuffed for the interrogation session again and stayed there until 23/11/2011 and was then transferred on the same day to Dammam General Prison. It is a prison where they usually hold criminals and murderers. After a couple days I was taken on Monday 28/11/2011 to the Bureau of Investigation and Public Prosecution for interrogation again and was sent back the same day to Dammam General Prison. I stayed in this prison until my release date, 08/13/2012, where I spent 264 days without any explanation or justification. In total, I spent 323 days in my second arrest with no charge or trial.

Dubaisi's crime was simply being Shia from Awamiyya, transporting computers and smartphones to his clients between towns in the Eastern Province, and writing about human rights. He explains:

> Since I am one of those activists in the society and had written a number of articles in independent media expressing my personal opinion and belief and also was a human rights and cultural activist, it is unlikely that the Saudi authorities would stop targeting me since they ended up trying a number of times to arrest me.

His participation in the Awamiyya Forum, a local debating club, and expression of criticism of the situation in Saudi Arabia, especially among his Shia co-religionists, made him suspect in the eyes of the Saudi security services. His articles, mostly highlighting inequality and discrimination among the Shia, published in a Shia online magazine, *Rasid*, alerted the authorities to his critical opinions.

Ali Dubaisi suspected that he would be arrested for a third time, as many of his relatives and friends had already been detained in 2013. His school friend Sayyid Akbar al-Shakhori was shot dead during a demonstration in Awamiyya, an event that saddened and shocked him.[39] He swiftly took the decision to leave with his wife and two children. He arrived in Germany and was granted asylum within a year.

Dubaisi's activism encompasses wider issues than those relevant to the Shia. He followed the cases of detainees from all regions, sects and ideologies. More recently, he highlighted the problem of unreturned bodies of executed prisoners whose relatives were unable to conduct appropriate funerals. While the body of Jamal Khashoggi is yet to be found and buried, if it is still intact, there are around eighty-two bodies held by the regime after executions that took place between 2016 and 2019.[40]

The efforts of Dubaisi complement those of ALQST, run by Yahya Assiri in London. Assiri and an older generation of exiles started providing an umbrella for various projects and media campaigns, one of which is to hold an annual conference for Saudis in the diaspora. Dubaisi welcomes the surge in support for human rights abroad, as 'no one organization is able to deal with the rising number of cases.' He works closely with Assiri, with whom he has an informal memorandum of cooperation. They share information about abuses in all regions of Saudi Arabia, occasionally meeting at UN forums in Geneva. One issue on which Dubaisi focuses is the return of bodies after executions by the regime. While this problem is of concern to all families of the executed, it is particularly relevant to those Shia whose funeral rites are culturally specific to the community. In September 2019, Dubaisi and Assiri used UN forums to put pressure on the regime to return the bodies of those executed inside Saudi prisons to their families. On 10 October 2019 a special event was planned, and the two activists worked together to highlight the cases of families who are unable to bury the bodies of their executed relatives.

Dubaisi hopes that the scattered efforts of exiles can come together under an institutional framework in which all movements, activists and dissidents coordinate their efforts. In his opinion, this will provide continuity and strength. Above all, the opposition will eventually turn into an international lobby that pressures both foreign governments and the Saudi regime to take steps to improve the abysmal human rights situation in the country. He laments that 'currently the opposition is in the process of debate, discussion and talk, but the regime has already taken the lead in pursuing a project of silencing all critical voices.' One important issue that the opposition should pursue 'is to pledge to accept pluralism and diversity' as a mechanism to unite. 'Without this, we will continue to be fragmented. We need more activists whose job is to engage in *taqrib* [bridging the divide] between various dissidents. As we lack the opportunity to engage in open conversations inside the country, we have to do this abroad.'

The geographical divides of the diaspora reflect certain ideological differences. In both London and Canada there is a tendency for dissent to have an Islamist-leaning agenda or a feminist project, while remaining open and inclusive of other trends. But the new Islamism is diluted and hybrid. None of the activists openly admit their affiliation to a specific Islamist trend, although many amongst them have a history of sympathizing with Islamist ideas. Under the rubric of human rights, activists are able to promote the cases of all detainees regardless of their political persuasions or sectarian affiliation. This also applies to the youth activism in Canada. In Dublin, Abdulaziz al-Muayyid openly declares that he is secularist. While most members of the old generation of Islamists engage with the new media forums run by the youth, one has not appeared in any show or conference that brings people together regardless of their ideologies. This is London-based Saad al-Faqih, a Salafi Islamist. However, he often sends a representative from his office in London, and his supporters and followers come to the annual conferences organized at Diwan London.

The young generation of exiles partially honours the work and struggles of the previous generation, especially the Islamists who had taken refuge abroad since the 1990s. Many of the people interviewed had been socialized into Islamist ideas and activism, especially since the 1990s. But they are unwilling to become blind followers of such oppositional discourse. They have a critical attitude towards Islamism in general and are willing to engage in *murajaat* (revisionist thinking) in order to learn from the previous generation and avoid their mistakes. In a recently broadcast YouTube show, Zahir al-Shihri[41] proposes evaluating the Saudi opposition in general. His first guest, Muhammad al-Qahtani, also in exile in London, denounces the Wahhabi tradition, although he is considered an Islamist. He regards it as a later Kharijite tradition that only sprang up in Arabia in the eighteenth century. In his words, 'its followers took up arms against the regime and developed into al-Qaida and the Islamic State'. He calls for a federal political system that incorporates all trends, Sunni, Shia, liberals and Islamists. He is followed by Hissa al-Madhi, mentioned in Chapter 6, who discusses the new young men and women activists. She insists that only a democratic framework can incorporate the diversity of Saudi opposition. She acknowledges that there are radicals within this exiled opposition. She also proposes that all peaceful opposition groups must unite under one banner and leadership. The inclusion of women promises to bridge the gender divide that has characterized Saudi mobilization for decades. Ali Dubaisi draws attention to the perils of other governments sponsoring the Saudi opposition, some of which attempt to dictate their agendas. The airing of this debate on the opposition sparked controversy among dissidents, who accused al-Shihri of destroying and undermining the opposition in exile.

As the sons and daughters come of age and start their own campaigns, older dissidents are drawn to them, as when Khashoggi reached out to al-Zahrani. On the proliferation of dissident voices, veteran Islamist Saad al-Faqih comments that this is a natural consequence of restricting all freedoms in the country:

> The crown prince provoked all sections of society because of his policies. Some people were already outside the country, but they openly started expressing objections to these policies while others fled the country. Those who dedicated all their lives to the opposition, together with those who left because of injustice inflicted on them personally, came together. The increase in the number of dissidents embarrasses the regime as it shows the world that its policies antagonize a diverse section of society. This will speed up change. As to the contradictory projects of the opposition, this may have negative consequences on the opposition's reputation and its performance abroad and inside the country.[42]

The proliferation of dissident voices comes at a time when individualism is apparently on the rise in Saudi Arabia in general and among the youth in particular. According to Moaddel, expressions of individualism among Saudi youth is higher than in any other Middle Eastern country that he surveyed:[43]

> [This surprising observation is] a reaction to the patriarchal values promoted by the dominant religious and political institutions. These values include the priority of parental authority over the children, obedience to religion, and religious injunction concerning the veil for women. Thus, this context turned patriarchy into a clear target of ideological attack, particularly by the youth, signifying the desirability of expressive individualistic values. Living in a relatively more prosperous economy, the Saudis have in fact been able to afford the lifestyle that is associated with expressive individualism.[44]

However, while the regime promotes a kind of populist Saudi nationalism to replace the dominant Islamic fundamentalism, it is important to mention that dissidents abroad tend to be critical of the new drive to limit political change to liberalization and entertainment, curbing the powers of the religious groups, especially the Islamist Sahwa, and the proliferation of social openness and superficial gender equality. Many of these young dissidents accept the social and gender reforms but are very critical of how this liberalism is juxtaposed with a politically repressive regime. Those who espouse liberalism tend to focus on the lack of freedom of speech and political representation, and on the opacity of regime policies and initiatives. The position of exiled dissidents is contrasted with that of Saudi youth inside the country, many of whom embraced and welcomed the social reforms of the crown prince, either because they had no choice or because they had impatiently awaited such a drive to 'normalize' Saudi society within the limits of its cultural, religious and social norms. But even those who welcome new entertainments such as the cinema argue that 'this alone does not solve existing social problems such as boredom and marginalisation'.[45]

While many young Saudis impatiently waited for the new social liberalization and have quickly become avid consumers of the entertainment industry, there are many others who question the logic of such a drive towards openness while the political system as a whole remains even more closed, restrictive and repressive.

Diaspora Politics

Saudi Arabia has had many dissidents since its creation. The project of state building was first challenged by the same people who had contributed to the Al Saud expansion. Later, in the 1950s and 1960s, a different opposition emerged as a wave of Arab nationalism, socialism and communism swept through the Arab world. But by the 1970s Islamism had displaced previous opposition and become the language of rebellion, reform and advice to the rulers. These three waves failed to accelerate the exodus abroad, although individual opposition figures sought refuge outside Saudi Arabia.

Since 2015, and for the first time in its modern history, the regime has pushed many young Saudis to seek exile. Its much-appreciated and praised scholarship programme exposed a young generation to different lifestyles and ideas. This highly interconnected generation became increasingly aware of restrictions on their freedom and of their inability to find jobs, housing and prosperity. At this point, many young activists decided to move from being students to asylum seekers. Others fled after they were threatened and intimidated by successive detentions, warnings and visits to intelligence and police stations. They flee a wealthy country with ample opportunities to realize their material dreams, leaving behind fathers and mothers who are subjected to punishment for the 'sins' of their sons. Many amongst this young and restless cohort experience serious restrictions on their freedoms and are still deprived of civil and political rights, although now they enjoy a relatively open social sphere.

At home, young people can only organize under the patronage of the regime and its many new institutions and initiatives. Independent opinions, let alone critical voices, are always muted. Exile, coupled with dedication to raising awareness of the plight of their generation under authoritarian and repressive rule, becomes a journey into a new and difficult life. Regrouping, at least virtually, and launching campaigns from abroad break the cycle of loneliness and guilt, adding meaning to their forced migration.

While a previous generation of dissidents adopted clear-cut ideologies to articulate their dissent, the new youth of Saudi Arabia who leave the country are willing to engage in hybrid discourses, transmitted mostly on social media. Their hybridity allows a certain solidarity among men and women scattered over several countries. While they guard their individualism, they nevertheless seek solidarity across ideological, gender and age divides. The new exiles congregate around the old fathers of dissent, without totally embracing the latter's point of view. Following the collapse of these old ideologies and paradigms of dissent, Saudi exiles are now reluctant to endorse them without revision and reassessment. However, they seem to be united by the pervasive repression that is affecting a cross-section of Saudi society: royals and commoners, Islamists and secularists, religious scholars and professionals, men and women. As the narrow margins of freedom of speech, association and mobilization, and the constant fear of detention become a lived experience, exiles abroad create a virtual microcosm of Saudi Arabia in its diversity and complexity. At the moment, exiles insist on cooperation, debate and solidarity, all articulated in their virtual diaspora polity abroad.

The context of repression, together with their inexperience in civil society activism, political party organizations and on-the-ground mobilization, makes joint action difficult. At the moment, exiles seem to focus on specific virtual campaigns to highlight grievances. Most of these aim to raise awareness, highlight injustice and puncture regime narratives about prosperity and security. The language of rights, anti-corruption, dignity, equality and justice dominates the rhetoric of these exiles as much as they inspired the crowds in Arab capitals during the 2011 uprisings. Exiles are gradually moving into limited action, as they now organize vigils and demonstrations outside Saudi embassies and consulates in Washington, London, Sydney and elsewhere. Local Arab activists in their host countries often support them. Gulf dissidents abroad who attend Saudi events and participate in demonstrations at Saudi embassies also embrace the kingdom's exiles. This Gulf cohort includes Kuwaitis, Omanis and Bahrainis. In recent years, Yemeni exiles joined Saudi vigils to protest at the destruction of their country since the Saudi airstrikes began in 2015.

Should these young people find themselves confronted with the opportunity to return to Saudi Arabia after the fall of the regime, amnesty or political reforms, the old divisions between Islamists and secularists, men and women, and individual and community would most probably resurface. At the moment, exiles seem to have no choice but to work together and must conceal or compromise their true beliefs and ideologies, if they subscribe to any other than a strong commitment to freedom, justice and dignity. Their small numbers, spread over several continents, and their determination to remain relevant to their own homeland force them to cooperate and engage in conversations with others, who may or may not share their commitment to a particular political project after the fall of the regime or its transformation, if both are possible in their lifetime.

Divisions within the diaspora remain and are fought on social media. Within the Islamist camp itself, pro-Wahhabis and Salafis differ from critical Islamist modernists. Many hardline feminists are very critical of Islamists abroad. Reconciliatory feminists are willing to work with moderate Islamists. In addition, hardline Salafis clash with Shia activists and refuse to cooperate with them. Such divisions persist in the diaspora despite efforts to achieve the solidarity and unity to which detained activists such as Walid Abu al-Khayr aspire. It is the decades of divisions purposefully encouraged by the regime that continue to plague politics in exile. Added to this is the fear and apprehension between exiles who have profound and justified suspicion vis-à-vis new, unknown activists who may be agents of the regime. The Saudi diaspora is just beginning to organize, in difficult and suspicious circumstances. It remains to be seen whether it will achieve national unity against the regime or become a critical mass that is taken more seriously by the international community or their compatriots at home.

THE FUTURE

The future of Saudi Arabia under the duality of reform and repression may seem bleak, as more young men and women flee the country in search of refuge. This is a challenge to a society unaccustomed to exile and forced migration. Fear settled on exiles following the murder of Khashoggi even after they reached relatively safe havens abroad. But soon the incident pushed other young Saudis inside the country to leave and become more vocal in their criticism of the regime. The mobilization of exiles to join demonstrations outside Saudi consulates in North America, Europe and Australia, in addition to lobbying international actors to pressure the regime to release prisoners of conscience, has only just begun. In addition to real activism, Saudi exiles became very active on social media, where they challenge regime promises and highlight serious abuses of human rights. While the incipient diaspora is still powerless, it proved to be an embarrassment for the regime. In fact, the murder of Khashoggi demonstrated the determination of the regime to silence Saudis even when they leave the country. Hacking social media accounts and posting threatening messages on exiles' accounts has become a deliberate policy to create fear and intimidation. Without a serious reconsideration of Saudi domestic politics and pressure from the international community, many Saudis will decide to flee the country and continue their struggle for a better life in their homeland from abroad. This has become a thorny issue between Saudi Arabia and its Western partners as more exiles seek refuge in countries that support the regime.

The era of Muhammad ibn Salman ushered in an unprecedented wave of repression, along with social and economic changes described as reform. Since 2015 domestic politics has revolved around social and economic liberalization while criminalizing any political discussion or debate. The crown prince wanted to roll back the state and move away from a state-centred, oil-dependent capitalist economy. However, in the process, he has appeared to increase state control over the economy, society, the military and the media. An autonomous or semi-autonomous public sphere quickly vanished as he introduced his own initiatives that target every aspect of public life, including the arts and entertainment. Controlled social change from above was imposed on a society deprived of the ability to stage resistance, engage in debate and express its own aspirations. Arguably, highly publicized social and economic initiatives seem to have failed to camouflage a sinister autocratic drive to silence all critical voices and narrow even further the margins of free speech.

In this book I have explored the past, stopping at important moments that have shaped the kingdom. I narrated the project of consolidating the state under the rule of the Al Saud early in the twentieth century with a view to demonstrating how this past stretches into the present, how it influences current calls for transformation, and how aspects of it continue to be both remembered and forgotten. The Al Saud are obviously proud of their efforts to build a state with the sword, but in recent years, and especially since the crown prince came to power, the regime is deliberately trying to remove embarrassing episodes of the past from the national consciousness, leaving only the parts that can be remembered without controversy. The prince is recreating

Saudi consciousness in ways that consolidate his own takeover of the state. He frames the past in a carefully controlled context, to be celebrated as a prelude to continuous progress in the present. He invites Saudis to selectively remember the past while forgetting its troubling and controversial aspects. This doctored version of the past glosses over the rationale and propaganda associated with the so-called reforms and their significance, not only for Saudis but also for the international community.

To understand how the new regime exercises power under the current crown prince, I included analysis of how the international community welcomed the newly branded prince and contributed to promoting a persuasive narrative about his top-down revolutionary reforms. The regime's power is inseparable from the international context in which it operates. It has always been so, as we saw in the first chapter, where the intervention of Britain was crucial to upsetting the balance of power among Arabian chiefs. Two aspects of the Saudi state distinguished it from the emerging post-colonial polities in the region. First, the invocation of a radical religious tradition was a crucial mechanism to launch the conquest of Arabia and subject it to the rule of the Al Saud under the pretext of purifying its religious practices. Second, while other Arab countries were founded on antagonism towards colonial powers and the subsequent liberation struggles, Saudi Arabia was in fact founded with British military and financial support. Saudis have no memory of colonial rule or any struggle for independence, as their leadership derived power from foreign support. The state project was initially resisted and challenged by those who were subjected to Saudi rule. But when oil resources started flowing into regime coffers, the project of consolidating the state became viable and durable.

After the discovery of oil, international actors such as Britain and later the United States became patrons of the realm, and the Al Saud rulers were described as 'vassals for good'. This influenced the production of knowledge about the country, which turned into 'knowledge in the time of oil', in which international media and scholarship continue to glorify previous and current Saudi monarchs by invoking the magical word 'reform'. This international context and the expectations of its most famous pundits exert pressure on the regime in ways that translate into specific forms of governmentality. The proliferation of global liberal discourses that encourage a kind of modernity defined in terms of demonstrating new forms of thinking and acting, new technologies of connectivity, artistic creations and consumption push the Saudi leadership to engage with issues defined as problematic. From religious conservatism to gender equality, the state translates world concerns into domestic policies, claiming to be solving urgent problems. However, this knowledge about past and present Saudi monarchs fails to even imagine an alternative polity in which Saudis can have rudimentary representative and elected government and political institutions. Saudi themselves have imagined such a polity, and have paid a high price, as we have seen in this book.

The narrow legitimacy base of the new crown prince even among his own kinsmen prompted a pervasive purge conducted against a whole range of political and financial rivals among the princes. The appropriation of private-sector funds, the detention of the financial elite, and the incarceration of influential princes under the guise of curbing corruption appeared as wise, popular initiatives, initially approved of by both outside observers and many Saudis. But the selective nature of the anti-corruption campaigns soon revealed them as a politically motivated move against potential rivals.

Western media's fascination with the prince, now branded as MBS, has helped to conceal the pervasive repression. Many observers justified it as inevitable and a necessary precondition for successful reforms in a society often described as socially conservative, religiously radical and economically lazy. Such discourses were inherently derived from older ones on the inevitability of oriental despotism, as they confirmed stereotypes about Saudis and royalty. The first were framed as conservative and the latter as progressive.

The repression was compounded by the failure to meet employment, housing and education targets, while publicity around entertainment, tourism and foreign investment painted a picture of a liberalized economy, long awaited by global markets and capital. A campaign to imagine a new Saudi nation that selectively remembers its past and dismisses its radical religion became essential as a cover-up for delayed achievements. A hawkish team of local aides and advisers ensured that projects to rebrand the nation and instil the spirit of creativity, innovation and connectivity with the outside world helped to spread propaganda. Branding Saudi Arabia accompanied the branding of the prince, now the celebrity Son King.

A new, aggressive Saudi nationalism was launched, intended above all to silence critical voices, which are readily described as enemies of the state, and to highlight the vitality and energy of the young reformer prince. The cult of Muhammad ibn Salman became dominant—above criticism, reprimand or scrutiny. While previous monarchs were also associated with a kind of domestic branding, the cult of the Son King was launched at the global level. This is simply because the crown prince's kingdom now needed to open up to global investors in the current international climate of cheap oil and economic liberalization. His many visions and transformation programmes were dependent on confidence in and subscription to his cult of personality.

Regime attempts to promote its desired vision of the nation, and the successive festivities and celebrations of its greatness, suffered from the usual shortcomings and contradictions of nationalism. The rhetoric of inclusion was accompanied by widespread exclusion. The diversity of Saudi Arabia was submerged in vague definitions of 'the nation'. In the past, sections of Saudi society such as tribal groups, religious minorities, women and immigrants were excluded from the nation on the basis of the bias and unchallenged power of those who unified it. The current version of Saudi nationalism perpetuates the old exclusion policies and creates new criteria for both inclusion and exclusion. Nationals are those loyal to the crown prince, while other critical voices are deemed outside the body of the nation, and a serious threat to its prosperity and well-being. As Saudis were indoctrinated in the legitimacy of killing for the faith when Al Saud rule was consolidated early in the twentieth century, now killing for the nation is promoted, to expunge foreign matter, critics and threats. Airstrikes on Yemen since 2015 served to consolidate the domestic front under the pretext of defending the nation against foreign enemies: the Houthis and their Iranian backers. Detentions at home were carried out in the name of the nation to rid it of those who communicate with foreign governments, talk to the global media without authorization, and of course those dissidents who flee the country under duress.

Saudi nationalism became a licence to silence criticism and label critics as traitors. Amidst this euphoria, the regime ordered the murder of one journalist who had previously been an ardent defender of the palace. Jamal Khashoggi was brutally murdered at the Saudi consulate in Istanbul in October 2018. In December 2019 the regime announced that the public prosecutor had sentenced five suspects to death. Saud al-Qahtani and Ahmad Asiri were both acquitted. The image of the crown prince was damaged, but not enough to make him a pariah. King Salman and his Western partners continued to support the new crown prince as if the crime had nothing to do with him. Saudis were not allowed to talk about the incident in public, as the regime pushed Khashoggi's sons to issue a statement to the effect that they were the only people entitled to discuss their father's murder. Saudi society was shocked by the brutality of the murder, but it was not allowed to express grief or ask questions. Emotions had to be suppressed, and their only legitimate expression was to support the kingdom against alleged traitors and restore confidence and trust in its own efforts to seek justice and punish those responsible for the crime. A form of funeral was held for Khashoggi, but without proper burial, as his body is still missing.

The crown prince not only suppressed the old Islamist movement but extended the repression to all aspects of civil life and freedom of speech in the kingdom. The Islamists had previously challenged the regime on various occasions, proposing their own reforms, signing petitions and criticizing domestic, regional and international policies, but with the exception of the Islamist opposition in exile, and the jihadis, Islamists inside the kingdom remained loyal to Al Saud rule in general. However, since 2015 a vigorous campaign of arrests, detentions and beheadings targeted both Sunni and Shia Islamist activists. By pledging to eradicate the Islamist Sahwa movement, the crown prince created a void that can only be filled by very loyal subjects, who refrain from voicing criticism against new initiatives, and violent jihadis. Islamists were described as being against the visible empowerment of women, the Yemen war, support for the military regime in Cairo, the privatization of state industries and the boycott of Qatar, among other divisive policies. On gender equality, the Council of Higher Ulama and regime religious scholars were the most vocal in denouncing Westernization, women driving and lifting the guardianship system. Loyal Islamists who remained out of prison expressed solidarity with the regime and defended its policies, as they had no choice. Those who failed to praise the regime and the crown prince were detained, as they had committed a crime of omission.

The regime was bewildered by the new activism of the Saudi feminist movement that began to form a national front, cutting across old ideological and sectarian divisions. While many of their demands were met as the regime appropriated their slogans and acted on them, their bold mobilization since 2011 frightened the regime as it realized that their voices had become global and their demands were not restricted to mitigating gender inequality. A broad section of this feminist movement has been targeted since 2017, as they continue to demand more rights and to scrutinize the new reforms. The regime wanted to take full credit for social changes, rather than acknowledging the efforts and campaigns of feminists. The women activists who crossed the gender divide, became active in national politics and demanded political representation, or who got involved in civil society mobilization that called for greater freedoms for all citizens, were sent to jail. They were described as agents of foreign governments, traitors or immoral women who did not respect Saudi values and tradition.

Other Saudis who simply expressed opinions with regard to specific policies, such as those who criticized the crown prince for floating the oil company Aramco, objected to the war in Yemen, or exposed the corruption of high-ranking officials, were simply silenced behind bars. While a few activists praised the new social openness, they were not satisfied by the limited reforms, as they argued that only political reform can guarantee a durable solution to the excesses of the regime and the problems of disenfranchised and marginalized citizens. As many of the reforms were suggested in reports by foreign management-consultancy firms, many Saudi citizens felt a sense of great exclusion. The regime showed no sign of consulting the very people affected by its reforms.

Social media played an important role even before 2015. Saudis used the internet and new communications technology to connect with each other in the absence of legitimate forums for discussion and debate. While they had always enjoyed political discussion in small, closed circles of relatives and friends, social media enabled them to reach a virtual community of Saudis and others. The abstract nation, whether religious or pan-Islamic, became a virtual reality in which membership is far-reaching and less costly. They aired their grievances, commented on domestic affairs and demanded services. A small minority called for the downfall of the regime and mobilized others to join protest both online and in reality. By 2015 most Saudis had become avid users of Twitter. The new prince recognized the subversive potential of the new platform and quickly appropriated it to launch his own propaganda and catch online dissidents. His personality cult was anchored in social media as his trolls and bots flooded the cyber-sphere not only with propaganda but also with intimidation. They spread fear and threats against dissenting voices. Many Saudis found themselves in prison simply for cyber-crimes, loosely defined as tarnishing the reputation of the king, spreading rumours and criticizing regime policies.

The duality of reform and repression pushed many men and women to leave the country. Since 2015 many Saudis who were threatened with detention or whose family members had been arrested have decided to seek asylum in other countries. Young women fled after the regime failed to protect them against abusive relatives. Young men of all political persuasions joined women exiles to establish institutions in the diaspora to support exiles and bring their many voices under one umbrella. New trends began to appear among exiles, who sought solidarity across generational, ideological and gender divides. Many expressed their support for others who did not share their political convictions. It seems that the diaspora is capable of staging a united front against the regime's increasing repression. Whether this diaspora will succeed in defining new national politics remains to be seen. Saudis have long been divided over the future of the country, but the current repression seems to unite them in exile, albeit temporarily.

While Muhammad ibn Salman continued to push for his economic and social reforms, both of which needed vast domestic wealth and international investment, in 2020 his reforms were seriously undermined by two global crises. Oil prices, which had been declining since 2014, continued a dramatic downward slide that undermined Saudi income from this important commodity. The crown prince contributed to this slide by continuing to pump oil into a sluggish global market following disagreement with Russia over production cuts. By May 2020 Saudi Aramco announced a 25 per cent fall in net income, thus depriving the crown prince of the funds needed to pursue his various projects, amongst them the famous NEOM city by the Red Sea.[1] The NEOM project was tarnished by the death of Abdulrahman al-Huwaiti, a native of the Red Sea territory on which the future NEOM city was planned. He refused to give away his land and property and was shot in his house during a confrontation with the police.

In the same month, Saudi Arabia announced that in July 2020 value added tax (VAT) would increase from 5 per cent to 15 per cent in anticipation of future budget deficits. Moreover, the state cost-of-living allowance paid to Saudis employed in the public sector was suspended to cut spending. This is just the beginning, as the government may be forced to resort to further measures, such as suspending employment in the public sector, cutting the salaries of existing state employees, or simply finding itself in the difficult situation of not being able to pay them at all.

With oil prices showing no sign of improvement throughout 2020, it is not certain that the new increase in VAT and the suspension of the living allowance will generate enough income for the state to compensate for serious losses. Both these measures are desperate attempts to increase revenues at a time when oil is increasingly becoming cheaper than water in the desert kingdom.

THE FUTURE

The political implications surpass these limited and desperate measures that in themselves will never be enough to halt the slide towards the unknown. The so-called Saudi social contract is believed to rest on a bargain. The government provides extensive services such as jobs in the public sector, education, housing and health. Under Muhammad ibn Salman, entertainment and income from tourism promise Saudis affluence and leisure. In return, citizens are expected to continue to pledge allegiance to the leadership, accepting their total political marginalization, disenfranchisement and even repression in the name of security and affluence. The crown prince, however, has continued to spend on projects abroad, for example initiating the acquisition of a football club in Britain, and promising Western countries, especially the USA, further arms deals amidst controversy and criticism.

This social contract was based on wishful thinking rather than an accurate assessment of state–society relations. Since the discovery of oil in 1933, Saudis have never stopped challenging their government—even in times of affluence and abundance, as we have seen in this book. Throughout the twentieth century, most opposition was articulated in ideological terms rather than being based on matters of domestic economic well-being. Both Saudi Arab nationalists and Islamists launched challenges to the state based on a discourse that concerns the identity of the state rather than its economy, finances or pledges to continue its vast welfare services. Nationalists challenged it on the basis of its connections with imperialist and Western projects, while Islamists preoccupied themselves with questions of authenticity, Islamic heritage and commitment to global Islamic revival, seeing oil in the hands of the state as an enabling mechanism to pursue such projects. Under such grand ideological projects, and while the state continued to pay citizens' salaries and provide sub-standard welfare services, the mismanagement of the economy persisted, and was elevated to new levels under the leadership of Muhammad ibn Salman.

However, the new economic hardship, brought about by the plundering of the country's wealth in the pursuit of futile projects, along with the introduction of new taxes, may raise fresh critical voices, of those suffering under new conditions that touch their own lives. How long can Saudis remain silent over their own impoverishment while at the same time they see the perpetuation of elite privileges, especially those of the crown prince?

Domestically, from Vision 2030 and the National Transformation Programmes to futuristic cities, billions of dollars were wasted without any accountability. Saudis are bound to lose their enthusiasm for grand mythical projects that are undoubtedly products of a vicious propaganda machine and the grandiose illusions of the crown prince.

As Saudis are subjected to new taxes and welfare cuts, many amongst them may shift their focus from the identity of the state and its worldview to their own destiny. The gradual erosion of state services and salaries, coupled with rising consumer prices and the prospect of prolonged poverty, will surely be the focus of a new era of opposition politics ushered in by the mismanagement of the leadership and its own narrow interests.

In addition to the current oil crisis, the Covid-19 pandemic reached Saudi Arabia early in 2020. By May the rate of infection was continuing to rise among the population, and even more so among the over 10 million immigrant workers. By August 2020, over 300,000 cases were reported and more than 3,000 deaths recorded, despite early measures to curb the spread of the virus.[2] Lockdowns and curfews were imposed in various cities. The lockdown resulted in the suspension of prayers in the Grand Mosque in Mecca, hitting the religious tourism that the crown prince had hoped would increase as part of economic diversification. In the period leading up to the 2020 Hajj, it became increasingly clear that Muslims would be unable to perform the annual pilgrimage in August, with the threat of infection, disrupted travel and successive lockdowns. The general tourism initiatives in other regions of the country received a serious blow as the infection ravaged many countries. The entertainment programme for 2020 was put on hold as Saudis retreated to the safety of their homes and international performers cancelled trips to Saudi Arabia.

In 2020, Saudi Arabia continued to detain peaceful activists who had been calling for change. Lujain al-Hathloul among others remains in prison, while Abdullah al-Hamid died in detention after being denied medical attention. The crown prince showed no sign that he was prepared to release prisoners of conscience in the face of the pandemic. With the world occupied with Covid-19, Saudi Arabia's repression continued at home.

The years-long war in Yemen was equally forgotten, as Saudi Arabia continued to pledge funds for rebuilding the devastated country on its southern border. Ceasefires were agreed in 2020, but there is still no sign that the Saudi airstrikes—and Houthi retaliation—were halted. Saudi Arabia remains mired in Yemen as the latter's ongoing economic hardship, exacerbated by the pandemic, continues to cause suffering for its people.

While reform may have appealed to many young Saudis and delayed open confrontation with the regime over repression, the current dual crisis of low oil prices and the pandemic may prove to be more serious and challenging. The crown prince may not be able to deliver on the promises he had made to create a new, open Saudi Arabia. The dwindling resources and the tarnished image of the prince immediately after the murder of Khashoggi created an atmosphere of mistrust in his projects. Saudis will watch how their leadership deals with the decreasing state revenues and the pandemic, but the crown prince may not, at least in the short term, be able to meet the high level of expectation that he has raised.

NOTES

INTRODUCTION: KNOWLEDGE IN THE TIME OF OIL

1. The best full account of the murder of Jamal Khashoggi so far is Jonathan Rugman, *The Killing in the Consulate: Investigating the Life and Death of Jamal Khashoggi*, London: Simon & Schuster, 2019.

2. On Saudi Islamism, see S. Lacroix, *Awakening Islam: Religious Dissent in Contemporary Saudi Arabia*, Cambridge, MA: Harvard University Press, 2011; N. Mouline, *The Clerics of Islam: Religious Authority and Political Power in Saudi Arabia*, New Haven: Yale University Press, 2014; and T. Hegghammer, *Jihad in Saudi Arabia: Violence and Pan-Islamism since 1979 in Saudi Arabia*, Cambridge: Cambridge University Press, 2011. For a critique of jihadi studies, see S. Alamer, 'Beyond Sectarianism and Ideology: Regionalism and Collective Political Action in Saudi Arabia,' in M. Al-Rasheed (ed.), *Salman's Legacy: The Dilemmas of a New Era in Saudi Arabia*, London: Hurst & Co., 2018, pp. 97–116.

3. A. Hanieh, *Money, Markets and Monarchies: The Gulf Cooperation Council and the Political Economy of the Contemporary World*, Cambridge: Cambridge University Press, 2018.

4. An exception to this is T. Matthiesen, 'Saudi Arabia and the Cold War', in M. Al-Rasheed (ed.), *Salman's Legacy: The Dilemmas of a New Era in Saudi Arabia*, London: Hurst & Co., 2018, pp. 217–33.

5. M. Yamani, *Changed Identities: The Challenge of the New Generation in Saudi Arabia*, London: Royal Institute of International Affairs, 2000.

6. P. Menoret, *Joyriding in Riyadh: Oil, Urbanism, and Road Revolt*, Cambridge: Cambridge University Press, 2014.

7. A. Le Renard, *A Society of Young Women: Opportunities of Place, Power and Reform in Saudi Arabia*, Stanford: Stanford University Press, 2014.

8. S. Foley, *The Arab Gulf State: Beyond Oil and Islam*, Boulder: Lynne Rienner, 2010 and *Changing Saudi Arabia: Art, Culture and Society in the Kingdom*, Boulder: Lynne Rienner, 2018.

9. M. Thompson, *Being Young, Male and Saudi: Identity and Politics in a Globalized Kingdom*, Cambridge: Cambridge University Press, 2019.

10. A. Hamidaddin, *Tweeted Heresies: Saudi Islam in Transformation*, Oxford: Oxford University Press, 2019.

11. H. al-Sudairy, *Modern Woman in the Kingdom of Saudi Arabia: Rights, Challenges, and Achievements*. Cambridge: Cambridge Scholars, 2017.

12. P. Veyne, *Bread and Circuses: Historical Sociology and Political Pluralism*, trans. B. Pearce, London: Penguin, 1992 [1976], p. 10.

13. Cited in P. Brantlinger, *Bread and Circuses: Theories of Mass Culture as Social Decay*, Ithaca: Cornell University Press, 1983, p. 22.

14. Veyne, *Bread and Circuses*, p. 10.

15. The best account on the cult of personality is Lisa Wedeen in her study of Syria. See *Ambiguities of Domination: Politics, Rhetoric, and Symbols in Contemporary Syria*, Chicago: University of Chicago Press, 1999.

16. K. Witfoggel, *Oriental Despotism: A Comparative Study of Total Power*, New Haven: Yale University Press, 1963.

17. S. H. Alatas, *The Myth of the Lazy Natives*, London: Routledge, 2010 (repr.).

18. N. Samin, *Of Sand and Soil: Genealogy and Tribal Belonging in Saudi Arabia*, Princeton: Princeton University Press, 2015.

19. For a general historical account of nationalism in Saudi Arabia, see M. Al-Rasheed, 'Gulf Leadership in the Arab World: From Nationalism to Hyper-Nationalism without "Political Dynamism"', in M. Owen Jones, R. Porter, and M. Valeri (eds.), *Gulfization of the Arab World*, Berlin: Gerlach Press, 2018, pp. 7–26.

20. On constructions of the nation in the Gulf and the Gulfization of the Arab world, see M. Owen Jones, R. Porter, and M. Valeri (eds.), *Gulfization of the Arab World*, Berlin: Gerlach Press, 2018.

21. E. Said, *Reflections on Exile and Other Literary and Cultural Essays*, London: Granta, 2012, p. 180.

22. Personal communication with L. Wynn and Ms Saffaa.
23. Over 10 million Saudis use Twitter. For detailed statistics on social media in Saudi Arabia see https://www.statista.com/statistics/242606/number-of-active-twitter-users-in-selected-countries. Other sources exaggerate the number of users and give a figure of 18 million. See https://www.globalmediainsight.com/blog/saudi-arabia-social-media-statistics/ (accessed 23 November 2019).
24. https://www.theguardian.com/technology/2019/nov/06/twitter-spy-saudi-arabia-workers-charged (accessed 25 November 2019).
25. On management consultancy work for the Saudi regime, see Chapter 7.
26. D. Eickelman and J. Anderson (eds.), *New Media in the Muslim World: The Emerging Public Sphere*, Bloomington and Indianapolis: Indiana University Press, 2003.
27. M. Lynch, *The Arab Uprisings Explained: New Contentious Politics in the Middle East*, New York: Columbia University Press, 2014.
28. 'Saudi Arabia Image Makers: A Troll Army and Twitter Insider', *The New York Times*, 20 October 2018, https://www.nytimes.com/2018/10/20/us/politics/saudi-image-campaign-twitter.html (accessed 27 November 2019).
29. G. Sheffer, *Diaspora Politics: At Home Abroad*, Cambridge: Cambridge University Press, 2003, p. 8.
30. For a full discussion of the regime forecast on future asylum seekers, see Chapter 7.
31. Sheffer, *Diaspora Politics*, p. 80.
32. Ibid., p. 30.
33. M. Al-Rasheed, 'Sectarianism as Counter-Revolution: Saudi Responses to the Arab Spring', in N. Hashemi and D. Postel (eds.), *Sectarianization: Mapping the New Politics of the Middle East*, London: Hurst & Co., 2017, pp. 143–58.
34. M. Al-Rasheed, *Politics in an Arabian Oasis: The Rashidi Tribal Dynasty*, London: I. B. Tauris, 1991.
35. M. Al-Rasheed, 'The Meaning of Marriage and Status in Exile: The Experience of Iraqi Women', *Journal of Refugee Studies*, vol. 6 (2) (1993), pp. 89–104; M. Al-Rasheed, 'The Myth of Return: Iraqi Arabs and Assyrian Refugees in London', *Journal of Refugee Studies*, vol. 7 (2/3)

(1994), pp. 199–219 and M. Al-Rasheed, *Iraqi Assyrian Christians in London: The Construction of Ethnicity*, London: Mellen Studies in Sociology, 1998.

36. L. Al-Rachid, 'L'Irak de l'embargo à l'occupation: dépérissement d'un ordre politique (1990–2003)', Paris: Institut d'Études Politiques de Paris, 2010.

37. M. Al-Rasheed and L. Al-Rasheed, 'The Politics of Encapsulation: Saudi Policy towards Tribal and Religious Opposition', *Middle Eastern Studies*, vol. 32 (1) (1996), pp. 96–119.

38. M. Al-Rasheed, 'Evading State Control: Political Protest and Technology in Saudi Arabia', in A. Cheater (ed.), *The Anthropology of Power*, ASA Monograph, London: Routledge, 1999, pp. 149–62.

39. M. Al-Rasheed, *Muted Modernists: The Struggle over Divine Politics in Saudi Arabia*, London: Hurst & Co., 2015.

1. BECOMING SAUDI ARABIA

1. On the controversy surrounding the national day celebrations, see M. Al-Rasheed, 'The Capture of Riyadh Revisited: Shaping Historical Imagination in Saudi Arabia', in M. Al-Rasheed and R. Vitalis (eds.), *Counter Narratives: History, Contemporary Society, and Politics in Saudi Arabia and Yemen*, New York: Palgrave Macmillan, 2004, pp. 183–200.

2. As the national day celebrations became spectacular occasions for 'legitimate fun', Saudi scholars and many Islamists called them *yawm al-wathan* (the day of the idols), as Wahhabi theology depicts such festivities as similar to the behaviour of *mushrikun* (polytheists) in the Arabian age of ignorance when people glorified their leaders.

3. Recordings circulated by Bader al-Asaker on Twitter @Badermasaker, 23 September 2019.

4. C. Leatherdale, *Britain and Saudi Arabia 1925–1939: The Imperial Oasis*, London: Frank Cass, 1983, p. 148.

5. General Authority for Statistics, Kingdom of Saudi Arabia, https://www.stats.gov.sa/en (accessed 7 April 2019).

6. On foreign labour, see F. De Bel-Air, 'Demography, Migration and Labour Market in Saudi Arabia', in Gulf Labour Markets, Migration and Population (GLMM), Gulf Research Centre, report no. 5, 2019.

7. M. Al-Rasheed, *Politics in an Arabian Oasis: The Rashidi Tribal Dynasty*, London: I. B. Tauris, 1991.

8. F. Anscombe, *The Ottoman Gulf: The Creation of Kuwait, Saudi Arabia and Qatar*, New York: Columbia University Press, 1997.

9. T. Matthiesen, *The Other Saudis: Shiism, Dissent and Sectarianism*, Cambridge: Cambridge University Press, 2015.

10. W. Ochsenwald, *Religion, Society and the State in Arabia: The Hijaz under Ottoman Control, 1840–1908*, Columbus: Ohio University Press, 1984.

11. M. Al-Rasheed, *A History of Saudi Arabia*, 2nd edn, Cambridge: Cambridge University Press, 2010.

12. On central Arabia before the rise of the first Saudi state, see U. al-Juhany, *Najd before the Salafi Reform Movement: Social, Political, and Religious Conditions during the Three Centuries Preceding the Rise of the First Saudi State*, Reading: Ithaca, 2002.

13. K. al-Dakhil, 'Social Origins of the Wahhabi Movement', Ph.D. thesis, University of California, 1998.

14. R. Vitalis, *America's Kingdom: Mythmaking on the Saudi Oil Frontier*, Stanford: Stanford University Press, 2006.

15. On the arrival of the Muslim Brotherhood in Saudi Arabia, see S. Lacroix, *Awakening Islam: Religious Discourse in Contemporary Saudi Arabia*, Cambridge, MA: Harvard University Press, 2011.

16. See T. Matthiesen, 'Saudi Arabia and the Cold War', in M. Al-Rasheed (ed.), *Salman's Legacy: The Dilemmas of a New Era*, London: Hurst & Co., 2018, pp. 217–33.

17. M. Farquhar, *Circuits of Faith: Migration, Education, and the Wahhabi Mission*, Stanford: Stanford University Press, 2016.

18. Centre for Biological Studies and Research, 'Girlfriend Shocked by Killing', *Desert Sun*, 27 March 1975, https://cdnc.ucr.edu/?a=d&d=DS19750327.2.28&e=———en——20——1——txt-txIN———1 (accessed 13 August 2020).

19. The so-called Sudaiyri Seven were the seven sons of Ibn Saud whose mother was from the Sudaiyri family, close friends of the royal household. Many observers of Saudi politics considered the seven senior princes, amongst them King Salman, as the most powerful cohort,

with unusual solidarity, as they were full brothers. In addition to King Fahd, Sudaiyri princes occupied the most senior and important jobs in the kingdom for several decades, including the Ministry of Interior (Prince Nayif), the governorate of Riyadh (Prince Salman), and the Ministry of Defence (Prince Sultan).

20. Al-Rasheed, *A History of Saudi Arabia*, p. 120.
21. M. Chulov, 'I Will Return Saudi Arabia to Moderate Islam, Says Crown Prince', *The Guardian*, 24 October 2017, https://www.theguardian.com/world/2017/oct/24/i-will-return-saudi-arabia-moderate-islam-crown-prince (accessed 19 April 2019).
22. T. Hegghammer, *Jihad in Saudi Arabia: Violence and Pan-Islamism since 1979*, Cambridge: Cambridge University Press, 2011.
23. M. Al-Rasheed, 'Saudi Internal Dilemmas and Regional Responses to the Arab Uprisings', in F. Gerges (ed.), *The New Middle East: Protest and Revolution in the Arab World*, Cambridge: Cambridge University Press, 2014, pp. 353–79.
24. A. Alaoudah, 'The Saudi State Manipulates Religious Discourse to Legitimize its Power and Undermine Independent Voices that may Pressure the State for Political Reform', Carnegie Endowment, 3 April 2018, https://carnegieendowment.org/sada/75971%20accessed%20 20%20April%202019 (accessed 19 April 2019).
25. See C. Bunzel, 'Wahhabism, Saudi Arabia and the Islamic State: Abdullah bin Jibrin and Turki al-Bin Ali', in M. Al-Rasheed (ed.), *Salman's Legacy: The Dilemmas of a New Era in Saudi Arabia*, London: Hurst & Co., 2018, pp. 183–213.
26. K. Kamel Daoud, 'Saudi Arabia, an ISIS That Has Made it', *The New York Times*, 20 November 2015, https://www.nytimes.com/2015/11/21/opinion/saudi-arabia-an-isis-that-has-made-it.html (accessed 7 April 2019). For an interesting discussion of the intersection between the Wahhabi movement and global jihadism, see Jarman, M. 2017, 'The Intersection between Wahhabism and Jihad', *Global Policy Journal*, July 2017, https://www.globalpolicyjournal.com/blog/06/07/2017/intersection-wahhabism-and-jihad (accessed 25 May 2019) and Bunzel, 'Wahhabism, Saudi Arabia, and the Islamic State'.
27. A survey of academic debates on the survival of the monarchy is dis-

cussed in M. Al-Rasheed, 'The Dilemmas of a New Era', in M. Al-Rasheed (ed.), *Salman's Legacy: The Dilemmas of a New Era in Saudi Arabia*, London: Hurst & Co., 2018, pp. 1–28.

28. See S. Yom and F. G. Gause III, 'Resilient Royals: How Arab Monarchies Hang On', *Journal of Democracy*, vol. 23 (4) (2012), pp. 74–88.

2. APOSTLES AND APOLOGISTS

1. Ignatius, 'Saudi Prince Could Jump-Start the Kingdom'.
2. Quoted in ibid.
3. E. Wald, 'The Promise and Perils of ARAMCO', *The New York Times*, 6 November 2019, https://www.nytimes.com/2019/11/06/opinion/saudi-aramco-public-offering-.html (accessed 6 November 2019).
4. 'Interview with Muhammad bin Salman', *The Economist*, 6 January 2016, https://www.economist.com/middle-east-and-africa/2016/01/06/transcript-interview-with-muhammad-bin-salman (accessed 15 November 2019).
5. T. Friedman, 'Saudi Arabia's Arab Spring, at Last', *The New York Times*, 23 November 2017, https://www.nytimes.com/2017/11/23/opinion/saudi-prince-mbs-arab-spring.html (accessed 10 February 2020).
6. 'Mohammed bin Salman, Strongman in the Making', *Financial Times*, 8 March 2018, https://www.ft.com/content/675ade40–22cc-11e8-ae48–60d3531b7d11 (accessed 10 February 2020).
7. Bernard Haykel, cited in 'Saudis are Still Stereotyped in the West', *Arab News*, 7 February 2014, https://www.arabnews.com/news/521931 (accessed 10 February 2020).
8. B. Haykel, 'The Rise of Saudi Arabia's Crown Prince Reveals a Harsh Truth', *Washington Post*, 22 January 2018, https://www.ndtv.com/opinion/the-rise-of-saudi-arabias-crown-prince-reveals-a-harsh-truth-1803422 (accessed 10 February 2020).
9. Ibid.
10. 'Ex-Twitter Employees Accused of Spying for Saudi Arabia', BBC, 7 November 2019, https://www.bbc.co.uk/news/world-us-canada-50324977 (accessed 7 November 2019).
11. Al-Rasheed, 'The Saudi Lie'.
12. A. Shihabi, 'The Need for Balance in Judging Saudi Arabia and its

Crown Prince', Arabia Foundation, https://www.arabiafoundation.org/saudi-arabia-the-gulf-states/the-need-for-balance-in-judging-saudi-arabia-and-its-crown-prince/ (accessed 11 November 2019). The Arabia Foundation is at https://www.arabiafoundation.org/ali-shihabi-articles?view=article&id=964.

13. 'Ouqubat mughalatha lil-niswiyat' [Harsh punishment for feminists], *al-Watan*, 11 November 2019.

14. Al-Rasheed, 'The Saudi Lie'.

15. Statement from President Donald J. Trump on Standing with Saudi Arabia, White House, 20 November 2018, https://www.whitehouse.gov/briefings-statements/statement-president-donald-j-trump-standing-saudi-arabia/ (accessed 7 November 2019).

16. Ibid.

17. G. Gause III, *After the Killing of Jamal Khashoggi: Muhammad bin Salman and the future of Saudi–US Relations*, CISI Briefs, 12 December 2018, https://www.csis.org/analysis/after-killing-jamal-khashoggi-muhammad-bin-salman-and-future-saudi-us-relations (accessed 10 February 2020).

18. J. Rugman, *The Killing in the Consulate: Investigating the Life and Death of Jamal Khashoggi*, London: Simon & Schuster, 2019.

19. Al-Rasheed, 'The Saudi Lie'.

20. Statement from President Donald J. Trump on Standing with Saudi Arabia, 20 November 2018.

21. Ibid.

3. THE SON KING AND THE 'MAN OF THE PALACE'

1. Interview with Hatice Cengiz, 14 June 2019.

2. J. Rugman, *The Killing in the Consulate: Investigating the Life and Death of Jamal Khashoggi*, London: Simon & Schuster, 2019.

3. United Nations Human Rights Council, *Annex to the Report of the Special Rapporteur on Extrajudicial, Summary or Arbitrary Executions: Investigation into the Unlawful Death of Mr. Jamal Khashoggi*, 19 June 2019, https://www.ohchr.org/EN/HRBodies/HRC/RegularSessions/Session41/Documents/A_HRC_41_CRP.1.docx (accessed 19 June 2019).

4. Jamal Khashoggi was interviewed on Walid ibn Talal's other television station, Rotana, https://youtu.be/W072HH7guVs (accessed 30 September 2019).

5. 'Jamal Khashoggi's Fiancée Speaks about Mourning and Freedom', *New Yorker*, 15 August 2019, https://www.newyorker.com/news/q-and-a/jamal-khashoggis-fiancee-speaks-about-mourning-and-freedom (accessed 20 August 2019).

6. J. Khashoggi, *Ihtilal al-souq al-saudi* [The occupation of the Saudi market]; *Rabi al-Arab, zaman al-ikhwan* [The Arab Spring: the time of the Brothers]; *Ro'yat muwatin 2030* [Citizen's Vision 2030].

7. Al-Khalij al-Jadid, 'Madawi Al-Rasheed: Jamil Farisi has principles that prevent him from selling the homeland', 9 September 2019, https://thenewkhalij.news/article/162960/مضاوي-الرشيد-عن-جميل-فارسي-صاحب-عقيدة-تمنعه-من-بيع-الوطن (accessed 4 March 2020).

8. United Nations Human Rights Council, *Annex to the Report of the Special Rapporteur on Extrajudicial, Summary or Arbitrary Executions*; 'Credible Evidence that Saudi Crown Prince is Liable for Khashoggi Killing—UN Report', *The Guardian*, 19 June 2019, https://www.theguardian.com/world/2019/jun/19/jamal-khashoggi-killing-saudi-crown-prince-mohammed-bin-salman-evidence-un-report (accessed 19 June 2019).

9. 'Credible Evidence that Saudi Crown Prince is Liable for Khashoggi Killing'.

10. Ibid.

11. Wemple, E., '"Enemy of the State": The Chilling and Familiar Term for Jamal Khashoggi in Trump Statement', 20 November 2018, *Washington Post*, https://www.washingtonpost.com/blogs/erik-wemple/wp/2018/11/20/enemy-of-the-state-the-chilling-and-familiar-term-for-jamal-khashoggi-in-trumps-statement/?utm_term=.badc-63caee8f (accessed 21 June 2019).

12. See M. Al-Rasheed, *Muted Modernists: The Struggle over Divine Politics in Saudi Arabia*, London: Hurst & Co., 2015.

13. Conversation with Nasir al-Said's wife and children, 12 June 2009.

14. M. Al-Rasheed, 'Mystique of Monarchy: The Magic of Royal Succession in Saudi Arabia', in M. Al-Rasheed (ed.), *Salman's Legacy: The*

Dilemmas of a New Era in Saudi Arabia, London: Hurst & Co., 2018, pp. 45–71.

15. The office of deputy crown prince was invented by King Abdullah, who feared a power vacuum should the ageing crown princes, Nayif and Sultan, die of old age and illness, which they did.

16. All references here draw on the prince's first interview on al-Arabiyya with Turki al-Dakhil on 25 April 2016, https://youtu.be/uhWfU-K0aizw (accessed 16 June 2019).

17. 'Full Transcript of the Interview with the Crown Prince Muhammad bin Salman', *The Economist*, 6 January 2016, https://www.economist.com/middle-east-and-africa/2016/01/06/transcript-interview-with-muhammad-bin-salman (accessed 16 June 2019).

18. The second mass execution during Muhammad ibn Salman's leadership as crown prince, of thirty-seven prisoners, took place in April 2019.

19. Al-Arabiyya, 25 April 2016, https://www.youtube.com/watch?v=jju7 ErdRot0 (accessed 18 June 2019).

20. M. Al-Rasheed, 'Saudi Arabia: Running into the Sand', *Prospect Magazine*, 12 October 2016, https://www.prospectmagazine.co.uk/magazine/saudi-arabia-oil-price-running-into-the-sand (accessed 27 June 2019).

21. Saudi Arabia, National Transformation Programme, 2018, https://vision2030.gov.sa/sites/default/files/attachments/NTP%20English%20Public%20Document_2810.pdf (accessed 26 June 2019).

22. King Abdulaziz City for Science and Technology (KACST), National Transformation Programme 2020, 2016, https://www.kacst.edu.sa/eng/stip/Pages/National-Transformation-Program.aspx (accessed 28 June 2019).

23. S. Kerr, 'Saudi Arabia Redrafts Crown Prince's Transformation Plan', *Financial Times*, 2 September 2017, https://www.ft.com/content/2cd73084–92e4–11e7-a9e6–11d2f0ebb7f0 (accessed 29 July 2019).

24. Saudi Arabia MiSK Foundation, https://misk.org.sa/en/ (accessed 29 June 2019).

25. Saudi Arabia General Entertainment Authority, https://www.gea.gov.sa/en/ (accessed 26 June 2019).

26. 'Nicki Minaj Pulls out of Saudi Arabia Festival after Backlash', BBC, 9 July 2019, https://www.bbc.com/news/world-middle-east-48930029 (accessed 10 July 2019).

4. THE NEW POPULIST NATIONALISM

1. N. Samin, *Of Sand and Soil: Genealogy and Tribal Belonging in Saudi Arabia*, Princeton: Princeton University Press, 2015, p. 14.
2. M. Thompson, *Being Young, Male and Saudi: Identity and Politics in a Globalised Kingdom*, Cambridge: Cambridge University Press, 2019, p. 21.
3. Samin, *Of Sand and Soil*, p. 14.
4. M. Thompson, 'The Impact of Globalization on Saudi Male Millennials: Identity Narratives', *Asian Affairs* (July 2019), pp. 1–22.
5. D. Commins, *The Wahhabi Movement and Saudi Arabia*, London: I. B. Tauris, 2002.
6. A. Hammond, *The Islamic Utopia: The Illusion of Reform in Saudi Arabia*, London: Pluto Press, 2012.
7. M. Al-Rasheed, *A Most Masculine State: Gender, Politics and Religion in Saudi Arabia*, Cambridge: Cambridge University Press, 2013, pp. 77–107.
8. Full details of the jihadi insurgency are in M. Al-Rasheed, *Contesting the Saudi State: Islamic Voices from a New Generation*, Cambridge: Cambridge University Press, 2007.
9. T. Hegghammer, *Jihad in Saudi Arabia: Violence and Pan-Islamism since 1979*, Cambridge: Cambridge University Press, 2011, p. 8.
10. On Saudi transnational networks, see M. Al-Rasheed (ed.), *Transnational Connections and the Arab Gulf*, London: Routledge, 2005; and M. Al-Rasheed (ed.), *Kingdom without Borders: Saudi Arabia's Political, Religious and Media Frontiers*, London: Hurst & Co., 2008.
11. M. Farquhar, *Circuits of Faith: Migration, Education, and the Wahhabi Mission*, Stanford: Stanford University Press, 2016.
12. Ibid., p. 20.
13. W. McCants, 'What the 1967 War Meant for Saudi Religious Exports', Brookings Institute, 2007, https://www.brookings.edu/blog/markaz/2017/05/30/what-the-1967-war-meant-for-saudi-religious-exports (accessed 1 May 2019).

14. A nascent Arab nationalist movement in the 1950s and 1960s was suppressed by the Saudi regime and its Western allies, mainly the USA. See R. Vitalis, *America's Kingdom: Mythmaking on the Saudi Oil Frontier*, Stanford: Stanford University Press, 2006.

15. T. Matthiesen, 'Saudi Arabia and the Cold War', in M. Al-Rasheed (ed.), *Salman's Legacy: The Dilemmas of a New Era*, London: Hurst & Co., 2018, pp. 217–33.

16. Ibid., p. 231.

17. 'Wahhabism was Spread at Behest of West during Cold War: Muhammad bin Salman', *The Tribune*, 30 March 2018, https://tribune.com.pk/story/1672777/3-wahhabism-spread-behest-west-cold-war-mohammed-bin-salman (accessed 1 May 2019).

18. M. Cioffoletti, 'Saudi Arabia Sings a Nationalist Tune', *Arab Gulf States Institute in Washington*, 7 January 2019, https://agsiw.org/saudi-arabia-sings-a-nationalist-tune/ (accessed 21 February 2020).

19. A. England and A. al-Omran, 'Nationalism on the Rise as Saudi Arabia seeks Sense of Identity', *Financial Times*, 7 May 2019.

20. E. Hussein, 'Saudi First: How Saudi Hyper-Nationalism is Transforming Saudi Arabia', European Council on Foreign Relations, 2019, https://www.ecfr.eu/publications/summary/saudi_first_how_hyper_nationalism_is_transforming_saudi_arabia (accessed 19 June 2019).

21. C. Jones, 'All the King's Consultants', *Foreign Affairs*, May/June 2019, https://www.foreignaffairs.com/articles/persian-gulf/2019–04–16/all-kings-consultants (accessed 29 July 2019).

22. P. Veyne, *Bread and Circuses: Historical Sociology and Political Pluralism*, trans. B. Pearce, London: Penguin, 1992 [1976].

23. Mansour al-Blushi defends Saudi nationalism on podcast, https://t.co/almqw6rI0u (accessed 14 October 2019).

24. Ibid.

25. Ibid.

26. U. Freitag, *Indian Ocean Migrants and State Formation in Hadhramout: Reforming the Homeland*, Leiden: Brill, 2003; P. Pétriat, *Le Négoce des Lieux Saints*, Paris: Publications de la Sorbonne, Pierre Vermeren, 2016.

27. On the Hadrami diaspora in Singapore and the Indian Ocean, see E. Ho, *The Graves of Tarim: Genealogy and Mobility in the Indian Ocean*, Berkeley: University of California Press, 2006.

28. Such views are expressed on http://www.saudishares.net/vb/-مايبحدث
في-بلادنا-هو-تنفيذ-الوطن-البديل-في-الحجاز501520- (accessed 10 June 2019).

29. N. Doaiji, 'From Hasm to Hazm: Saudi Feminism beyond Patriarchal bargaining', in M. Al-Rasheed (ed.), *Salman's Legacy: The Dilemmas of a New Era in Saudi Arabia*, London: Hurst & Co., 2018, pp. 117–44.

30. The story of Ghada al-Fadl was publicized on several Twitter accounts and in *The Independent*: see https://www.independent.co.uk/news/world/middle-east/saudi-arabia-mother-greece-twitter-help-danger-woman-children-ghada-allfadl-a8922576.html (accessed 23 May 2019).

31. 'Saudi's Image Makers: A Troll Army and a Twitter Insider', *The New York Times*, 20 October 2018, https://www.nytimes.com/2018/10/20/us/politics/saudi-image-campaign-twitter.html (accessed 20 September 2019).

32. Author interview with Sultan al-Abdali, 8 October 2019.

33. Author interview with Ahmad ibn Said, 10 October 2019.

34. In defence of nationalism in general, see S. al-Amer, *Hal al-ihtimam bi al-qawmiyya takhaluf?* [Is concern with nationalism backwardness?], 30 September 2015, http://www.alhayat.com/article/827392//تلفزيون
هل-الاهتمام-بالقومية-تخلف (accessed 9 October 2019).

35. Al-Amer responds to a podcast promoting a specific defence of Saudi nationalism and attacking Arab nationalism, aired in this podcast by Mansour al-Blushi, a defender of Saudi nationalism and its divorce from its Arab surroundings: https://t.co/almqw6rI0u (accessed 14 October 2019).

36. S. al-Amer, 'Iflas al-inizaliyya al-saoudiyya' [The bankruptcy of Saudi isolationists], 2019, article made available to the author by al-Amer.

37. On the Tanwiri modernists and Abdullah al-Maliki, see M. Al-Rasheed, *Muted Modernists: The Struggle over Divine Politics in Saudi Arabia*, London: Hurst & Co., 2015.

38. This section draws on al-Amer's Arabic articles in both *Ewan24* and *al-Taqrir*. Links are not available now as both sites were shut down after the detention of their founders, Abdullah al-Maliki and Sultan al-Jamri. The articles were made available to me by Sultan al-Amer.

39. S. al-Amer, 2016, https://fnjan.thmanyah.com/66 (accessed 8 October 2019).

40. Not all colonial forces suppressed Arab nationalism. In fact, during the First World War Britain encouraged rebellion against the Ottoman Empire in Arab lands on the pretext of Arab sovereignty. It also encouraged the formation of the Arab League after the Second World War. The USA also encouraged self-determination among the people who were freed from Ottoman domination in the First World War. It was only during Nasser's era in Egypt and after the 1956 war that Arab nationalism expectedly became anti-colonial and in favour of nationalizing economic assets and, in its Nasserite version, began to be seen as an 'enemy' of the West.

41. S. al-Amer, *Fi Tarikh al-ourouba* [A history of Arabism], Beirut: Jusour, 2016, pp. 132–33.

42. On Saudi Arabia and the 1948 Israeli–Arab war, see M. Al-Rasheed, 'Saudi Arabia and the 1948 War: Beyond Official History', in E. Rogan and A. Shlaim (eds.), *The War for Palestine*, Cambridge: Cambridge University Press, 2007, pp. 228–47.

43. Al-Amer, *Fi Tarikh al-ourouba*, p. 162.

44. N. Partrick, *Nationalism in the Gulf States*, LSE, Centre for the Study of Global Governance, no. 5, 2009; also in D. Held and K. Ulrichsen (eds.), *The Transformation of the Gulf: Politics, Economics and the Global Order*, Abingdon: Routledge, 2012, pp. 47–65.

45. 'Why Saudi Arabia is Embracing a New Nationalism', *Stratfor*, 4 January 2019, https://worldview.stratfor.com/article/why-saudi-arabia-embracing-new-nationalism (accessed 24 February 2020).

5. THE SUB-NATIONALS: DIVERSITY AND EXCLUSION

1. The surge in tribal genealogies is discussed in A. Al-Fahad, 'Rootless Trees: Genealogical Politics in Saudi Arabia', in B. Haykel, T. Hegghammer, and D. Lacroix (eds.), *Saudi Arabia in Transition: Insights on Social, Political, Economic and Religious Change*, Cambridge: Cambridge University Press, 2015, pp. 263–91.

2. N. Samin, *Of Sand or Soil: Genealogy and Tribal Belonging in Saudi Arabia*, Princeton: Princeton University Press, 2015, p. 2.

3. On the vanishing tribal world and its poetic representations under the new state, see A. Al-Fahad, 'Raiders and Traders: A Poet's Lament on

the End of the Bedouin Heroic Age', in Haykel et al. (eds.), *Saudi Arabia in Transition*, pp. 231–62.

4. The use and later discharge of the Bedouin tribal groups during the formation of the Saudi state and the rise of the *hadari* (sedentary) communities are discussed in Al-Fahad, A., 'The Imama vs. the Iqal: Hadari–Bedouin Conflict and the Formation of the Saudi State', in M. Al-Rasheed and R. Vitalis (eds.), *Counter-Narratives: History, Contemporary Society, and Politics in Saudi Arabia and Yemen*, New York: Palgrave, 2004, pp. 35–75.

5. S. Maisel, 'The Resurgent Tribal Agenda in Saudi Arabia', 2015, https://agsiw.org/wp-content/uploads/2015/07/Maisel_Resurgent-Tribal-Agenda.pdf (accessed 15 May 2019).

6. Al-Fahad, 'Rootless Trees'.

7. P. Ménoret, 'The Municipal Elections in Saudi Arabia 2005: First Steps on Democratic Paths,' *Bulletin of the Arab Reform Initiative*, 27 December 2005, https://www.arab-reform.net/publication/the-municipal-elections-in-saudi-arabia-2005/ (accessed 29 February 2020).

8. Samin, *Of Sand or Soil*, p. 11.

9. N. Samin, 'Kafa'a fi l-Nasab in Saudi Arabia: Islamic Law, Tribal Custom, and Social Change', *Journal of Arabian Studies*, vol. 2 (2) (2012), pp. 109–26.

10. http://www.alhayat.com/article/780057/-تكافؤ-النسب-من-منصور-وفاطمة-إلى-قاضي-العينة (accessed 16 May 2019).

11. https://www.youtube.com/watch?v=qpWDNMqLuoA&feature=youtu.be (accessed 16 May 2019).

12. See, for example, the official web forum of Otaiba: http://www.otaibah.net/m/ and the YouTube channel of Qahtan: https://youtu.be/hIOLXigZQOw (both accessed 20 May 2019).

13. Human Rights Watch, 'Saudi Arabia: Reveal Poet's Whereabouts', 2018, https://www.hrw.org/news/2018/06/13/saudi-arabia-reveal-young-poets-whereabouts (accessed 21 May 2019).

14. https://www.alaraby.co.uk//medianews/2017/8/21/-ما-قصة-وسم-السعودية-تعترف-بقتل-الرشيد-وما-علاقة-سعود-القحطاني-به (accessed 15 May 2019).

15. Samin, *Of Sand or Soil*, pp. 188–9.

16. M. Al-Rasheed, *A History of Saudi Arabia*, 2nd edn, Cambridge: Cambridge University Press, 2010, pp. 15–19.

17. 'Al-Saud are from Banu Hanifa min Wail bin Rabia', *al-Riyadh*, 2008, http://www.alriyadh.com/337287 (accessed 14 May 2019).

18. Samin, *Of Sand or Soil*, p. 195.

19. M. al-Sunaytan, *al-Nukhab al-saudiyya: dirasa fi l-tahawulata wa al-ikhfaqat* [Saudi elites: a study of changes and shortcomings], Beirut: Markaz Dirasat al-Wihda al-Arabiyya, 2004; M. al-Sunaytan, *al-Saoudiyya al-siyasi wa al-qabila* [Saudi Arabia: politics and the tribe], Beirut: al-Shabaka al-Arabiyya lil-Abhath wa al-Nashr, 2008.

20. 'Saudi Prince Guilty of Servant's Murder', *The Guardian*, 19 October 2010, https://www.theguardian.com/uk/2010/oct/19/saudi-prince-servant-murder-guilty (accessed 19 May 2019).

21. *Middle East Eye*, 1 May 2019, https://www.middleeasteye.net/video/saudi-official-accused-racism-after-ignoring-black-saudi-children-awards-ceremony (accessed 1 June 2019).

22. Alamer, S. 2018. 'Beyond Sectarianism and Ideology: Regionalism and Collective Political Action in Saudi Arabia', in M. Al-Rasheed (ed.), *Salman's Legacy: The Dilemmas of a New Era in Saudi Arabia*, London: Hurst & Co., 2018, pp. 97–116.

23. M. Yamani, 'Evading the Habits of a Life Time: The Adaptation of Hejazi Dress to the New Social Order', in N. Lindisfarne-Tapper and B. Ingham (eds.), *Languages of Dress in the Middle East*, London: Curzon, 1997, pp. 55–66.

24. https://ipfs.io/ipfs/QmXoypizjW3WknFiJnKLwHCnL72vedxjQkDDP1mXWo6uco/wiki/Muhammad_Alawi_al-Maliki.html (accessed 25 May 2019).

25. On the history of intolerance towards folkloric and healing practices, see E. Doumato, *Getting God's Ear: Women, Islam, and Healing in Saudi Arabia and the Gulf*, New York: Columbia University Press, 2000.

26. N. Mouline, *Les clercs de l'Islam: Autorité religieuse et pouvoir politique en Arabia Saoudite, xviii–xxi siècle*, Paris: PUF, 2011, p. 234.

27. F. Ibrahim, *The Shi'is of Saudi Arabia*, London: Saqi, 2006; B. Ibrahim and M. al-Sadiq, *al-Hirak al-shii fi al-saoudiyya* [Shia mobilization in Saudi Arabia], Beirut: Arab Network for Research and Publishing,

2013; T. Matthiesen, *The Other Saudis: Shiism, Dissent and Sectarianism*, Cambridge: Cambridge University Press, 2015.

28. M. Al-Rasheed, *A Most Masculine State: Gender, Politics and Religion in Saudi Arabia*, Cambridge: Cambridge University Press, 2013, p. 124.

29. There is a full discussion of the Wahhabi clerics' fatwas on the exclusion of the Shia and others concerning marriage in ibid., pp. 120–5.

30. On Shia intellectuals and history writing projects, see J. Determann, *Historiography in Saudi Arabia: Globalization and the State in the Middle East*, London: I. B. Tauris, 2014.

31. On how the Saudi regime used sectarianism to undermine the Shia protest movement in 2011 and thwart the Arab uprisings, see M. Al-Rasheed, 'Sectarianism as Counter-Revolution: Saudi Responses to the Arab Spring', in N. Hashemi and D. Postel (eds.), *Sectarianization: Mapping the New Politics of the Middle East*, Oxford: Oxford University Press, 2017, pp. 143–58. For an alternative interpretation of the Shia protest movement, see Alamer, 'Beyond Sectarianism and Ideology'.

32. Author interview with Taha al-Hijji, 25 September 2019.

33. Author interview with Saudi dissident, 24 September 2019.

34. Author interview with Abu Hadi al-Yami in exile, 11 June 2019.

35. Matthiessen, *The Other Saudis*.

36. Mamdouh al-Harbi, https://hawamer.com/vb/hawamer1171531 (accessed 30 May 2019).

37. @azyaam (accessed 30 May 2019).

38. Human Rights Watch 2008, *The Ismailis of Saudi Arabia: Second Class Citizens*, 2008, https://www.hrw.org/report/2008/09/22/ismailis-najran/second-class-saudi-citizens (accessed 13 August 2020).

39. Ibid., pp. 25–8.

40. Ibid.

41. Author interview with Abu Hadi al-Yami in exile, 11 June 2019.

42. Y. Farouk, 'Quieting the Home Front', 31 July 2019, Carnegie Middle East Centre, https://carnegie-mec.org/diwan/79597?lang=en (accessed 31 July 2019).

43. Author interview with Abu Hadi al-Yami in exile, 11 June 2019.

44. F. De Bel-Air, *Demography, Migration and Labour Market in Saudi Arabia*, 2019, http://gulfmigration.org/media/pubs/exno/GLMM_EN_2018_05.pdf%20 (accessed 13 August 2020).

45. Human Rights Watch, *Saudi Arabia: Domestic Workers Face Harsh Abuses*, 2008, https://www.hrw.org/news/2008/07/08/saudi-arabia-domestic-workers-face-harsh-abuses (accessed 16 June 2019).

46. Personal communication with John, April 2019. To protect the identities of both John and Jawahir, the electronic campaign that John started in support of Jawahir is not cited here.

47. M. Al-Rasheed, *Contesting the Saudi State: Islamic Voices from a New Generation*, Cambridge: Cambridge University Press, 2007.

48. In the past, the Saudi regime sentenced several British citizens to prison for making alcohol and selling it in the country. Reports about torture in prison to extract confessions were released to the press. Eventually, the prisoners were released and repatriated to Britain. However, John could have faced adultery charges, punishable by execution. This is exactly what happened to a Saudi princess and her Saudi commoner lover, who were executed in a public square during King Khalid's reign. The story was dramatized in a film, entitled *Death of a Princess*, and aired on British and other television stations. For further details on the princess and her lover, see Al-Rasheed, *A Most Masculine State*.

49. N. Woolcock and A. La Guardia, 'Freed "Bomber" Tells of Torture in Saudi Jail', *The Telegraph*, 9 August 2000, https://www.telegraph.co.uk/news/worldnews/middleeast/saudiarabia/1438410/Freed-bomber-tells-of-torture-in-Saudi-jail.html (accessed 9 June 2019).

50. C. Jones, 'All the King's Consultants: The Perils of Advising Authoritarians', *Foreign Affairs*, 2019, https://www.foreignaffairs.com/articles/persian-gulf/2019–04–16/all-kings-consultants (accessed 5 June 2019).

51. S. Hertog, 'Challenges to the Saudi Distributional State in the Age of Austerity', in M. Al-Rasheed (ed.), *Salman's Legacy: The Dilemmas of a New Era in Saudi Arabia*, London: Hurst & Co., 2018, pp. 73–98.

52. Gulf Business, 'Saudi Shoura Council Approved New Green Card Residency Scheme for Expats', 2019, https://gulfbusiness.com/saudis-shoura-council-approves-new-green-card-residency-scheme-expats/ (accessed 4 June 2019).

53. Laura Alho promotes tourism in Saudi Arabia on Twitter. See @blue-abaya

54. Amani al-Ahmadi 2019 @amani_aal (accessed 6 June 201).

55. C. Lacadet and M. Tafesse Tilkamu, 'The Expulsion of Ethiopian Workers from Saudi Arabia (2012–2014)', *Annales d'Ethiopie*, 2016, pp. 225–43, https://www.persee.fr/doc/ethio_0066–2127_2016_num_31_1_1633 (accessed 8 June 2019).

56. In 2018, over 660,000 foreigners left the country, and the number reached a record level of over a million in 2019. See A. al-Omran, 'Record Numbers of Foreign Workers are Leaving Saudi Arabia', *Financial Times*, 10 July 2018, https://www.ft.com/content/c710cf30–8441–11e8-a29d-73e3d454535d, and K. Fahim, 'Saudi Arabia Encouraged Foreign Workers to Leave—and Struggling after So Many Did', *Washington Post*, 2 February 2019, https://www.washingtonpost.com/world/saudi-arabia-encouraged-foreign-workers-to-leave——and-is-struggling-after-so-many-did/2019/02/01/07e34e12-a548–11e8-ad6f-080770dcddc2_story.html?utm_term=.16628a78593a (both accessed 5 June 2019).

57. M. Ahmad, 'Thailand Takes Steps to Repatriate 5000 Citizens Working in Saudi Arabia', *Benar News*, 20 July 2018, https://www.benarnews.org/english/news/thai/thailand-employment-07202018161911.html (accessed 10 June 2019).

6. WOMEN AND RIGHTS

1. H. al-Fassi, 'al-Huriyya al-akadimiyya fi jamiat al-khalij' [Academic freedom in Gulf universities], report, Gulf Centre for Development Policies, 2018.

2. H. al-Fassi, 'Saudi Women and Islamic Discourse: Selected Examples of Saudi Feminists', *Journal of Women of the Middle East and the Islamic World*, vol. 14 (2016), pp. 187–206.

3. Author interview with Hissa al-Madhi, 26 April 2019.

4. On the 1990s campaigns against the driving ban, see M. Al-Rasheed, *A Most Masculine State: Gender, Politics and Religion in Saudi Arabia*, Cambridge: Cambridge University Press, 2013.

5. For an excellent and detailed account, see N. Doaiji, 'From Hasm to Hazm: Saudi Feminism beyond Patriarchal Bargaining', in M. Al-Rasheed (ed.), *Salman's Legacy: The Dilemmas of a New Era in Saudi Arabia*, London: Hurst & Co., 2018, pp. 117–44.

6. Two reports published by Human Rights Watch in 2008 and 2016 highlighted the restrictions of the guardianship system, thus globalizing Saudi women's struggle against one of the most restrictive legal obligations that place women under the control of male guardians, known as *muhram*. See Human Rights Watch, *Perpetual Minors: Human Rights Abuses Stemming from Male Guardianship and Sex Segregation in Saudi Arabia*, New York: HRW, 2008 and Human Rights Watch, *Boxed In: Women and Saudi Arabia's Guardianship*, 16 July 2016, https://www.hrw.org/report/2016/07/16/boxed/women-and-saudi-arabias-male-guardianship-system (accessed 15 September 2017).

7. https://www.spa.gov.sa/viewstory.php?lang=ar&newsid=1671323 (accessed 13 August 2020).

8. See 12 June 2012 petition, https://www.ipetitions.com/petition/women2drive-17jun2012 (accessed March 2019).

9. A. Alaodah, 'State-Sponsored Fatwas in Saudi Arabia', Carnegie Endowment for International Peace, 3 April 2018, https://carnegieendowment.org/sada/75971%20 (accessed 13 August 2020).

10. https://saudiwoman.me (accessed 28 July 2019).

11. For a list of names of women campaigners, see Iman al-Nafjan, https://saudiwoman.me (accessed 20 April 2019).

12. https://edition.cnn.com/2019/01/31/opinions/walid-alhathloul-opinion-intl/index.html (accessed 30 April 2019). Walid went as far as testifying to Congress to draw attention to the plight of his sister: https://www.middleeastmonitor.com/20190321-brother-of-detained-saudi-activist-lojain-al-hathloul-speaks-before-congress/ (accessed 19 August 2019).

13. D. Malik, 'Ms Saffaa: Protest Art and the Fledgling Saudi Arabia Women's Rights Movement', *The Guardian*, 16 October 2016, https://www.theguardian.com/artanddesign/2016/dec/01/ms-saffaa-on-protest-art-and-iammyownguardian-dont-say-saudi-women-dont-have-a-voice (accessed 20 April 2019).

14. Author interview with Ms Saffaa, 22 April 2019. All personal information about Ms Saffaa draws on information she gave me during the interview.

15. Many of Ms Saffaa's art pieces are displayed on Instagram: https://

www.instagram.com/mssaffaa, and her blog: https://saffaa.wordpress.com (both accessed 13 August 2020).

16. S. Hassanein, 'I am my Own Guardian: Reflections on Resistance Art', *Journal of Middle East Women's Studies*, vol. 14 (2) (July 2018), pp. 236–41.

17. On art in Saudi Arabia under Muhammad ibn Salman's patronage, see S. Foley, *Changing Saudi Arabia: Art, Culture and Society in the Kingdom*, Boulder: Lynne Rienner, 2019.

18. 'Some Saudi Women are Secretly Deserting their Country', *The Economist*, 16 March 2017, https://www.economist.com/news/middle-east-and-africa/21718871-women-are-fed-up-being-treated-children-some-saudi-women-are-secretly (accessed 13 August 2020).

19. *Middle East Monitor*, https://www.middleeastmonitor.com/20190424-pull-inhuman-women-monitoring-app-runaway-saudi-sisters-tell-tech-giants (accessed 26 April 2019).

20. 'Some Saudi Women are Secretly Deserting their Country', *The Economist*, 16 March 2017, https://www.economist.com/news/middle-east-and-africa/21718871-women-are-fed-up-being-treated-children-some-saudi-women-are-secretly (accessed 18 August 2017).

21. *The Independent*, 'At Least 1000 Women Flee Saudi Arabia Every Year Because of Sexism', 21 March 2017, https://www.independent.co.uk/news/world/middle-east/saudi-arabia-women-flee-sexism-at-least-thousand-a-year-a7642041.html, and M. Al-Rasheed, 'Why Women are Fleeing Mohammed Ben Salman's Saudi Arabia', *Middle East Eye*, 24 January 2019, https://www.middleeasteye.net/opinion/why-women-are-fleeing-mohammed-bin-salmans-saudi-arabia (both accessed 14 August 2020).

22. M. al-Sharif, *Daring to Drive: The Young Saudi Woman who Stood up to a Kingdom of Men*, New York: Simon & Schuster, 2017.

23. Human Rights Watch, *Boxed In*.

24. Ibid.

25. Issa al-Gaith @IssaAlgaith, 20 June 2019.

26. Sheikh Sulayman al-Majid and Muhammad al-Muqrin, both on https://oktob.io/posts/11443 (accessed 23 April 2019).

27. Author interview with Saudi Islamist, 22 April 2019.

28. R. al-Baz, *Défigurée: Quand un crime passionnel eviant affaire d'état*, Paris: Michael Lafon, 2008.

29. Hala al-Dosari, 'The Saudi National Transformation Program: What's in it for Women?', http://www.agsiw.org/the-saudi-national-transformation-program-whats-in-it-for-women (accessed 7 March 2017).

30. H. al-Sudairy, *Modern Woman in the Kingdom of Saudi Arabia: Rights, Challenges and Achievements*, Cambridge: Cambridge Scholars Publishing, 2017.

31. Saudi Arabia criminalized comparisons in the press that highlight common ground between the country and IS in Mosul and Raqqa. See 'What Happens after One Man Compares Saudi Arabia to Islamic State', BBC, 1 December 2015, http://www.bbc.co.uk/news/blogs-trending-34966066 (accessed 4 September 2017).

32. Hala al-Dosari, 'The Saudi National Transformation Program: What's in it for Women?', http://www.agsiw.org/the-saudi-national-transformation-program-whats-in-it-for-women (accessed 7 March 2017).

33. The following paragraphs are based on an author interview with Hala al-Dosari, 24 April 2019.

34. 'Saudis Plan to Ease Travel Restrictions on Women', *Wall Street Journal*, 11 July 2019, https://www.wsj.com/articles/saudis-plan-to-ease-travel-restrictions-on-women-11562837401 (accessed 19 July 2019).

7. YOUNG AND RESTLESS

1. Saudi Arabia received just over 2,000 applications for asylum between 2000 and 2018, mainly from Syria: World Data, 'Asylum Seekers and Refugees in Saudi Arabia', https://www.worlddata.info/asia/saudi-arabia/asylum.php (accessed 4 September 2019).

2. 'Thousands of Gulf Arabs are Abandoning their Homeland', *The Economist*, 19 January 2019, https://www.economist.com/middle-east-and-africa/2019/01/19/thousands-of-gulf-arabs-are-abandoning-their-homeland (accessed 20 September 2019).

3. A. al-Omran, 'Saudi Arabia Revives Efforts to Draw Dissidents Home', *Financial Times*, 14 July 2019, https://www.ft.com/content/21e93b02-a185-11e9-a282-2df48f366f7d (accessed 4 March 2020).

4. M. al-Sharif, 'The Saudi Diaspora of Dissidents in Exile is Fighting Back', *Washington Post*, 1 October 2019, https://www.washingtonpost.com/opinions/2019/09/30/saudi-diaspora-dissidents-exile-are-fighting-back (accessed 5 October 2019).
5. MiSK Foundation, https://misk.org.sa/en/ (accessed 15 September 2019).
6. L. Quran, 'Saudi Students in the US Say their Government Watches their Every Move', PBS NewsHour, 6 November 2019, https://www.pbs.org/newshour/world/saudi-students-in-u-s-say-their-government-watches-their-every-move (accessed 10 November 2019).
7. Princes who challenged Salman in 2015 were severely punished. See M. Al-Rasheed, 'Mystique of Monarchy: The Magic of Royal Succession in Saudi Arabia', in M. Al-Rasheed (ed.), *Salman's Legacy: The Dilemmas of a New Era in Saudi Arabia*, London: Hurst & Co., 2018, pp. 45–71.
8. D. Sheppard et al., 'Saudi Arabia Bullies Wealthy Families to Pump Cash into IPO', *Financial Times*, 20 September 2019, https://www.ft.com/content/e9fe2862-dada-11e9-8f9b-77216ebe1f17 (accessed 29 September 2019).
9. https://youtu.be/o2o0u7jbTbY (accessed 7 July 2019).
10. Discussion with author, Sabtiyya, YouTube show, 20 September 2019.
11. K. al-Saud, *Mamlakat al-samt wa al-istibdad* [Kingdom of silence and repression], n.p., 2019.
12. R. El Mawy, 'Saudi Arabia's Missing Princes', BBC, 15 August 2017, https://www.bbc.co.uk/news/magazine-40926963 (accessed 28 September 2019).
13. http://www.diwan.tv/ (accessed 8 August 2019).
14. https://alqst.org/eng/ (accessed 19 September 2019).
15. Conversation with author, 24 September 2019.
16. https://www.aljazeera.com/news/2018/12/saudi-opposition-joins-forces-london-tackle-oppression-181210182434052.html (13 August 2020).
17. On art, see S. Foley, *Changing Saudi Arabia: Art, Culture, and Society in the Kingdom*, Boulder: Lynne Reinner, 2019.
18. @TurkiHAlhamad1
19. T. Matthiesen, 'Marxists in the Land of the Two Holy Places: The

Communist Party of Saudi Arabia', *Journal of Cold War Studies* (forthcoming).

20. M. al-Sudairi, 'Marx's Arabian Apostles: The Rise and Fall of the Saudi Communist Movement', *Middle East Journal*, vol. 73 (3) (2019), pp. 438–57.

21. M. Al-Rasheed, *Muted Modernists: The Struggle over Divine Politics in Saudi Arabia*, London: Hurst & Co., 2015.

22. 'To Escape Repression, Critics are Leaving the Gulf', *The Economist*, 22 July 2017, https://www.economist.com/middle-east-and-africa/2017/07/22/to-escape-repression-critics-are-leaving-the-gulf (accessed 23 September 2019).

23. For an assessment of digital activism as resistance site, see S. Ofori-Parku and D. Moscato, 'Hashtag Activism as a Form of Political Action: A Qualitative Analysis of the #BringBackOurGirls Campaign in Nigerian, UK, and US Press', *International Journal of Communication*, vol. 12 (2018), pp. 2480–2502.

24. Author's interview with Abdullah al-Awdah, 30 September 2019.

25. A. Alaoudh, 'My Father Called for Reform in Saudi Arabia: Now he Faces Death', *The Guardian*, 13 August 2019, https://www.theguardian.com/commentisfree/2019/aug/13/saudi-arabia-salman-al-odah-arrest-death-sentence (accessed 30 September 2019).

26. Author's interview with Abdullah al-Awdah, 30 September 2019.

27. S. Hertog, 'Challenges to the Saudi Distributional State in the Age of Austerity', in M. Al-Rasheed (ed.), *Salman's Legacy: The Dilemmas of a New Era in Saudi Arabia*, London: Hurst & Co., 2018, pp. 73–98.

28. C. Jones, 'All the King's Consultants', May/June 2019, *Foreign Affairs*, https://www.foreignaffairs.com/articles/persian-gulf/2019-04-16/all-kings-consultants (accessed 5 October 2019).

29. On rumours and Mujtahid, see Al-Rasheed, 'Mystique of Monarchy'.

30. L. Hamdan, 'White Nightclub Shuts Down on Opening Night', *Arabian Business*, 16 June 2019, https://www.arabianbusiness.com/travel-hospitality/422138-saudi-alcohol-free-nightclub-shuts-down-on-opening-night (accessed 16 June 2019).

31. https://citizenlab.ca (accessed 26 July 2019).

32. https://youtu.be/A1xgYWxl6fQ (accessed 8 August 2019).

33. Author interview with Omar al-Zahrani, 11 September 2019.
34. Fitna, https://youtu.be/WEFM0xlJI-c (accessed 4 September 2019).
35. Fi al-Khaliyya, https://youtu.be/Uogj57b_qUU (accessed 13 September 2019).
36. Author interview with Abdullah al-Juraywi, 9 September 2019.
37. European–Saudi Organization for Human Rights: https://www.esohr.org/en/ (accessed 7 September 2019).
38. Author interview with Ali Dubaisi, 24 September 2019. All quotations draw on the interview and his personal document in support of his asylum application in Germany, which he made available to the author.
39. The shooting and death of Shakhori as documented by friends: https://www.youtube.com/watch?v=tdlW_xxUj10 (accessed 6 September 2019).
40. Author interview with Ali Dubaisi, 23 September 2019.
41. Khabaya al-Muaradha [Hidden affairs of the opposition], https://www.youtube.com/watch?v=vZZBJuzOXks (accessed 24 September 2019).
42. Author interview with Saad al-Faqih, 25 September 2019.
43. M. Moaddel, *The Clash of Values: Islamic Fundamentalism versus Liberal Nationalism*, New York: Columbia University Press, 2020.
44. Ibid., p. 52.
45. On attitudes of Saudi youth inside the country, see M. Thompson, *Being Young, Male and Saudi: Identity and Politics in a Globalized Kingdom*, Cambridge: Cambridge University Press, 2019.

THE FUTURE

1. 'Saudi Aramco First Quarter Profit Slides 25% as the Collapse in Oil Prices Bites', CNBC, 12 May 2020, https://www.cnbc.com/2020/05/12/saudi-aramcos-profit-slides-25percent-in-the-first-quarter-as-collapse-in-oil-prices-bites.html (accessed 16 May 2020).
2. 'Saudi Arabia's Coronavirus Cases Top 50,000', Reuters, 16 May 2020, https://www.reuters.com/article/us-health-coronavirus-saudi-idUSK-BN22S0L7 (accessed 13 August 2020).

SELECT BIBLIOGRAPHY

Alamer, S., 'Beyond Sectarianism and Ideology: Regionalism and Collective Political Action in Saudi Arabia,' in M. Al-Rasheed (ed.), *Salman's Legacy: The Dilemmas of a New Era in Saudi Arabia*, London: Hurst & Co., 2018, pp. 97–116.

———, *Fi Tarikh al-ourouba* [A history of Arabism], Beirut: Jusour, 2016.

Alatas, S. H., *The Myth of the Lazy Natives*, London: Routledge, 2010 (repr.).

Anscombe, F., *The Ottoman Gulf: The Creation of Kuwait, Saudi Arabia and Qatar*, New York: Columbia University Press, 1997.

al-Baz, R., *Défigurée: quand un crime passionnel devient affaire d'état*, Paris: Michel Lafon, 2008.

Brantlinger, P., *Bread and Circuses: Theories of Mass Culture as Social Decay*, Ithaca: Cornell University Press, 1983.

Bunzel, C., 'Wahhabism, Saudi Arabia and the Islamic State: Abdullah bin Jibrin and Turki al-Bin Ali', in M. Al-Rasheed (ed.), *Salman's Legacy: The Dilemmas of a New Era in Saudi Arabia*, London: Hurst & Co., 2018, pp. 183–213.

Commins, D., *The Wahhabi Movement and Saudi Arabia*, London: I. B. Tauris, 2002.

al-Dakhil, K., 'Social Origins of the Wahhabi Movement', Ph.D. thesis, University of California, 1998.

Determann, J., *Historiography in Saudi Arabia: Globalization and the State in the Middle East*, London: I. B. Tauris, 2014.

Doaiji, N., 'From Hasm to Hazm: Saudi Feminism beyond Patriarchal Bargaining', in M. Al-Rasheed (ed.), *Salman's Legacy: The Dilemmas of a New Era in Saudi Arabia*, London: Hurst & Co., 2018, pp. 117–44.

Doumato, E., *Getting God's Ear: Women, Islam, and Healing in Saudi Arabia and the Gulf*, New York: Columbia University Press, 2000.

Eickelman, D., and J. Anderson (eds.), *New Media in the Muslim World: The Emerging Public Sphere*, Bloomington and Indianapolis: Indiana University Press, 2003.

Al-Fahad, A., 'The Imama vs. the Iqal: Hadari–Bedouin Conflict and the Formation of the Saudi State', in M. Al-Rasheed and R. Vitalis (eds.), *Counter-Narratives: History, Contemporary Society, and Politics in Saudi Arabia and Yemen*, New York: Palgrave, 2004, pp. 35–75.

Al-Fahad, A., 'Raiders and Traders: A Poet's Lament on the End of the Bedouin Heroic Age', in B. Haykel, T. Hegghammer, and D. Lacroix (eds.), *Saudi Arabia in Transition: Insights on Social, Political, Economic and Religious Change*, Cambridge: Cambridge University Press, 2015, pp. 231–62.

———, 'Rootless Trees: Genealogical Politics in Saudi Arabia', in B. Haykel, T. Hegghammer, and D. Lacroix (eds.), *Saudi Arabia in Transition: Insights on Social, Political, Economic and Religious Change*, Cambridge: Cambridge University Press, 2015, pp. 263–91.

Farquhar, M., *Circuits of Faith: Migration, Education, and the Wahhabi Mission*, Stanford: Stanford University Press, 2016.

al-Fassi, H., 'Saudi Women and Islamic Discourse: Selected Examples of Saudi Feminists', *Journal of Women of the Middle East and the Islamic World*, vol. 14 (2016), pp. 187–206.

Foley, S., *The Arab Gulf State: Beyond Oil and Islam*, Boulder: Lynne Rienner, 2010.

———, *Changing Saudi Arabia: Art, Culture and Society in the Kingdom*, Boulder: Lynne Rienner, 2019.

Freitag, U., *Indian Ocean Migrants and State Formation in Hadhramout: Reforming the Homeland*, Leiden: Brill, 2003.

Hamidaddin, A., *Tweeted Heresies: Saudi Islam in Transformation*, Oxford: Oxford University Press, 2019.

Hammond, A., *The Islamic Utopia: The Illusion of Reform in Saudi Arabia*, London: Pluto Press, 2012.

SELECT BIBLIOGRAPHY

Hanieh, A., *Money, Markets and Monarchies: The Gulf Cooperation Council and the Political Economy of the Contemporary World*, Cambridge: Cambridge University Press, 2018.

Hassanein, S., 'I Am My Own Guardian: Reflections on Resistance Art', *Journal of Middle East Women's Studies*, vol. 14 (2) (July 2018), pp. 236–41.

Haykel, B., T. Hegghammer, and D. Lacroix (eds.), *Saudi Arabia in Transition: Insights on Social, Political, Economic and Religious Change*, Cambridge: Cambridge University Press, 2015.

Hegghammer, T., *Jihad in Saudi Arabia: Violence and Pan-Islamism since 1979 in Saudi Arabia*, Cambridge: Cambridge University Press, 2011.

Hertog, S., 'Challenges to the Saudi Distributional State in the Age of Austerity', in M. Al-Rasheed (ed.), *Salman's Legacy: The Dilemmas of a New Era in Saudi Arabia*, London: Hurst & Co., 2018, pp. 73–98.

Ho, E., *The Graves of Tarim: Genealogy and Mobility in the Indian Ocean*, Berkeley: University of California Press, 2006.

Ibrahim, B. and M. al-Sadiq, *al-Hirak al-shii fi al-saoudiyya* [Shia mobilization in Saudi Arabia], Beirut: Arab Network for Research and Publishing, 2013.

Ibrahim, F., *The Shi'is of Saudi Arabia*, London: Saqi, 2006.

al-Juhany, U., *Najd before the Salafi Reform Movement: Social, Political, and Religious Conditions during the Three Centuries Preceding the Rise of the First Saudi State*, Reading: Ithaca, 2002.

Lacroix, S., *Awakening Islam: Religious Dissent in Contemporary Saudi Arabia*, Cambridge, MA: Harvard University Press, 2011.

Leatherdale, C., *Britain and Saudi Arabia 1925–1939: The Imperial Oasis*, London: Frank Cass, 1983.

Le Renard, A., *A Society of Young Women: Opportunities of Place, Power and Reform in Saudi Arabia*, Stanford: Stanford University Press, 2014.

Lynch, M., *The Arab Uprisings Explained: New Contentious Politics in the Middle East*, New York: Columbia University Press, 2014.

Matthiesen, T., *The Other Saudis: Shiism, Dissent and Sectarianism*, Cambridge: Cambridge University Press, 2015.

———, 'Saudi Arabia and the Cold War', in M. Al-Rasheed (ed.), *Salman's Legacy: The Dilemmas of a New Era in Saudi Arabia*, London: Hurst & Co., 2018, pp. 217–33.

SELECT BIBLIOGRAPHY

———, 'Marxists in the Land of the Two Holy Places: The Communist Party of Saudi Arabia', *Journal of Cold War Studies* (forthcoming).

Menoret, P., *Joyriding in Riyadh: Oil, Urbanism, and Road Revolt*, Cambridge: Cambridge University Press, 2014.

Moaddel, M., *The Clash of Values: Islamic Fundamentalism versus Liberal Nationalism*, New York: Columbia University Press, 2020.

Mouline, N., *Les clercs de l'Islam: Autorité religieuse et pouvoir politique en Arabia Saoudite, xviii–xxi siècle*, Paris: PUF, 2011; trans. as *The Clerics of Islam: Religious Authority and Political Power in Saudi Arabia*, New Haven: Yale University Press, 2014.

Ochsenwald, W., *Religion, Society and the State in Arabia: The Hijaz under Ottoman Control, 1840–1908*, Columbus: Ohio University Press, 1984.

Ofori-Parku, S. and D. Moscato, 'Hashtag Activism as a Form of Political Action: A Qualitative Analysis of the #BringBackOurGirls Campaign in Nigerian, UK, and US Press', *International Journal of Communication*, vol. 12 (2018), pp. 2480–2502.

Owen Jones, M., R. Porter, and M. Valeri (eds.), *Gulfization of the Arab World*, Berlin: Gerlach Press, 2018.

Pétriat, P., *Le Négoce des Lieux Saints*, Paris: Publications de la Sorbonne, Pierre Vermeren, 2016.

Podeh, E., 'Saudi Arabia and Israel: From Secret to Public Engagement', *Middle East Journal*, vol. 72 (4) (2018), pp. 563–86.

Al-Rachid, L., 'L'Irak de l'embargo à l'occupation: dépérissement d'un ordre politique (1990–2003)', Paris: Institut d'Études Politiques de Paris, 2010.

Al-Rasheed, M., *Politics in an Arabian Oasis: The Rashidi Tribal Dynasty*, London: I. B. Tauris, 1991.

———, *Iraqi Assyrian Christians in London: The Construction of Ethnicity*, London: Mellen Studies in Sociology, 1998.

———, *Contesting the Saudi State: Islamic Voices from a New Generation*, Cambridge: Cambridge University Press, 2007.

———, *A History of Saudi Arabia*, 2nd edn, Cambridge: Cambridge University Press, 2010.

———, *A Most Masculine State: Gender, Politics and Religion in Saudi Arabia*, Cambridge: Cambridge University Press, 2013.

SELECT BIBLIOGRAPHY

———, *Muted Modernists: The Struggle over Divine Politics in Saudi Arabia*, London: Hurst & Co., 2015.

———, 'Evading State Control: Political Protest and Technology in Saudi Arabia', in A. Cheater (ed.), *The Anthropology of Power*, ASA Monograph, London: Routledge, 1999, pp. 149–62.

———, 'The Capture of Riyadh Revisited: Shaping Historical Imagination in Saudi Arabia', in M. Al-Rasheed and R. Vitalis (eds.), *Counter-Narratives: History, Contemporary Society, and Politics in Saudi Arabia and Yemen*, New York: Palgrave, 2004, pp. 183–200.

———, 'Saudi Arabia and the 1948 War: Beyond Official History', in E. Rogan and A. Shlaim (eds.), *The War for Palestine*, Cambridge: Cambridge University Press, 2007, pp. 228–47.

———, 'Saudi Internal Dilemmas and Regional Responses to the Arab Uprisings', in F. Gerges (ed.), *The New Middle East: Protest and Revolution in the Arab World*, Cambridge: Cambridge University Press, 2014, pp. 353–79.

———, 'Sectarianism as Counter-Revolution: Saudi Responses to the Arab Spring', in N. Hashemi and D. Postel (eds.), *Sectarianization: Mapping the New Politics of the Middle East*, London: Hurst & Co., 2017, pp. 143–58.

———, 'The Dilemmas of a New Era', in M. Al-Rasheed (ed.), *Salman's Legacy: The Dilemmas of a New Era in Saudi Arabia*, London: Hurst & Co., 2018, pp. 1–28.

———, 'Mystique of Monarchy: The Magic of Royal Succession in Saudi Arabia', in M. Al-Rasheed (ed.), *Salman's Legacy: The Dilemmas of a New Era in Saudi Arabia*, London: Hurst & Co., 2018, pp. 45–71.

———, 'Gulf Leadership in the Arab World: From Nationalism to Hyper-Nationalism without "Political Dynamism"', in M. Owen Jones, R. Porter and M. Valeri, *Gulfization of the Arab World*, Berlin: Gerlach Press, 2018, pp. 7–26.

———, 'The Meaning of Marriage and Status in Exile: The Experience of Iraqi Women', *Journal of Refugee Studies*, vol. 6 (2) (1993), pp. 89–104.

———, 'The Myth of Return: Iraqi Arabs and Assyrian Refugees in London', *Journal of Refugee Studies*, vol. 7 (2/3) (1994), pp. 199–219.

Al-Rasheed, M. (ed.), *Transnational Connections and the Arab Gulf*, London: Routledge, 2005.

———, *Kingdom without Borders: Saudi Arabia's Political, Religious and Media Frontiers*, London: Hurst & Co., 2008.

———, *Salman's Legacy: The Dilemmas of a New Era*, London: Hurst & Co., 2018.

Al-Rasheed, M., and L. Al-Rasheed, 'The Politics of Encapsulation: Saudi Policy towards Tribal and Religious Opposition', *Middle Eastern Studies*, vol. 32 (1) (1996), pp. 96–119.

Al-Rasheed, M., and R. Vitalis (eds.), *Counter Narratives: History, Contemporary Society, and Politics in Saudi Arabia and Yemen*, New York: Palgrave Macmillan, 2004.

Rugman, J., *The Killing in the Consulate: Investigating the Life and Death of Jamal Khashoggi*, London: Simon & Schuster, 2019.

Said, E., *Reflections on Exile and Other Literary and Cultural Essays*, London: Granta, 2012.

Samin, N., *Of Sand and Soil: Genealogy and Tribal Belonging in Saudi Arabia*, Princeton: Princeton University Press, 2015.

———, 'Kafa'a fi l-Nasab in Saudi Arabia: Islamic Law, Tribal Custom, and Social Change', *Journal of Arabian Studies*, vol. 2 (2) (2012), pp. 109–26.

al-Saud, K., *Mamlakat al-samt wa al-istibdad* [Kingdom of silence and repression], n.p., 2019.

al-Sharif, M., *Daring to Drive: The Young Saudi Woman who Stood up to a Kingdom of Men*, New York: Simon & Schuster, 2017.

Sheffer, G., *Diaspora Politics: At Home Abroad*, Cambridge: Cambridge University Press, 2003.

al-Sudairi, M., 'Marx's Arabian Apostles: The Rise and Fall of the Saudi Communist Movement', *Middle East Journal*, vol. 73 (3) (2019), pp. 438–57.

al-Sudairy, H., *Modern Woman in the Kingdom of Saudi Arabia: Rights, Challenges, and Achievements*. Cambridge: Cambridge Scholars, 2017.

al-Sunaytan, M., *al-Nukhab al-saudiyya: dirasa fi l-tahawulata wa al-ikhfaqat* [Saudi elites: a study of changes and shortcomings], Beirut: Markaz Dirasat al-Wihda al-Arabiyya, 2004.

———, *al-Saoudiyya al-siyasi wa al-qabila* [Saudi Arabia: politics and the tribe], Beirut: al-Shabaka al-Arabiyya lil-Abhath wa al-Nashr, 2008.

SELECT BIBLIOGRAPHY

Thompson, M., *Being Young, Male and Saudi: Identity and Politics in a Globalized Kingdom*, Cambridge: Cambridge University Press, 2019.

———, 'The Impact of Globalization on Saudi Male Millennials: Identity Narratives', *Asian Affairs* (July 2019), pp. 1–22.

Veyne, P., *Bread and Circuses: Historical Sociology and Political Pluralism*, trans. B. Pearce, London: Penguin, 1992 [1976]

Vitalis, R., *America's Kingdom: Mythmaking on the Saudi Oil Frontier*, Stanford: Stanford University Press, 2006.

Wedeen, L., *Ambiguities of Domination: Politics, Rhetoric, and Symbols in Contemporary Syria*, Chicago: University of Chicago Press, 1999.

Witfoggel, K., *Oriental Despotism: A Comparative Study of Total Power*, New Haven: Yale University Press, 1963.

Yamani, M., *Changed Identities: The Challenge of the New Generation in Saudi Arabia*, London: Royal Institute of International Affairs, 2000.

———, 'Evading the Habits of a Life Time: The Adaptation of Hejazi Dress to the New Social Order', in N. Lindisfarne-Tapper and B. Ingham (eds.), *Languages of Dress in the Middle East*, London: Curzon, 1997, pp. 55–66.

Yom, S. and F. G. Gause III, 'Resilient Royals: How Arab Monarchies Hang On', *Journal of Democracy*, vol. 23 (4) (2012), pp. 74–88.

INDEX

INDEX

INDEX

Consultative Council, 202, 228, 257, 264, 265
Convention against Torture, 117
Council of Economic Development Affairs, 126
Council of Higher Ulama, 71, 210–11, 329
Covid-19 pandemic (2019–20), 334–5
Cox, Sir Percy, 42
cult of personality, 5–9, 91, 100
  globalization of, 86, 88, 91, 94, 95, 100
  Khashoggi murder and, 94–5, 122
  women and, 91
cyber-sphere, 14–18, 30, 281
  activism and, 14–18, 289, 293–7, 319, 330–1
  Arab uprisings (2011) and, 16, 23, 156
  diaspora and, 19–20, 22–3, 28, 295–7, 300–310, 321, 323
  festivities and, 36
  Khashoggi and, 104
  Muhammad ibn Salman and, 7, 9, 12, 13, 36, 86, 90, 228, 280
  nationalism and, 12, 15, 119, 161, 164, 167, 171, 177, 280
  al-Qahtani and, 171, 195, 280
  racism, debates on, 206
  surveillance, 16–17, 86, 91, 294, 301, 331
  tourism and, 86, 229

tribal poetry on, 201
tribalism and, 193
trolls, 12, 22, 91, 119, 123, 171, 182, 297, 298, 331
  women and, 13, 14, 17, 20, 234, 238, 247, 251–3, 263

al-Dakhil, Abdul Aziz, 90
al-Dakhil, Turki, 128
al-Damini, Ali, 113, 283
death squads, 109, 119, 120, 122, 125, 172–3
diaspora, 4, 15, 18–24, 26–30, 271–80, 282, 318–21
  activism, 20–21, 23–4, 28, 33, 273, 295, 297, 298, 300–310, 315
  conferences, 277–8, 293, 304, 309, 315
  cyber-sphere and, 19–20, 22–3, 28, 295–7, 300–310, 321, 323
  family members of, 21–2, 289, 291–2, 305
  feminists, labelling as, 22
  jihadis, labelling as, 22
  Khashoggi murder and, 19, 21, 96, 272, 278, 279, 308–9, 316, 323
  political views, 293, 315, 318–21
  students, 32, 274–5, 290–93, 298, 299, 300–310, 318–19
  traitor narrative, 23, 306
  women, 19–20, 22–3, 238–40, 245–56, 267, 269, 298

INDEX

Diriyyah (town), 7, 115, 159
Diriyyah Emirate (1744–1818), 36, 45–8, 182, 309
Diwan London, 277, 293, 304, 309, 315
diyya, 193–4
Doaiji, Nora, 169
al-Dosari, Ghanim, 288, 294
al-Dosari, Hala, 249, 266–8, 278
driving, women and, 242–4, 249
   campaigns, 13, 14, 32, 70, 237, 240, 241, 242–4, 255, 264, 298
   employment and, 266
   Islamists and, 162
   lifting of ban (2017–18), 32, 134, 147–8, 171, 237, 242–3, 329
   religious nationalism and, 147–8
   satire on, 17
   Western media and, 81, 83, 84, 88, 89, 95, 97
Dubaisi, Ali, 214, 310–16
al-Duwaish, Faisal, 51–2

Eastern Province
   Arab uprisings (2011), 24, 71, 156
   genealogy in, 191
   Ibn Saud's conquest (1913–15), 38, 43
   Ismailis in, 221
   local identities in, 182, 183
   oil industry, 55, 57, 65, 215

   Shia in, 38, 65, 71, 156, 182, 208, 211, 215, 313
education, 57–60, 281, 327, 333
   Abdullah's reforms (2005–15), 71
   international students, 71, 224, 227, 241, 242, 245, 254, 274
   ISIS and, 73
   Khashoggi on, 113
   pan-Islamism and, 150, 152
   religious nationalism and, 143, 147, 148, 149
   Shia and, 213, 214
   slaves and, 204
   sponsorship worldwide, 59, 66, 69
   tribes and, 191, 202
   women, 58, 241, 242, 245, 254, 256, 259, 260, 268
Egypt
   Camp David Agreement (1979), 66–7
   coup d'état (2013), 72, 304
   hegemony, 179
   Islamism in, 58, 60, 72, 97
   migration from, 57, 58
   Muslim Brotherhood, 58, 72
   Nasserism, 58, 97, 152, 179, 350 n.40
   October War (1973), 61
   Revolution (2011), 69, 70, 100, 306
   United Arab Republic (1958–71), 59
   Wahhabi War (1811–18), 42, 47–8

375

INDEX

INDEX

Hashemite family, 39, 40, 42, 43, 44, 52
al-Hashimi, Muhammad, 199
HASM, *see* Civil and Political Rights Association
al-Hassan, Hamza, 27, 137, 213, 216, 286
Hassanein, Saffaa, 245
al-Hathloul, Lujain, 173, 243, 264, 270, 294, 299, 335
al-Hawali, Safar, 151, 156, 173, 286
al-Hayat, 104, 290
Haykel, Bernard, 84–5
al-Hijji, Taha, 214
Hijra, 35
al-Hiwar TV, 275
Hizb al-Tahrir, 286
Hizb al-Ummah, 156
Hizbollah, 119
al-Hmami, Ali, 218
al-Hodeif, Muhammad, 110–11
holy cities, 3, 39, 59, 143–4
    beggars in, 205–6
    Covid-19 pandemic (2020), 335
    Grand Mosque siege (1979), 63–5, 66, 160, 197, 200
    Houthis and, 168
    immigration to, 167, 204, 231
    legitimacy of control, 97, 150, 151–2
    local identity, 182, 209
    Ottoman rule (1517–1925), 39–40
    pan-Islamism and, 150, 151–2

pilgrimage to, *see under* pilgrimage
    radical Islam and, 97, 222
    Wahhabi attack (1803–4), 46–7
    World War I (1914–18), 40, 41
Houthis, 53, 72, 92, 168–9, 221–3, 328, 335
al-Howaiyder, Wajiha, 243
Human Rights Watch, 219, 256, 267
Hussein, Saddam, 66, 68
Hussein, Sharif of Mecca, 41, 43, 52
al-Huthloul, Alya, 244
al-Huthloul, Walid, 244
Huwaitat tribe, 42
al-Huwaiti, Abdulrahman, 332

ibn Abd al-Wahhab, Muhammad, 45, 46, 201
ibn Baz, Abdul Aziz, 153
Ibn Bijad, Sultan, 51
ibn Hanbal, Ahmad, 55
Ibn Hithlaiyn, 51
ibn Huthloul, Turki, 222
ibn Ibrahim, Muhammad, 211
ibn Juluwi, Abdul Aziz, 222
ibn Rashid, Abd al-Aziz (al-Jinaza), 195
ibn Rashid, Muhammad, 37, 43
ibn Said, Ahmad, 176–7
Ibn Saud, King of Saudi Arabia (r. 1932–1953), 36–44, 48–56, 58, 143, 149
    Britain, relations with, 36–44, 49–55, 74–5, 82–3, 325

INDEX

INDEX

INDEX

Muhammad Ali, Wali of Egypt, 42, 47
Muhammad ibn Nayif, Crown Prince, 10, 70, 124, 125, 207, 277, 297
Muhammad ibn Salman, Crown Prince, 1, 2, 5–6
  anti-corruption campaign (2017), 94–5, 119, 125–6
  Aramco privatization, 80, 81, 90, 128–9, 133
  borrowing, 132
  Crown Prince accession (2017), 10, 53, 77, 123–5
  cult of personality, see cult of personality
  cyber-sphere presence, 13, 36, 86, 91, 280
  detention campaign, 134
  entertainment and, see under entertainment
  Islamists, repression of, 95–6
  Khashoggi murder (2018), 9, 12, 31, 86, 92–4, 116, 118, 127
  Mecca summits (2019), 127
  MiSK, 84, 134–5, 274, 280, 294
  moderate Islam, return to, 64, 133–4
  National Transformation Programme, 87, 133, 222, 296, 334
  populist nationalism, 12–13, 85
  positions, 125–6
  on radical Islam, 64, 96
  religious police and, 84, 134
  UK visit (2018), 8, 83, 87
  US visits (2017), 87
  Vision 2030, see Vision 2030
  Western media and, 79–100
  women's rights and, 82, 84, 88, 89, 96, 98, 134
  Yemen War (2015–), 72, 91–2, 127
Muhammad Reza Pahlavi, Shah of Iran, 65
al-Muharib, Ruqiyya, 280
Mujtahid, 296–7
municipal elections, 188, 236
Munif, Abdulrahman, 136, 178
Muntada Hawamer al-Boursa al-Saoudiyya, 218
Muqrin ibn Abd al-Aziz, Crown Prince, 10, 123, 206–7
al-Muqrin, Abdul Aziz, 68
al-Murrah tribe, 48, 201
Mursi, Muhammad, 72
Muslim Brotherhood, 58, 120, 163, 237, 285, 292, 302
  criminalization (2014), 155, 237
  in Egypt, 58, 72
  Khashoggi and, 136
Muslim World League, 152
al-Mustaqilla, 199
Mutair tribe, 51
al-Mutairi, Muhammad, 165, 166

Nabateans, 235

INDEX

al-Nafjan, Iman, 243, 244, 266, 280
al-Najjar, Umayma, 249
Najran, 185, 218–25
Nasser, Gamal Abdel, 58, 59, 60, 98
Nasserism, 115, 181, 285
Nassif, Sahar, 255
National Day, 35, 174–6, 182, 294, 340 n.2
National Guard, 56, 96, 125, 196–7
National Transformation Programme (NTP), 87, 133, 222, 296, 334
nationalism, 4, 12–13, 31–2, 85, 118, 138, 139–82
  archaeological sites and, 159–60
  cyber-sphere and, 12, 15, 119, 161, 164, 167, 171, 177, 280
  death squads and, 172–3
  diaspora and, 23, 173–80
  employment and, 162, 165, 175, 178
  immigration and, 112, 165–7, 175
  foreign management consul-tants and, 89
  Khashoggi and, 112, 115
  marriage and, 169–70
  pan-Arabism, 58–60, 75, 95, 179–80
  pan-Islamism, 150–54, 159, 160
  religious nationalism, 142–50, 159, 160

  treason and, *see* treason
  ultra-nationalism, 112, 118, 120, 167, 170, 173, 226
  Wahhabism and, 60
  watani, 163, 171–2
  women and, 169–71, 174
  Yemen War and, 168, 169, 170, 172, 176, 328
Nayif ibn Abd al-Aziz, Crown Prince, 9, 128
NEOM City, 332
al-Nimr, Nimr, 121, 128, 212–13, 286

oaths of allegiance (*bay'a*), 144, 145
October War (1973), 61
oil, 2–3, 4, 5, 18, 31, 55–6, 75, 76, 325, 332
  Aramco privatization, 80–82, 90, 113, 128, 132–3, 275
  dependence on, 6, 8, 85
  discovery (1933), 39, 55
  in eastern region, 55, 57, 65, 208, 211, 215
  embargo (1973), 61, 62–3
  Faisal, reign of (1964–1975), 59, 60, 61
  'laziness' and, 11
  post-oil economy, 128–9, 130, 132, 158, 169, 170, 227, 263, 281
  price shock (2014), 128, 129, 132, 224, 230, 332
  Saud, reign of (1953–64), 56, 57, 58

385

INDEX

Vision 2030 programme,
128–9, 132–3
welfare and, 70, 269
Omari, Muhammad, 278
Otaibi, Juhayman, 63, 197, 200
Otaibi, Maryam, 251–3
Otaibi, Sarah, 249
Ottoman Empire (1299–1922),
36–42, 45–6, 55, 350 n.40

Pahlavi, Shah Mohammad Reza,
65
Pakistan, 60, 67, 75, 141, 153,
185, 220
Palestine, 40, 67, 103, 164, 175,
176, 179–80
Islamism in, 60
Israel established (1948), 59
migration from, 57
nationalists and, 164, 175, 176
refugees, 59
al-Said kidnapping (1979), 122
pan-Islamism, 59, 138, 142,
150–54, 155, 157, 159, 160,
163, 176
Pelham, Nicolas, 299
Philby, St John, 40, 55, 83
Philippines, 185, 250, 254, 286
pilgrimage, 3, 35
beggars and, 206
Covid-19 pandemic (2020), 335
education curriculum and, 147
Grand Mosque siege (1979),
63–5
Great Depression period
(1929–39), 54

immigration and, 204, 206, 231
nationalism and, 157, 164
Ottoman period (1517–1925),
40, 41, 47
slavery and, 204
Vision 2030 and, 130
Wahhabis and, 47
poetry, 9
dissidents, 16, 25, 26, 91
Mecca and, 157
National Day celebrations, 35,
182
tribal, 170, 193, 194–6, 197–8,
201

al-Qadafi, Muammar, 69
al-Qahtani, Maha, 249
al-Qahtani, Muhammad, 63, 98,
114, 156, 278, 315
al-Qahtani, Saud, 118–20
Khashoggi murder (2018), 116,
118–19, 181, 328
social media presence, 171,
195, 280
Rasheed funeral tweet (2017),
195
Ritz Carlton incident (2017),
119
'traitors', targeting of, 119–20,
171, 181, 291, 302
tribal ancestry, 190
al-Qaida, 54, 67–9, 110, 146, 153,
221, 284, 286, 316
Nayif assassination attempt
(2009), 124

INDEX

INDEX

Awdah and, 292
Ghathami and, 283
Zahrani and, 302
al-Said, Ahmad ibn Rashid, 278
Said, Edward, 12
al-Said, Nasir, 25, 136
Saif al-Islam, Prince, 277
al-Saif, Tawfiq, 27, 137, 215, 286
al-Saiyari, Talal, 217
Salafism, 109, 210, 217, 221,
   284–6, 302, 320
Saleh, Ali Abdullah, 69, 72, 231
Salman, King of Saudi Arabia
   (r. 2015–), 8, 10, 158
   accession to throne (2015), 74,
      76–7, 240, 290
   Alzheimer's rumours, 127
   beheadings, approval of, 145
   Crown Prince appointment
      (2017), 10, 53, 77, 123–5,
      207, 240
   Diriyyah, restoration of, 159
   Faisal's assassination (1975), 62
   genealogy, views on, 199–200
   al-Hathloul's petition (2016),
      244
   Muhammad ibn Nayif sacking
      (2018), 277
   Khalid ibn Farhan on, 276
   Khashoggi murder (2018), 127,
      328
   'King of Decisiveness', 8, 74,
      172
   and religious police, 242
   Soviet–Afghan War (1979–89),
      153

and women's rights, 192, 264
Yemen War (2015–), 72, 74,
   172
Samin, Nadav, 139, 185, 198–9,
   200
Saud Abd al-Aziz ibn Naser,
   Prince, 205
Saud, King of Saudi Arabia
   (r. 1953–64), 56, 58–9
September 11 attacks (2001), 68,
   69, 79, 108, 114, 154
al-Shaibani, Sami, 206
al-Shair, Ali, 122
Shakespear, William, 40
al-Shakhori, Sayyid Akbar, 313
al-Shammari, Muhammad
   Nakhlan, 163
sharha, 186
al-Sharif, Manal, 243, 249, 255,
   264
Shayba, Muhammad Yahya, 218
Sheffer, Gabriel, 20
al-Sheikh, Abdul Aziz, 71, 201,
   243
al-Sheikh, Muhammad, 178
al-Sheikh, Turki, 135
Shia Islam, 18, 76, 84, 183, 189,
   207–8, 211–16, 305, 310–16
   Arab uprisings (2011), 71, 156,
      212, 310
   Ashura, 213, 215
   diaspora, 26–7, 137, 273, 277,
      278, 286
   in Eastern Province, 38, 65, 71,
      156, 182, 208, 211, 215, 313

INDEX

INDEX

INDEX

Yemen War (2015) and, 31,
221–2
Walid ibn Talal, Prince, 108, 125
Watfa, 62
welfare, 5, 70, 71, 76, 88, 170,
227, 263, 333–4
Vision 2030 programme, 128,
131, 269
women and, 241, 255, 260
women, 2, 3–4, 22, 32, 71, 85, 97,
109, 123, 233–70
abuse of, 13, 14, 85, 244,
245, 249, 251, 254–5, 258,
260–61, 269–70
activism, 13, 233–70
Arab uprisings (2011), 70
diaspora, 19–20, 22–3, 27–9,
32, 238–40, 245–56, 267,
269, 298
dress code, 73, 148, 170–71,
184, 236, 245, 317
driving rights, see driving,
women and
education of, 58
emigration, 5, 14, 19, 97, 235,
247, 250–56, 260, 263, 270,
294
employment of, see employment of women
feminism, see feminism
festivals and, 174, 198
foreign consultants and, 89, 227
global media and, 15
guardianship system, see guardianship system
healing practices, 210

marriage, see under marriage
nationalism and, 148, 169, 174,
198
religious nationalism and, 144,
147–8
as sabaya, 221
sports, 89, 170
tourism promotion and, 90
travel abroad, 133, 147, 171,
246, 256, 259, 268, 269
treason accusations, 13, 238,
244, 245, 330
tribalism and, 190–91, 193,
202–3
veiling, 73, 148, 170–71, 236,
245, 317
welfare system and, 241, 255,
260
World War I (1914–18), 38–44,
350 n.40
World War II (1939–45), 3, 55

xenophobia, 165, 166, 181, 202,
230

Yahya, Imam, 53
Yam tribe, 216, 217, 219, 222
Yamani, Ahmad Zaki, 61
Yamani, Mai, 3, 209
al-Yami, Abu Hadi, 217
Yemen
Covid-19 pandemic (2020), 335
diaspora and, 320
Gulf War (1990–91), 231
Houthi takeover (2014), 72, 92
immigration from, 167

393